D1617518

The Bloody Flag

THE CALIFORNIA WORLD HISTORY LIBRARY

Edited by Edmund Burke III, Kenneth Pomeranz, and Patricia Seed

The Bloody Flag

MUTINY IN THE AGE OF ATLANTIC REVOLUTION

Niklas Frykman

UNIVERSITY OF CALIFORNIA PRESS

University of California Press
Oakland, California

© 2020 by Niklas Frykman

Library of Congress Cataloging-in-Publication Data

Names: Frykman, Niklas, author.
Title: The bloody flag : mutiny in the age of Atlantic revolution /
    Niklas Frykman.
Other titles: 0 California world history library ;
Description: Oakland, California : University of California Press, [2020] |
    Series: 1 California world history lib | Includes bibliographical
    references and in
Identifiers: LCCN 2019052052 (print) | LCCN 201905 (ebook) |
    ISBN 9780520355477 (cloth) | ISBN 9780520975927 (epub)
Subjects:
Classification: LCC HN49.R33 .F79 2020 (print) | LCC HN49.R33 (ebook) |
    DDC 303.48/4—dc23
LC record available at https://lccn.loc.gov/2019052052
LC ebook record available at https://lccn.loc.gov/2019052053

Manufactured in the United States of America

29 28 27 26 25 24 23 22 21 20
10 9 8 7 6 5 4 3 2 1

For Jasper and Michelle

The publisher and the University of California Press Foundation gratefully acknowledge the generous support of the Peter Booth Wiley Endowment Fund in History.

CONTENTS

ILLUSTRATIONS

FIGURES

MAPS

ACKNOWLEDGMENTS

This book has taken a long time to write. Initial research started in 2003, a few months after the United States-led invasion of Iraq appeared to crush the alter-globalization movement's hopes for a different, less violent world. To counter the darkness of that hopeless moment, it seemed to me an urgent task to learn as much as there was to know about the history of resistance among frontline troops. But as the project evolved, and the perpetual war in the global South was joined by a sustained political crisis in the global North, I began to see that the history of late eighteenth-century naval mutinies also held important lessons about class, nationalism, and revolutionary politics. This book, I hope, succeeds in sharing some of those lessons. Not unlike Rebecca Solnit's notion of a paradise built in hell, the history of maritime radicalism in the revolutionary era, with its extraordinary political creativity in the midst of catastrophic turmoil, can perhaps contribute a small measure of historical depth and inspiration to the radical democratic renewal we so urgently require.

Throughout my education, I have been fortunate to learn from many inspiring teachers: Jon Carver at Lima (Ohio) Senior High School, who first showed me how much joy the study of history could bring; Eric Schroeder at the University of California, Davis, who taught me the importance of taking the experience of fighting men seriously; the late Alun Howkins at the University of Sussex, who introduced me to the marvelous world of the British Marxist historians; and, finally, my friend, mentor, and comrade Marcus Rediker at the University of Pittsburgh, whose work and unwavering support has meant more to me than words can convey. His cheerful hatred for the state of the world, matched by his remarkable ability to see its enduring beauty, continues to be a source of inspiration. Whatever virtue the reader may see in the pages that follow is in large part owed to what Marcus has taught me.

I have had the privilege to teach in two outstanding History departments, first at Claremont McKenna College and then at the University of Pittsburgh. In both places I thank friends and colleagues for their insatiable curiosity about all things old, especially Lisa Cody, Lily Geismer, and Diana Selig at CMC, and George Reid Andrews, Michel Gobat, Holger Hoock, Patrick Manning, Carla Nappi, James Pickett, Lara Putnam, Pernille Røge, Rob Ruck, Scott Smith, Gregor Thum, Liann Tsoukas, Molly Warsh, and Mari Webel at Pitt. I especially thank Kathy Gibson, Cynthia Graf, Patty Landon, and Grace Tomcho for making Pitt's History Department work, and for making it the special place that it is.

I have enjoyed many moments of collegiality, generosity, and intellectual friendship during the time I worked on this book. For discussions large and small, I thank Clare Anderson, Richard Blakemore, Pepijn Brandon, Jaap Bruijn, Denver Brunsman, George Caffentzis, Lucy Capes, Matilde Cazzola, Titas Chakraborty, John Clegg, Isaac Curtis, James Davey, John Donoghue, Thierry Drapeau, Seymour Drescher, Silvia Federici, Wendy Goldman, Van Beck Hall, Christina Heatherton, Lex Heerma van Voss, Johan Heinsen, Steve Hindle, Evelyn Jennings, Sylvie Kleinman, Isaac Land, Marcel van der Linden, Peter Linebaugh, Chris Magra, John Markoff, Hamish Maxwell-Stewart, Michael McDonnell, Matthias van Rossum, Pavlos Roufos, Anita Rupprecht, Jonathan Scott, Pierre Serna, Phil Stern, David Struthers, Nicole Ulrich, Bruce Venarde, Carsten Voss, Peter Way, Carl Wennerlind, and Kenyon Zimmer. Special thanks go to Matthieu Ferradou, Tim Murtagh, and Nathan Perl-Rosenthal, who generously shared transcripts from their own archival adventures with me. All the participants of the "Mutiny and Maritime Radicalism in the Age of Revolution" conference at the International Institute of Social History in Amsterdam in 2011 and the "Free and Unfree Labor in Atlantic and Indian Ocean Port Cities" conference at the University of Pittsburgh in 2016 contributed more to this book than they could possibly know. Vince Brown, Billy Smith, Peter Wood, Kathleen Wilson, and two anonymous readers carefully combed through the entire manuscript and helped me see things in it I had never thought about. Hélène Palma and Phil Deloole generously volunteered to photograph the round robin petition that appears in the conclusion. Finally, my heartfelt thanks go to Niels Hooper, Kathleen MacDougall, Robin Manley, Emilia Thiuri, and everyone else at University of California Press who has helped make this book a reality.

Many institutions have financially supported this project during its long gestation. I am grateful to the History Department at the University of

Pittsburgh, the Kenneth P. Dietrich School of Arts and Sciences at the University of Pittsburgh, the University Center for International Studies at the University of Pittsburgh, the William L. Clements Library at the University of Michigan, the Huntington Library in San Marino, the American Historical Association, the Sweden-America Foundation, the American Council of Learned Societies, the Dean of Faculty's Office at Claremont McKenna College, and the Richard D. and Mary Jane Edwards Endowed Publication Fund for their support.

Most importantly of all, I thank my family, near and far. My parents, AnnChristin and Lars, have not been bewildered nearly enough by their youngest son's decision to move halfway around the world to study ill-behaved eighteenth-century sailors for years on end. For this and so much else besides, tack, mamma och pappa. Jasper Horton Frykman made me happier than I thought I could be, but he did not exactly help with the timely completion of this book. His mother, Michelle Horton, more than made up for that. Thank you. For that, and so much more. And yes, now we finally can talk about something else.

Some parts of chapters 1, 3, and 5 previously appeared in "Seamen on late eighteenth-century European warships," *International Review of Social History* 54 (2009): 67–93; "The mutiny on the Hermione: Warfare, revolution, and treason in the Royal Navy," *Journal of Social History* 44, no. 1 (2010): 159–187; and "Connections between mutinies in European navies," in *Mutiny and Maritime Radicalism in the Age of Revolution: A Global Survey,* edited by Clare Anderson, Niklas Frykman, Lex Heerma van Voss, and Marcus Rediker, 87–107 (Cambridge: Cambridge University Press, 2014). I am grateful to Cambridge University Press and Oxford University Press for permission to republish these sections here.

Introduction: Like a Ship on Fire

The sea smells bad.
This is not because of the mud, however.
The sea smells of sailors, it smells of democracy.

—JACQUES RANCIÈRE,
On the Shores of Politics (2007)

THE BATTLE OF CAMPERDOWN ON OCTOBER II, 1797 was one of the hardest fought victories the British Royal Navy won during the French Revolutionary Wars. In most major engagements, the British outkilled their enemies by a vast margin—from the First of June 1794 to the Battle of Trafalgar in 1805, on average by a proportion of about six to one—but against the Dutch at Camperdown the losses were more evenly balanced. Unlike French and Spanish gun crews, who were trained to aim for the masts and rigging in order to immobilize the enemy's ships, the Dutch adopted the British tactic of pounding the hull with broadsides until there no longer were enough men left standing to return fire. At Camperdown, it took about three hours of close-range combat before the slower-firing Dutch were forced to surrender. Most of their sixteen ships were damaged beyond repair, their hulls shot through, masts and rigging destroyed. Some were on fire, and three ships would eventually sink. Of the 7,157 Dutch seamen who had sailed into battle, 620 now lay weltering in each other's gore; another 520 were already dead. They had sold their lives dearly. The British, who had entered the fight with 8,221 men, suffered 228 men dead and 812 wounded, many of them invalids for life.[1]

When news of the carnage reached Amsterdam, Dutch naval authorities breathed a sigh of relief. Their men had fought with bravery and dedication against a much superior enemy, and that was not something anyone had been able to count on. Morale below deck had been rotten for months, and before the battle many officers had worried that disaffected crews might refuse orders and turn their guns on the quarterdeck instead. It would not have been the first time. Just over a year before, a Dutch squadron at anchor in Saldanha Bay had been forced to surrender to the British after a council of war came to the conclusion that the crews, if ordered to fight, were as likely "to shoot and kill their own officers as fire on the enemy." When the decision to surrender was announced, violent riots erupted on several of the ships. Officers and their supporters among the crews were beaten up, and some murdered. Afterwards, the majority of Dutch sailors switched sides and joined the Royal Navy, and some even ended up on the British ships that fought the Dutch at Camperdown the following year.[2]

A few months after the Saldanha Bay surrender, a British spy reported that the French government had become so concerned about their Dutch allies "that they have shipped on board of every Dutch ship of the line such a number of French troops as they think sufficient to maintain discipline and enforce Patriotism." Not surprisingly, the decision to use French troops to enforce Dutch patriotism only added to the breakdown of discipline. Right before the battle, a group of French soldiers on the *Hector* were discovered as they plotted to assassinate the ship's commander, while two days later a sailor was executed on the flagship *Vrijheid* for murdering a soldier. He was sorry, he said before dying, for there were two more he would have liked to kill. On the *Kortenaar,* meanwhile, counter-revolutionary agitators were discovered with orange ribbons in their possessions, signifying their continued loyalty to the overthrown Stadtholder William V, who from his exile in Britain had called upon Dutch troops to aid the British war effort by rising up against the revolutionary Batavian regime.[3]

As they prepared for the battle in the early fall of 1797, British Admiralty officials had no idea of just how much disorder there was in the Dutch fleet. But it probably would not have made much difference had they known, for their own crews were just as unreliable. Of the sixteen ships that eventually sailed into battle at Camperdown, ten had participated in the fleet mutinies that rocked the Royal Navy's home command earlier that year. From Cork in the west all the way to Great Yarmouth in the east, over 40,000 men on more than a hundred ships had raised the blood-red flag of mutiny and for two months refused to do the work of war. It became the largest, best organized, most sustained working-class offensive in eighteenth-century Britain. At the Nore anchorage, where the rebellion peaked in late May, the mutineers proclaimed a "floating republic," established a complex hierarchical committee system staffed by instantly recallable delegates to serve as their legislative branch, elected a president as their executive, and used a jury-based court system as their judiciary. When the government refused to negotiate, some of the insurgents suggested taking the ships to sea and handing them over to the nearest enemy, but in the end the mutiny collapsed before any of the ships could sail. In the chaos that ensued, several dozen mutineers fled to France and the Batavian Republic, and some even appear to have made their way onboard the Dutch ships that fought the British at Camperdown a few months later.[4]

With the memory of the great mutiny still fresh in their minds, British admiralty and high government officials were just as relieved as their Dutch counterparts when news of Camperdown arrived in London. The battle's unusual ferocity and high death toll seemed to suggest that Jack Tar had finally come to his senses and was looking for redemption, and that in its pursuit he was willing to kill and die like never before. The government seized the opportunity to stage a series of bombastic victory celebrations. Parliament voted funds for a monument at St. Paul's, Admiral Duncan was ennobled Viscount Camperdown, all first lieutenants in his fleet were promoted to the rank of master and commander, and a variety of little-known medieval titles were resurrected to further honor the display of martial valor. The most persistent theme that emerged from the celebrations was that victory in the battle had owed entirely to the fact that every single sailor onboard the king's ships, from the commander in chief down to the lowest cabin boy, had fulfilled without fail the duties expected of his particular station. To underscore the point, the grand Naval Thanksgiving procession that snaked its way through London towards St. Paul's Cathedral on December 19, 1797 included as its central component the reenactment of the properly constituted hierarchies that governed patriotic service at sea: following behind the rugged warrior-hero Duncan came individual ship delegations from his fleet, each consisting of one lieutenant trailed by one master's mate, two midshipmen, three marines, and five common seamen. The message was clear: order had been restored, and with everyone once again content and fixed in their proper place, the Royal Navy ruled the waves.[5]

In renouncing the egalitarian principles that had flourished during the floating republic at the Nore, the government-backed celebrations that followed the British victory at Camperdown drew on an ancient trope that associated the sea and those who made a living upon its waves and along its shores with the potential for political unrest and social collapse. Plato, for example, used the metaphor of a mutinous ship to denounce democratic forms of rule, painting a dystopian image of a bickering, drunken crew, unwilling to recognize their own limitations and too jealous to admit that others might be more skilled in the intricate art of navigation. And so, Plato concluded, "they sail the way you'd expect people like that to sail." Centuries later, when political philosophers in ancient Rome elaborated on the same theme, hatred of democracy was often tempered with a stronger emphasis on the fragility of the "ship of state," and the need for all members of society to pull together and do their duty in order to ensure its safe passage through a world in which it was constantly beset by hostile forces. However, as with Plato's more openly antidemocratic use of the trope, the evocation of a state of emergency as the permanent condition of political society similarly served to naturalize the need for strong governments, hierarchical forms of rule, and unquestioned submission to authority.[6]

The trope reemerged following Europe's early modern turn towards the sea, and it was especially prominent in periods of political crisis. In 1798, for example, Finland-Swedish poet and one-time revolutionary enthusiast Frans Michael Franzén used it in a mournful denunciation of the Enlightenment's culminating decade. "A terrifying beauty," he began,

> This century already has passed us by,
> Like a ship on fire,
> Casting its luster and horror,
> On the night-dark river's shore.
> In vain did humanity hope to see,
> It carefully carrying Peace
> To meet with Truth and Liberty;
> Nothing but ruins mark its course.

Franzén was not the first to reflect on the consequences of the French Revolution with the metaphor of a ship in distress, drifting towards catastrophe. A few years earlier, in 1792, as France proclaimed itself a republic and began the world anew, German philosopher Johann Gottfried Herder consoled himself with the idea that the national characters of Germany and France were as vastly different as the solid earth and the fluid sea, and that therefore "we can observe the French Revolution as if it were a shipwreck on

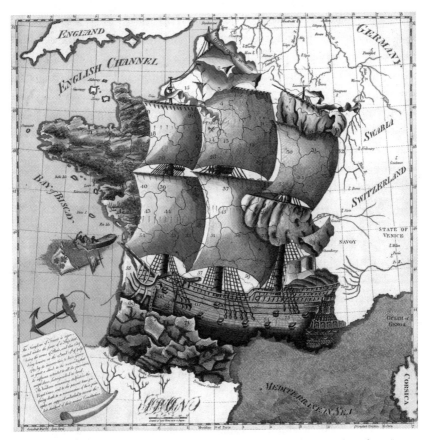

FIGURE I. British propaganda print depicting the revolutionary French "ship of state" as an abandoned warship, London, 1796. Courtesy of the Geography and Map Division, Library of Congress, Washington, DC.

the open, foreign sea, witnessed from the safety of the shore." A similar vision of French revolutionary collapse appeared in a 1796 British propaganda print, which depicted the French republic as a warship adrift, its quarterdeck empty and abandoned, anchor cable torn, sails fluttering wildly in the winds, the *fleur-de-lis* thrown overboard, and flying from its foretop a red flag of rebellion, running like a thick stream of blood from Paris out into the sea.[7]

For many of those who throughout the centuries used the "ship of state" trope to theorize the nature of political power, shipboard society was not just a conveniently intuitive metaphor with which to attack democratic forms of rule. It also often reflected the authors' own unhappy experiences with the mutinous inhabitants of the waterfront. Based on the experience of his own family's struggles with the rebellious sailors gathered in the port of Piraeus, Plato argued that proximity to the sea naturally fostered social and political unrest, and he therefore pronounced that a well-governed city must be located as far inland as possible, away from the sea and the undesirable elements it threw up on the shore. His student Aristotle also saw the dangers of political instability that cosmopolitan seafarers and merchants brought to a city, but these were outweighed, he thought, by the commercial and military advantages of sea-power. He therefore recommended that the city's dependence on maritime resource extraction and commerce, as well as on the workers whose labor made it possible, instead be managed and supervised with care.[8]

Two millennia later, Aristotle's early modern followers recognized his concerns as their own. Political thinkers, especially in England and the Netherlands, often celebrated their nation's liberty, strength, and prosperity as the natural consequence of sea-power. And yet, they never quite managed to overcome the fear of disorder that was associated with those who lived along the coasts and made their living afloat. Their fears were not without cause. As revolution began to ricochet back and forth across the Atlantic in the middle of the eighteenth century, the same maritime workers whose labor had transformed the once-peripheral northwestern European coast into the core of the capitalist world-economy were often at the forefront of the revolutionary movements that now threatened to unravel European imperial power overseas.[9]

In 1746, Boston seafarers resisted an attempt to coerce them into the Royal Navy and thus triggered the first urban insurrection on the road to the American Revolution, a road that eventually was paved with dozens of riots in port cities up and down the North American seaboard, throughout the Caribbean, and even in the imperial capital itself. In 1768, Thames river workers ceased work and symbolically struck the sails of their vessels, gifting the global labor movement with the evocative word "strike" for its most important form of struggle. In the late winter of 1770, Crispus Attucks, a seafarer of both Native American and African descent, was gunned down by a detachment of British troops in Boston, and thus became the first martyr of the American Revolution. Five years later, slave ship sailors in Liverpool rebelled against their wage-suppressing employers, dragged cannons off their ships, and, with the red flag flying high, bombarded the city's mercantile exchange. When mobs tore apart London during nearly a week of rioting in the summer of 1780, workers connected to the river and the seven seas beyond came flooding out of their neighborhoods, attacked the houses of rich, and demolished London's central prison-house, freeing all those locked up inside.[10]

In the 1790s, when tens of thousands were coerced to serve in the French Revolutionary Wars at sea, the radicalism of seafaring workers escalated to previously unprecedented heights. Governed by a form of martial law that afforded naval seamen none of the protections against state violence enjoyed by their compatriots on shore, warships had always been spaces of intensely concentrated social conflict. Before the 1790s, however, the balance of power was heavily in the officer corps' favor, and naval seamen therefore rarely mutinied in pursuit of better conditions. They chose to simply run away instead. All that changed when revolution gripped France at the end of the 1780s. Virtually overnight, port cities along both the Atlantic and Mediterranean coasts became leading centers of radicalization, sending out disruptive impulses to the colonies overseas and amplifying them as they came bouncing back towards the imperial core. Across the French Atlantic empire, warship crews turned on their aristocratic officers, endlessly questioned the legitimacy of their rule, and with increasing confidence and consequence disregarded orders whenever they feared them to be out of step with the revolutionary movement on land.

When the revolutionary turmoil took more violent and chaotic turns, and the foundations of political authority on both sides of the Atlantic began to crumble, French warship crews often had no choice but to assert their own collective will as the only reliable source of political legitimacy at sea. After four years of revolution, coinciding with the Jacobins' rise to power in metropolitan France and the destruction of slavery in the colonies overseas, control over the shipping lanes and naval stations that held together the French Atlantic empire had effectively devolved into the hands of common seamen. To outsiders, that devolution of power often appeared as just a never-ending series of mindless mutinies and provocations, easy fodder for counter-revolutionary propagandists who mocked as ludicrous the idea that ordinary seamen ought to be granted any degree of political authority at all. And yet, the chaos obscured what in reality was a serious attempt to articulate a claim to popular sovereignty onboard ship that had profound implications for the structure of French imperial power overseas.

The project to make the French navy a truly republican fighting force did not long survive the outbreak of war and the onset of the Terror in 1793. Soon, however, major conflicts erupted onboard the ships of the Dutch navy. Following the combined French invasion and domestic

de Vinck

LE JACOBIN ' ROYALISTE

Après avoir longtems gouverné les Galleres?
Maintenant il voudrait gouverner les affaires.

FIGURE 2. French political cartoon that draws on the anti-democratic "ship of state" trope to disparage the radical Jacobin republic, Paris, n.d. Caption: "Le Jacobin royaliste: après avoir longtems gouverné les galleres maintenant il voudrait gouverner les affaires." Courtesy of the Bibliothèque nationale de France.

revolution that overthrew the Orangist regime and created the Batavian Republic in 1795, seamen in the Dutch fleet almost immediately launched a series of violent, treasonous mutinies. Unlike the French navy, where the majority of sailors were native-born conscripts who fought for their place within the reconstituted imperial nation, the Dutch navy had long relied on foreign-born volunteers with purely contractual ties to the nation they served. When initial promises of post-revolutionary reforms were not met, many seamen in the Dutch navy considered themselves no longer bound by the terms of service to which they had agreed and soon took extreme measures to escape.

When large-scale mutinies erupted in the British navy not long afterwards, both the French emphasis on popular sovereignty and the Dutch insistence on consent reappeared, but in a context of increasingly confrontational struggles over shipboard working conditions. Ever since the Royal Navy had embarked on a course of aggressive expansion in the 1740s, bringing wide-ranging reforms to maximize the exploitation of all available resources, relations between officers and crews onboard ship had gone into steep decline. Most importantly, where previously officers and men had been allowed to serve together for the duration of a war, they now faced each other as strangers who temporarily served together in one ship before being transferred into another. Reduced to feeling like replaceable cogs in a vast imperial war machine, sailors began to experience a consciousness of class that prefigured its broader appearance during the industrial revolution on land.

The great, fleetwide strikes in the spring of 1797 turned that consciousness of class into a material force. But contradicting the well-worn attempt to discredit revolutionary movements on shore with evocative images of anarchy at sea, when British fleet mutineers seized control of over a hundred vessels, they developed a sophisticated constitutional order that brought together the egalitarian culture of North Atlantic maritime communities with contemporary forms of revolutionary republicanism, and then refracted both through their experience of class conflict onboard ship. This experiment in self-government only lasted for a few weeks, but for those who participated in the mutinies, it was a transformative experience. For a brief moment, they had turned the Royal Navy into a floating republic, replaced their despotic officers with democratic assemblies below deck, and the unrelenting terror of the lash with debate and popular consent.

After two months, the insurrection collapsed, and a wave of punitive terror took the lower deck in its grip. Dozens of men were executed and publicly tortured, and hundreds more were thrown into prison and sent to penal colonies overseas. But the continued demand for manpower at sea and the continued globalization of naval warfare ensured that the experience and lessons of the fleet mutinies spread around the world, together with the bitter memory of their repression. Strike-like mutinies suddenly disappeared from the arsenal of the lower deck, and a wave of violent, retaliatory mutinies surged through the ships of the Royal Navy instead. Following the influx of large numbers of hardline Irish republican seamen, who planned to steal several of the Royal Navy's warships in coordination with the 1798 Rebellion in Ireland, the lower deck's murderous rage against the officer corps was briefly given a renewed political focus, but that more radical form of lower deck republicanism also soon collapsed. Another round of even more extreme punitive violence finally crushed the lower deck's insurrectionary spirit for good.

From the outbreak of the French Revolution in 1789 to the brief pause in the global wars it spawned in 1802, the French, Dutch, and British navies experienced over 150 single-ship mutinies, as well as half a dozen fleet mutinies that lasted from a few days to several months and involved between 3,000 and 40,000 men each time. While conflicts in each navy followed their own trajectory, in the latter half of the 1790s overlapping waves of revolt flowed together into a single revolutionary surge, genuinely Atlantic in both origin and scope. By the time the mutinous surge broke in the early 1800s, between one-third and one-half of the approximately 200,000 men mobilized across all three fleets had participated in at least one mutiny, many of them in several, and some even on ships in different navies. This book tells their forgotten story.

The history of mutiny in the revolutionary era is of course not completely unknown, but the sheer scale of unrest, its sophistication, and political significance has previously been obscured by attempts to write about it primarily from the perspective of individual navies. This was not always the case. When Herman Melville turned to the British fleet mutinies of 1797 in *Billy Budd,* he wrote that "reasonable discontent growing out of practical grievances in the fleet had been ignited into irrational combustion as by live cinders blown across the Channel from France in flames." Melville's vision of a revolutionary wildfire spreading across the sea was not entirely fanciful. The mutineers of 1797 inherited a rich tradition of lower deck struggle that fed on experiences not just in the British navy, but in all those in which the cosmopolitan, ocean-wandering crews who came together in the spring of 1797 had previously served. While it is often difficult to trace direct lines of influence, it is clear that the mutineers of the 1790s shared in a radical and cosmopolitan political culture that reached across navies, a culture that was influenced by traditions neither wholly of the land nor of the sea, but instead combined elements of both. Crowded out by the belligerent, terrestrial nationalism of the nineteenth and twentieth centuries, that radical maritime culture seems to have disappeared nearly without a trace. And yet, the long-term legacies of maritime radicalism include some the most powerful symbols in the canon of revolutionary struggle: as the floating republic collapsed into defeat, the red flag that had flown continuously from the masts of the mutinous fleet went on to become the most important symbol of class struggle, economic justice, and republican liberty worldwide.[11]

ONE

Barbaric Industry

ON NOVEMBER 26, 1793, around two o'clock in the afternoon, Johan Sigfrid Schedvin was suddenly brought face to face with the reality of revolutionary warfare at sea. Standing on the deck of the Swedish frigate *Eurydice*, the young naval surgeon watched as the nearby warship *Scipion* was consumed by fire, before it eventually exploded "with a horrible boom, spreading a rain of fire across the anchorage." It was, Schedvin later wrote, "an event without equal—my God!—what a ghastly scene for a man to behold." According to an anonymous eyewitness onboard a British warship anchoring nearby, the explosion onboard the French 74-gun ship *Scipion* sent up a column of smoke to a height of some 600 yards, "intersected with flames, and during several minutes the whole horizon seemed to be on fire." The blast wave that followed "resembled the effect of the most dreadful shock of an earthquake," shattering "an immense number of windowpanes" in Livorno's portside neighborhoods, more than three miles away. By daybreak, all that was left of the *Scipion* was a small piece of the hull floating in the water, "full of coals, and covered with dead corpses." The exact number of dead was never determined, but it appears that approximately 150 of the ship's 600 crewmembers had been either roasted alive, suffocated, drowned, or torn to shreds by the explosion. Bodies, as well as body parts, Schedvin noted, were washing up against Livorno's seawalls for weeks to come.[1]

Fire inspired almost hysterical terror in all those who went to sea in wooden ships of war. In this case, it also inspired heroic solidarity. When thick black smoke first appeared above the *Scipion,* followed shortly afterwards by the firing of its emergency cannons to summon aid, neighboring ships—British, Spanish, Neapolitan, and Swedish—all scrambled their boats to help evacuate the crew. Despite the danger of not knowing when the ship's powder magazine would blow up, and not knowing that the *Scipion* carried an additional three hundred barrels of gunpowder in its storerooms, the rescuers raced towards the floating inferno as fast as they could. "We had barely reached halfway when the flames broke through the deck, and consumed the masts," Schedvin later recalled. "It looked desperate beyond all imagination." Not only did the fire burn through the rigging with terrifying speed, the *Scipion*'s guns began firing uncontrollably from the heat. Many of them were loaded with grapeshot, an extraordinarily nasty form of anti-personnel ammunition that turned a ship's cannons into giant shotguns firing iron balls the size of eggs. Despite the bombardment, Schedvin's boat managed to save 31 men, and altogether over 400 were successfully evacuated. But eventually the wildly firing guns forced the rescuers to retreat, and to abandon more than 100 men onboard the blazing ship. Schedvin watched in horror as tide and winds slowly pulled the *Scipion* through the roadstead and out to sea. "I can barely describe the awful things I saw," he later wrote. "To see people clinging to the side of the ship like ants; and those at the bottom being trampled into the water by the weight of those on top—to see naked men coming out of the flames, half fried—it was horrible."[2]

Line-of-battle ships like the 74-gun *Scipion* were the world's most powerful weapons of war. Each one possessed more firepower than Napoleon's entire army had available at the Battle of Austerlitz in 1805, and they were built strong enough to withstand hours of intensive close-range combat. But against fire they had virtually no defenses. Constructed out of approximately 150,000 cubic feet of seasoned timber (the equivalent of about 3,000 mature trees), several dozen miles of hemp rope, much of it covered in tar, and tons of equally flammable canvas sail, it took surprisingly little to reduce even the most imposing man-of-war to a burning death trap. In May 1795, the British 98-gun ship *Boyne* was destroyed when a single piece of burning cartridge paper drifted off the poop deck and into the Admiral's vacant cabin below, setting fire first to a few sheets of paper lying out, and eventually to the ship itself. The fire, as on the *Scipion,* burned its way through the quarterdeck and then moved up into the rigging, quickly spreading along miles of cordage and setting fire to masts and yards, before it turned around and made its way down, slowly burning through each successive deck, until finally after several hours the flames reached the ship's fully stocked, lead-lined powder room. By the time it exploded and obliterated the ship, most of the crew had been evacuated. Other crews were not so lucky. The fire that broke out on the massive 110-gun ship *Queen Charlotte* in early 1800 also burned for several hours before it reached the powder magazine, but as no other ships were close enough to lend aid, only those few who managed to crowd into the *Queen Charlotte*'s own boats escaped the inevitable explosion. Nearly seven hundred men perished when the ship finally blew up.[3]

In most cases, ships caught fire because of carelessness, often just a small mistake that ended in catastrophe. But the *Scipion* inferno was different. The fire that destroyed the ship was started on purpose, a calculated act of terror that dramatically escalated the conflicts that had raged onboard the ships of the French navy since 1789. Three months before the explosion, the *Scipion*'s officers and the majority of the crew had betrayed the republic and declared themselves for the Bourbon restoration, replaced the revolutionary tricolor flying from the mast with the royal white, and then joined forces with the British-led coalition that occupied the French Mediterranean fleet's home port of Toulon. In the months that followed, the *Scipion* was part of a small Anglo-Spanish-French squadron that sought to clear French republican shipping from the western Mediterranean and thus cut off the grain imports that many people in southern France depended on for their daily bread.[4]

In Genoa, in early October, the *Scipion* led an unprovoked attack against the republican frigate *Modeste*—in port to negotiate the purchase of over a million livres worth of flour—slaughtered several of its crew members, injured others, and took the rest prisoner. A few weeks later, the *Scipion* was sent to Livorno in order to help carry war materiel and five thousand Austrian troops back to Toulon. It was probably while loading gun powder that someone—sources suggest prisoners from the *Modeste,* aided by loyal republicans among the *Scipion*'s own crew—first had the idea of setting fire to the ship in the hope of blowing the royalists to hell, and then with a little bit of luck spread the conflagration to the Spanish and British warships anchoring nearby. When the fire erupted, the arsonists simply hid among the victims, and then launched a mutiny onboard the ship that rescued them. When they finally arrived back home in France, the revolutionary government celebrated their uncompromising brutality in defense of the republic as an act of true patriotism.[5]

For the Swedish naval surgeon Schedvin, the destruction of the *Scipion* was an unsettling event. More than just the horrors of what he had witnessed, he struggled to reconcile his enthusiastic support for the French Republic with the visceral reality of revolutionary warfare at sea. In the months he had spent onboard the *Eurydice* before coming to Livorno, Schedvin had used his diary to ponder and pontificate on the inevitable progress of enlightened revolution, against British tyranny at sea, against slavery, against religion and superstition, and above all for *liberté, égalité,* and *fraternité.* But in the weeks that followed the explosion, with blackened bloated body parts floating almost daily past the ship, he appears to have gradually descended into a depression. On Christmas day 1793, he recorded in his diary a strangely moving comparison between humanity's fate and the meaningless life of a fly. Two days later, on December 27, he drily noted that Toulon had been reconquered by the forces of the republic, and after that he fell completely silent for two months.[6]

Schedvin wrote his first diary entry on August 28, 1793, shortly after the *Eurydice* dropped anchor off Dover following a difficult, month-long slog across the North Sea. Part of a small squadron of warships, the *Eurydice* had orders to accompany a convoy of Swedish merchantmen sailing to the Mediterranean, where it was to help protect the neutrality of the country's maritime trade now that tensions between Europe's major powers had once again escalated into open warfare. It was a mostly symbolic mission, for the navy still had not recovered from its poorly planned and badly executed attack on Russia in 1788. The resulting war, which dragged on for three disastrous years before ending with a treaty that simply reestablished the *status quo ante bellum,* destroyed about a third of the Swedish navy's deep-sea-going ships, and cost the country around 50,000 dead and wounded. Some of the battles, like the two war-ending clashes at Viborg and Svensksund, were fought with exceptional brutality, but most of the dead were victims of a harrowing typhus epidemic that originated on a captured Russian warship. Just as the war was drawing to a close in the summer of 1790, disaster struck again when a fire and a series of massive gunpowder explosions ripped through the navy's home base of Karlskrona, leaving nearly half the town in ashes and over 3,000 people homeless.[7]

By the time France declared war on Britain in early 1793, and the *Eurydice* was sent to protect Swedish merchantmen abroad, the navy had collapsed into near irrelevance. As if to confirm its insignificance, just five days after the *Eurydice* arrived at Dover, British authorities unceremoniously seized one of the merchant ships under its protection. It had been bound for France and was therefore, according to Britain's self-serving interpretation of international law, by definition carrying war material, which made the vessel legally liable for seizure. The *Eurydice*'s officers were beside themselves when they heard the news, but there was nothing they could do about it. Whatever the legal niceties, and whatever the established rights of neutral traders, Britain was determined to wage total war on revolutionary France, completely sever its maritime trade, steal its overseas possessions, and drive its metropolitan population into economic misery.[8]

Schedvin was astonished by the British government's ruthlessness. The violation of the rights of foreign merchants was bad enough, he thought, but what really shocked him was the brutality with which the Royal Navy's press gangs tore through the anchorage off Dover. Hundreds of men were dragged kicking and screaming off their ships to satisfy the navy's voracious demand for manpower, which, like everywhere else, over recent decades had grown to an almost unsustainable level. British success in the wars of the 1740s and 1750s had prompted France and Spain to launch campaigns to expand their fleets in the early 1760s, which in turn had sucked every other European power with overseas interests and aspirations into a rapidly escalating naval arms race. The fleets of France, Spain, and the United Provinces all nearly doubled in size between 1760 and 1790, while the Russian navy grew at twice that rate. By contrast, the already vastly superior British navy initially shrunk by approximately 11 percent in the late 1760s and early 1770s, but the War for American Independence triggered a renewed round of expansion, producing a 40 percent growth spurt over the next fifteen years. All told, when large-scale hostilities commenced in the early 1790s, European navies were ready to send some 600 line-of-battle ships, almost as many frigates, and nearly 2,000 smaller vessels into combat. Together they packed over 60,000 guns, ten times the number of moveable artillery pieces then in use by the continent's land armies, and required approximately 350,000 men to operate, equivalent to almost all the skilled manpower available in the North Atlantic.[9]

Service onboard warships was deeply unpopular, and the frequency of wars in the late eighteenth century made it even more so. In contrast to early modern armies, which employed large numbers of specialized workers for whose skills there was little demand in the civilian sectors of the economy, eighteenth-century navies satisfied their manpower requirements by drawing on the same pool of skilled maritime labor that also supplied the merchant marine and the fisheries. But the number of workers in that pool grew nowhere near as fast as the navies that demanded their labor. Already in the early 1780s, the Dutch navy barely managed to scrape together two-thirds of the men it needed to fight the fourth and final Anglo-Dutch War (1780–84), and that only after closing a number of commercial ports and offering extra

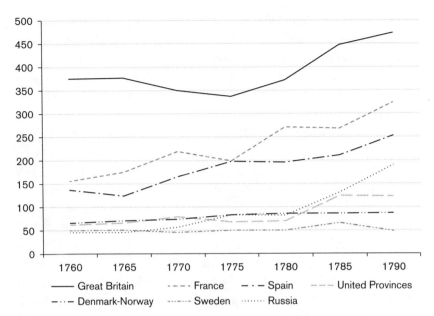

FIGURE 3. Size of European sailing navies, 1760–1790 (per displacement in 1,000 tons). Source of data: Jan Glete, *Navies and Nations: Warships, Navies, and State Building in Europe and America, 1500–1860* (Stockholm: Almqvist and Wiksell, 1993), 2:311.

bonuses to newly unemployed mariners willing to volunteer for service onboard a warship. Likewise, Britain and France only with great difficulty were able to force enough men into service during the American War of Independence (1775–83), and they both emerged from the war in the mid-1780s with even greater needs. And still they kept building more warships. By the time France declared war on all the crowned heads of Europe in 1792, both fleets had manpower requirements roughly equivalent to each country's entire population of seafarers.[10]

The decision not to create a permanent workforce meant that waging war at sea hinged on each navy's ability to shift mariners quickly and efficiently from civilian to naval employment in times of war. The challenge was usually not about numbers, since rumors of war tended to depress civilian deep-sea shipping, which in turn drove unemployed mariners to look for work wherever they could find it. Instead, the problem was how to secure those highly skilled men who already had experience serving onboard a warship and therefore could form the core around which to quickly rebuild a ship's crew. But as the wages that highly skilled mariners could earn in the merchant service usually shot up whenever war broke out, while the pay offered by most navies remained stable and low, the question became how best to capture and coerce them into the state's service at the precise moment when it was most in their economic self-interest to avoid it.[11]

Britain's Royal Navy solved this problem through impressment: whenever war threatened, the Privy Council issued the Admiralty with warrants, and His Majesty's press gangs came sweeping through port towns and roadsteads, abducting as many mariners as they could get their hands on, and then forcing them into whatever warship stood in need of their services. Press gangs also routinely intercepted and stripped inbound merchant ships of their crews, a practice Schedvin witnessed firsthand when the *Eurydice* anchored near Dover. "It works as follows," he wrote. "When a merchant vessel drops anchor, immediately a sloop with armed men is dispatched, who take all useful seamen.... The unlucky ones are immediately taken onboard a warship, and even though they may have been away from home and friends for ever so long, they are not allowed to set foot on land." When Schedvin together with the *Eurydice*'s officers paid a customary visit to the British 74-gun *Tremendous,* he came away haunted by the "sadness and desperation" of the four hundred newly pressed men he had seen onboard. "Impressment is unbelievably violent," he wrote in his diary that night, "an injury to the rights of man. I do not understand how it can exist in civilized countries, or in the ports of so-called free nations."[12]

Neither could many Britons, who fought impressment tooth and nail. Between 1738 and 1805, attempts to press in the British Isles triggered over six hundred affrays, approximately a quarter of which involved serious violence, and about 10 percent ended with at least one fatality. And all this even though Britain was home to Europe's largest population of seafarers, and the navy's demand for manpower never quite exhausted available supply. Still, press gangs were constantly on the hunt for new recruits, for the government's long-term strategic plan demanded not only a rapidly growing navy, but also a capacity to deploy at full strength without undermining the ability of the British merchant fleet to keep sailing during wartime. As a result, at the outbreak of war the demand for seamen nearly doubled overnight. To help ease the crisis and encourage foreign mariners to take the place of British seamen pressed from the merchant service into the navy, Parliament for the duration of hostilities routinely raised the peacetime cap on foreign-born crew members onboard British merchant ships from 25 to 75 percent. But it was never enough, and with each war, press gangs ravaged coastal communities ever more thoroughly. Seaman William Richardson later remembered that in 1795 press gangs had almost brought his hometown of Shields to a complete standstill: "My brother and I went on shore, but found Shields not that merry place we had hitherto known it; every one looked gloomy and sad on account of nearly all the young men being pressed and taken away." This was a mere two years into a war that was to last for twenty more.[13]

Most governments preferred their own country's mariners to man the navy. But with the escalation of the naval arms race, that was often no longer a viable option, and the number of foreign-born crew members increased steadily in most navies. On the *Hermione,* which in most respects was an ordinary British frigate, only 50 percent of the crew came from England by 1797, 20 percent from within the empire, another 20 percent from Ireland, and 10 percent from eleven different countries around the Atlantic rim. Such a distribution appears to have become common in the late eighteenth-century British navy, but it was nothing compared to the role that foreign-born men played in the Dutch service, where they often accounted for 70 percent or more of a crew.[14]

Unique among major navies, the Dutch admiralties did not operate their own recruitment system and instead relied on the same network of private labor brokers that also supplied the ships of the Dutch East India Company and other state-related and private enterprises. Known as *zielverkopers* (sellers of souls), these brokers were usually boardinghouse keepers who specifically sought out newly arrived sailors, offered them food and shelter on credit, and then, once they had built up enough debt, pushed them onto the first short-crewed ship they could find. In return, they collected the man's customary two-month advance, and if the debt exceeded that amount, as it usually did, also a promissory note issued by the navy that gave the bearer first claim to the man's future earnings.[15]

By converting naval service into a form of debt peonage, the Dutch navy was usually able to raise enough men to meet its needs, but it had no way of singling out and forcing the most highly skilled men into service. During the country's seventeenth-century "Golden Age," this was not much of a problem since its high-wage economy was able to attract enough skilled migrant mariners from across the North and Baltic Sea regions for whom service onboard a Dutch warship was a comparatively attractive and well-paid option. By the eighteenth century, however, the country's relative decline was strongly reflected in its underfunded, corruption-riddled, and disease-ravaged navy: service onboard its ships was now widely considered among the worst jobs in the republic, accepted only by the most desperate and destitute, who by the end of the century were often recently arrived migrants from the landlocked heartlands of the Holy Roman Empire. Their numbers onboard Dutch warships eventually became so large that communication between officers and crews sometimes proved difficult. In 1799, for example, Captain van Grootenray of the *Kortenaar* complained that he was unable to issue orders to his crew, for almost all of them were fresh recruits from eastern Europe. Worse still, their efforts at Dutch language acquisition had apparently ceased with the word *sold* (wages), but that one word, van Grootenray reported, they used over and over again.[16]

In response to the growing shortage of skilled manpower across Europe, navies looked increasingly to subject populations in its overseas possessions for new recruits. While sailors of south and southeast Asian descent ("lascars") served primarily onboard the ships of Europe's various East India Company fleets, mariners of African descent worked across all the maritime industries, including state-owned warships. Their flexible status within the system of European nationality law, and the permanent threat of enslavement that hung above their heads, made them attractive recruits. For example, when Britain's Royal Navy pressed in the colonies, black men were considered subjects of the crown, and therefore legally liable to be impressed. At the same time, when the Royal Navy captured black men serving onboard enemy warships, they did not consider them enemy subjects, and thus were able to offer them a choice between imprisonment or service in the navy. Many chose the latter. By the early 1780s, the latest date for which there are reliable estimates, "black Jacks" accounted for 5 to 10 percent of the Royal Navy's total manpower.[17]

Outside of the Mediterranean, where enslaved rowers still powered some of the remaining galley fleets, navies did not officially employ slaves as regular sailors, and anyone recruited as a common rating and entered into the books was implicitly understood to be free. Ironically, therefore, while many white European mariners denounced coerced naval service as a form of slavery, footloose slaves throughout the greater Caribbean saw warships as a possible path to personal emancipation. If runaways were discovered to have been recruited under false pretenses—a common occurrence, since recruitment agents had little incentive to investigate the legal status of anyone willing to serve—they were discharged back into the hands of their enslavers. But the likelihood of that happening decreased dramatically once a ship left port, and especially if it was bound for Europe, where naval officers sometimes made sure to formally secure the freedom of those who had served under them.[18]

However, black mariners were never safe. Even in England, where Lord Chief Justice Mansfield's 1772 Somerset decision made it illegal to take slaves out of the country against their will, the kidnapping, enslavement, and removal of free black people continued for decades. One of Schedvin's ship-mates, for example, was a fifteen-year-old boy who as a child had been kid-napped in London, taken to Sweden, and then sold to Captain von Platen as a personal servant. The boy, who was given the humiliating name Figaro, refused to acknowledge his enslavement and ran away when the *Eurydice* dropped anchor off Dover, hoping, he later explained, to make his way to London in order to find his father. But instead he was recaptured and beaten.[19]

In contrast to most of its northern European counterparts, the French navy largely resisted the drift towards greater reliance on foreign-born crew members, in part because its manning system was fundamentally based on a reciprocal arrangement between the king and his subjects in the maritime provinces. Under the *système des classes,* as it eventually came to be known, every French mariner and worker somehow connected to the sea or one the kingdom's navigable rivers was required by law to register their name with a regional commissioner, who, depending on the man's family status, placed him into one of three or four classes. During peacetime, members of each class were expected to remain available for service every third or fourth year, and during that year were strictly forbidden from working onboard civilian craft. In times of war, when usually the members of several classes were needed for service all at once, the classes were called up in succession, always starting with the class whose members had the least number of dependents and whose death or incapacity therefore would impose the smallest burden on their home communities.[20]

In return for their cooperation with the *système des classes,* the state pro-vided mariners with a rudimentary social security system, including invalid care, old-age pensions, support for war-widows, free education for their chil-dren, and financial support for the conscript's family while he was at sea. But despite these benefits, the system was deeply unpopular. In peacetime, more men than necessary were forced into service, which led to pointless make-work, and in wartime the system of mobilizing by class broke down com-pletely, since the navy never managed to attract many volunteers and there-fore often had to mobilize all of its classed men at once. Naval wages in both peacetime and wartime remained significantly below those of the merchant marine, and the administration of benefits, which theoretically was meant to compensate for some of the difference, was unreliable at best. Meanwhile, resistance to the *système* was met with brutal repression. The failure to register, the refusal to serve when called up, and even emigration abroad or away from the coast were all treated as desertion, punishable by perpetual "galley slavery," which by the late eighteenth century meant a lifetime of uncompensated heavy labor in the royal dockyards.[21]

The navy could have eased some of the pressure had its narrow conception of nationality not excluded a significant proportion of French mariners, especially along the Mediterranean coast and in the Flanders borderlands where many maritime communities were of unusually mixed heritage. Even in Toulon, home base of the navy's Mediterranean fleet, the population was dizzyingly diverse. Henri Lauvergne, who grew up in the bourgeois part of town, remembered the feeling of alienation that beset him whenever he ventured into the working-class neighborhoods near the waterfront, where "one felt more out of place than in Turkey.... Here one spoke low *Provençal*, the corrupted idiom of our coasts, bad Italian, Genoese, Corsican, what have you! All the nations that live by the sea were here represented." Many of the mixed-heritage mariners who roamed the streets of Toulon, Marseilles, Bordeaux, or any of the other ports in the kingdom were happy enough to sail as Frenchmen in peacetime onboard the ships of the country's merchant fleet, thus earning high wages in return for helping shipowners meet the mercantilist requirement that crews be made up predominately of French seamen. But whenever naval recruiters came calling, many of them suddenly remembered their allegiance to the Republic of Genoa, the Grand Duke of Tuscany, or his most Catholic Majesty, the King of Spain, and thus they escaped conscription into naval war-work.[22]

France was unique in the extent to which it let xenophobia influence its naval recruitment system. In contrast to almost every other major European navy, which reacted to the escalating demand for manpower in the second half of the eighteenth century by increasingly competing for men from abroad, French naval administrators turned inward instead, pushing the officially defined area within which seafaring conscripts may be found far up the country's navigable rivers, and then swelling the number of potential recruits still further by including workers with only the most marginal and indirect connections to any kind of aquatic activity. By the end of the old regime, state authorities had declared about a quarter of metropolitan France to be officially close enough to the water's edge for its male working-age population to be subject to conscription.[23]

Violent resistance to this aggressive expansion of the state's claim to people's labor and liberties erupted almost immediately, especially in those peripheral areas where central state authority remained weak. Throughout the southwest, which had only recently been integrated into the *système des classes,* whole communities rose in open revolt against the attempt to force local men into the navy during both the Seven Years' War and the War for American Independence. But even around Toulon, the country's oldest war-port, anti-conscription resistance at the beginning of the Seven Years' War was so fierce that the navy was forced to order a *levée générale,* a rough equivalent to the indiscriminate emergency hunt for sailors that the British navy referred to as a "hot press." By the time of the next major mobilization in the 1770s, naval service had become so unpopular that desertion rates shot up to previously unimaginable heights. At the first rumor of war, thousands of people fled away from the coasts and across borders, feigned illness, and even mutilated themselves. Some ran away to join the army just to avoid service onboard ship. In Brest, over four thousand men failed to show up for service and several ships were unable to sail. In Toulon, the navy ordered another *levée générale,* and when that failed to yield enough men, recruiters rounded up local peas-ants, which triggered widespread rioting and drove the rural population even deeper into its disaffection with the king and his ministers.[24]

The increased reliance on landsmen was part of a broader transformation of Europe's maritime industries in the eighteenth century. By the 1780s, more than half of all registered seamen in France were first generation mariners, and in the deep-sea trades their proportion was higher still. This was a con-sequence of technical changes, foremost in the size of ocean-going vessels, as well as the complexity of their rigging, which together undermined the importance of seamen's craft skills and put an increased premium on simple muscle power instead. The proportion of able seamen on board transatlantic merchantmen consequently declined by as much as 33 to 50 percent in the middle years of the century, and in their place came cheaper, lower-skilled workers without much or any experience of the sea.[25]

The same tendency was even more strongly marked onboard warships, which throughout the century were packed with ever more guns, and there-fore required ever more men to fire them. In the late seventeenth-century, a ship of the line had a crew of approximately 500 men; one hundred years later crews of 750 were common, and up to 900 far from unheard of. Since few of these men were needed to sail the ship, and the skills necessary for firing the guns were easily learned, navies had no difficulty absorbing and training large numbers of landsmen. But there was an upper limit. Commander Evertsen found nearly 80 German and Polish landsmen amongst his crew of 120 when he assumed his position on the Dutch frigate *Scipio* in the summer of 1797. To put to sea, Evertsen estimated that he needed another 16 actual seamen, plus a handful of petty officers. That still would have left him with nearly 60 percent landsmen, a figure far higher than was considered desirable in the British navy. There, ideally, the proportion of landsmen and boys was to be kept below 25 percent. At the same time, it was only considered necessary to have 25 percent experienced and able seamen on board, while the remaining 50 percent could safely be made up of low-skilled common ratings, often recent landsmen themselves.[26]

To help meet the growing demand for labor, which by the late eighteenth century was emerging ever more clearly as a bottleneck in the further expansion of fleets, several European states took steps to systematically transform landsmen into seamen. In Sweden, for example, the *rotering* system required every local community along the coasts to provide the navy with one *båtsman* (ship man) each, which in most cases they did by recruiting a landless peasant and providing him with a cottage and a small plot of land in return for his willingness to serve on their behalf. The advantage of this system was the speed with which the fleet could reliably mobilize for war, since *båtsmän* were prohibited from leaving their communities for more than three days unless explicitly permitted to do so by their local admiralty agent. But the disadvantage was that many of the men thus raised were inexperienced and unskilled. The admiralty periodically made efforts to encourage *båtsmän* to gain maritime experience by signing on with merchant ships during their off years, but after 1733 only 10 percent of the total were allowed to be away at any one time, and of those only one-third were permitted to go beyond the Baltic Sea.[27]

Paradoxically, the fear was that once *båtsmän* gained enough experience to work as skilled mariners, they might desert while abroad, to either Britain or the United Provinces, where they could earn far higher wages than they did in the Swedish king's service. At mid-century, therefore, a decree determined that any *båtsman* who wished to go to sea would have to leave behind a deposit of 100 daler in silver coins, a sum far beyond the means of an average mariner. The revised articles of war issued in 1755 also prescribed ferocious punishments for *båtsmän* who ran away. During peacetime, and if there was no intention of leaving the country, the first offense was punished with running the gauntlet seven laps, or 32 lashes with either the cat-o'-nine-tails or a birch rod. The second offense was punished with nine laps or 40 lashes, followed by a lifetime of hard labor. If a *båtsman* ran away during wartime, or if his intention was to go abroad, the punishment was death.[28]

Several European navies also created institutions that took in orphaned pauper children and bred them into naval recruits. One such institution, Britain's Marine Society, provided the Royal Navy with almost 10 percent of its manpower during the French Revolutionary and Napoleonic Wars. These numbers paled, however, next to the flood of landless peasants who washed onto European warships during the 1790s and early 1800s. Rapid population growth, coupled with the continuing enclosures of common land, the monetization of rural social relations, and the commercialization of agricultural production brought forth a vast landless surplus population, highly mobile, and desperate for work. Europe's roads were clogged with men and women seeking a living, and while most of these roads led into the rapidly expanding slums of the cities, there were others that led to the coast and from there out to sea. There is a striking correlation, for instance, between the large number of landless peasants in Bohemia in the last quarter of the eighteenth century—estimated at 40 to 60 percent of the total population—and the substantial presence of Bohemians in the Dutch navy at the same time. Similar developments were underway in Ireland, where peasants flooded into the British navy, and rural France where they filled the lower decks of their own country's fleet.[29]

However, despite the influx of landsmen, those born and bred to the sea remained the largest group to serve onboard European warships. They came from two relatively distinct maritime sectors. One was made up of the men of the deep-sea trades who sailed out across the world's oceans to carry back capital and commodities to Europe's major port cities. These were the proletarianized mariners whose dreary lives were turned into the well-known stereotypes of Jack Tar, Jean Matelot, and Jan Maat: deracinated, spendthrift, childlike, and impulsive. Their working conditions had been steadily deteriorating since the late Middle Ages, when they had been conceived of in both custom and in law as subordinate but equal partners in a risky venture. By the late eighteenth century, they had instead become interchangeable "hands," hired and fired by their capitalist employers in accordance with the fluctuating demands of the market.[30]

In the other sector, that of local fishing and short-distance merchant shipping, the patriarchal relations of old-regime rural Europe still prevailed. Crews were small, hierarchies flat, cargo ownership often shared, and the powers of the captain limited both by custom and the force of communal disapproval in their home port, usually a small town or village where most of the crewmen lived with their families. For many of the young men working in the green and brown water industries (i.e., coastal and riverine shipping), seafaring was only a temporary part-time occupation that filled out what otherwise might have been idle periods during the agricultural year. Only a very few continued to work at sea once they reached middle age.[31]

Movement between both sectors of the maritime labor market for a long time was limited, but as transoceanic shipping grew more capital intensive throughout the eighteenth century, and the industry was ever more concentrated in a smaller number of major ports, thousands of men made a shift from the shallow to the deep-water trades, and with that often into lifelong careers as wage-earning proletarians at sea. The near-permanent warfare that raged across the world's oceans from the War of Austrian Succession in the 1740s to the end of the Napoleonic Wars in the mid-1810s, and the expansion of the multiple coercive recruitment systems that supplied warships with workers by the tens of thousands, shock proletarianized many more.[32]

Wooden ships of war were machines of staggering complexity. Voltaire, in *A Philosophical Dictionary*, could think of no better examples of the achievements of "Man" than warships and operas: "Here we represent a tragedy in music; there we kill one another on the high seas of another hemisphere with a thousand pieces of cannon. The opera, and a ship of war of the first rank, always astonish my imagination." Schedvin, after watching the *Eurydice*'s gun crews practice their craft, likewise marveled that "one can hardly imagine a more beautiful scene than a ship under full sail firing a broadside . . . but in order to enjoy it one had better not remember that humans invented cannon balls and powder in order to destroy and murder their equals." War at sea, Schedvin concluded, truly represented "the height of barbaric industry," a perverse testament to humanity's evil genius.[33]

Everyone who first entered onboard a man-of-war was overcome by a profound sense of wonder. Whatever their life may have been before— middle-class *philosophe* or experienced mariner, landless peasant or unemployed artisan—never before had they been in so alien and artificial an environment. Only very rarely in the eighteenth century did hundreds of men work together in one place, let alone coordinate their labor to operate a

FIGURE 4. Painting by Johannes Swertner of a French three-decker under full sail, 1770. Courtesy of the Rijksmuseum, Amsterdam.

single machine, as they did onboard a warship. Few people had experience with industrial labor discipline, and most barely accepted that the clock might have anything to do with when they ought to be working. But coming onboard a warship, new recruits suddenly found themselves in a miniature mass society, with hundreds of men toiling in unremitting twenty-four-hour work cycles, under constant supervision by their officers, their every activity standardized, closely coordinated, and precisely defined by watch, station, and maneuver. Hierarchies were rigidly drawn and brutally enforced, and all formal power concentrated in the single figure of the captain, whose unchecked will flowed out through the officer corps before cascading down to the disempowered "hands" on the lower deck.[34]

While a vast number of finely graded social distinctions separated an admiral from the lowliest seaman, shipboard society basically consisted of four groups. On top were the commissioned officers, the inhabitants of the quarterdeck, who under the leadership of the ship's commander enjoyed virtually unlimited powers onboard. They were drawn mostly from the prosperous middle classes or the aristocracy, although in the post-revolutionary French and Dutch navies, where most members of the old officer corps were judged politically unreliable, officers sometimes also rose up from the ranks. Below the commissioned officers came the warrant and petty officers, a mix of experienced seamen and trained craftsmen, such as caulkers, coopers, carpenters, gunners, and sailmakers, as well as what might be described as shipboard service workers, including chaplains, surgeons, schoolmasters, and cooks. Particularly the seamen among them were often career navy men who had slowly built up their position through years of loyal service. Socially, most of them belonged to the lower deck, but thanks to their experience, skill, and strategic position within shipboard society, they generally were treated with respect by the commissioned officer corps. The same could not be said about the largest group onboard, the common seamen. These were at best seen as dumb instruments of their officers' will, and at worst as unruly, drunken saboteurs. They were usually divided into two or three ranks, depending on their experience and training, and though some advanced up into the petty officer corps, shipboard social mobility was limited once a man was rated as an able seaman. The fourth and final group were the marines, the onboard police force that protected the quarterdeck. These were often of proletarian and foreign origin, unskilled, and widely disrespected by all others onboard.[35]

Most ships at sea operated a two-watch system: the crew, excepting the shipboard artisan classes, were divided into two identical groups that came on and off duty every four hours. Within both watches, the men were assigned to a part of the ship, reflecting their predominant area of labor. The highest skilled men were sent up into the tops, where they spent long hours in wind and weather handling the sails. When a man grew too old for the tops, he usually migrated to the forecastle, where the duties included the front-most set of sails and the anchor. Less experienced seamen and landsmen were ordered either into the ship's midsection (the waist) or its rear-most part (the afterguard), where they pulled the heavy ropes and braces that lifted and lowered the major yards and sails of the ship, looked after the livestock, and pumped bilge water. In addition to a watch and a part of the ship, each man also had a number of stations which clearly defined his exact duty for a large number of standard maneuvers, such as mooring and unmooring, weighing, tacking and wearing, lowering and squaring yards, and so forth. In battle, nearly the entire crew was assigned to the gundeck, each man again fulfilling a clearly defined role at a specific gun.[36]

From about mid-century onwards, some navies introduced divisions and squads to facilitate greater social control on their larger vessels. Under this system, the crew was broken up into small groups of men and put under the immediate supervision of an officer who was held responsible for their good behavior, cleanliness, and general seaman-like development. The Swedish navy went one step further towards individualized surveillance, issuing each man with a *förhållningsbok* (behavior book), in which was recorded his experience, training, rating, and disciplinary history. He was expected to carry it with him throughout his naval career and always present it to a new commander upon first mustering.[37]

Yet despite such innovations, the primary mechanism for social control remained the unceasing rounds of never-ending labor on board. The day's work onboard a typical British warship began at four in the morning, when one of the two watches was ordered to commence holy-stoning the deck, one of the most odious activities on board: "Here the men suffer from being obliged to kneel down on the wetted deck, and a gravelly sort of sand strewed over it. To perform this work, they kneel with their bare knees, rubbing the deck with a stone and the sand, the grit of which is often very injurious." This continued for three and a half hours until breakfast, after which the other watch was set to holy-stoning for four hours. The crew detested this incessant cleaning of the decks, especially in the winter months, but captains nevertheless continued to order it, because there quite simply was little else for the crew to do.[38]

Warships had up to ten times as many men onboard as most merchantmen of a similar size, which meant that in almost all situations except for combat they were excessively overcrewed. Lieutenant Thomas Hodgskin, who went from naval officer to socialist pioneer in the early nineteenth century, explained that a captain was constantly, obsessively thinking of ways to put his men to work, for he feared that idleness would lead to reflection and he worried that "reflection should make them compare their situation with the rest of their countrymen, with what they themselves once were, and that this reflection should rouse them to vengeance for oppression." And so sailors were kept busy with make-work, holy-stoning the deck or endless drills at small arms or the great guns, both of which the men found only slightly less objectionable.[39]

The crew ate dinner between noon and one, after which one of the watches went back on duty, usually attending to various necessary maintenance tasks, or yet more drilling, while the other watch was given leisure-time until supper at four. Two half-watches of two hours length followed, making sure that the order of on-duty, off-duty was reversed for the following twenty-four-hour period. Finally, between eight and nine, the hammocks were ordered down and the men of one watch sent to sleep. The watches changed at midnight and again at four in the morning, when the first watch of the day once again began the pointless task of scrubbing the decks.[40]

Except for a few hours of eating, drinking, and yarning in the late afternoon, seamen's daily lives were thus mostly consumed by disagreeable tasks or smothered in mind-numbing boredom. When writing his autobiography, Samuel Leech vividly remembered the many lonely hours he had spent on duty as a topman: "Often have I stood two hours, and, sometimes, when my shipmates have forgotten to relieve me, four long, tedious hours, on the royal yard, or the top-gallant yard, without a man to converse with. Here, overcome with fatigue and want of sleep, I have fallen into a dreamy, dozy state, from which I was roused by a lee lurch of the ship." The only thing worse than the boredom, he concluded, was "to be compelled to stand on these crazy elevations, when half dead with sea-sickness."[41]

But even these discomforts paled in comparison to "the King of Terrors," those rare bursts of intense violence that ruptured the tedium of everyday life and left men traumatized, wounded, or dead. When battle commenced, the ships' gundecks became an inferno: broadsides were unleashed with eardrum-bursting roars, the smoke and fire from dozens of great guns saturating the air. When cannonballs struck the hull of a ship, footlong heavy wooden splinters tore loose on the inside, severing arms and legs, smashing skulls, and cutting torsos in two as they slashed and hurtled their way across the tightly packed deck. If the battle lasted for several hours, the gundeck took on the look of a "slaughterhouse": scores of men dead and dying, heaps of unrecognizable human flesh piled high, blood streaming out the scuppers and into the sea. Down in the hold, the ship's doctor tried to salvage what he could: "The stifled groans, the figures of the surgeon and his mates, their bare arms and faces smeared with blood, the dead and dying all round, some in the last agonies of death, and others screaming under the amputating knife, formed a horrid scene of misery, and made a hideous contrast to the 'pomp, pride, and circumstance of glorious war.'"[42]

With hundreds of men packed together into a small space for long periods of time, the majority of them serving against their will, and made to work in ways that violated customary expectations in almost every other contemporary occupation, the maintenance of discipline onboard warships was never an easy matter. Naval theorists found comfort in thinking of shipboard society as "a great machine," operated but by a single human agent, the captain. Seamen, in this vision, were nothing more than "a wheel, a band, or a crank, all moving with wonderful regularity and precision." But reality was different. Instead of the interlocking wheels of discipline imagined by the theorists, "one universal system of terror" prevailed on many ships. The men were either unwilling or unable to function like cogs in a machine. They made mistakes, they were slow, they grumbled, and they complained. Orders frequently had to be accompanied by the "flesh carpenters"—the boatswain and his mates—beating the crew with their rattan canes and ropes' ends to speed up execution.[43]

If seamen committed a breach of the ship's many rules, the most common punishment in most navies was flogging with the cat-o'-nine-tails, a whip with nine separate two-foot-long cords, each reinforced with several knots. The legal maximum amount of lashes the captain could order without a court-martial varied from navy to navy (in the British navy it was twelve, and in the Danish navy twenty-seven). But most violations could be broken down into many constituent parts, and each one punished with that number of lashes. The frequency of such corrective floggings varied from ship to ship, but the average was around once every ten to fifteen days. More serious violations, ranging from derelictions of duty via buggery to mutiny, were tried by courts-martial, and these had, depending on the navy, a terrifying arsenal of punishments available to them, including solitary confinement, hard labor, pillorying, ducking, branding, pulling out of tongues, severing of hands, keel-hauling, running the gauntlet, flogging round the fleet, hanging, gibbeting, drowning, decapitation, decimation, arquebusing, and breaking on the wheel. Most of these punishments were rarely applied, but at least in the British navy, hangings and floggings round the fleet with up to eight hundred lashes were quite common, as was ducking and hard labor in the Dutch navy.[44]

Punishments that were deemed to be excessive or unfair often made crews resentful and rebellious, but they also drove men into despair, and even suicide. Soon after leaving Dover, for instance, Schedvin recorded the death of Jacob Skomakare, a *båtsman* from the central Swedish province of Södermanland, where he left behind a wife and a child. Skomakare's death appeared to be an accident—he was aloft, lost his grip, fell overboard, and drowned—but Schedvin afterwards reflected that "punishments here are as frequent as dinner. The same man who today fell into the sea was recently punished for not cleaning his mess gear; and he often spoke about suicide. In this case, who has a right to judge him?"[45]

The history of trauma, mental illness, and suicide has received little attention from historians of Europe's early modern war-fleets, but indications are that all of them were common. Samuel Leech recorded in his memoirs the case of ward-room steward Hill:

> This man came on board with a resolute purpose to give satisfaction, if possible, to his superiors. He tried his utmost in vain. He was still scolded and cursed, until his condition seemed unendurable. One morning a boy entered the after ward-room, when the first object that met his astonished eye was the body of the steward, all ghastly and bleeding. He had cut his throat and lay weltering in his gore.

Other men in Hill's situation turned their violence outward and became homicidal instead. Johan Baptist Ernaúw, a twenty-seven-year-old Piedmontese soldier on the Dutch warship *Medemblink,* fell into such a deep bout of depression after repeatedly watching innocent men being beaten by their officers that he tried to blow up the powder room and kill everyone onboard. For this he earned a sentence of three times keel-hauling, followed by a severe flogging, after which he was put ashore and banished for life. It was not a sentence likely to have benefitted his mental health. Indeed, men who survived such tortures were often left so severely traumatized that they were like walking ghosts, at times completely detached from reality. "We had many such on board our frigate," Samuel Leech remembered, "their laughs sounded empty, and sometimes their look became suddenly vacant in the midst of hilarity. It was the whip entering the soul anew."[46]

It is impossible to know how many such men wandered the decks of late eighteenth-century warships. In the British navy, the number of officially recognized "naval lunatics" rose steadily during the wars of the 1790s and early 1800s (in Hoxton House, one of the asylums used by the navy, the total climbed from 39 in 1794 to a peak of 238 in 1813). Of course, these numbers are minuscule in comparison to the thousands of men mobilized, but a man would clearly have had to be severely incapacitated before he was removed from service and locked into an asylum. Virtually all patients with a naval background in Haslar hospital, some of whom in 1824 had been there for decades already, were categorized as "incurable," and their behavior ranged from "generally quiet" and "extremely loquacious but inoffensive" to "turbulent," "noisy and violent," and "extremely violent."[47]

The feeling of having completely lost control of one's life was responsible for an inordinate amount of stress below deck, and some men were overwhelmed by it. Louis Garneray, a French sailor who went on to become a famous painter, and who as a young man was incarcerated for nine years in British prison hulks, noted that a particular form of insanity gripped some of his fellow prisoners of war:

> At sea, doesn't *rafaler* or *affaler* mean to lower away or to be caught in a squall? Well! A *rafalé* is a fellow who is completely down and under the weather. Your *rafalé* now, to return to the subject, is above all a gambler at cards, but that's nothing. What he lacks is dignity. We have only a few of them here, herded together like filthy wild beasts. We hardly ever have dealings with them, but there's one hulk where they have about two hundred of them. First of all the *rafalés* sell all of their belongings. They have neither hammocks nor bedclothes. To keep themselves warm they sleep huddled together, just like sardines, on the planks of the deck. . . . Your real *rafalé* has no breeches, coat or shirt in this world. He goes bare, stark naked!

The *rafalés*' powerful addiction to gambling probably was a form of sublimation, a way of channeling the experience of no longer controlling the course of their lives back into an arena in which they at least were able to freely choose to constantly risk it all.[48]

This sense of living an utterly unpredictable life, one in which death lurks around the corner each and every day, perhaps was most strongly felt in the prison hulks, but every person who went to sea during the age of sail experienced it to a greater or lesser degree. Professional seamen often coped with these fears by wholeheartedly embracing the unpredictable dangers of their lives. "I have read somewhere," explained Samuel Kelly,

> that seamen are neither reckoned among the living nor the dead, their whole lives being spent in jeopardy. No sooner is one peril over, but another comes rolling on, like the waves of a full grown sea. In the Atlantic one fright after another undermines the most robust constitution and brings an apparent old age in the prime of life. No trouble softens their hard obdurate hearts, but as soon as the danger is past they return in the greatest avidity to practice wickedness and blaspheme their Maker and preserver.

Ned Ward added that "no man can have a greater contempt for death, for every day [the seaman] constantly shits upon his own grave, and dreads a storm no more, than he does a broken head, when drunk."[49]

Outside observers often found it difficult to understand the culture of the lower deck, and the apparent contempt with which sailors treated mortal dangers struck onlookers as irrational, even offensive. After two men had fallen from aloft and drowned in the space of just three days onboard the *Eurydice,* Schedvin exploded in his diary that "this happened because of carelessness, and yet—only two minutes later, just as the captain was busy warning and reminding the men to be cautious—another *båtsman* almost fell from the same spot. God only knows to what one can liken the heedlessness and carelessness of these people?" Since both accidents happened during a storm, it is not clear that recklessness really was to blame, since Schedvin, who probably never went aloft, and certainly not during rough weather, most likely had no comprehension of just how hard and exhausting it was to work high above a swaying deck in howling wind and frigid rain. The anonymous author of *Life On Board a Man-of-War* recalled one gale in the Irish Sea when "the wind was so strong that it nearly took the breath from me, while the rain and the spray from the sea kept me completely drenched. I became so sick of this job, that I scarcely cared whether I held on for my own safety or not."[50]

Beyond the dangers of accidental death and the risk of imprisonment, the combined operation of the international maritime labor market's multiple and overlapping coercive labor recruitment systems added a further element of instability to life at sea, especially during wartime. Having already spent nine years continuously away from home at sea, the twenty-two-year-old James Durand was finally on his way back to Milford, Connecticut, when he was pressed by the British, who did not release him for another seven years: "Despair so completely seized on my frame, after so many hardships and disappointments, that I lost all relish for the world, and for the first 12 days I was on board, my whole victualing would not have amounted to one ration. . . . I had been now nine years from home, in hopes of always reaching that place, so necessary to my happiness, but I now wholly despaired." His countryman, John Edsall, had a similar experience in 1812 when a British press master at the Downs tore up his protection certificate—his proof of American citizenship—and then forced him into the *Burlette:* "I began now to despair; my wanderings appeared to be likely to have no termination. I did not like to look forward, and a retrospective glance, the reader will agree with me in saying, was not one calculated to cure sore eyes."[51]

Sailors like Durand and Edsall, who spent extended periods of time at sea, were sometimes overcome by a peculiar form of severe homesickness known as calenture, which killed an unknown number of people by deluding them into believing that the sea around them was in fact a luscious pasture, or "the green fields of home." Dr. William Oliver, who observed a man seized by calenture in 1693, believed that such attacks were most common at night, and

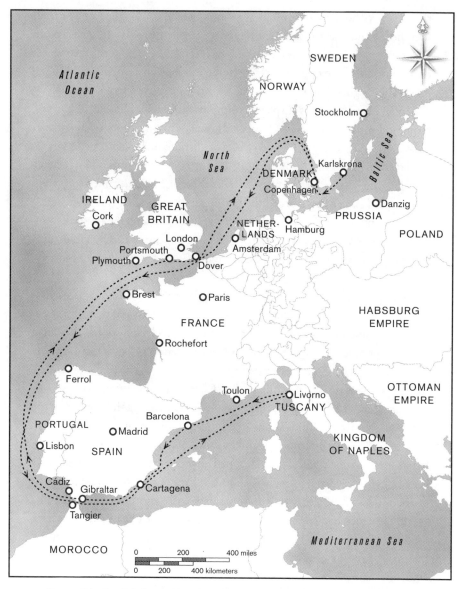

MAP 1. Route of the Swedish frigate *Eurydice*, May 1793 to September 1794, between its home port of Karlskrona in the Baltic and Livorno in the Mediterranean. Map designed by Gerry Krieg.

that men without their comrades' knowledge simply crawled out of their hammocks and over the side. On the *Eurydice,* calenture was unlikely a problem, for usually it took calm, cloudless days to induce it, and the crew experienced few of those once the frigate heaved anchor on September 5, headed down the English Channel, and out into the Atlantic Ocean. But scurvy, which in its early stages displays symptoms similar to those of calenture, brought down a man in mid-October. Thomas Trotter, who used his time as a slave ship surgeon to study the effects of chronic malnourishment, in particular insufficient intake of Vitamin C, described the symptoms of scurvy as a "longing desire for fresh vegetables, after being for some time deprived of them. This I have often marked the harbinger of scurvy. . . . It is more or less an attendant on the disease; and not only amuses [the affected person's] waking hours with thoughts of green fields and rivers of pure water, but in dreams they are tantalized with the same ideas, and on waking nothing is as mortifying as the disappointment."[52]

The *Eurydice*'s voyage down the French, Portuguese, and Spanish coasts was accompanied by nearly uninterrupted rain and gales, and the sailors were soon exhausted by having to work the ship under such conditions. They were hardly ever able to dry out their clothes and hammocks, which not only increased the risk of scurvy but also opened the crew to the epidemic disease they most likely picked up while visiting Cartagena. Schedvin, characteristically uninterested in his chosen profession as ship surgeon, did not record the name of the disease, but yellow fever and bubonic plague were common throughout the Mediterranean, and both were highly contagious and often lethal. By the time the *Eurydice* dropped anchor at the quarantine facilities in the port of Livorno, fifty men, almost a third of the crew, were incapacitated, and two had already died. Three days later, another two died, and a further five men had fallen so gravely ill that they were taken to the lazaretto ashore. It is unknown whether they survived, but they did not return on board. On December 6, ten days after the explosion onboard the *Scipion,* the epidemic claimed its final victim.[53]

The *Eurydice* spent the next three months mostly at anchor off Livorno or showing flag around the Ligurian Sea, before getting ready to convoy a number of merchant ships back to Scandinavian waters at the beginning of March 1794. The weather turned foul before they even passed through the

Straits of Gibraltar in mid-April, and after that they barely had two successive days of good, steady winds. In early May, somewhere to the west of Portugal, they were battered by a storm that lasted for several days, followed by one day of good weather, and another week of hard winds and rough seas. On May 23, they finally staggered into Spithead, the Royal Navy's anchorage off Portsmouth. The ship was badly damaged, and water and provisions were running low. After a week of emergency repairs, they got underway for the final run home, and once again they were hit by gale-force winds and driving rain as they struggled up the English Channel and across the North Sea, and then through the Skaggerak and Kattegat Sounds. Finally, on June 12, they dropped anchor off Elsinore in northern Denmark. Both ship and crew were close to their breaking points.[54]

But they were not yet home. During the *Eurydice*'s nearly year-long sojourn to the Mediterranean, British efforts to close down the direct trade between Scandinavia and revolutionary France had grown even more aggressive, and to counter the Royal Navy's dominance over North Sea shipping lanes, Denmark and Sweden had concluded an armed neutrality convention in late March 1794. By the terms of the treaty, both countries agreed to mobilize a joint fleet of sixteen ships of the line and several smaller vessels for patrol duty throughout the North Sea that summer. The *Eurydice,* instead of being allowed home for a refit and change of crew, was ordered to make sail for Copenhagen to join the combined Swedish-Danish fleet.[55]

Captain von Platen was beside himself. The ship had sprung a leak, and after so many weeks of hard weather, its sails and rigging were in no state to brave the winds of the North Sea. As for the crew, he noted, it was a miracle that not a single man had died since leaving Livorno, for their clothing had long since rotted and fallen off their bodies. He was not exaggerating. Von Platen's superior commander, Vice-Admiral Clas Wachtmeister, confirmed in a letter to the Royal Naval Committee that many of the *Eurydice*'s crew really were stark naked: no shirts, no shoes, not even pants. Cables and anchors were also missing onboard, as was brandy, and it was only a question of time before the men would fall ill again in such conditions. "Complaints," von Platen added in another letter, "have been both general and strong, and I, for one, cannot condemn them or consider them in a state of mutiny, since there is no other alternative for people who are expected to go naked into the North Sea."[56]

Despite working conditions that often bordered on the intolerable, mutinies appear to have been rare onboard eighteenth-century warships. The Dutch East India Company, for example, suffered through nearly dozen violent conflicts between 1750 and 1795, while the Dutch Navy experienced only a single, relatively orderly mutiny in the same period. The French experience was similar. Between 1706 and 1788, a period during which both the size and fortune of the navy oscillated wildly, shipboard conflicts only five times escalated to the point of triggering an official prosecution for mutiny. The French privateering fleet, by contrast, experienced five times as many mutinies (25), merchantmen more than four times as many (22), and even the deep-sea fisheries two and half times as many (13). The same picture is true for the British deep-sea industries: while the merchant marine had a well-earned reputation for shipboard conflict, the navy experienced only six full-scale mutinies between 1755 and 1789, a period that stretched across two major wars.[57]

There are, however, good reasons to assume, and anecdotal evidence to suggest, that the actual incidence of mutiny was higher than official prosecutions would indicate. Indeed, much like the ritualized subsistence rioting that was endemic throughout much of eighteenth-century Europe, eruptions of turbulent protest appear to have been fairly common onboard warships. A crew might throw an anonymous petition complaining over the late payment of wages onto the quarterdeck, or instigate murmuring campaigns against particular officers, hold illegal assemblies below deck over the poor quality of food, or even on occasion riot for shore leave. But as long as a discontented crew did not violate certain basic principles—for instance, by putting forward wild demands unsanctioned by custom—commanders were unlikely to react with arrests and formal charges. Many simply took the view that shipboard tensions were inevitable and their periodic release therefore desirable: if the men were willing to accept the risks that came with a potential charge of mutiny, their grievances were probably real and had better be redressed, if for no other reason than to assure the continued functioning of the service.[58]

The reluctance to prosecute lower deck troublemakers was also motived by self-interest. Commanding officers were generally held to be responsible for everything that happened onboard their ships, including breakdowns of discipline. In order therefore to avoid earning a reputation as a poor leader of men, and thereby endanger future promotions to more lucrative or prestigious posts, commanders had a keen interest in resolving shipboard conflicts as informally as possible, perhaps through negotiation or by punishing ringleaders without recourse to official, and therefore record-generating, judicial proceedings. Admiralty and government officials for the most part did not mind the informality of these arrangements, as they reinforced the individual captain's personal authority over his crew, which since the founding of modern navies in the sixteenth and seventeenth centuries had been the corner-stone of naval governance.[59]

In addition to the officer corps' desire to defuse lower deck discontent before it reached the stage of violent insurrection, several other factors combined to make mutinies onboard warships less likely to occur and more difficult to succeed than on any other type of vessel. First, warships were enormously crowded spaces, with virtually no opportunity for more than a tiny handful of conspirators to meet at any one time without attracting the attention of snitches and spies. Second, warships usually carried a detachment of infantrymen or specialized marine troops whose primary duty when not engaged in combat was to police the lower deck and guard against mutiny bubbling up from below. The size and composition of these detachments varied over time, between vessels, and from navy to navy, but generally they accounted for approximately 15 percent of a crew. Finally, even if the risks of discovery in the planning phase and the high chance of failure during the rising itself were not enough, the dangers that came with success might scare potential mutineers away. Even following successful mutinies, those identified as ringleaders rarely escaped completely unscathed.[60]

Rather than take such a risk, either by unlawful petitioning or outright mutiny, most men who found a particular situation no longer tolerable preferred simply to run away. It was the mariner's traditional response. Since many of his long-standing social bonds were severed when recruiters forced him into a ship that sailed halfway around the world, leaping overboard and making a run for it when an opportunity arose was often easy. And judging from the numbers of men who ran, there was no shortage of such opportunities. According to Admiral Nelson's calculations, some 42,000 British seamen took "French leave" between 1793 and 1802, a figure that is all the more impressive when recalling that the overall strength of the service in 1800 was just under 120,000. In the French and Dutch navies, the situation was even more extreme, in part because the British blockade kept their fleets bottled up in port for long periods of time, thus giving their seamen plenty of opportunities to desert. Thousands of French seamen ran away, rejoined their families, or linked up with brigand bands. Mass desertions in Brest grew to such proportions that the commune periodically felt compelled to close the city's gates in order to prevent anyone from leaving town. It did not help. Deserting seamen simply landed outside of the walls. By 1799, the Atlantic fleet was over 8,000 men short, while the Mediterranean fleet was missing a full third of its regular complement. Eventually, the back country harbored so many deserters that the government sent the hated *colonnes mobiles* against them, but that too proved useless. Mass desertions continued unabated until the end of the wars.[61]

Despite their angry muttering, the *Eurydice*'s exhausted crew also refused the risk of mutiny. A few men deserted in Copenhagen, and others were discharged ill, but most stuck around, and by early August it became clear that they probably would not be ordered to cruise in the North Sea that summer after all. The Danes, as usual, had trouble mobilizing sufficient manpower on short notice, and that spring and summer it may have been especially difficult, for Copenhagen had been hit over the past couple of years by a series of strikes and riots that reached their violent peak in 1794. In 1792, a group of seamen unloaded their class resentment against a former comrade who had become a merchant. "Listen here, you dog," they told him, "you were once a seaman like us but now you have become a merchant." The altercation quickly escalated into a major riot when the mob turned its anger on a detachment of soldiers who had arrested one of the seamen. In early 1793, on the day that news of the execution of Louis XVI reached Copenhagen, the *Posthusfejde* ("Post Office Fight") erupted after a student fought an army officer outside of the post office. Soon large crowds "of servants and the lowest scum" attacked both city hall and the police chief's official residence. A year later, almost to the day, between 500 and 800 carpenters in the naval dockyard rioted after a number of their comrades had been detained for trying to leave the yard without permission. Fifty-one men were arrested, and seventeen of them punished with hard labor and public floggings. And in the summer of 1794, as riots and strikes spread among carpenters' apprentices in a number of northern German ports, those in Copenhagen joined in. Sympathy strikes quickly spread to other crafts, first to the masons, and then to the tailors, joiners, and bakers.[62]

Seamen, about one-tenth of the Danish capital's population of 100,000 people, were among the most enthusiastic participants in these struggles. Perhaps members of the *Eurydice*'s crew went ashore and released some of the frustrations that otherwise might have led to a mutiny onboard. It is equally possible, however, that Captain von Platen's vocal sympathy for their plight—his complaints to the Admiralty eventually earned him a stern rebuke—may have blunted the crew's anger at their abominable working conditions. At anchor in a foreign port, and with a commander who was on their side, it is not readily apparent what purpose a mutiny really could have served. Demands for clothing, wages, and provisions were pointless, because they knew that neither von Platen nor any of the other Swedish commanders at Copenhagen had access to them. Had the *Eurydice* been ordered into the North Sea that summer, desperation perhaps would have seized the crew. But in the end, they only took a brief swing around nearby Öresund in early September and then headed home to Karlskrona, where the crew finally were discharged after spending nearly fifteen months in their derelict ship.[63]

Schedvin never returned to the sea. While he remained an enthusiast for revolution, during his year onboard the *Eurydice* he had developed a harder, angrier, more pessimistic view of the great social and political convulsions that were underway all around him. The explosion of the *Scipion* had brought him face to face with the violent reality of revolutionary warfare, and he spent his remaining months onboard the *Eurydice* pondering its implications. As the crew fought wind and weather to steer the ship north along the Bay of Biscay's western edge and then up through the Channel, Schedvin remained below, feverishly reading his way through Abbé Raynal's anti-imperialist *History of the Two Indies*. Studying Europe's long history of exploitation and violence overseas, he finally understood the origin of the forces that had begun to wreak such terrible havoc across the continent. Unless the colonies were destroyed, and the system of plantation slavery ended, he concluded, ill-gotten treasure would continue to feed the forces of European reaction and cripple the progress of enlightened revolution.[64]

In his diary, Schedvin gives no indication that he ever discussed these ideas with anyone onboard, including Captain von Platen's enslaved personal servant Figaro, who certainly would have agreed with his condemnation of Europe's colonial system. Nor does Schedvin appear to have ever spoken much with the common crewmen, whose strange behavior he continued to view with incomprehension. And yet, when naval seamen thought about their working conditions—torn from home, forced onto ships, made to labor under threats of violence—they sometimes described their own lot as a form of slavery. Even if this was mostly rhetorical, they knew of what they spoke. Few people traveled as widely as they, and even fewer had quite so many opportunities to study and compare the various forms of coerced labor that pumped capital and commodities into the European world economy. Others, who also knew of what they were speaking, agreed. After witnessing a flogging onboard the *Lynx* man-of-war, Hugh Crow, a notorious slave ship captain, concluded that "severity, if not cruelty . . . must be employed to keep slaves in order and subordination, whether they be black or white; and there is not, in my opinion, a shade of difference between them, save in their respective complexions." Even enslaved people sometimes thought of seamen as rather similar to themselves. In Kingston in the late 1780s, Crow overheard a black man cursing "the law for floggey negro man and poor woman, and poor buckra sailor, and red-back soldier man."[65]

Schedvin, and many other middle-class revolutionaries like him, failed to see the connection. But like the enslaved workers of the greater Caribbean, naval seamen were routinely beaten within an inch of their lives if they sought to improve the conditions they worked under. Unlike plantation workers, however, sailors found it fairly easy to get away from an especially disagreeable situation, and they did so in huge numbers during the wars of the 1790s. In part, the spike in desertions was probably due to the vastly increased number of forcibly recruited landsmen who found life at sea intolerable and tried to make their way home. But this was often difficult unless they happened to be stationed in home waters. Having lost their wages by running away, they had few resources to sustain themselves for long, and in most cases economic pressure or predatory recruitment soon forced them back into service onboard another ship.

But it was not just desertions that reached unprecedented levels in the 1790s. As ancient thrones came tumbling down and plantation islands went up in flames, naval mutinies, which had been rare for nearly a century, suddenly tore like wildfire through one fleet after another. Not since the mid-seventeenth century, also a time of all-consuming war and revolution, had naval seamen acted with such determination to improve their conditions through collective, offensive action. On hundreds of ships, the lower deck rose up, turned their guns on the quarterdeck, formed committees, elected delegates, and overthrew the absolute rule of captains. These mutinies began when revolution first shook the French Atlantic empire in 1789.

Who Will Command This Empire?

WHEN NEWS OF THE DECEMBER 1, 1789 insurrection in Toulon reached Paris, Pierre-Victor Malouet instantly understood the stakes. The Toulon dockyard, together with its counterparts in Brest and Rochefort, had been at the forefront of efforts to restore French naval might after its collapse in the Seven Years' War (1756–63). The rebuilt fleet had delivered an impressive performance during the War for American Independence (1775–83), and afterwards continued to expand until finally, in 1789, France ranked alongside Britain as only one of two naval superpowers in the world. But the rearmament effort had not been cheap. The country's costly participation in the American war had pushed the already ailing state into a full-blown financial crisis, and even though funds kept trickling into the navy, its expansion and day-to-day operations were largely financed on credit. By 1789, the navy had run up debts of over 400 million francs.[1]

Pierre-Victor Malouet's direct involvement with the navy had begun in 1781, when his long ascent within the Ministry of the Marine finally culminated with his appointment as the highest-ranking civilian administrator of the Toulon dockyard. During his nearly decade-long tenure as intendant, Malouet helped implement a series of wage-slashing reforms that pushed working-class Toulon to the edge of penury but allowed the dockyard to keep operating on an ever-expanding scale despite facing increasingly severe fiscal constraints. Most importantly, in the mid-1780s, the dockyard embarked on a major privatization program. From now on, every task that could be fulfilled by the private sector was outsourced to a contractor, with the result that the dockyard was able to reduce its directly employed workforce of three thousand by approximately two-thirds. Most workers, however, simply continued in their old position within the dockyard, but because they were now employed by a private contractor, they no longer enjoyed the generous set of benefits that service in the king's navy had provided, including guaranteed employment, free hospital treatment, contributory insurance schemes, free firewood, and, in times of need, bread from the dockyard's own bakery.[2]

With nearly half of the city's adult male population employed in the naval dockyard, and almost everyone else indirectly reliant on government funds flowing out of the Arsenal and into the local service economy, Toulon's fortunes, in good times and in bad, were closely tied to those of the central state. The reforms of mid-1780s therefore hit the city's wage-dependent working class hard. And the government's fiscal collapse in late 1788, followed by the worst winter anyone could remember, hit them even harder. They soon struck back. Following a furious hunger riot that only just stopped short of literal class warfare on March 23–24, 1789, and the plebeian takeover of the city's *milice bourgeois* and its transformation into a belligerent National Guard unit during the summer, Toulon's previously acquiescent working class emerged as a violent revolutionary force. After having dominated the city's political life for almost three centuries, members of the naval officer corps suddenly found themselves in deeply hostile territory.[3]

By fall, Commandant Albert de Rions began fearing the build-up of dual power even inside the dockyard itself. To undermine it, he decided to force a preemptive confrontation between workers organized in the revolutionary National Guard and members of the navy's own militarized elite unit, the *cannonier-matelots* (naval artillery men). But the plan that was intended to forestall a limited insurrection inside the dockyard instead triggered a much broader urban revolt that drew a majority of Toulon's radicalized working class into its chaotic orbit. When the *cannonier-matelots* refused orders to open fire on a mixed mob of residents and workers, and instead sided with their comrades in the National Guard, and then helped them beat up and throw Rions and several of the town's highest-ranking naval officers into prison, the die was cast: far from smothering the insurgency inside the dockyard, the involvement of naval seamen spread it from shore to ship and brought decades of social peace in the king's navy to a sudden, spectacular halt. On December 1, 1789, the lower deck of the French royal navy, the second most powerful fleet in the world, joined the revolution.[4]

This was far more than just a local matter. From Toulon, as well as from its Atlantic sister ports of Brest, Rochefort, and Lorient, the crown projected its naval power overseas, dispatching warships, troops, and administrators to ensure that French capital and commodities circulated safely within

European waters and out across the oceans, to the rich ports of India, to Africa's slave coast, to the islands of the Caribbean plantation zone, and then back again to the thriving commercial ports of the metropolis. The cities that were directly linked through maritime trade with the colonies overseas experienced among the highest levels of economic growth in late eighteenth-century France, or indeed Europe as a whole. This was also one of the very few sectors in the national economy that continued to boom and feed the state with revenue throughout the 1780s. When news of the December 1 insurrection therefore first began to spread, it induced panic in all those whose fortunes were tied to the sea, and to the slave-worked plantations overseas. A group of naval officers in Rochefort wrote to the Minister of the Marine to demand the most severe punishment for the insurgents, for otherwise, they warned, "all discipline will be destroyed, the multitude will henceforth make the law. The ports, the ships of war, even merchantmen, will be exposed to mutinies and insurrections."[5]

Pierre-Victor Malouet agreed. By the time of the December 1 revolt, he had left Toulon for Paris, but as a member of the newly constituted National Assembly he retained a keen interest in safeguarding the continued prosperity of the French colonial empire. When official news of the insurrection was announced in the National Assembly on December 7, Malouet sprang to his feet. While broadly sympathetic with the struggle for political reform, ideally towards something that approximated the British constitutional monarchy, Malouet did not believe that low-level war-workers should have any role in this process. In Toulon, however, dockyard workers and sailors had somehow come to believe "that it is up to them to make the law; and that every act of authority is an injustice; that all discipline is an insult to the rights of the people; that no man holding office can have authority or dignity; and finally, that liberty means to dare all."[6]

What made the appearance of anarchy a problem of such gravity was that the far-flung French empire had no choice but to depend on the same people who had just collapsed the established order in Toulon to maintain and continue the movement of ships between metropolitan France and its colonies overseas. Knowing that many of his fellow representatives were sympathetic to the insurgents, Malouet begged them to consider the consequences if the overthrow of Commandant de Rions was not condemned in the strongest terms. "Messieurs," he demanded to know, "what will become of government, the authority of law, and on what foundations will public liberty rest? And who, ultimately, will command this empire?" This was the question that agitated the career imperial administrator Malouet most of all. But it would take several years before he finally got an answer.[7]

On January 1, 1790, just a month after the Toulon insurrection, Captain de la Gallissonnière of the 74-gun ship *Léopard* predicted that his crew would mutiny sometime around the end of July. "It is my duty," he reported to the Minister of the Marine, "to warn you that one cannot count on this crew if they remain in the colony past the month of July, at which point it will be very important in order to avoid revolts that the ships on this station be relieved." Earlier that day, he reported, the crew had come together in an unauthorized assembly, mulled over their several grievances, and then presented Gallissonnière with a single, pressing demand: the ship, they warned, had better return to France before the onset of "the bad season," the annual summer downpour period which drove illness and mortality rates sky-high among European sailors in the Caribbean. Gallissonnière, who enjoyed good relations with his men and emphasized that they had acted towards him in a manner that was "not in the least reprehensible," knew that this was serious ultimatum. As conscripts during peacetime, they were only supposed to serve one year at sea for every three or four at home, but by January 1790 the crew had already spent twenty-one months onboard the *Léopard,* thirteen of them in Saint-Domingue. Since leaving Toulon, they had not been paid at all, and before that only a single month's wages. It was particularly the many fathers amongst them, noted Captain de la Gallissonnière, who grew increasingly dissatisfied. It did not help, he continued, that the men have "perfect knowledge" of the "constant troubles in France."[8]

The *Léopard* had sailed from Toulon in late October 1788, and its crew therefore had missed the horrid winter of 1788–89 and the revolutionary upheavals that followed. Yet the dense merchant traffic between France and its West Indian possessions guaranteed that even if only a few naval vessels were deployed that year, news of the "constant troubles" at home quickly spread throughout the empire. During 1789 alone, 18,460 mariners on 710 French vessels arrived in Saint-Domingue, and while the majority of these came from Bordeaux and Nantes, France's major Atlantic seaports, many also came from Toulon's close neighbor Marseille, which during the 1780s increased its West Indian trade six-fold. The crew of the *Léopard* was therefore able to follow, with only a few weeks' delay, the growing hardships their friends and families suffered back home—the runaway inflation rate, the shortages of food, the bourgeois attempt to hijack the revolution, the March 23 riots, the mounting tensions throughout the summer, the rumors of counter-revolutionary massacres in the weeks following the fall of the Bastille, the formation of a National Guard unit, and finally the complete breakdown of established military discipline during the December 1 insurrection that ended with the overthrow and imprisonment of Commandant de Rions. It is hardly surprising that the men onboard the *Léopard* were eager to get back to Toulon, and quickly, without having to endure another season of sickness in the colonies.[9]

There was no sign that the Department of the Marine intended to relieve the ships on the Saint-Domingue station anytime soon. In June, Gallissonnière wrote again to emphasize the urgency of having his men sent home no later than the middle of July. On some ships, the crews had already started murmuring about rising up and forcing their ships to sail for France, whether they were replaced or not. "It is possible," Gallissonnière admitted, "that this noise is false and has been spread by ill-intentioned spirits . . . but bad examples are contagious." The crew of the *Sensible* was openly threatening mutiny, and a volunteer seaman on the *Sans Souci,* recently arrived from Brest, had been trying to incite the crew to rise on their officers ever since the ship left France. Even worse, before sailing the man had had the audacity to complain of bad treatment at the hand of his captain, not to Brest's naval authorities, which would have been bad enough, but to the officers of the town's revolutionary municipality. As in Toulon, Brest's naval war-workers had moved rapidly from mob violence in the spring of 1789 to the formation of a National Guard unit by the late summer, undermining the navy's chain of command as they first strengthened and then radicalized the town's civil authorities. In Saint-Domingue, where a small and divided ruling class of 31,000 whites and 28,000 free people of color held down 465,000 slaves, the threat of contagion from such an example was understandably felt to be a serious one. Gallissonnière, as station commander, immediately ordered the man on the *Sans Souci* disembarked and sent back to France.[10]

This did nothing to halt the progress of the revolution in Saint-Domingue, nor to prevent Gallissonnière's men from eventually becoming entangled in it. Tensions between different factions in the colony had grown throughout the spring, and by July the supporters of two rival assemblies—one at Saint-Marc in the west, the other at Cap Français (or Le Cap) in the north—were rapidly sliding towards armed confrontation. Initial unity in driving the most hated royal bureaucrats from the colony and loosening the metropolitan hold on the

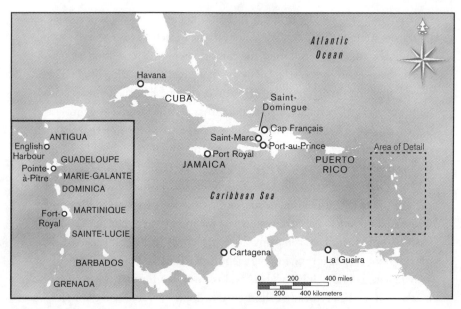

MAP 2. French Caribbean ports in the early 1790s. Map designed by Gerry Krieg.

island's economic life soon gave way to divisions of race and class among Saint-Domingue's revolutionaries. When orders for the election of a temporary consultative colonial assembly arrived in January 1790, the *petits blancs* (white laborers, smallholders, shopkeepers, artisans, clerks, overseers, and the like) seized the opportunity to move against their rich white planter allies, the so-called *blancs-blancs* (the white whites), whose domination of the colony's social, political, and economic life they deeply resented. Small whites, alongside coffee and indigo planters from the western and southern provinces involved in the inter-imperial contraband trade, used violence, intimidation, and their superiority of numbers over the wealthy sugar planters of the north to secure a majority in the new assembly. They promptly reconfigured it into a permanent General Assembly and asserted the right to initiate all legislation that concerned the government of the colony. In response, the *blancs-blancs* of the north, together with their merchant and lawyer allies in the northern Provincial Assembly at Le Cap, drew closer to the class of people the small whites hated the most, the free people of color, many of whom were wealthy plantation owners and therefore simultaneously of an economically superior class and a racially inferior caste.[11]

In Paris, meanwhile, the National Assembly, well aware of the enormous profits that could be lost by meddling with the old regime's colonial system, sought a politically acceptable way of quarantining the revolution in metro-politan France, keeping its universalism away from the racial slave system of the plantation islands. Saint-Domingue alone produced half of the world's coffee, more sugar than Jamaica, Cuba, and Brazil combined, and in 1790 purchased almost half of the 97,860 slaves that European and American trad-ers sent across the Atlantic that year. The colony was the most productive and profitable piece of land in the entire Atlantic system. It played a crucial role in the French imperial economy even before the state bankruptcy and finan-cial crisis of the late 1780s; afterwards, as the plantation economy kept boom-ing and expanding, its importance only grew. If the radical egalitarianism of the Declaration of the Rights of Man and the Citizen—"all men are born and remain equal in rights"—were allowed to escape beyond French shores and touch upon the slave plantation islands overseas, French capitalism, built on a foundation of colonial exploitation, transoceanic exchange, and metro-politan accumulation, would suddenly lose the bedrock upon which it stood: racial slavery.[12]

Therefore, on March 8, 1790, the National Assembly passed a decree which declared that while "considering the colonies as a part of the French empire and desiring for them to enjoy the fruits of the happy regeneration that here has taken place," the intention most certainly was not "to subject them to laws which could prove incompatible with their local and particular customs." The decree left internal colonial governance to local assemblies, "freely elected by the citizens"—a category which may or may not include free people of color—but it strictly prohibited "innovations in any branch of commerce, either direct or indirect, between France and its colonies." Finally, it erected a protective shield around the institution of slavery by putting "colonials and their property under the particular safeguard of the nation, and whoever works to create an insurrection against them is declared a crimi-nal against the nation."[13]

The deputies of the self-declared General Assembly at Saint-Marc greeted the arrival of the March 8 decree with outrage. The assembly had been elected with an exceptionally broad franchise—all white males resident for at least a year in the colony were admitted—but the instructions for implementation that accompanied the March 8 decree not only suggested the possibility of political rights for free people of color, it introduced property and tax-paying require-ments for voting which once again excluded many of the newly enfranchised small whites. Members of the assembly announced that they would rather die than cede political power to "a bastard and degenerate race." A campaign of violence against free people of color quickly ensued, culminating at the end of April in two decrees that forcibly confined them to their parishes. Shortly afterwards, on May 28, the General Assembly put forward what it called "the fundamental principles of the constitution of Saint-Domingue," in which it declared itself sovereign over all affairs internal to the colony, and assumed a significant say in those that concerned its external trade relations.[14]

Enemies of the Saint-Marc assembly seized the opportunity to hurl charges of separatism and treason. Opposition centered in the Provincial Assembly of the North at Le Cap, dominated by *blancs-blancs,* which now allied itself with what remained of the colonial government. Together they began to prepare for a military offensive. The General Assembly at Saint-Marc responded in kind, and both sides now claimed sovereignty over the king's forces stationed in the colony. But while the Le Cap assembly worked through the old imperial command structures, the *petits blancs* patriots in Saint-Marc declared their enemies traitors and used the network of revolutionary municipalities and regional committees to appeal directly to the troops. This proved largely fruitless amongst the soldiers in the colonial regiments, but the sailors in the Port-au-Prince squadron, and especially those onboard the flagship *Léopard,* appeared willing to be "seduced by the insinuations of the General Assembly of the Colony meeting at Saint-Marc and the secret machinations of the Committee of the West at Port-au-Prince."[15]

Gallissonnière knew that a mutiny amongst his men could have devastating consequences. His squadron, led by the flagship *Léopard,* provided the all-important naval screen that secured the circulation of slaves and tropical commodities in and out of Port-au-Prince, Saint-Domingue's administrative capital and its second most important commercial harbor. When Gallissonnière had first alerted his superiors to the risk of insurrection in his squadron at the beginning of the year, he had been careful to emphasize that "until this moment the mariners embarked on the king's ships have taken no side in the troubles that exist here, however agitated they may have become. If they no longer were to recognize their commander, one cannot imagine the level of disorder to which things would be carried. It is all the more dangerous," he concluded, "that they are able to ravage both sea and land." Indeed, with only about two thousand royal soldiers in the colony, the *Léopard* alone, with its 74 guns and hundreds of men trained at small arms, had the power to tip the balance of military force in favor of the Saint-Marc assembly if the crew chose to violate orders and intervene on its behalf.[16]

Hoping to prevent just that, on July 27 Gallissonnière ordered the *Léopard* to prepare to sail for Le Cap the next day. But before the ship could get underway, he received a decree from the Saint-Marc assembly forbidding him to leave the Port-au-Prince roadstead until further notice. Gallissonnière, who did not recognize the General Assembly as legitimate, immediately ordered all unauthorized communication with the shore shut down, and in the course of the day intercepted at least three packages addressed to various petty officers, each containing multiple copies of the decree. The crew was wavering. In the afternoon, they had appeared happy enough with the prospect of sailing that night, but by nine o'clock in the evening Gallissonnière was told a conspiracy was underway to refuse orders. An hour later there was enough turmoil in the ship that he gave up all hope of being obeyed that night. He delayed the departure, "flattering myself," as he put it, "with the notion that the leaders of the cabal would be less audacious in the morning."[17]

He flattered himself in vain. When ordered to raise the topsail the next evening, the recalcitrant crew first reacted sluggishly, and then one by one they began murmuring, their voices rising louder, until finally the boatswain was forced to pipe for silence over their repeated shouts of "*non, non, non!*" Gallissonnière reasoned with them, threatened them, reassured them, but when the order for raising the topsail was given again, it was met with another round of "*non, non, non!*" The captain then ordered one of the leading mutineers arrested, but "the whole crew took his side . . . shouting that he should be released." They told Gallissonnière that the ship would not sail without orders from the regional Committee of the West, dominated by the *petits blancs* of Port-au-Prince. "We are to be used to spill the blood of citizens," the sailors protested, "and that we will not do. The [Port-au-Prince royal infantry] regiment is planning to butcher the town." Gallissonnière tried to assure them that nothing of the sort was planned, but the crew again told him that "we want to stay here to defend the citizens of Port-au-Prince." Gallissonnière made a final attempt at being obeyed, but he was laughed off the deck when someone replied to his order to raise the topsail with "Fine, we'll raise the topsail, but the anchor stays where it is, so why even raise the topsail?" Gallissonnière left the ship shortly afterwards, along with most of his officers.[18]

Mutiny onboard the *Léopard* in itself did not avert the risk of a massacre, and the very night Gallissonnière abandoned the ship, July 29, the Chevalier de Maudit, colonel of Port-au-Prince's royal regiment, received orders from the colonial government to dissolve, with force if necessary, the Committee of the West, before moving his troops to Saint-Marc, where they were to rendezvous with the regiment sent from Le Cap. The next day, as Maudit was mobilizing his troops, the *Léopard*'s crew sent Gallissonnière a letter, inviting him and his fellow officers to return to the ship which, in the crew's opinion, "they [had] abandoned without any reason whatsoever." The mutineers continued by assuring their captain that "we do not lack that respect which is due to you. But we have the honor to observe that if you fail to come back onboard the ship, it is up to the crew, in the final instance, to elect (from amongst the few remaining officers) a captain in order to guarantee the preservation of the ship which ought to be dear to all good Frenchmen."[19]

The crew, of course, had no such right. Hierarchies onboard warships were clearly defined, and in case a commander was unable to exercise his duties, responsibility simply devolved down the chain of command to the next available officer. At the same time, the crew's assertion was not without precedent. Before the seventeenth-century creation of modern navies, European shipping ventures were usually cooperative undertakings, in which ship masters were understood, in custom as well as in law, to be only the first among equals (*primus inter pares*). This principle, intended to protect the property of stay-at-home merchants and shipowners against incompetent or self-interested masters in an era of expanding maritime trade, made its way into medieval maritime law codes. The thirteenth-century *Rôles d'Oléron,* for example, established a carefully calibrated shipboard social order that balanced the rights of the master to be obeyed against the rights of the crew to be consulted in all important decisions while the ship was abroad. The co-participatory nature of these arrangements could be taken quite far, and in some cases, they survived well into the early modern period. For example, German sea regulations from 1614 determined that a master could only punish members of the crew for mutiny if two ordinary seamen agreed with him—if they did not, there was no mutiny, but simply a case of the master being outvoted by the crew.[20]

It is in the context of these submerged traditions that the *Léopard* mutiny might be understood. The crew clearly felt a powerful sense of responsibility to act according to the will and in the interest of "all Frenchmen," the shipowner to whom both captain and crew separately would have to be able to justify their actions while abroad. To Gallissonnière, the crew's collective refusal of an order was a decisive breach of military discipline, which had to be restored through either formal pardon or punishment. In contrast, the crew saw it as a legitimate disagreement at a moment of grave danger, which therefore called for collective deliberation and decision-making. From the crew's perspective, this dispute in itself did not undermine the captain's ability to exercise his authority in the future, but his permanent abandonment of the ship did.

Gallissonnière had no other option. Because the crew had thrown in their lot with the General Assembly at Saint-Marc, he told them, they had become "traitors to France, and henceforth could no longer be commanded by Frenchmen." Neither he nor his officers would therefore resume command as long as the crew remained "determined to renounce their fatherland and do every possible evil in trying to squander the beautiful colony of St. Domingue." There is no clearer proof of their treason, he told them, than their unanimous refusal to sail for France. However, having consulted with the military council at Port-au-Prince, Gallissonnière was willing to forgive and forget if they immediately returned to duty, raised the topsail, lifted the anchor, and then, finally, and without delay, sailed for France.[21]

No one really believed the charge of treason, least of all Gallissonnière. In his report on the mutiny, he even argued that "the crew of the warship Léopard is infinitely more unfortunate than guilty. They were truly persuaded that in taking the side of the assembly in St. Marc and against the government and officer corps, they were serving the good cause. They certainly are not disenchanted with France." Gallissonnière was right. Knowing they were able to intervene decisively in the conflict between the insurgent small-white patriots and the armed forces of the government put the Léopard's crew in a difficult bind. They had to weigh, on the one hand, the increasingly doubtful legitimacy of those long-established institutions that officially represented the French imperial government in the colonies, including the naval officer corps, against, on the other hand, the claim of a newly constituted, locally elected colonial assembly. By the summer of 1790, over a year after the fall of the Bastille, it was no longer obviously clear which of these was the true embodiment of the French nation overseas.[22]

Because the General Assembly was elected without the participation of free people of color, and its deputies remained fanatically opposed to their civic emancipation, the Léopard mutiny has often been interpreted as simply motivated by racism. But its politics were more complex than that. Whatever they may have thought on the question of racial equality, the crew was most of all concerned with preventing what they perceived to be an imminent slaughter of their fellow citizens in Port-au-Prince and Saint-Marc. Indeed, soon after Gallissonnière charged the crew with treason to France, they renamed their ship *Le Sauveur des Français* (The Savior of the French), thus meeting his demand for submission to the imperial nation, as it was embodied in the old regime's military and colonial hierarchies, with a commitment to defend the regenerated nation's new constitutive political subject, the French people. Saint-Domingue's governor, the Comte de Peinier, recognized immediately the dangerous political implications of that step. "All must be sacrificed," he roared at Gallissonnière, "to remove this ship which could become the cause of the loss of the colony if the crew, even after having renounced them, cling to principles which are difficult to destroy while they remain in St. Domingue."[23]

When the *Léopard* again refused to sail for France—the name change does not appear to have stuck—Governor de Peinier ordered Port-au-Prince's fort and harbor batteries to prepare red-hot shot for a bombardment of the ship, hoping the threat of an inferno would finally drive them away. On the *Léopard,* the crew watched the preparations in disbelief. Red-hot shot was rarely used against enemies, and certainly never against fellow citizens, be they ever so mutinous. The seamen quickly informed Gallissonnière that in order to maintain "peace and harmony between the two parties," none of the remaining officers would be allowed off the ship. The next day, having elected "with one voice" the *Léopard*'s second lieutenant to replace Gallissonnière as captain, the crew took the ship to sea and hurried towards Saint-Marc, where the General Assembly had issued a desperate proclamation: "In the name of the Nation, the Law, the King, and the imperiled French part of Saint-Domingue—union, force, haste, and courage! The infamous [Governor] Peinier, the execrable [Colonel] Maudit have accomplished their vile project: they have soaked their hands in the blood of citizens. To arms!"[24]

Two small armies were converging on Saint-Marc, one from Le Cap, the other from Port-au-Prince. Since both were preparing to lay siege to the town, the military situation was overwhelmingly against the forces of the General Assembly, which consisted of just one detachment of soldiers, some ragtag National Guardsmen, and a few of the town's braver civilians. The arrival of the *Léopard* did little to change this. Sticking to their commitment to act only as protectors, the crew announced that while they were ready "to defend the assembly until the last drop of their blood, they would not act offensively in its name against its enemies." This refusal drove the final nail into the coffin of the General Assembly. Eighty-five of its members, most of those still remaining at Saint-Marc, together with ninety soldiers that had defected from the Port-au-Prince regiment, abandoned the town and boarded the *Léopard,* which immediately heaved its anchor, raised its sails, and set course for Brest. Five weeks later, on September 14, they finally arrived back in France. It had been nearly two years since the ship and its crew had sailed from Toulon.[25]

The crew of the *Léopard,* on station in the West Indies, had carefully begun the process of reconstructing the revolutionary navy from below—rejecting the absolute authority of the royally appointed officer corps, electing their own captain, diverting the chain of command and finding a new source of legitimacy in locally elected assemblies. Meanwhile, in Paris, the National Assembly's *Comité de Marine* set about the same project from above. Created in October 1789, the committee was charged with reviewing the composition of the naval officer corps, the fleet's administrative structure, its manning system, and its disciplinary regime. Where necessary, the committee was to suggest new rules and regulations, "founded on reason" and agreeable with a "free constitution." Its first two proposals—a bill suggesting minor changes to the manning system, and another reconfiguring the balance between civil and military administrators—were considered ill-conceived by the full assembly. Only after the committee had been expanded with several members of the maritime bourgeoisie did it successfully begin to send bills to the floor. On June 26, the new constitutional principles of the navy were passed into law, which turned the fleet into an instrument of the nation's will, dedicated to the protection of French commerce and overseas colonization. Budgetary control was firmly lodged with the National Assembly, and while the king remained the fleet's commander in chief, all other positions within the navy were theoretically thrown open to every qualified citizen. With that, naval policy was brought into line with the May 19 abolition of the nobility, although it would take some time before commoners were actually able to ascend the quarterdeck in meaningful numbers.[26]

These were important innovations, but they paled in comparison with the committee's next proposal: a completely new *Code Pénal Maritime,* which it presented to the National Assembly on August 16. The *Comité de Marine* rejected the existing code, largely unchanged since the reign of King Louis XIV, as "a work of despotism, as incomplete as it is rigorous." Inspired by the ideas of Enlightenment penology that were rapidly winning converts among European reformers, the committee went on to list its shortcomings: "there are no gradations in punishment, excessive severity, death and galley service pronounced for offences that can be excused by human weakness, and crimes which religion alone ought to sanction expose the unlucky or insane perpetrator to the most ferocious punishments." Despite these oppressive laws, order was maintained in the fleet, the committee argued, because officers and men had reached a tacit agreement to disregard them in favor of a more harmonious paternalist relationship. This had worked surprisingly well: "custom has instilled [in the men] a nearly religious respect for authority, arbitrary but always exercised with tenderness and moderation, which takes the place of laws that are never executed." But living as they now did under "a free Constitution," the time had come to abolish this system of personal, arbitrary, and extra-legal rule, and replace it with the supreme authority of the law.[27]

The new *Code Pénal Maritime* contained two major innovations. First, when it came to determining a man's guilt, trial by jury replaced the naval court-martial. This introduced the principle of popular sovereignty into a process which traditionally had been dominated by the officer corps. An accused seaman, instead of facing a panel made up of only his superior officers, now pleaded to a jury composed of one commissioned officer, three warrant officers, and three of his fellow *matelots*. In addition, the accused man would be allowed to choose one defender from amongst the crew. His commanding officer was completely removed from the whole process, except at the very end when, in his role as the nation's highest representative on board, he was given "the beautiful right" of being able to show mercy by commuting the sentence to a lesser one. It was an arrangement, the committee believed, "truly based in civil liberty, and honorable to a free people."[28]

Second, the new code tightly regulated, defined, and precisely graded the range of punishments that could be imposed on a guilty man. Here, it distinguished between "disciplinary" and "afflictive" punishments. The former were incurred for a very broad range of minor offences, such as drunkenness, fighting, absence without leave, or lighting an unauthorized fire below deck. These were all far too small to warrant a trial, and the captain was therefore given the flexibility of choosing an appropriate punishment from a very narrow list of options. Such arbitrariness was not ideal, the committee conceded, but since the aim was correction and not retribution, only mild punishments, such as withholding the wine ration for a few days or forcing a man to wear a foot-ring with a trailing chain, were permitted. The code also urged the captain to exercise all possible restraint and understanding, and to behave towards his crew as mercifully as a father would towards his children.[29]

Violations that called for "afflictive" punishments were a different matter altogether: "here all uncertainty disappears; the punishment is as precise as the crime." Indeed, most of the new code consisted of a long list of serious shipboard offences that were matched with precisely defined punishments, many of them as gruesome as anything contained in the old regulations, including flogging, ducking, and running the gauntlet. Once a jury issued a guilty verdict, the punishments would automatically be imposed by the majestic objectivity of the law, except for those crimes that demanded the death penalty or galley service, in which case a "martial council" composed of high-ranking naval officers would have to confirm the verdict by a 7–4 majority (for galley service) or an 8–3 majority (for the death penalty).[30]

The new *Code Pénal Maritime* was well intentioned, informed by humanitarian ideals, and unrivalled amongst eighteenth-century naval articles of war in its application of Enlightenment penal philosophy. But it did not live up to its stated purpose of bringing the internal governance of the navy fully into the modern constitutional era. Instead, it created for the navy a hybrid legal space that combined in complex and contradictory ways elements of both old-regime authoritarianism and post-revolutionary republicanism. For example, it confirmed the captain in the arbitrary and personal nature of his power, even as it severely restricted its scope, leaving him only with the ability to pardon and to correct as he saw fit. On the flipside, through the introduction of jury trials, the "people" gained those unlimited powers to punish wrongdoing that the captain had lost, but under the new code those powers were so tightly regulated as to remove almost all flexibility from their application. Ironically, therefore, while the arbitrary exercise of power was associated in the new code with mildness, understanding, and forgiveness, popular sovereignty and the rule of law were identified with mercilessness and spectacular forms of punitive violence carried over from the old regime. This confused muddling of elements had the effect of re-inscribing into law the principle that immediately beyond French shores a different legal order prevailed, a principle long since institutionalized in the Department of the Marine's responsibility for both the navy and the colonies. But in contrast to the National Assembly's March 8 decree, which simply excluded colonial slavery from the political regeneration that swept through French institutions in 1790, the new *Code Pénal Maritime* sought to reconcile the old-regime navy's "colonial" form of governance with the recognition that those who lived below deck and toiled up in the shrouds were now fellow citizens.[31]

When the new *Code Pénal Maritime* was officially announced on September 6, 1790, seamen reacted with outrage. At Brest, home to the navy's Atlantic fleet and its largest, most important dockyard, the announcement triggered a fleet mutiny. Trouble began on the *America*, spread to the flagship *Majesteux*, and from there to all the other warships in the roadstead. Soon between 1,500 and 2,000 seamen had seized control of their ships' boats and were rowing towards Brest. Shopkeepers boarded up their stores for fear of looting, and the panic-stricken municipal authorities ordered troops to be assembled and armed in their barracks, ready to meet violence with violence. But that was not what the mutineers had in mind. Instead, they held an orderly march through town, and when they arrived at the Hôtel de Ville they asked for permission to present the municipality with a list of grievances regarding the new code. Thirty men, two representatives from each of the fifteen crews present, were invited to speak in the chamber.[32]

The men had three complaints. First, they thought it completely unacceptable that the new code allowed boatswains and their mates to continue carrying ropes' ends as symbols of their office. These were traditionally used to dole out random subjudicial punishment beatings, a practice intended to remind ordinary seamen of their powerlessness, and therefore totally inappropriate for the regenerated navy, especially when some kind of insignia would do just as well for a distinguishing mark. Second, the crews' representatives complained that despite the new code's restrictions on the application of "afflictive" punishments, some of them remained unacceptably out of proportion to the crime, such as ducking for bringing alcohol on board, or the death penalty for even just lightly striking an officer.[33]

Finally, they objected to the new "disciplinary" punishment of being forced to wear a foot-ring with a trailing chain, which replaced the old irons that stapled a man to the deck. This, they argued, was degrading. Being forced to wear the ring and chain was a punishment associated with "galley slaves," who by the late eighteenth century were no longer enslaved rowers but convicts condemned to a lifetime of hard labor in the naval dockyards. However, imposing the ring and chain on naval seamen inevitably brought to mind the history of galley slavery, which originated in the enslavement of previously free volunteer rowers during a similar period of endemic warfare and severe labor shortages in the fifteenth- and sixteenth-century western Mediterranean. To the seamen of the fleet, the ring and chain was therefore a symbol for the fragility of their freedom at sea, for their continued confinement into a separate legal sphere, and for the dreadful horizon of slavery towards which they might yet be driven.[34]

Overall, the message was clear: the new code did not go nearly far enough in dismantling quarterdeck tyranny. By taking their complaints to the municipality and not up the navy's chain of command, the seamen also signaled their rejection of the semi-colonial legal sphere the new code had created for them. Much like the *Léopard*'s crew had done at Port-au-Prince, the mutineers in Brest instead sought to put themselves under the regular jurisdiction of locally elected, civilian authorities on shore. The municipality, however, did not accept their submission to its authority and simply passed on their complaints to Commandant de Rions, Brest's highest ranking naval officer, who in turn forwarded them to the next higher level of civil authority above himself, the National Assembly, which finally responded with a testy decree a week later.[35]

"Some lost men," it grumbled, "have misunderstood the happy dispositions of the Assembly's decree, and, confused about the intentions behind a number of articles, have overlooked how the new code, given to them with paternal solicitude, is gentler and more just than the rigorous and arbitrary regime by which they have been governed." The assembly went on to reject the complaints put forward by Rions in the men's name. The rope's end, it declared with a surprising lack of reforming spirit, had been used since time immemorial in the French and every other European navy, and therefore one should only be concerned with preventing its abuse. As for the foot-ring with the trailing chain, its intention was to replace the painful and unhealthy punishment of being put in irons on deck, and hence there really could be no legitimate complaints about it. This was an extremely mild punishment, the assembly explained, and in no way should it be construed as a degradation. The decree did not address the issue of disproportionately severe punishments.[36]

Rions had warned the assembly that the mutineers' complaints needed to be taken seriously—preferably two commissioners should be sent to Brest to deal with them directly—or the whole fleet must be disarmed, and the men dispersed. The assembly dismissed his concerns. The revolt was far from a general one among the crews, it claimed in a report on the matter, and most likely "enemies of the Constitution (because unfortunately these are everywhere)" were responsible for spreading the seeds of discontent, targeting in particular "newly recruited seamen, men lacking in training and only barely exercised in discipline, who can very easily be entangled by error and sugges- tion." The assembly was persuaded "that all true mariners remained faithful to military discipline, [and] that the confidence which the seamen have in their commander, as well as their sense of duty, is sufficient for maintaining that exact subordination which has always been the sign of a free people."[37]

It was a remarkably tone-deaf response, almost perfectly designed to deepen the conflict between state authorities and crews. The complaints about the new code clearly came from men steeped in their profession and its traditions. These were men, moreover, who regularly braved the war-torn, storm-tossed waters of the North Atlantic and therefore did not need land-lubbing legislators to lecture them on the importance of shipboard discipline. They were well aware of the need for proper submission to authority so as not to endanger the ship and everyone in it. At the same time, as a "free people," they expected that authority to be legitimate. And that, it increasingly appeared, was not the case with their royally appointed officers.[38]

At Brest, much like at Toulon, the naval officer corps had always been viewed as a powerful alien imposition, and it only made matters worse that virtually all of them had a noble pedigree. Following the July 1789 outbreak of the revolution, suspicion against them mounted quickly, and when they refused to let their men participate in the nationwide oath-swearing ceremo- nies that accompanied the July 14 Feast of the Federation, muttering was finally transformed into open hostility, and not just on the coast. The influen- tial newspaper *Révolutions de Paris* exploded with rage, damning Brest's naval authorities for cloaking their town in silence while all over France, and indeed the rest of Europe, people came together to celebrate the first anniversary of this new dawn of liberty. Echoing Emmanuel-Joseph Sieyès's famous judg- ment on the aristocracy, the paper charged the naval officer corps with having made themselves irrevocably into "strangers to their country." "It is high time," it concluded, "that the National Assembly takes on the task of regenerating that part of the military to which we have entrusted the safety of our coasts."[39]

The danger of an unreconstructed officer corps dominated by the aristoc- racy appeared to be confirmed the very next month when, on August 31, 1790, the Marquis de Bouillé used 4,500 troops to put down an army mutiny that had erupted over pay arrears and disciplinary matters at Nancy, in the north- eastern province of Lorraine. One mutinous soldier was broken on the wheel, 22 hanged, and 41 condemned to thirty years galley service each at Brest. The *Affaire de Nancy* became a major scandal, and on the national political scene it effectively marked the end of the Marquis de Lafayette's attempt to forge a coalition between progressive members of the aristocracy and the revolutionary bourgeoisie. Individual nobles had already been implicated in counterrevolutionary plots over the preceding months, but following the events at Nancy the whole aristocratic class became firmly identified with organized, violent reaction. Lafayette himself, "the hero of two worlds, the man who became immortal in the cause of liberty," was denounced by Jean-Paul Marat in his *L'Ami du Peuple* as "the leader of the counter-revolutionaries and the inspiration of all the conspiracies against our beloved country."[40]

Into this atmosphere of rising class anger the National Assembly released its new *Code Pénal Maritime,* and though guided by Enlightenment principles, in its attempt to construct a hybrid legal regime for the navy it failed to take into account that the longstanding paternalist bonds between aristocratic officers and plebeian men were already damaged beyond repair. Seamen now considered themselves equal citizens of the French nation, which is why they complained about the new code to the elected municipality and not to their commanders. As citizens, they expected to be treated with dignity and respect. Many of the seamen who served in the fleet were no longer willing to participate in the demeaning illusion of their commander as "the head of a large family who chastises with tender, even fatherly corrections those of his children who have strayed into error." Such undignified pretense was especially intolerable when the imagined father figure was in fact a politically suspect aristocrat, to whom the new code granted arbitrary powers not only to punish but to degrade those citizens who fell under his command. "There is no point in revolution," an article in *Révolutions de Paris* argued, "as long as the active forces of the empire continue to be directed by commanders known or suspected of being enemies of public liberty. What confidence can they inspire? What obedience can they exact from those who are destined to serve under their command when their conduct and their manifest opinions give the soldier a thousand reasons to believe that it is dangerous to march under their banner?" The brutal suppression of the army mutiny at Nancy— forty-one participants were now incarcerated in Brest's Pontaniou prison— provided more than enough evidence that the danger was real.[41]

Before the National Assembly even had the opportunity to dismiss the seamen's complaints against the new *Code Pénal Maritime,* another mutiny broke out at Brest. On September 11, the crew of the *Ferme* refused to weigh anchor and set sail for the West Indies at the head of a small squadron of eight vessels. There had been long delays in their departure, and the three months' advance pay the crew received when first coming on board had already been used up. In order to put to sea, they demanded, "with *sang-froid*," another two months' worth of wages. Despite the protests that had rocked the fleet only a week before, this direct refusal of an order to sail was a significant escalation of the conflict between quarterdeck and forecastle. Throwing in its lot once again with the naval authorities, the municipality worried that "the spirit of insubordination in the fleet is reaching an alarming level, and one cannot ignore the frightful consequences that could ensue, for the Nation in general, and for the city of Brest in particular." Graphic threats of punishment soon broke the mutiny, and after the ship's petty officers returned to duty, its detachment of soldiers soon followed, and eventually its common crewmen as well. But the *Ferme* still could not sail, for the very next day, September 14, the *Léopard* arrived and thus brought the radicalism of the Saint-Domingue revolution to the fleet in Brest.[42]

Not knowing how they would be received in France, the *Léopard*'s crew had drafted a careful petition to the king in which they downplayed the significance of what had taken place at Port-au-Prince and Saint-Marc. "Your faithful subjects composing the crew of your ship the *Léopard*," they wrote,

> were, in Saint-Domingue, forced to make the cruel choice between treason to the nation or disobedience to their commanders. They were forced to choose the latter. Monsieur de la Gallissonnière, our captain, abandoned us with nearly his whole officer corps. Monsieur de Santo Domingo, our second in command, replaced him, and with him at the helm we returned the ship to your orders. We hope, Sir, that our conduct will not be seen to be either against you or against the corps of naval officers.

These *fleur-de-lis*-draped assurances of continued loyalty most likely were meant in earnest, but the deferential tone did not obscure the quiet confidence with which the crew presumed to be better judges of what might constitute treason to the nation than their own royally appointed, socially superior officers. The crew—composed of common sailors, fishermen, artisans, laborers—in effect told the king that obeying the men he had invested with his authority would be, in their opinion, to condone, even aid, murder and treason. Mutiny therefore had become a moral and political imperative.[43]

Upon their arrival at Brest, the people onboard the *Léopard*, both the crew and the deputies of the General Assembly, did not even bother reporting to Brest's naval intendant, M. Redon de Beaupréau, but headed straight for the municipality instead. Redon, not exactly hiding his irritation, wrote to the Minister of the Marine that "I do not know what they talked about, but I can see that it made a strong impression, since the municipality and the district marched with them, ahead of a large detachment of National Guardsmen, volunteer seamen with their swords drawn, and music, cannon-fire, and church-bells ringing. I will give you a more detailed report when I am better informed." Similar scenes of celebration repeated themselves over and over again in the coming days. Seamen, municipal officers, local Jacobins, and the deputies from Saint-Domingue affirmed and re-affirmed their friendship and solidarity, with gallons of cider and rousing toasts—"Long live the nation and the King!", "Long live the deputies from Saint-Domingue!" and "Long live the Municipality and the Friends of the Constitution!" The people of Brest "fought each other for the honor to receive and celebrate them in their homes."[44]

News of the "execrable affair" in Saint-Domingue spread fast, and it seemed to confirm all the suspicions against the forces of the aristocratic counter-revolution which now attached themselves more firmly than ever to the naval officer corps. Rumors soon swirled through the fleet that the Vicomte de Marigny, the navy's second highest ranking officer at Brest, was about to take a squadron to Saint-Domingue, "to bring to reason and cut to pieces the partisans of the general assembly of the colony." In response, someone erected gallows in de Marigny's front yard one night, a reminder of what might happen if he ordered the fleet to sail. The municipal authorities condemned this as a "blood-thirsty affront," but they too had their suspicions about his orders and forbade the *Ferme* to sail.[45]

The municipality's intervention was mostly an empty gesture, for discipline throughout the fleet was in a state of collapse. Only four days after the arrival of the *Léopard*, a group of Brest naval officers sent the Minister of the Marine a desperate plea, informing him that "anarchy and insubordination reign among the crews of our ships. The officers who command them are totally unable to make them respect the laws; the commander-in-chief himself is publicly disobeyed; one dares to insult him on the very ship that flies his standard." On the *Patriote*, "a great fermentation" broke out when a drunken and "seditious" seaman from the *Léopard* was ordered off the ship. Captain d'Entrecasteaux's crew feared the man was to be punished, so they told their captain that he had no right to make up laws, and that the man under no cir-

PORT DE BREST. *INSURRECTION DES VAISSEAUX DE LÉOPARD ET L'AMÉRICA.*
en Septembre 1790

FIGURE 5. Painting of the mutinous ships *Léopard* and *America* at the port of Brest in September 1790, after the *Léopard*'s return from Saint-Domingue, Paris 1802. Courtesy of the Bibliothèque nationale de France.

cumstances must be harmed. When d'Entrecasteaux reminded them of their oath of loyalty, they denied having ever taken one, and, in any case, "they were the strongest, they make the law." In that case, Captain d'Entrecasteaux told them, he was forced to resign his post. "So much the better!" the crew hollered. "Long live the nation! The aristocrats to the lamp-post!"[46]

Commandant de Rions came on board the next day, assuring everyone that there had been no plans to punish the man from the *Léopard*. He had merely been ordered back to his own ship to sober up. But unfortunately, the leader of the previous day's mutiny would now have to go to prison. The crew just taunted Rions in response: "He will not go," they told him, "He will not go!" When Rions asked for a show of hands to see if anyone on board would obey him, not a single hand went up. Upon returning to his flagship, the *Majesteux,* he learned that the ship's detachment of soldiers was refusing to do regular duty, and for that they too had gone unpunished. "In vain did I tell my officers that subordination still reigns in the fleet," he reflected, "but my mouth was unable to convince them of what I myself no longer believed."[47]

Rions was finished, and he knew it. On September 20, a week after serious troubles had erupted in the fleet, the municipality described to its deputies in Paris how Rions's men had openly turned on him: "You cannot imagine to which point they have carried their animosity towards the general; they loudly proclaim that they do not want him, that he is an aristocrat." Two and a half weeks later, Rions resigned his command. But his resignation did little to lessen the anti-aristocratic fury that now burned through the fleet. Only ten days later, his temporary replacement, the former Vicomte de Souillac, informed the Minister that his officers were forced to listen almost daily to shouts of "*les aristocrates à la lanterne* and a thousand other horrors."[48]

The National Assembly finally followed Rions's advice and dispatched two royal commissioners with extraordinary powers to reestablish order in the fleet. They also ordered anyone who had been on the *Léopard* as far away from Brest as possible, demobilizing the crew, sending the men back to their home departments, and commanding the deputies of the General Assembly to come to Paris. The commissioners were authorized to call on the municipality and "all agents of the public force" in their efforts to "reestablish discipline and subordination in the squadron." Brest's influential Jacobin club, having wavered for a month between its dislike for the aristocratic officer corps, its ambivalent support for the incipient *sans-cullotisme* of the lower deck, and its powerful concern for an orderly, bourgeois-led revolution, finally threw its support behind the commissioners and proposed to lead a procession through the fleet, exhorting the crews "in the name of *la Patrie,* which we must all defend, in the name of liberty, which together we have won, to obey the Nation and to obey the commanders, who derive their powers from her." For two full days, members of the Jacobin club, together with the royal commissioners, representatives of the municipality, the National Guard, dockyard workers, soldiers of the royal and colonial regiments, the corps of volunteer seamen, and even the company of invalids went from ship to mutinous ship, passionately appealing to the seamen's sense of duty, and threatening doom and destruction to the fatherland if they continued to cripple its defenses.[49]

Onboard each ship they read out an address that sought to convince the crews that their conflict with the aristocratic officer corps, their refusal to sail for the West Indies, and their rampant resistance to any kind of punishment threatened the revolutionary experiment they claimed to be supporting. The address opened by reminding the crews that under the new constitution taking shape aristocratic power had actually already been broken, for everyone was now equal under the law. To illustrate the universality of that principle, and that in fact it extended beyond metropolitan shores to include French-flagged warships at sea, the address moved on to discuss the new *Code Pénal Maritime.* In contrast to the National Assembly, which when challenged about the new code's insufficient egalitarianism had reverted to the language of paternalism and sought to justify its authoritarian elements with reference to the age-old customs and conditions of life at sea, the Brest address instead emphasized the constitutional continuity between shore and ship, and pointed in particular to the participatory nature of the judicial process that the new code had introduced: "Neither the caprices of a commander, nor his passions any longer preside over judgments, and no longer arbitrarily decide over the life and honor of a citizen. The punishments prescribed by the Law can only be inflicted by your comrades, after your brothers have recognized and declared the accused guilty."[50]

However, in return for being granted equality in the process of adjudicating the law, the new constitution, onboard ship as well as on shore, also imposed a universal duty of submission to that law, without which there could be no union, no liberty, and no safety. This meant that those legally invested with the authority to command obedience must indeed be obeyed, for otherwise liberty inevitably decayed into license. Seamen really ought to understand that better than most, the address continued: "Suppose yourselves in a storm—if order does not reign onboard, if the captain does not have the powers to enforce his commands, if everyone believes to have the right to give orders, no one thinks himself required to obey; everyone wants to do a different maneuver, and none is done; all the while the storm intensifies, the danger grows, and the ship is lost." And that indeed was the prospect facing France at that very moment: "The National Assembly is the pilot of this great vessel, all Frenchmen are its seamen: we all have our stations, and we may only move by the order of those who govern us. But if—deaf to their voices, rebels to their orders—we refuse to obey, we become the authors of a general loss; and the ship, at the mercy of the waves and the storm, is lost."[51]

By framing the stakes of the seamen's struggle in terms of the familiar "ship of state" trope, thereby elevating in importance the politics of shipboard governance and linking it to questions of national survival, the address intended to honor the mutinous crews, and to flatter them back into obedience. But in doing so, it also perpetuated the insulting stereotype that portrayed ordinary seamen as too irresponsible to be capable of acting together without the firm guidance of a competent helmsman, even when their lives depended on it.

Still, on many of the ships in the roadstead, the crews appear to have been seduced by the grand spectacle of national unity that was enacted for their benefit. "Citizens embraced each other," reported an officer of Brest's municipality, "men and officers shed tears for one another." But on several other ships, the crews remained guarded, leaving members of the procession "with some concern about their sincerity" as they made their way to the next vessel. The two royal commissioners nevertheless were quick to claim success. "The sailors," they boasted to the National Assembly, "in an outpouring of most lively joy, affirm their attachment to both their officers and their captains; everywhere one hears the joyful shout: Long live the nation, the law, and the King! All orders are now executed with the greatest possible care."[52]

The reality onboard many of the ships was rather different. The day after the commissioners had dispatched their excited report to Paris, provisional commandant de Souillac reminded them that on several vessels officers and loyal men doing their duty had been violently attacked, and the majority of the crews were shielding and hiding the attackers. On one ship an officer had even died under suspicious circumstances after being struck on the head by a heavy object dropped from aloft. Even on those ships where the crew had returned to duty, the undermining and sidelining of the officer corps continued, as did the struggle for popular control over the judicial process.[53]

On the *Superbe,* members of the crew took it upon themselves to arrest a drunk man who was trying to reignite the mutiny. The captain, presented with this *fait accompli,* helplessly relinquished his right to decide on a punishment, and the crew took the man to the municipality, which in turn stuck him in prison. A few days later, members of the crew issued a public statement in which they affirmed their rediscovered conviction "that insubordination is the most dangerous poison to any branch in the service.... Consequently, our masters, sailors, volunteer seamen, and soldiers of all classes and all grades promise to discard and extirpate from amongst ourselves the last vestige of this dark vice, unanimously to obey all of our commanders and to entrust ourselves to their wisdom." This, no doubt, their captain was happy to hear, except that it probably would have been even more reassuring had it actually been addressed to him, and not to the local Jacobin club, which the crew evidently thought a more appropriate addressee for their pledge of fidelity.[54]

The arrival of a new commandant on November 10 once again escalated the conflict between officers and men. Louis-Antoine (formerly Comte de) Bougainville was not the type of officer who took an interest in reasoning, negotiating, or fraternally celebrating with his fellow citizens before the mast. "Every day," he thundered, "brings an insurrection more or less intense." Before he even had the opportunity to raise his standard on the *Majesteux,* he was informed of a "grave mutiny" onboard the 74-gun ship *Dugué-Trouin.* After a man was put in irons for stealing some wine, a number of his comrades broke him out, and when a detachment of soldiers arrived, "quite a large number of men used force to prevent him being taken to Pontaniou [prison]." The soldiers eventually won the stand-off, and the man, along with several of the mutineers, was incarcerated on shore. The very next day, Bougainville gave orders to crush "a very forceful insurrection" on the *Temeraire* and ordered four men thrown into prison.[55]

A few days later, the crews of the *America* and the frigate *Surveillante* unsuccessfully launched an insurrection, which Bougainville, in a show of paternal grace, was at first willing to forgive, but when members of the *America*'s crew broke an arrested mutineer out of his irons and threw the shackles into the sea, the commandant struck back. He ordered seventeen mutineers arrested for having "incited or participated in all the insurrections which for the past three months have rendered the *America* one of the worst examples in the fleet." He them had them conducted to the *bureau des classes* (naval conscription office), where their names were formally removed from the list, legally barring them from all future employment at sea, military and civilian. After that, the guards marched the men beyond the city's walls, and slammed its gates shut behind them. Bougainville announced to the entire fleet that "notes have been sent to their respective departments and to all commercial ports, which . . . will be careful not to employ such perverse men as the navy was forced to reject from its bosom." He quickly followed up with a chilling order in which he threatened to start executing people if complete subordination did not immediately return to the fleet.[56]

Bougainville was under pressure to prepare a major fleet to sail for Martinique, where colonial patriots and royalist planters threatened to plunge the island into civil war, but he worried that the rampant anti-authoritarianism of his men might stoke rather than choke the fires of colonial revolution. Demonstrative punishments, such as destroying the livelihood of the seventeen *America* mutineers, had a "salutary effect," Bougainville claimed, but it was not enough to reestablish discipline. Only a week later, on November 26, yet another insurrection broke out, on the *Jupiter* this time, and once again the spark came when the crew tried to protect "a very insubordinate man" from his "just punishment." No matter the crime or the consequences, the lower deck's refusal to cooperate with the judicial process set out in the new code by now seemed almost absolute. To counter the solidarity and undermine the trust that made this resistance possible, Bougainville ordered a number of the most unruly crews broken up, removing the most "gangrenous men" from the squadron bound for the West Indies, and replacing them with "good subjects, who want nothing but employment." The newly reconstituted crews, he hoped, would know that their families' subsistence at Brest depended on their continued good behavior on board, and act accordingly.[57]

Bougainville also worried that difficulties in provisioning the fleet—expected to carry over 6,000 troops on five transports, as well as the crews of fourteen warships, up to 3,500 men—would give his discontented crews a new issue to rally around. The required amount of provisions was enormous: the seamen alone needed for the three-month voyage approximately 555,000 pints of wine, 330,000 lb. biscuit, 160,000 lb. flour, 82,000 lb. salt pork, 6,500 lb. salt beef, 8,000 lb. cod, 12,000 lb. cheese, 10,500 lb. vegetables, 8,000 lb. rice, 26,000 lb. peas, 26,000 lb. beans, 26,000 lb. broad beans, 6,000 lb. oil, 17,500 lb. vinegar, 16,500 lb. salt, 175 lb. mustard, and 875 lb. candles. On December 10, Bougainville pleaded with the minister to ensure that his fleet was supplied, in full and on time, so that his men were given no "pretext" whatsoever to pass "from murmuring to insurrection . . . either through innovations or through shortages in the objects which constitute their legal rations." Nevertheless, only two weeks later, shortages forced Bougainville to order the substitution of *eau-de-vie* for the men's daily lunch ration of wine, an "innovation" which did indeed trigger mutinies on several ships. The most forward among the men were immediately arrested and imprisoned, but it nonetheless took four days to reestablish order in the fleet. The incident confirmed Bougainville's belief that disorder had become endemic, and with further shortages expected throughout the winter this was unlikely to change. "The murmurings, the refusals of order, the open insults of superior officers, both by able seamen and petty officers, who ought always to be models of subordination for the other men in the crew: examples of these are multiplying and sadly they prove that the spirit which was believed to have disappeared still exists and is perhaps in some manner incurable, infected as it is by the venom of insubordination."[58]

In fact, large-scale unrest quite suddenly died off as actual infections devastated the fleet during the winter months. The ships were overcrowded, wet, cold, and unsanitary, and the men bored, malnourished, and dirty—ideal conditions for breeding all kinds of disease, both physical and mental. Illness rates exploded towards the end of November, and by December 1, between 1,400 and 1,500 men had already been taken off the ships and brought to the dockyard's hospital. Numbers kept rising, and on December 10 Bougainville admitted that among the men in the roadstead "innumerable are sick, and they truly suffer." He failed to specify the diseases, but most likely they included various respiratory ailments, digestive disorders, dysentery, skin infections, rheumatism, fevers, and perhaps even early cases of typhoid, which would rage with harrowing force at Brest a few years later, killing over eight thousand men and sending tens of thousands more to the hospital in 1793 and 1794. Bougainville, concerned most of all with "the humors of insurrection" that might fester on his disease-ridden ships, was not above exploiting the epidemic as a disciplinary tool, punishing mutinous crews by keeping them cooped up on board while granting those obedient to their officers shore leave to recuperate their strength.[59]

The mood throughout the fleet was a foul one when the squadron bound for Martinique finally heaved anchor at the end of January 1791. The weather had remained numbingly cold, wet winds lashed the roadstead, and there had been reports of ships lost at sea. Illness rates gave no indication of leveling off, and it had been weeks since the crews had last received their full legal rations. Many of those bound for the open sea also harbored severe doubts about their mission in the islands, and about the real intentions of their aristocratic officers. What might they order their men to do off Martinique? Was the squadron to be made a tool of the aristocratic party or its colonial equivalent, the *blancs-blancs?* Would the men be ordered to spill the blood of fellow citizens, and then be denounced both at home and abroad as counter-revolutionaries, as had happened to the crew of the *Illustre* only a few months before? When ordered by Governor Damas to blockade the port of Saint-Pierre, Martinique's insurgent patriot stronghold, revolutionaries had denounced the *Illustre* as a floating Bastille. The insult apparently stung, for shortly afterwards the crew mutinied and forced their commander to return the ship to Brest. They arrived there less than two months after the *Léopard* had carried a similar tale of colonial counter-revolution, quarterdeck treachery, and lower deck mutiny back from across the Atlantic.[60]

When the squadron reached Martinique and dropped anchor off Fort-Royal in mid-March, the situation hardly reassured them. As on Saint-Domingue, news of the revolution in France had encouraged Martinique's planter-dominated colonial assembly to claim legislative authority over the island's commercial life. As their first order of business they had opened the ports to merchantmen of all nations, in the hope that greater competition would force down the cost of imports and raise the price of sugar. But opposition to these plans quickly congealed in the island's port towns, where an alliance of revolutionary *petits blancs* and colonial merchants, whose businesses had been nurtured and protected by the old regime's mercantilist system, seized local government and accused the planters of separatism. The newly formed revolutionary municipality of Saint-Pierre then issued a call to arms, inviting small-white patriots from other French islands to come and assist in the struggle against the counter-revolutionary planter class. The colonial government, meanwhile, wavered back and forth between the two sides, but finally sided with the *blancs-blancs* after a small-white race riot in early June left several free-colored militiamen dead. Even though the planters pushed to dismantle the mercantilist system and assert their own legislative autonomy, the patriots' belligerent *sans-cullotisme* and fanatic racism now appeared as a far more immediate threat to the stability of the colonial regime. During the summer, Governor Damas ordered his troops to impose order and restore regular government in the colony. But following a mutiny among soldiers of the Martinique regiment in support of imprisoned patriots awaiting deportation, full-blown civil war between the two sides broke out in early September 1790.[61]

The 74-gunship *Ferme* and the frigate *Embuscade,* at the head of a small group of transports carrying around five thousand troops, arrived off Martinique on November 1 and were immediately drawn into the fighting to relieve the colonial government's badly beleaguered forces. After delivering much-needed food supplies to the governor's troops at Gros-Morne, the *Embuscade* and *Ferme,* together with a small group of corvettes, spent most of the winter months choking off Fort-Royal and Saint-Pierre, both of them patriot strongholds. They repeatedly bombarded both towns as well as other settlements along the coast, intercepted and seized inbound merchantmen, and tried to capture a fleet of small, fast privateers that repeatedly managed to swarm out despite the blockades. By the time the squadron that sailed from Brest in January arrived in the middle of March 1791, the small naval detachment commanded by Chevalier de Rivière, captain of the *Ferme,* was credited with having prevented a patriot victory throughout the colony. But that was a feat that many of those who had just arrived from France thought far from commendable.[62]

In June, Rivière complained that "since the arrival of the force destined for this colony, ill-intentioned men have tried to excite the crews of the other ships against my crew and that of the Embuscade." In truth, it took no outside agitators to stir up trouble with Rivière's men. Even though most of them willingly participated in combat, especially after the shore batteries at Saint-Pierre had fired red-hot shot at them in early January, there had been continuous, low-level unrest on both ships ever since they had arrived in the colony in early November. On February 15, finally, "a very great fermentation" broke out on the *Ferme* after Rivière ordered the distribution of prize money from the sale of a number of captured enemy merchantmen and privateers. In dividing up the profits, Rivière intended to follow the law, which allocated one-third to the navy's invalid fund, one-third to the ship's commissioned officer corps, and one-third to its warrant officers and crew, who together composed about 90 percent of the ship's population. The protesters demanded that all receive an equal share instead, regardless of rank or position, but Rivière refused. In that case, they informed him, he could keep the money until the National Assembly had a chance to consider the matter.[63]

Rivière noted that the detachment of Norman soldiers onboard appeared to be "the engine of the fermentation." This may not have been a coincidence. Normandy had long been one of the most important centers of French privateering, a form of state-licensed but privately operated enemy commerce-raiding that in France had survived largely unchanged since the medieval period. Like most medieval shipping, it was based on the principle of shared risks and shared profits. The exact distribution of prize money varied across time and space, but it was always significantly more equitable than in the navy. By the late eighteenth century, two-thirds of net profits customarily went to the ship's outfitter and his financiers, and the remaining third to the crew. This made a privateer crew's overall share the same as in the navy, but given that they were at most one-tenth the size of those onboard a 74-gunship like the *Ferme,* the individual share of a common crew member was, accordingly, at least ten times larger. It is therefore not surprising that men socialized in the world of Norman privateering would take the lead in the struggle against the grossly unequal distribution of prize money that prevailed in the navy, especially as those who benefitted from it did so purely because of their office, which until very recently had only been open to those of noble blood. Moreover, unlike outfitters and financiers in the privateering business, naval officers had no more invested in a voyage than the lowest ship's boy, nor did they enter into any greater risks that would justify their much larger share.[64]

Even though the majority of the *Ferme's* crew accepted their prescribed share of prize money the day after the protest, the Norman soldiers continued to hold out, "carrying on with the most seditious speeches." After being informed that they had also misbehaved when given shore liberty, Rivière made a last attempt to recall them to duty. He succeeded only partially, and in response decided to select for combat duty on shore the "most seditious spirits that attempt to raise a rebellion on board of my ship." As soon as Governor Damas asked the captain for reinforcements on March 5, Rivière happily sent him the unruliest of his Norman soldiers. "Their future conduct," he remarked, "proved how ill-intentioned they were; for, not only did they break through the bounds of subordination and formally refused to obey their officers, but they allowed themselves excesses and pushed their insolence to the point of firing on their own commander." When asked to take them back on board, Rivière refused.[65]

Discipline amongst the majority of Rivière's men held for some time after the arrival of the Brest squadron in mid-March 1791, but by summer there were signs of serious discontent, especially on the *Embuscade*. Illness and mortality rates were escalating with the onset of the rainy season, and the constant subversive appeals from radicals in other ships were beginning to take their toll. Following a truce between the rival factions fighting for control of the colony, the crews of the *Ferme* and the *Embuscade* for the first time since their arrival six months earlier came into sustained contact with merchant seamen and colonial patriots ashore. "At Fort-Royal," Captain d'Orléans of the *Embuscade* complained, "both naval and merchant vessels wintered. Long periods of inactivity, idleness, free and daily communications with the shore all favored the projects of seduction and corruption that the ill-intentioned aimed mainly at the crews of the Ferme and the Embuscade, since they had remained loyal and seemingly unshakeable." Now, however, their loyalty was beginning to shake. Discussions with *petits blancs* patriots ashore and their comrades onboard merchant ships led many of them to doubt their mission. It dawned on them that by obeying orders and fighting on behalf of Martinique's planter class during the winter's hostilities, they may well have helped the colonial counter-revolution, and this worried them profoundly. In late August, the crew of the *Embuscade* "expressed the desire to return to France in order to bring clarity to their situation." A month later, when Captain d'Orléans instead ordered the ship to prepare for a cruise to Guadeloupe, the crew gathered on the forecastle and "imperatively and tumultuously" told him that they would sail for France, with or without his blessing. D'Orléans and all his officers were disarmed and confined to their quarters. The next day the *Embuscade* put to sea.[66]

The crew wrote a formal report on the mutiny, which they conveyed to the National Assembly upon their arrival off Rochefort a few weeks later. "This day, 30 September 1791," they wrote,

> we have communicated to the captain in an unanimous voice our desire to return to France rather than sail to Basse-Terre Guadeloupe; given that we are uncertain about our mission, relative to the troubles which presently reign at Pointe-à-Pitre as well as at Sainte-Lucie, and that we under no circumstances want to commit the same hostilities against our brothers as those for which we already have been reproached, according to letters dated July 15, in which our past conduct is reproached and which mention that we have been denounced in all the clubs of the kingdom as treasonous criminals, we have decided to sail for France.

In a competing report, Rivière pleaded with the National Assembly to punish the *Embuscade* mutineers "rigorously," lest he lose control of his own crew on the *Ferme* as well. But his cries fell on deaf ears in Paris. Under the pretense that the mutiny was covered by an amnesty for political crimes whose deadline had in fact passed, the National Assembly decided that the crew of the *Embuscade* could not legally be tried by court-martial, nor be sent back to the West Indies as a form of extra-judicial punishment (this had been Captain d'Orléans' idea). The mutiny, in other words, had received the nation's highest sanction.[67]

Rivière, meanwhile, was left to fight a rising tide of disobedience, sedition, and even violence among his men. On January 4, 1792, Jean-Baptiste Bouanchaud of the *Lily* was sentenced to three years of galley service for rebelling against Captain Maucler and raising a cutlass against First Lieutenant Odiette. The judgment was nailed to the masts of all ships at anchor in Martinique, as well as distributed to all naval stations and French commercial ports throughout the Caribbean. But it does not appear to have done much good. By June, Rivière was forced to remove twenty-four "insolent" men from his own already severely undermanned ship. Then on October 17, Claude-Antoine Girard of the *Ferme* was sentenced to death by firing squad on a floating pontoon amidst the ships of the squadron for conspiring with soldiers of the Fort-Bourbon garrison to rise on their respective officers and overthrow the authority of the king in the colony. Two of his co-conspirators, François Groffelin and Claude Miche, were to be branded with the letters "GAL" (short for *galérien,* or galley slave) on their shoulders and afterwards conveyed to France for a lifetime of hard labor in the naval dockyards. François Chapelle, Jean Maffet, Jacques le Tanneur, Jacques-Robert Cotte, and Vincent Cotentin were sentenced to running the gauntlet, four rounds each, and then barred for life from all legal employment at sea.[68]

The unusual brutality of these last verdicts grew from Rivière's decision the month before to side with the governors and colonial assemblies of Martinique and Guadeloupe and openly commit himself to counter-revolution. The royalist coup began with the turning away of a squadron of small warships and transports that came to implement the Legislative Assembly's decree of April 4, 1792. The decree's most important provision was to rectify the contradictory position of free people of color by finally guaranteeing their full citizenship rights throughout the empire, a step, as metropolitan authorities well knew, that would meet with outrage amongst colonial *petits blancs* patriots. Already ill-disposed towards free people of color for reasons of class envy and race hatred, colonial patriots detested them even more for having sided with the *blancs-blancs* during the revolutionary struggles that had thrown Martinique into civil war only two years before. In order therefore to guarantee its full implementation, the metropolitan government decided to send a force of two thousand National Guardsmen along with the decree. This, in turn, alienated the planters and their friends in the colonial governments, who otherwise had no problem with a decree that gave their allies the vote. But the prospect of having large numbers of proletarian National Guardsmen run riot in the colony terrified the planters, especially since it was only to be expected that sooner or later the Guardsmen would side with the revolutionary *petits blancs,* whatever their orders might be. With only around 10,600 white inhabitants in Martinique, a force of 2,000 armed and motivated soldiers would easily tilt the balance of forces in favor of the patriots.[69]

Fearful of the troops coming from France, Guadeloupe's and Martinique's colonial assemblies resolved to implement the decree of April 4 in every detail on their own. When the small squadron carrying the National Guard units, special commissioners, and new governors for all the French Windward Islands arrived off Fort-Royal on September 16, they were refused permission to anchor and disembark the troops. A volley of red-hot shot from the shore batteries emphasized how deadly serious the colonists were. They invited the commissioners to come ashore and ascertain that all laws were being followed to the dot in the island, but after that they would have to sail away again. The commissioners naturally rejected this proposal as unacceptable, and in response were told they had better leave then or be prepared to fight as enemies against Rivière's superior forces. The squadron had no choice but to make sail, and after they were met with gunfire off Basse-Terre in Guadeloupe as well, most of the ships headed for Saint-Domingue.[70]

Meanwhile, one of Rivière's captains, Mallevault of the *Calipso* frigate, picked up a rumor, apparently originating in the British island of Montserrat, that Austrian and Prussian troops had crushed the revolution and fully reestablished Louis XVI's royal authority. Mallevault, a keen royalist, enthusiastically embraced the rumor as fact, immediately replaced the hated tricolor with the king's royal white, and then fired a twenty-one-shot salute. White flags soon went up all over Guadeloupe and Martinique, and whoever refused to fly it or sport a white cockade was treated as a traitor. Slave ship captain Jean-François Landolphe was told a day outside of Port-à-Pitre by Lieutenant Duval of the *Perdrix* that he would have to switch flags if he wanted to enter the harbor. Landolphe instead ordered the revolutionary tricolor nailed to the mast of his slave ship. For that, and his refusal to wear the white cockade, he spent the next three months confined to his ship in harbor. He was allowed to disembark his slaves and lodge them in "an immense warehouse."[71]

Unlike captains in the merchant service, most naval officers were quick to support what rapidly exploded into a colonial counter-revolution. Lieutenant Duval of the *Perdrix* was in fact one of only two commanders who refused the white flag and took their vessels to France instead. Most common crewmen, as well as most *petits blancs,* appear to have opposed the royalist counter-revolution. When Captain Mallevault, for instance, laid claim to the *Bienvenue,* which had sought the protection of the British at St. Kitts, the crew rioted, smashed up the ship, and abandoned it for the beach. Shortly afterwards, Rivière was faced with the anti-royalist conspiracy onboard his flagship that resulted in the brutal court-martial sentences of October 17. Later that month, large numbers of *petits blancs* radicals fled Guadeloupe and Martinique, first for the British island of Dominica, later for the French islands of Marie-Galante and Sainte-Lucie. By December, following the arrival of the staunchly republican Captain Lacrosse on the *Félicité* frigate, Rivière's own men began to run away, stealing small vessels to reach Sainte-Lucie, where Lacrosse had established his headquarters.[72]

Lacrosse had sailed from Brest on October 24, 1792, before the *Perdrix* had brought news to France of the counter-revolution brewing in the Caribbean. His original mission was to explain to the colonists the events that had led to the overthrow of the king, and to encourage them to love the republic, a task that turned out to be trickier than he probably expected. However, despite or perhaps because of the royalist rebellions in Martinique and Guadeloupe, colonial patriot refugees on the other islands greeted his arrival with extravagant celebrations. On Dominica, where Lacrosse went first, the British governor soon demanded that he leave, lest all this talk of liberty should inspire the slaves to rise on their own oppressors. On Sainte-Lucie, where he went next, revolutionary fever gripped the populace: the *bonnet rouge* was on everybody's head, liberty trees went up all over the colony, and the inhabitants sang the Marseillaise until they were hoarse. At the height of their excitement they decided to rename the island La Fidèle, the Faithful One.[73]

From here, Lacrosse flooded Guadeloupe and Martinique with republican propaganda, promising pardons to all commoners who crossed over into the republican camp. The royalist elites were rapidly losing support, even among many of the free people of color, and on December 20 a popular insurrection broke out in Pointe-à-Pitre on Guadeloupe. A crowd made up largely of free people of color was soon joined by rebellious soldiers who had refused the oath to the king. Sailors fleeing the warships in the roadstead joined in as well, along with merchant seamen who had been forced to fly the white flag "with indignation." Together, they demanded that the revolutionary tricolor once again be raised in the colony. On December 24, seamen from the *Bonne Mère,* a merchantman just arrived from Bordeaux, streamed into town shouting "Down with the White Flag, or Death!" During the night, hundreds of men descended from the surrounding mountains and in three columns attacked the town, leaving many dead and wounded. After the insurrectionists, with the help of a group of mutinous naval artillery men, routed a detachment of royalist troops sent from Basse-Terre, the royalists abandoned the island for Martinique. On January 4, the tricolor finally billowed over Basse-Terre once again. The next day, Lacrosse sailed into the harbor of Pointe-à-Pitre with a gigantic red cap of liberty dangling from the mainmast of his ship, the *Félicité.* After that, it only took another week for the royalist government in Martinique to collapse as well. On January 12, Rivière took on board Martinique's governor Béhague, eighteen ennobled planters, the president of the colonial assembly, six militia commanders, ten deputies, as well as several priests. Together with a small squadron, they sailed for Spanish

Trinidad, where Rivière surrendered the four ships under his command and asked for asylum. It was duly granted.[74]

Rivière's failure to enforce obedience amongst the crews of his squadron played a crucial role in the counter-revolutionary coup's defeat. The men had learned their lesson. Ever since being denounced for obeying orders to fight on the side of the planters in Martinique's 1790–91 civil war, they had remained suspicious, and were continuously watching out for any sign of falling out of step with the revolution at home. Many had therefore resisted the royalist counter-revolution from the very beginning, either by murmuring and complaining, plotting insurrection, or simply running away. When Lacrosse showed up with his single frigate in early December 1792, Rivière could not get his squadron, consisting of one 74-gunship, two frigates, and three corvettes, to put to sea and fight him. Too many men had left already, and most of those who remained were not exactly enthusiastic. Even the free-colored seamen were showing signs of wavering, and once Lacrosse announced that the new French republican empire intended to destroy all racial designations by replacing them, once and for all, with the single name of citizen, they too deserted in large numbers and joined the republican side. In the end Rivière was only able to get his remaining men to work by continuously pointing pistols at them.[75]

But the popular enthusiasm that ushered in the new republican regime and drove the uppermost layer of royalists from Martinique in early January 1793 did not last long. It soon gave way, once again, to vicious factional infighting. The already tenuous alliance between bourgeois merchants and port city radicals was rapidly disintegrating, even as royalists together with British agents were plotting a second rebellion in northern Martinique. When the revolt finally erupted in April, the weak and unpopular administration led by General Rochambeau was forced to rely on free-colored troops and armed slaves to defeat it, a move that alienated even the politically radical but fanatically racist small-white patriots who clung to the republican regime the longest. In response, the regime became more repressive, and by late summer jails and prison ships were filling up with suspected counter-revolutionaries, a category which by now included almost everyone opposed to the administration. In October, the Revolutionary Tribunal would begin its bloody work on the island.[76]

Throughout the summer, the impeccably republican crew of the *Félicité* grew increasingly confused and irritated as they watched the depressing spectacle of colonial revolutionary politics unfold, and they soon lost all sense of purpose and belief in their mission. In late July, they asked Captain Lacrosse to take them home. A month later, on August 27, they forced him to do so. "As long as we had real enemies to fight," they explained in a long declaration signed by almost every member of the crew, "we would have considered it cowardice of speaking about a return to France." But as things stood, the colony was hopelessly divided into factions, each fighting for their own advantage, with no regard for the common good. "The factions are tearing [the colony] apart; the whites are on one side, the free people of color on the other side. And then there are the slaves, who were promised in the hour of utmost danger more liberty than one today, now that the danger has passed, is willing to grant them."[77]

The *Félicité*'s crew did not know what to do. Their original mission had been to bring news of the republic to the Windward Islands, and to protect the rights of its newest citizens, the free people of color. But doing that had put them on a collision course with the small-white patriots, who were not only the republic's staunchest local defenders, they were also people very much like themselves. The majority of the small-white population was young, male, and used to working at sea, or close to port. Many of them were recent immigrants, sometimes from the very same regions that also supplied the navy with its conscripts. They shared the same anti-elitist politics, and the same distrust of aristocratic, counter-revolutionary plotters, of whom there were many in the colony. Rochambeau's administration had become surrounded by opportunists, big planters and merchants who pretended to be patriots but who in reality hated the idea of equality, "having for that word a repugnance so strong that they would sacrifice nearly all before accepting it." But instead of fighting to purge the colony of these last vestiges of the old regime, small-white patriots had instead turned their wrath on the free people of color, whose insistence on complete equality as guaranteed by the decree of April 4 they perceived as an existential threat to their own fragile position within the colonial order.[78]

The *Félicité* mutineers emphasized that their decision to force a return to France had nothing to do with "Citizen Captain Lacrosse," who continued to enjoy their highest esteem and fullest confidence. Even so, while they knew they owed him obedience, the crew ultimately felt responsible to their "fellow citizens" in France. And they trusted them to recognize that the mutiny, though illegal, was motivated neither by ignorance nor cowardice, but by a genuine fear of unwittingly aiding the counter-revolution, as so many other crews sent to the West Indies had done before them. "The nature of the crisis in which the colony finds itself is such," they argued, "and the path forward so slippery, that the danger of choosing this or that party appears equally great on all sides." Obeying their initial orders to support and protect the rights of the free-colored citizens would now mean taking up arms against the small whites. But the small whites were the only ones able to prevent the colony from being delivered up, once again, into the hands of the counter-revolution, a threat that seemed to emanate most strongly from the factions surrounding General Rochambeau, who, to make matters even worse, was the *Félicité*'s local commander-in-chief. All options were bad. "It therefore seems best," the mutineers concluded, "to steer for France."[79]

The seriousness and sophistication of the *Félicité* mutineers' declaration belies the image of anarchy and chaos, of liberty decayed into license that Pierre-Victor Malouet and other holdovers from the old regime sought to associate with the revolutionary navy. Like those of the *Léopard,* the *Illustre,* and the *Embuscade* before them, the crew onboard the *Félicité* did not take lightly its decision to violate orders, abandon the colony, and sail for home. They took seriously their mission "to protect maritime commerce and the national possessions in the different parts of the globe," but at the same time they refused to be simply unthinking cogs in that vast imperial war machine by which Paris projected its power overseas. Experience had taught them to question their orders, for all too often in the past treacherous officers and officials had exploited the blind obedience of well-intentioned crews and made them into unsuspecting tools of the counter-revolution. Seamen on the Windward Island station knew this better than most.[80]

But fear of quarterdeck treason was only a part of it. Captain Lacrosse genuinely enjoyed the trust and high esteem of his men, yet they still decided that their desire to return home overrode his orders to remain in the colony. This decision did not come out of nowhere. Ever since the navy's strictly hier-archical system of subordination and obedience had fallen apart during the December 1, 1789 insurrection in Toulon, seamen throughout the fleet had struggled to establish the crew's collective will as the new sovereign onboard ship. On the *Léopard,* mutineers asserted the right to elect a replacement for the captain who had abandoned them. At Brest, on ship after mutinous ship, crews refused to cooperate with the new jury system under the reformed *Code Pénal Maritime* and aggressively shielded their comrades from arrest. And finally, on the *Félicité,* the tone of quiet and polite confidence with which the crew justified the mutiny suggests that after four years of revolution the citizens below deck had come to consider it their right ultimately to decide over their ship's operations.

The crew's presumption that each man onboard, whether citizen captain or citizen sailor, should have an equal vote when it came to the fundamental decisions regarding the ship's voyage recalled the old maritime custom of collective decision-making in moments of crisis that had been repressed with the militarization of naval warfare in the seventeenth century. At the same time, with its emphasis on equality and its unapologetic insistence on the right to mutiny despite what the law might say, the *Félicité* declaration also reflected the growing influence of radically democratic plebeian republicanism that flourished in urban centers around the Atlantic world. Ever since the factional infighting in Saint-Domingue had forced a division between officer and men onboard the king's ships stationed in the Windward islands, the contradictions of colonial revolution had supplied the fuel which allowed these two traditions—maritime collectivism and urban working-class republicanism—to cross-fertilize and fuse amongst the conscripted mariners, laborers, peasants, and artisans dwelling together below deck. Deprived of reliable leadership, yet forced to take a stance in relation to the violence that broke out first in Saint-Domingue, then in Martinique and Guadeloupe, naval seamen, on the *Léopard,* on the *Illustre,* on the *Embuscade,* and finally on the *Félicité,* sought legitimacy for their political choices in combining the submerged traditions of the sea with the new language of popular sovereignty that had flooded onto the ships during their stays at Brest, Toulon, and Port-au-Prince.[81]

One can speculate whether the disappointment that the radicals onboard the *Félicité* experienced with Martinique's patriot movement may not have sprung from the same mingling of maritime experience and revolutionary enthusiasm when they asked: "Are not the free people of color our brothers?" Next to equality, fraternal solidarity ranked at the very top of the list of revolutionary values most treasured by radical urban working-class republicans. But it was no less esteemed in those exclusively male micro-societies that plowed across the seven seas, where men from many different nations, continents, and races habitually referred to each other as brothers, and often established bonds close enough to verge on fictive kinship. It therefore seems likely that the refusal of Martinique's small whites to accept the "new citizens" as their revolutionary brothers was especially disappointing to the lower deck cosmopolitans onboard the *Félicité.*[82]

When the mutineers on the *Léopard* sailed away from Saint-Marc and steered for home in the summer of 1790, they had felt compelled to emphasize "that the motive for their actions in Saint-Domingue was the preservation of this beautiful part of France." Three years later off Martinique, their equally mutinous brothers onboard the *Félicité* no longer appeared sure that the effort was really worth it. They were not alone. Earlier that summer, crews onboard the ships of the Saint-Domingue squadron had joined in the June 20, 1793 small-white patriot insurrection that left Cap Français reduced to rubble and littered with anywhere between 3,000 and 10,000 corpses. Only the *America,* whose crew had played a leading role in the struggle over the new *Code Pénal Maritime* at Brest in the summer of 1790, as well as in the assault on the aristocratic officer corps later that year, refused to join in the insurrection. Unlike the other ships in the squadron, it had only recently arrived in the colony and the crew therefore did not share the others' sense of solidarity with the small-white patriot movement, whose fanatic resistance to free-colored equality was driving Saint-Domingue towards the June 20 explosion. But even the reliably republican crew of the *America* soon gave up. After the destruction of Cap Français, conditions onboard the ship became intolerable. The rainy season was looming, the number of men already on the sick list was rising fast, and there was not enough food to adequately provision them. But whenever the crew went ashore in search of victuals, they were driven back into their boats by "negroes and mulattoes." On July 23, 1793, fed up by the irreconcilable contradictions of what rapidly was developing into a revolutionary race war, the crew ordered their captain to raise anchor and steer for France.[83]

That summer, Pierre-Victor Malouet, by now safely ensconced in British exile, finally had his answer: the empire was no longer under anyone's command. Initially, naval seamen had played an important role in destabilizing the old-regime empire, just as Malouet had predicted. But as the revolution radicalized, these same mariners often took it upon themselves to uphold the principles of metropolitan *sans-culotte* republicanism in the deeply divided West Indian slave plantation islands. Doing so, they faced a hopeless challenge. When the *America* and the *Félicité* finally abandoned their posts and sailed eastward across the Atlantic in the late summer of 1793, they left Saint-Domingue and the Windward Islands without naval protection. But whatever concern for the fate of the colonies they still retained most likely faded fast, for the survival of France itself was now at stake. In January 1793, Spain and Portugal had joined the coalition against revolutionary France, and on February 1 the National Convention declared war on Britain and the Dutch Republic. Every major fleet in the Atlantic was now mobilizing for war against the French navy.

THREE

Demons Dancing in a Furnace

THE WAR THAT BEGAN IN 1793, and then raged with only a brief intermission for twenty-two years, brought enormous hardship to the lower deck. While Europe put to sea fleets that were larger and more powerful than anything the world had ever seen, many of the ships were old, and some were in a poor state of repair. Ships that urgently needed extensive overhauling before they were battle-ready were often sent out to fight anyway. Moreau de Jonnès, who fought in the war's first major engagement on June 1, 1794—known in Britain as the Glorious First of June, and in France as the Battle of 13 Prairial—later recalled that many of the French ships were what old sailors called "drowners," worn-out vessels with worm-eaten, barnacle-covered hulls, and so leaky that they were "often only kept afloat by their pumps."[1]

De Jonnès's own ship, the 74-gun *Jemappes,* had its brittle fore- and mainmasts blown away early in the battle, and then became a sitting target for the British three-decker *Queen,* which drew up across its defenseless stern and started pouring in broadsides, massacring its crew as if shooting fish in a barrel. "It was really equivalent to hitting a man when he was down, murdering the wounded and mutilating the dead," de Jonnès remembered. "In the position in which we were none of our guns would bear, and we had no alternative but to allow ourselves to be shot to bits without resistance." British cannon balls crashed through the *Jemappes*'s lower decks, dismounting guns and smashing bodies. One shot found its way into the hold and there created "an appalling slaughter" amongst the wounded waiting to be treated by the ship's surgeon. Louis Garneray, who fought his first naval battle soon afterwards, recalled a similar scene when after two hours of close-range combat the crew, "blinded by the smoke, overwhelmed by the burning heat . . . threw off their clothes and came to resemble a pack of demons dancing in a furnace. Most of them were completely covered in blood after having tripped over the corpses of their dead comrades lying between the guns. It was horrifying to behold."[2]

Combat, on this scale at least, was mercifully rare. But even during the tedious day-to-day operations that dominated life in the service, working onboard wooden ships of war put a huge strain on the crews. Samuel Kelly recalled sailing on one drowner that required round-the-clock pumping simply to keep it afloat, and from that constant toil "some of our seamen's hands had lost pieces of skin, and had wounds on their palms nearly as large as a sixpence." John Hoxse was on another vessel where the men were "reduced almost to skeletons by such incessant labor." In Saint Mary's Sound, off the Scilly Isles, William Spavens saw a ship come in "which had been out so long, that her bottom was quite green, and her sails and rigging bleached white; the crew were so emaciated with continual fatigue, and their strength so much exhausted, that they could scarcely hold themselves on the yards; and one of them was so weak that he fell from the main yard as the ship came into the Sound."[3]

Every year during the French Revolutionary Wars, the Royal Navy alone lost around 1,700 seamen to fatal accidents onboard. But a far larger number, at least 2,600 men on average, died annually from disease. Elsewhere, conditions were even worse. In France, over 8,000 people died when typhus tore through Brest in the winter of 1793–94, and this was not the only time or place an epidemic raged out of control. Insufficient funding, underdeveloped distribution networks, primitive food preservation techniques, and a reluctance to accept recent discoveries in nutritional science made it difficult for most navies to provision their warships adequately, and many seamen were therefore left chronically malnourished, and sometimes in a state of semi-starvation. Their weakened bodies became fertile breeding grounds for disease. The total number of dead from scurvy, yellow fever, malaria, dysentery, chicken pox, typhus, influenza, and even bubonic plague has never been calculated, but it was certainly in the tens of thousands.[4]

Wartime working conditions were broadly similar across most navies, but the willingness of ordinary seamen to endure them varied considerably according to the political context. In France, where control over the nation's seaborne defenses to a significant degree had devolved into the hands of common sailors, the lower deck was prepared to suffer dreadful depredations for as long as they believed their sacrifices served the interests of the French Republic as they understood them. When after the fall of the Jacobin regime in the late summer of 1794 that was no longer the case, they bitterly withdrew their support. The rate of desertion and migration away from the coasts escalated to new heights.

Seamen in the Dutch navy, by contrast, experienced the Batavian Revolution from the outset as one imposed from above, and were therefore without the sense of common purpose that initially motivated their French republican counterparts. Since a majority of them were foreign-born volunteers, they felt next to no loyalty to the new Batavian regime that asked them to fight in a quixotic battle against Britain's far superior Royal Navy. Indeed, many of them interpreted the overthrow of the Orangist state as having cancelled the contract that bound them to the Orangist navy, and the refusal of their new Batavian officers to release them from service only deepened their disaffection. As a result, the need to enforce order and obedience onboard ship actually increased the rate of punishments after the revolution, with predictable consequences for the lower deck's already rotten morale. It was not long before the Batavian navy began losing men through desertion at an even more spectacular rate than its old-regime predecessor.[5]

The British navy had the advantage of mobilizing for war without simultaneously having to worry about the impact of civil war and social revolution on its ability to maintain order onboard ship, or to provide sufficient provisions, naval stores, and other war materiel to keep its ships afloat and ready to fight. But despite allocating vast sums to the navy after its shock defeat in the War for American Independence, by the time large-scale naval conflict once again erupted in 1793, Britain had not been able to achieve its strategic goal of building and maintaining a navy the size of its two closest competitors combined. The Royal Navy therefore mobilized for war and stretched and strained available resources with the same feverish urgency as its much weaker rivals. Like them, it also experienced an unprecedented explosion of discontent.

However, in contrast to the unrest that rocked the French and Dutch navies after the revolutions of 1789 and 1795, in the British navy the lower deck's anger over intolerable working conditions was not diluted by the same kind of political conflicts that weakened their solidarity elsewhere. While malcontents in the French and Dutch navies often chose desertion as an individual or small-group response, ironically, it was the lower deck of the counter-revolutionary British navy that during the first four years of the war developed the most militant and sophisticated tradition of collective action.

The outbreak of war in 1793 triggered a surge of frenzied activity as each navy scrambled to raise and deploy available seamen as rapidly and efficiently as possible. In France, the challenge must have appeared almost insurmountable. The destruction of Cap Français in late June 1793 ruined the most important branch of French Atlantic commerce and sent several of the metropole's port cities and their hinterlands into steep decline, dragging the country's already battered economy even closer towards collapse. At the same time, metropolitan France was faced with three invading armies on three different fronts and was simultaneously torn apart by two major domestic rebellions, one centered on the rural Vendée region in the far west, the other on urban areas in the southeast. In late August 1793, the so-called "Federalist revolt" turned into catastrophic treason when the ships of the Mediterranean fleet stood aside while Toulon's counter-revolutionary municipal elite invited British and Spanish forces to occupy the town and take control of its naval dockyard and the warships anchored in the harbor. When news of the surrender reached the Atlantic fleet in Quiberon Bay, discipline collapsed completely. Convinced their current mission was a counter-revolutionary plot to keep them away from Brest, so it could likewise be surrendered to the enemy, the crews demanded an immediate return to port in order to prepare for its defense. To prevent the mutiny from drifting into armed rebellion, and the officers from losing even the pretense of authority over the fleet, the ships made sail and returned to Brest.[6]

But the French navy's problems did not end there. In contrast to the sense of republican duty its seamen generally observed while on station in the overseas colonies, discipline in the home command had deteriorated into a state of near anarchy. Whatever orders they were given, French seamen often responded with "*un refus general.*" Strikes erupted constantly, there were frequent acts of sabotage onboard ship, mysterious fires broke out in the dockyards, and individual officers suffered violent attacks, usually on shore and under the cover of darkness. Absenteeism and desertion escalated to ever new heights, and there was little anyone could do about it. When in May 1793 the *Engagéante* received orders to chase down a British privateer that cruised just offshore from Lorient, only about a hundred of its 260 men appeared onboard. And when subsequently Commandant de Secqville appointed a jury to investigate and try the guilty according to the procedures laid out in the new *Code Pénal Maritime,* not a single man was convicted, which in turn led the crew to openly mock and disparage the impotence of the law, for which crime de Secqville likewise failed to secure a conviction.[7]

It was not an isolated case. Ever since the introduction of the new *Code Pénal Maritime* in 1790, letters had come pouring into the Ministry of the Marine in which officers complained that the replacement of courts-martial with trials by jury had made it impossible for them to uphold proper military discipline onboard ship. As it turned out, contrary to the *Comité de Marine*'s hope that participation in the judicial process would give ordinary seamen a sense of shared responsibility for the maintenance of good order onboard, the prospect of being tried by one's all too forgiving peers completely failed to instill that "healthy fear" which officers believed to lie at the foundation of all shipboard discipline.[8]

The *Comité de Marine*'s reform of the conscription system suffered a similar fate. Early in 1790, as part of its sweeping regeneration of the fleet, the committee had initially planned to abolish the *système des classes,* but upon further review determined that there was in fact no alternative that balanced respect for the liberties of French citizens with the necessity for cost-effective recruitment as well as the old regime's system of conscription. Impressment, the committee found, while obviously convenient in a society as fundamentally oriented towards the sea as the British island nation, was simply offensive to the liberties of a free people and therefore completely out of the question for France. However, its polar opposite, a permanently employed all-volunteer corps, was both cost-prohibitive and self-defeating for a navy as large as the French, as it would necessarily starve the merchant marine of its already scarce labor force, and thus undermine the purpose of having a deep-sea-going navy in the first place. As none of the alternatives managed to strike a better balance between the military needs of the nation and the rights of the nation's citizen-mariners, the committee deemed the *système des classes* to still be the best possible recruitment system for the French navy. This was especially true, the committee maintained, after a final reform effort under the old regime had made the system less compulsory by allowing mariners under twenty-four years of age to "declass" themselves if they decided to turn their back on the sea for good. The committee's proposal, passed into law on January 7, 1791, consequently retained almost all features of the old system, except that it made even more population groups with only the most remote connections to the sea subject to its requirements.[9]

But even as members of the *Comité de Marine* continued the previous regime's practice of continuously expanding the geographical area and number of people subject to conscription, they wondered whether such targeted state coercion was in fact reconcilable with the principles of a free constitution. On the one hand, the nation had a right to expect all citizens to serve the common interest to the best of their abilities, and that was particularly true for those citizens who possessed abilities that were critical to its security, such as skilled mariners. On the other hand, when not serving the king onboard ship or in the royal dockyards, those who the law defined as maritime laborers were simply ordinary citizens who possessed a particular skill and happened to live in a particular area. It was clearly a violation of their rights to simply appropriate their labor and move them by administrative fiat from civil into martial law jurisdiction.[10]

To resolve this contradiction, the committee proposed to give maritime laborers influence over the procedure that transformed them from citizen into servant of the crown by granting them the right to elect their local *syndic,* the low-level administrator responsible for the registration and mobilization of eligible men in a given district. In theory at least, the introduction of *syndics élus* (elected conscription officers) was meant to ensure that the revolutionary principle of popular sovereignty was upheld all the way to the water's edge, thus treating maritime laborers as equal citizens when not in service, without endangering the mechanism that, at the outbreak of war, pushed them from shore to ship, and into the jurisdiction of the *Code Pénal Maritime.*[11]

However, the introduction of *syndics élus* proved no more successful than the newly established jury trials in binding the loyalties of French mariners to the navy, for as it turned out they simply elected *syndics* who were likely to drag their feet and call up as few local men for service as possible. More important for solving the recruitment issue than this partial assimilation of maritime laborers to ordinary terrestrial citizens was therefore the continued reverse expansion of the state's coercive claim made originally only on the labor of genuine seafarers to an ever-wider swath of the metropolitan population. Already well underway in the final years of the old regime, that process approached its logical conclusion when the National Convention passed the *levée des 300,000* in late February 1793, hoping to mobilize three hundred thousand men for both the army and the navy by laying strict quotas on every single French department. It was followed in September of the same year by the more famous *levée en masse* that quite simply imposed military service obligations onto the whole population, including the rich who previously had been able to buy replacements.[12]

The militarization of French civil society was a double-edged sword for mariners. On the one hand, it represented the generalization of the special service requirements that for centuries had been laid only on communities along the maritime peripheries. This more equal sharing of the burden appears to have been welcomed, even if the actual number of war-workers raised fell far short of the theoretical maximum. On the other hand, the state's far more aggressive requisitioning of military labor that began in 1793–94 made it more difficult than it had been under the old *système des classes* for local communities to shield their young men from service, and it also offered no privileges or exemptions in return for their cooperation. With several of the coastal departments that traditionally had supplied the navy with a disproportionate share of their conscripts already drifting into counter-revolutionary disaffection, including Brittany and the Vendée, this imposition of an even more demanding recruitment system escalated diffuse unrest into organized, violent resistance, and eventually outright civil war.[13]

Coupled with the increasing militarization of French civil society on land came the rollback of popular sovereignty at sea. In early November 1793, Jeanbon Saint-André, whom the National Convention had chosen to regenerate the navy and prepare it for war with Britain, announced an addendum to the existing *Code Pénal Maritime* that replaced trial by jury with an appointed disciplinary council in all cases involving disobedience, the questioning or refusal of orders, all forms of unauthorized assembly, collective petitioning, political speech, absenteeism, and disorderly conduct. Reflecting the Jacobin republic's growing authoritarianism, the revised code was intended to push back against the political autonomy that since 1789 had flourished onboard ship and to replace it once again with the principle of complete, unquestioning obedience to all orders, in all circumstances.[14]

However, in contrast to the rules that had governed the old regime's navy, the principle of complete submission now explicitly included the officer corps. Not only did Article 1 of the new code make officers personally responsible for the maintenance of good order among their subordinates, like everyone else within the naval hierarchy they in turn were made completely subordinate to the political authorities above them. Saint-André, who mostly blamed the reactionary officer corps for the dissolution of discipline in the post-revolutionary navy, explained in a blunt speech that accompanied the introduction of the revised code that "you demand subordination among the crews, and with good reason. Where subordination no longer reigns, there is neither order nor unity and the most formidable forces are delivered up to the enemy like a timid, dispersed, defenseless herd. But for subordination to reign, you yourself must set the example; in order for the seamen to obey you, you must obey your own master first." In supplementary legislation announced just a few weeks before the great fleet battle on the First of June 1794, Saint-André further restricted the autonomy of ship commanders by ordering the death penalty for any officer who failed, was slow to act on, or did not respond at all to signals he received from other ships. Such a law, Saint-André explained, "by its just severity promises the nation that the scandals and the crimes of the old navy, where one could frequently see commanders abandoning their superiors, do not reproduce themselves in the regenerated navy of the Republic."[15]

In contrast to the cold suspicion with which he treated the officer corps, Saint-André believed that the citizens below deck were naturally inclined to obey the authority of the nation and its legitimate representatives, in port as well as onboard ship. However, given the officer corps' plotting and their many counter-revolutionary betrayals, he told the crews in a separate speech marking the introduction of the revised code that he understood why they had come to distrust their superiors, and why all too often they had felt compelled to take matters into their own collective hands. But that was then. With a purged and regenerated officer corps, with commanders who will be "severe without pride, just without passion, and inflexible towards the guilty," it was time once again for all men to take their assigned places, and for each one of them to do their duty, and nothing but their duty. To emphasize that all matters of command were once again to be left to the officer corps, the revised code determined that especially serious cases of disobedience— for example petitions, assemblies, and mutinies aimed at changing course or forcing a return to port—would henceforth be adjudicated by a Revolutionary Tribunal on shore. Mutiny, in other words, from now on would be treated as a counter-revolutionary crime.[16]

Saint-André was determined to ensure that the revised *Code Pénal Maritime* would not be received onboard ship as just another dead letter, like so many other post-revolutionary reforms before it. When therefore four members of the *America*'s crew were sentenced to death for mutiny under the new rules in early January 1794, Saint-André seized the moment to make his point. The *America*'s crew was among the most consistently radical and republican in the navy. They had been among the leading agitators against the introduction of the new code in 1790, and they had taken an active role in driving royalist officers out of the navy and into exile in 1791–92. In 1793, they had sided with the revolutionary authority of the representatives-on-mission in Saint-Domingue, Léger-Félicité Sonthonax and Étienne Polverel, and under their orders bombarded the small-white insurgents of Port-au-Prince. Subsequently they had refused to join the June 20 insurrection that destroyed Cap Français, and they were the only

French warship that did not afterwards flee to the United States. Instead, once their mission had lost all purpose, they mutinied and forced a return to France, as so many other republican crews demoralized by the irreconcilable contradictions of colonial revolution had done before them.[17]

From Saint-André's perspective, the *America* crew's impeccable republican track record must have made them ideal for a demonstration of the blind inflexibility of revolutionary justice, and the deadly seriousness of the demand for complete submission that the revised version of the code had introduced. After being condemned to death, the four *America* mutineers were immediately rowed out to a floating guillotine in the middle of the Brest roadstead and there executed in front of the whole fleet. It was a carefully staged demonstration of power. The decision to execute the guilty not by hanging, as was traditionally done in the French navy, but onboard a floating guillotine sent an unmistakable message: the principle of popular sovereignty onboard ship that the 1790 code had introduced in order to blunt the force of maritime martial law would henceforth be replaced by the sharp edge of terrestrial revolutionary justice.[18]

As the campaign to reimpose hierarchy and obedience unfolded, ordinary seamen were often targeted by the new law for their continued insistence on popular sovereignty as a fundamental principle of shipboard governance. As so often before, that insistence most frequently took the form of direct interventions to prevent punishments from taking place. Three of the four *America* mutineers, for instance, had tried to stop the punishment of a shipmate accused of insubordination. In other cases, it was enough to lament the decline of popular control in more general terms. François Grard, for example, a twenty-four-year-old former stonemason serving as a marine artillery soldier in Brest, was sentenced to death by the Revolutionary Tribunal for having dared to complain that "democracy is lost," and for threatening to run away to the war-torn Vendée region to escape the navy and its recruitment officers.[19]

There was also counter-revolutionary resistance to the transformation of the navy under Saint-André. In those cases, however, the accused tended to be petty officers and other career naval men rather than ordinary seamen. The fourth *America* mutineer, for instance, was a surgeon's mate who was sentenced to death for royalism and treason. Similarly, Jean-Joseph Algant, a thirty-year-old carpenter, was sentenced to death in April 1794 for shouting "*Vive le Roi!*" A month earlier, François Legouy, quartermaster onboard the *Impétueux,* was killed for failing to celebrate the retaking of Toulon from the British, for having refused to swear a patriotic oath, and for having said that he would rather work for the aristocrats and the emigres than for the republic.[20]

Similarly, Jean-Jacques-François Levée, carpenter onboard the *Félicité*, was executed for having harangued "a considerable mob" in the hope of convincing them that they would be better off serving the English, and that if everyone was of his mind, it would not be difficult to seize the ship and sail it across the Channel. But for the vast majority of French mariners, especially on the Atlantic coast where memories of British naval aggression ran deep, this was a step too far. For despite their unhappiness with Saint-André's heavy-handed regime, it was undeniable that in the short term the remilitarization of work relations in the dockyards and onboard ship, coupled with the influx of new recruits from all over France, helped create a sense of widely shared national sacrifice that stimulated such extraordinary levels of activity that within just a few short months the revolutionary fleet was ready to meet and fight the mighty Royal Navy at sea.[21]

And it was not a minute too soon. The fleet that sailed from Brest in mid-May had orders to draw the attention of Lord Howe's Channel fleet away from a huge convoy of merchant ships that carried desperately needed grain from the United States to France. However unruly, and however prone to desertion under normal circumstances, the crews onboard the French warships understood that the convoy's failure to get through would likely trigger famine at home, collapse the war effort, and spell the end of the revolutionary republic. And so they fought with remarkable courage when finally they met the far superior British fleet on June 1, 1794 (or 13 Prairial in Year II of French Liberty according to the newly introduced revolutionary calendar). Most famously, early in the battle the *Vengeur du Peuple* ("Avenger of the People") became entangled with the *Brunswick,* and for three hours was battered at point-blank range by the better equipped, more highly trained Royal Navy gun crews. Eventually, the pounding caused the ships to break free from each other, and as the *Vengeur* drifted off, with scores of men already dead and dozens of shot-holes near the waterline, the British *Ramillies* pulled up and unleashed another barrage on its masts, which destabilized the *Vengeur*'s hull, and with that sealed the fate of its crew. Despite the surviving men's desperate efforts at the pumps, the *Vengeur* went down, dragging nearly 350 crewmen to a watery grave. One eyewitness claimed that as the ship sank, in the final moments when all hope for a rescue was gone, "we heard some of our comrades still making prayers for the welfare of their country; the last cries of these unfortunates were: 'Vive la République!' They died uttering them."[22]

FIGURE 6. *Vengeur de Peuple* goes down at the end of the Battle of 13 Prairial, Year II; painting by Yves-Marie Le Gouaz and Nicolas-Marie Ozanne, "Combat du Vengeur" (1800). Courtesy of the Bibliothèque nationale de France.

Though immortalized almost immediately as a characteristic example of French republican martial valor, the self-sacrifice of the *Vengeur*'s crew in reality represented only a fleeting moment of patriotic unity, and only a brief suspension of the lower deck's growing alienation from the militarized republican naval establishment that looked increasingly like its royal predecessor. Once the radical Jacobin republic fell and openly counter-revolutionary forces took control of the reconstructed state in the late summer of 1794, anti-conscription resistance and desertion again became phenomena so widespread that the government threatened to garrison troops in the homes of all those who failed to show up for service onboard ship. At Toulon, where seamen and dockyard workers briefly rose in revolt to halt the slide into counter-revolution in the spring of 1795, the navy was soon hemorrhaging men at so staggering a rate that the government could think of no better solution than to order the fleet out to sea to stop the men from leaving.[23]

In contrast to the soldiers of the French Republic, who went on to conquer most of continental Europe, a large proportion of French sailors simply refused to fight on its behalf after the spring of 1794. Further reforms to the recruitment system all proved equally incapable of mobilizing a sufficiently large number of seafarers for service in the fleet, and eventually the navy began filling empty berths with soldiers transferred from the army instead. While many of these men had next to no seagoing experience, they were considered much more obedient than seamen, and it was hoped they would at least be able to work the guns below deck, the most labor-intensive task onboard ship. But their inexperience only accelerated the navy's post-revolutionary collapse. In 1795, a number of frigates in the Mediterranean fleet were forced to surrender without firing a single shot, because the majority of their landlubbing gunners were simply too seasick to fight. In other cases, the consequences were much worse. During the Battle of Genoa in mid-March 1795, the crew of the 80-gun *Ça Ira,* composed of 187 seamen and 496 soldiers, was overwhelmed by their enemies' superior seamanship, and in just a few hours suffered almost 500 men dead and wounded. It was a new low.[24]

As French soldiers invaded the United Provinces in 1795, they managed to capture most of the Dutch fleet at anchor. Had they not been able to add those desperately needed ships and sailors to the French war effort, the republic's naval power would likely have collapsed that same year. In itself, of course, the prize was not exactly a glorious one. Once the world's most powerful fleet, by the mid-1770s the Dutch navy had fallen behind even the small Danish fleet, and far behind those of Spain, France, and Britain. A brief expansion effort in the early 1780s collapsed under the financial and organizational strains of the Fourth Anglo-Dutch War (1780–84), and once the country became virtually a British protectorate in 1787, funding for the navy's deep-sea fleet dried up almost completely. Essential maintenance and even the victualing of the crews were neglected. Conditions onboard many of the ships soon became close to intolerable.[25]

By the time French troops under General Pichegru stormed north across the frozen river Waal in the winter of 1794–95, and in just a few short weeks overran the United Provinces, morale below deck had grown so bad that thousands of Dutch seamen simply wandered off their ships, sometimes demolishing them first. At the onset of spring, the *Staaten Generaal,* ordinarily with a complement of 550 men, only had 122 left onboard, while the *Delft,* with a regular crew of 350 men, only had 10. The *Castor* and the *Princess Frederika Louisa Wilhelmina,* both large frigates with a complement of 270 men, only had 22 and 7 men left respectively, and the *Hector* of the same size was completely deserted, as were many smaller vessels, such as the *St. Lucie* and *La Lurette* gunboats. The once mighty Dutch navy had become a ghost fleet.[26]

Following the French invasion, Dutch patriots overthrew Stadtholder William V, Prince of Orange, and in the ruins of his regime proclaimed the Batavian Republic. It now became a matter of great urgency to prevent the further collapse of the state's maritime defenses, for the country suddenly found itself dragged into war with Britain. The Treaty of The Hague, which French emissaries forced the new government to sign on May 16, 1795, not only imposed land cessions along the southern Dutch border, a large indemnity payment for the country's past participation in the First Coalition against France, and a huge low-interest loan to its new ally, it also forced the Dutch to maintain a French occupation force of 25,000 troops and commit at least a dozen ships of the line and eighteen frigates to the joint Franco-Dutch war effort against Britain. To make matters worse, Britain immediately retaliated by capturing seven, until very recently allied, Dutch warships at anchor in British ports, which was the equivalent of losing a major fleet battle before the war had even started.[27]

Despite the enormity of the challenge, the provisional government's *Comité tot Zaken van der Marine* (Committee on Naval Affairs) moved quickly to undertake a series of reforms in the hope of speeding along the fleet's combat-readiness. First of all, it dissolved and united under its own authority the five autonomous admiralties that together had formed, and with their constant bickering significantly weakened, the navy of the United Provinces. Next, to enforce revolutionary loyalty in the fleet's upper ranks, the committee dissolved the entire commissioned officer corps, re-employed those of impeccable political reputation, promoted petty officers up the ranks, and hired commanders from the merchant service to fill vacant spots on the navy's quarterdeck.[28]

But as the fierce struggles in Brest in 1790–91 had shown, it was not enough to replace the old officer corps with politically and socially more palatable commanders. The lower deck demanded truly revolutionary changes to the system of discipline as well. Finally, therefore, as in France, in order to make Dutch naval service less repulsive, the old fleet's brutal articles of war were replaced with a new code that restricted the power of captains to impose extra-judicial punishments and simultaneously opened up the composition of courts-martial to common seamen and petty officers. Some of the more spectacularly vicious punishments, such as keelhauling or tying a man convicted of murder to his victim and then throwing both overboard, were abolished, though for cases deemed serious the new articles retained a number of very severe punishments. Jan van der Pot, for instance, was sentenced on November 9, 1795, to lose his position as quartermaster on the *Dordrecht,* to be put in the pillory with a noose around his neck, to be severely beaten with oars, to be branded, to spend fifty years doing hard labor in a penitentiary, and afterwards to be banned from the territory of the republic for the remainder of his natural life. His shipmate, Hendrik van der Hoer, was sentenced to two hundred cane strokes, ten years of hard labor in a penitentiary, and then to be exiled from the republic for twenty years. Their crime: together with others, they had demanded an advance on their wages, and threatened not to weigh anchor without it.[29]

The Batavian navy inherited from its predecessor admiralties virtually empty war-chests and a fleet that required at least five million guilders in repairs and essential supplies to fight a war. As it was, the navy could barely afford to pay its sailors, and raising wages was completely out of the question, even though everyone knew that was the only way to get sufficient numbers of qualified men back onboard the empty ships. The old navy had purposely kept wages low on the assumption that it would prevent seamen from deserting— the idea being that with no money to spend, they would have nowhere to go—but low pay also discouraged men from signing up in the first place and thus created a chronic manpower shortage which now, on the eve of a major war, suddenly became acute. Promises of pardons and amnesties for those who had left their ships during the chaos of the revolution enticed only a few to return onboard, and the newly increased signing bonuses attracted only the low-quality recruits that had long filled the lower deck of the old navy.[30]

Recruitment remained slow, and only after the provisional government finally made extensive promises of imminent wage increases and improved conditions, including better food, free clothing, and more financial support for war widows, did the number of new recruits finally begin to creep up late in the fall of 1795. Of course, the Batavian state's catastrophic financial situation made a mockery of these promises. But that was a problem that would have to wait, for the navy was under pressure to assemble and put to sea a major fleet to secure the allegiance of the Dutch overseas colonies, which the exiled Stadtholder William V had formally transferred to the British for temporary safekeeping. Only the governors of Malacca, Amboina, and West Sumatra obeyed his orders, but the British lost no time conquering most of the remaining Dutch possessions in Asia anyway. In September 1795, they grabbed the strategically crucial Cape colony in southern Africa as well, and then seized Demerara on South America's Caribbean coast a few months later.[31]

In the fall and winter of 1795–96, people in the mother country had no idea how quickly the empire was collapsing around them as they scrambled to get a fleet underway to prevent just that from happening. It took months to assemble enough ships, supplies, sailors, and soldiers to create, by mid-January, a modest fleet of eight ships of the line, seven frigates, and a number of smaller support vessels. Several more weeks of bad weather stalled the fleet until late February, and even then, they were battered and scattered by a severe storm barely two weeks out. Their orders were to sail north around the tip of the British Isles together, and then split into two squadrons, one bound for Surinam, the other for the Cape of Good Hope. Most of the ships eventually managed to regroup after the storm, but the *Jason* frigate was so badly damaged that Captain Donckum judged it unsafe to continue across the Atlantic. He got permission to take the ship to the nearest port for emergency repairs.[32]

The *Jason* had barely arrived in the neutral Norwegian port of Trondheim before fourteen men, nearly 10 percent of the crew, deserted. But that was the least of Donckum's concerns, for also riding at anchor in Trondheim were four Dutch East India Company (VOC) ships and two naval vessels, all six of them defiantly flying the colors of the overthrown Orangist regime. Donckum tried to prevail with the ships' commanders to lower their flags and acknowledge the Batavian Republic's authority, but they mocked him and encouraged their men to sing pro-Orangist songs extra loud whenever he complained. The morale on the *Jason*'s lower deck grew noticeably worse during their stay in Trondheim, and Donckum was glad when after two very difficult months he finally was able to order the ship to sea again.[33]

A week later the crew revolted. Early in the morning of June 4, five men— Sergeant Steijner, Corporals Meijer and Bavius, and two seamen, Cardeves and Solomon Leslie—attacked Donckum in his cabin, disarmed and confined him, while another group knocked out the lieutenant of the watch. Soon all the ship's officers were confined, and the helmsman was ordered to turn the ship around and make sail straight for Scotland's craggy west coast. After that, the mutineers broke into the spirit room and got so terribly drunk that when they finally arrived at their destination, which turned out to be Greenock near Glasgow, several of them had to be admitted to hospital to cure "Fevers brought on by excess in drinking spirituous Liquors." The rest officially surrendered the ship, and after a few weeks of celebration, most of them asked to be permitted to join the British army. Some, including the leading mutineers, entered the Royal Navy instead. Others made their way back to the Netherlands, where some were discovered and arrested, and at

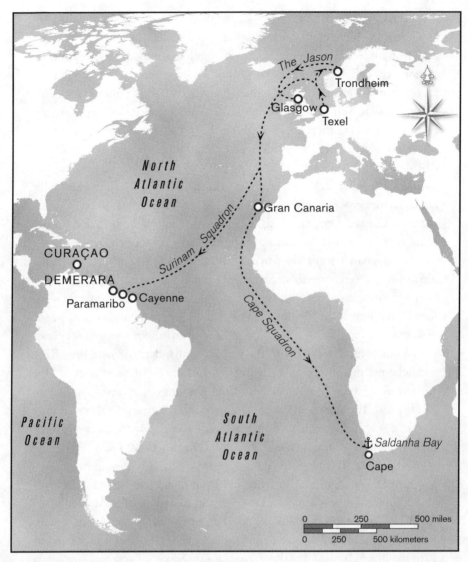

MAP 3. Routes of the Batavian navy's Surinam and Cape squadrons, January to August 1796. Map designed by Gerry Krieg.

least one hanged with the words "oath-breaking traitor" mounted atop the gallows. Thirty-six members of the crew, including all officers save for one midshipman, chose to become prisoners of war, and the few common seamen among them were sent into the hulks at Chatham. In a strange twist of fate, they were joined at Chatham by the fourteen men who had deserted at

Trondheim, who subsequently had been captured by the British onboard a Dutch merchantman on their way back to the republic.[34]

Captain Donckum, who himself remained a prisoner of war until 1799, afterwards knew exactly who to blame for the mutiny, and it was not himself. The frigate's common crewmen, he charged, were almost all "runaways and deserters," and even the soldiers onboard, usually the ones tasked with maintaining order and discipline, were themselves convicted deserters who were forced to serve in the Surinam squadron as a punishment. And as if that was not yet bad enough, nearly all the petty officers belonged to the counter-revolutionary "Orange party," and they continuously egged on the crew to be disobedient to the quarterdeck. Once the *Jason* was separated from the fleet, Donckum argued, mutiny was virtually inevitable. He had hoped the "orange flame," that he had noticed already at the Texel anchorage in north Holland, would burn itself out as the fleet made its way across the Atlantic. Instead, the crews of the ships that anchored alongside the *Jason* at Trondheim provided the flame with new fuel. Their provocations eventually pushed his already unreliable and quarrelsome crew over the edge into mutiny and treason.[35]

Donckum's explanation, while obviously self-serving, was nonetheless plausible, for the *Jason* was not the only ship in which the survival of pro-Orangist sentiment among the crew led to constant and sometimes serious trouble in the years following the revolution. On the *Cerebus,* first carpenter Klaas Scheepmakers was arrested for shouting out *"Oranje Boven!"* (Hail Orange!), and Jan Christian Ludeman, boatswain of the *Furie,* was tried for mocking and cursing the representatives of the Batavian regime and admitting support for the Prince of Orange. The second surgeon of the *Kortenaar,* Johannes Kamperdijk, was found with an orange ribbon in his possession. More worrisome, six disgruntled men on the *Otter*—a quartermaster, a sergeant, three soldiers, and a seaman—planned to arm the captured crew of the British brig *Lord Chichester,* rise on their officers, if necessary kill them, and afterwards flee to England, where they hoped to join the Stadtholder's service. The conspiracy was betrayed, and four of the men were executed and two severely flogged and thrown into prison for fifteen years. After being forced to watch the punishments of the *Otter* conspirators, the crew of the *Monnikkendam* suddenly grew truculent, and seventeen self-professed Orangist loyalists were arrested for singing "insurrectionary songs," holding illegal assemblies, beating up "stinking patriots" below deck, threatening not to fight against the English, and promising instead to murder their officers ("traitors," "patriotic beasts"), and then hand the ship over to the enemy. They also tattooed each other with portraits of the Stadtholder and a variety of Orangist slogans, such as *"Viva Oranje"* and *"P.V.O.B."* (an acronym for *"Prins van Oranje Boven,"* or "Hail to the Prince of Orange!").[36]

As had been the case in the French navy, counter-revolutionary sentiments were especially strong amongst the petty officer corps and other career naval men. The seventeen men arrested on the *Monnikkendam,* for instance, included two warrant officers, four quartermasters, a constable's mate, the ship's third master, and a cooper, as well as three seamen whose ages suggest that they looked back on long careers at sea. These men had ample reason to resent the new regime, for most career naval men like them had long ago attached themselves to a commander and through many years of loyal service steadily advanced up the ranks to their current positions. When the Committee on Naval Affairs therefore dissolved the entire commissioned officer corps for being politically suspect, it also, with the stroke of a pen, destroyed the patronage system that had structured the career paths of hundreds of the most highly skilled and dedicated workers in the service. Their anger and bitterness caused enormous damage, and their unwillingness to put their experience at the service of the Batavian Republic was an irreplaceable loss.[37]

But most of the men who worked onboard the ships of the Batavian navy had no such investment in the service, and despite Captain Donckum's attempt to place the majority of the blame for the *Jason* mutiny on counter-revolutionary agitation, he did admit that his crew in fact had quite specific grievances. Many had joined the navy before the revolution and thus not signed up to serve under the flag of the Batavian Republic. However, they had continued on board, trusting the new regime to honor its promises in regard to the payment of back wages accumulated before the revolution. These promises had not been fulfilled, and the mutineers therefore felt the navy had unilaterally violated the contract that bound them together. Considering the dreadful conditions they were expected to work under—they pointed to food cooked with seawater, reduced meat and water rations, overwork, and quarterdeck brutality—they saw no compelling reason to continue in the service, especially as they knew of the terrifying disease environment that awaited them in Dutch Guyana.[38]

The *Jason's* muster book was lost or destroyed during the mutiny, and it is therefore impossible to know how many of the crew had really been onboard already before the revolution. But in other cases where similar charges of broken promises emerged from below deck, no such ambiguity existed. This was especially true for the crews who served in the colonies at the time of the revolution, and whose loyalty to the new regime was often secured with insincere promises. Two days after his arrival in Surinam on May 13, 1796, for instance, Vice Admiral Braak called together the crews who had been there since 1794 and asked them to swear an oath of fidelity to the new Batavian regime. This oath, he assured them, was entirely voluntary, but even if they refused, they still would have to remain on their ships until they were ordered back to Europe, which probably would happen within the next six or seven months. The only difference was that without the oath they obviously would not be paid for their service, since the new regime could hardly be expected to honor the old regime's obligations, especially to people who remained loyal to it. With that threat hanging over their heads, and with the assurance that soon they would return home, most of the crews swore the oath.[39]

Six months passed, then seven, eight, nine, ten, eleven, and finally twelve, and still there was no sign that they would sail for Europe anytime soon. In response, one hundred crewmen of the frigate *Vertrouwen* wrote to Captain Hartsinck, Vice Admiral Braak's successor as station commander, to demand their immediate discharge. When they took the oath over a year ago, they reminded him, it had been with the explicit understanding that

> they would return to the fatherland within 6–7 months, and there receive their discharge, whether the four years were up or not [that they originally had signed up to serve under the old regime], and they would receive all their earned wages and a regular letter of discharge. Even though we had signed up for four years, the new oath supersedes that promise, and, in fact, we were not obliged even to swear it and rightfully could have taken a discharge then, and therefore it is proper now to most humbly ask that this condition be honored. By now, moreover, we have served out our four years.[40]

Hartsinck dismissed the complaint. He called together all the squadron's commanders and ordered them to inform their crews that there never had been a condition attached to the swearing of the new oath. What they at the time may have understood to be a promise to sail for Europe within six or seven months, he explained, was in reality only a prediction of what was likely to happen. But as it turned out, events unfolded differently, and there could not be any talk of a mass discharge. If anyone had a problem with that, Hartsinck continued, he recommended they be reminded of the articles of war, which they had sworn to obey, and especially of those sections that dealt with failure to follow orders.[41]

It is not difficult to understand the crews' eagerness to leave. Surinam was easily one of the most horrible places within the European orbit, a "space of death" so vile it troubled even Voltaire's pathologically optimistic character Candide. As well as home to one of the hemisphere's most notoriously brutal plantation regimes—graphically depicted in John Gabriel Stedman's *Narrative of a Five Years' Expedition Against the Revolted Negroes of Surinam*—the "wild coast" was also an unparalleled killer of unseasoned white men. High humidity combined with a merciless sun turned the whole colony into a festering sore. Those afflicted only by fevers, dysentery, diarrhea, or rheumatism were the lucky ones, for thousands of newcomers were wasted in constantly recurring epidemics of chicken pox and yellow fever, and by the mid-eighteenth century even leprosy had become common.[42]

Disease ravaged Surinam's small naval station. Already in the summer of 1795, a full year before the arrival of the relief squadron, illness had cut down so many sailors that the colony's maritime defenses were near collapse. On one of the station's four vessels, the 16-gun brig *Thetis,* virtually the entire crew had died. Some months later, station commander Captain S. A. van Overfelt reported that on the frigate *Erff Prins,* ordinarily with a complement of 300 men, only 80 were left onboard, and 60 of those were too sick to work. By March 1796, not enough officers were left alive even to constitute a regular court-martial. Vice Admiral Braak's squadron brought temporary relief in May, but also scores of new victims. Braak himself was dead within three months, and by October 330 men of the squadron's complement of 1,597 were sick, and an unknown number dead. By January 1797, 326 men were sick, and the squadron short an additional 81 men. By July, the number of sick had fallen to 246, but the squadron was now short another 145 men, many of them dead and some of them deserted.[43]

Before the relief squadron arrived, Overfelt had begun exploring the possibility of drafting black men to fill the many empty berths onboard the *Erff Prins* frigate, and he even raised the idea of pardoning African-born soldiers who had been sold into slavery as punishment for desertion from Dutch colonial regiments. However, Paramaribo's chief of police very firmly made him "understand the impossibility of supplementing the said frigate's crew with negroes." The Surinam authorities were understandably apprehensive of giving blacks a critical role in the colony's defense, given that a major combined slave-maroon insurrection had only just erupted in neighboring Demerara, along with another major slave revolt in Curaçao. Officials were also afraid, and they had been for quite some time, that disgruntled European sailors would make common cause with the slaves. Several years earlier, some kind of problem arose when a disaffected seaman was put ashore after being punished with keelhauling followed by a severe flogging. In response, colonial officials requested the Admiralty henceforth stop the practice of discharging mutinous and disobedient sailors in the colonies, where they will become "vagabonds, and thus have the opportunity to mix with the slaves." Ending the practice, they insisted, was necessary for "the preservation of unity."[44]

After the Batavian Republic joined France as an ally in 1795, fears of unrest intensified among local authorities, for the colony now became a safe haven for commerce-raiding French privateers, whose numbers had exploded after the abolition of slavery in the French empire on February 4, 1794. Compensating for the collapse of French naval power in the Caribbean, and to help stoke subversive anti-slavery insurgencies in the British colonies, French republican authorities in many colonies went out of their way to encourage former slaves to join the irregular war at sea. Their call was heard. In Guadeloupe alone, which together with French Guyana became one of the centers of republican privateering, around 3,500 former slaves took to the sea as privateersmen and helped capture or destroy over 1,800 enemy ships between 1795 and 1799.[45]

Unlike their white shipmates, who mostly went privateering for personal gain, former slaves often considered their service under the banner of the French Republic as part of the broader war against slavery, sometimes in a very direct sense. Not only did black privateersmen have every reason to expect that a British victory in the Caribbean would lead to the reintroduction of slavery in the French colonies, but for many of them, even just losing a single battle against a British warship or privateer might result in their own re-enslavement. Even then, however, their struggle against slavery was not always over. In the spring of 1794, for example, Pierre Guy, a captured black privateersman, led a mutiny onboard two British transport vessels that carried black republican prisoners of war away from Guadeloupe and back into slavery. After the successful insurrection, the mutineers sailed across the Atlantic to Rochefort, and from there sent a letter of thanks to the National Convention for having abolished slavery and "elevated them to the dignity of French citizens."[46]

Some black republican privateers had an even more expansive understanding of revolutionary solidarity. On the eve of the Irish Rising of 1803, the crew of a French-licensed privateer originally from Saint-Domingue was so moved by witnessing the Bastille Day festivities in Ireland—"celebrating the anniversary of the French Revolution, and the deliverance of enslaved peoples"—that they decided to smuggle pike heads from France to the rebels in Dublin, and then join the insurrection "to overthrow the English government in Ireland." When the rebellion fell apart, they made their escape and resumed privateering.[47]

Local authorities in Dutch Surinam were obviously not thrilled with the arrival of French republican privateers in the colony, for unlike their French allies, whose ships they had no choice but to welcome in their ports, the Batavian government had no intention of abolishing slavery in the Dutch empire. Captain Hartsinck, who took over as station commander after Vice Admiral Braak's death, therefore worried about the consequences of having black privateersmen, whom he called Cayenne negroes, sharing their experiences of life beyond slavery with local blacks. Even if it were possible to prevail on their commanders not to grant black crew members shore leave in Surinam, they still would be able to communicate with the slave lightermen and shipwrights who worked in the harbor, and with black seamen onboard other merchant ships that visited the port. That latter group had already drawn Hartsinck's ire after it was discovered that a black sailor onboard the American merchantman *Franklin* had tried to help a deserter from the brig *Snelheid* escape from Surinam.[48]

Desertion rates had always been fairly high at the Surinam station, but after Captain Hartsinck openly went back on his predecessor's promise to return the veteran crews to Europe, escape attempts increased significantly. But Surinam was a difficult place to get away from. Paramaribo's harbor was closely monitored, and those who tried to make it overland to one of the neighboring colonies, French Guyana or British-occupied Demerara, often suffered a painful death, as the jungle slowly sapped their strength. In some cases, they had to contend with hostile maroon communities. In other cases, they encountered Native Americans who exploited their inexperience with the alien jungle environment. Jan le Clerk, Gerriet Hutte, his brother Isaac, and Jan Wax, all deserters from the *Kemphaan,* were recaptured when a group of Indians, who pretended to lead them to British-occupied Demerara, took them to the nearest Dutch warship instead, and presumably were given a reward for their troubles. Jan Wax and Gerriet Hutte were hanged, and the other two were severely flogged, branded, condemned to labor in a chain-gang for two years, followed by a lifetime ban from the territories of the Batavian Republic.[49]

Surinam's financial troubles, and the lack of support from the metropole, made it difficult to maintain order amongst the crews by any means other than harsh discipline. Hartsinck could not even afford to keep his fleet in a decent state of repair, and one ship after another literally fell apart. The *Vertrouwen* frigate, judged to be in a "good" condition in January 1797, was considered only "decent" six months later, and already "questionable" a few months after that. Morale among the crews deteriorated even faster. The seamen were rarely paid, and when they were, Surinam's runaway inflation made their money almost worthless. Many could not afford to replace the slops that rotted off their bodies in the tropical heat. The sheer brutality of everyday life, and the absence of any real hope of escape, eventually pushed some crews to contemplate murdering their officers and running off with their ship to the nearest enemy port. On the *Havick* schooner, where the crew was forced to steal food, alcohol, and even linen to fashion trousers and shirts for themselves, a full third of the crew conspired to rise on their officers, either shoot them or throw them overboard, and then take the ship to Demerara. But their plan was found out, and six men were sentenced to severe cane beatings and hard labor, while another three were confined in irons for eight days.[50]

In the Batavian fleet's Cape of Good Hope squadron, lower deck morale collapsed even more spectacularly than in Surinam. There was already trouble before the squadron left the republic in late February 1796, for many of the hastily raised recruits were undernourished and in poor health. During the fleet's long wait for decent weather conditions at the Texel anchorage, their various diseases had time to incubate and spread amongst the tightly packed crews. In early March, after the ships had been at sea for barely two weeks, the flagship *Dordrecht* already counted 90 men on its sick list, and several dead. By the time the squadron reached the Canary Islands off the northwest African coast in mid-April, 42 men had died on the *Dordrecht,* 31 on the *Trompe,* 15 on the *Revolutie,* 13 each on the *Braave* and *Bellona,* 10 on the *Castor,* 3 on the *Sireene,* and one on the VOC ship *Vrouw Maria.* The squadron also had 317 men on the sick list, approximately 14 percent of its overall strength.[51]

Discipline onboard the short-handed ships became ferocious, and as soon as the squadron dropped anchor off Gran Canaria, men began to desert in droves. In response, Vice-Admiral Lucas cancelled all shore leave, even for the sick, and he ordered three captured deserters hanged and another two flogged through the fleet with four hundred lashes each. Soon afterwards, when Lucas announced that, due to the high cost of provisions in the islands, he would not be able to pay the men their promised wages, there was grumbling throughout the squadron, and onboard the *Revolutie* even a minor riot. Lieutenant Colonel Henry, who accompanied the expedition at the head of a detachment of French soldiers, worried where this level of open dissatisfaction might lead. He was not surprised, however. The men, he wrote, were constantly told about "the Revolution" and "the Freedom" that allegedly flowed from it, yet the same old vicious discipline continued to determine their everyday lives. Boatswain's mates still patrolled the decks with rope ends and they still brutalized the men at random, completely out of proportion and without due process. Nor had the men's wages gone up, and all the old abuses and tricks that were used to deny them the little they were owed continued as well. When news of the squadron's fate finally reached Holland the next summer, J. P. G., publisher of the staunchly republican *Nationaale Bataafse Courant,* agreed with Henry's assessment: "If one promises something to men of this class and fails to follow through, that creates dissatisfaction, and then it takes but an insignificant trifle that is not to their liking and there will be an insurrection."[52]

When the revolt finally came, it was triggered by something a little more serious than a mere trifle. The squadron left the Canaries, much delayed, on May 29 and as it slowly drew close to the Cape in late July, news arrived that the British had taken the colony the previous fall. With nearly exhausted provisions and once again rapidly growing sick lists—on the *Sireene* a full third of the crew was incapacitated, on the *Trompe* 29 men had died since leaving Gran Canaria, many of them from scurvy, and on the flagship *Dordrecht* another 18 men were dead—Vice-Admiral Lucas had no choice but to order the squadron to anchor in Saldanha Bay, some seventy miles north of the Cape. Within days, a powerful squadron of eleven Royal Navy warships shut down the entrance to the bay, and thousands of redcoats commenced a bombardment with red-hot shot from the shore. The Dutch squadron was hopelessly outmatched. The British warships had more than twice as many guns as the Dutch, and together with the troops on shore nearly 7,500 more men. On the *Trompe, Braave, Sireene, Havick,* and the *Bellona,* the crews were nonetheless willing to fight, even though illness, death, and desertion had so weakened them that they could only man a fraction of their guns.[53]

But on the flagship *Dordrecht,* the *Revolutie,* and the *Castor,* three of the squadron's most powerful ships, discipline collapsed. Dozens of men took off with their weapons to join the enemy, and on the *Castor* and *Revolutie* large-scale violence erupted. Officers feared for their lives, many were ritually humiliated, and several nearly murdered. On the *Castor*, Orangist mutineers cursed their officers for being "damned sons of Batavian freedom" and promised them to "break your necks in liberty and fraternity," but others on the same ship sang songs about "the god-damned William of Orange the traitor." Eventually Patriots and Orangists came to blows. Several men were murdered, some stabbed to death, a few thrown overboard and drowned, and yet others knocked around the head and slashed with broken bottles. The *Castor*'s boatswain Hendrik Prins, boatswain's mate Jurrie Mate, and second constable Jacob Popkes were beaten so savagely that it was hard to identify them afterwards. The violence raged on for a day and a half, and when its fury finally was spent, the exhausted squadron quietly surrendered to the British.[54]

When news of the surrender reached the Batavian Republic a few months later, there were suggestions that perhaps the 1795 purge of the naval officer corps had not gone far enough, and that in fact the squadron's commanders had willingly delivered themselves up to the British in order to undermine the revolution. It seemed suspicious that they had not taken any steps to secure the entrance to the bay with shore batteries, even though it must have been clear to them that the Royal Navy would show up sooner rather than later. Equally odd, when the first British advance parties arrived to drive the Dutch from the bay's two watering places, Vice-Admiral Lucas denied a request from Lieutenant Colonel Henry to land six hundred men to fight them off, which would at least have given the squadron the chance to take on enough water to put to sea. Worst of all, why had they not challenged the British squadron to a fight and thus at least been able to damage some the enemy's ships, even if their defeat was a foregone conclusion?[55]

Lucas, aware that such questions would inevitably come, explained that he quite simply had lost faith in his men. If given half a chance, they deserted, so he could not risk putting anyone ashore, and when he called a council of war to determine whether to surrender or fight, it unanimously concluded that the crews were as likely "to shoot and kill their own officers as fire on the enemy." Some of the other officers in the squadron tried to blame pro-Orangist agitators below deck, but Lucas knew better: his men were not for or against anything, they were "faithless." Many of them had not been off their ships since going onboard at the Texel anchorage the previous winter and they had thus been cooped up for seven, eight, or nine months, constantly surrounded by disease and death. What kept them at their duty for so long despite the daily misery was the hope that at the Cape they finally would receive some of their long overdue wages, which they planned to spend with abandon in that famous "tavern of the seas." When news arrived that the British had taken the colony, even that last bit of hope for temporary relief evaporated, and in bitterness, anger, and disappointment they erupted into violence. Lieutenant Colonel Henry also put little stock in the idea that Orangism had animated many of the mutineers, for they remembered perfectly well, he claimed, that conditions in the old Orangist navy had not been any better than they were now. Angry at all the broken promises of improvement, they now turned on their new officers, professing loyalty to the old regime simply as a way of undermining the legitimacy of the officers' rule.[56]

After the surrender, a small number of men immediately joined the Royal Navy—mostly those, it seems, with genuine Orangist convictions—while the majority had no desire to get back onboard a warship anytime soon. But the British, desperately short of manpower themselves, were not about to let a bounty of nearly two thousand seamen slip out of their grasp. By the terms of the capitulation treaty, Admiral Elphinstone promised Lucas that all those who chose to become prisoners of war would be brought "by the most speedy and convenient conveyances to Europe." But two weeks later he reported to the Admiralty his belief that the "many foreigners not native dutch or french" who had been part of the squadron could be prevailed upon to join the British service. To Lucas' intense irritation, Elphinstone delayed sending the prisoners for several months, and he cunningly arranged for celebrations of made-up British naval victories, then plied the prisoners with drink and let loose his recruiters among them. By early November nearly 75 percent of the Dutch prisoners had signed on with the British, either for service on Royal Navy or East India Company ships, or to work the docks at the Cape. When the prisoner of war cartel finally sailed for Europe on December 6, only 220 men were onboard. One hundred twenty-eight men who were too weak to brave the many months at sea remained behind in hospital, 33 were left in prison for unknown reasons and everyone else, somewhere around 1,500 men, had switched sides and joined the British.[57]

Climbing aboard a Royal Navy warship for the first time, the defecting sailors can hardly have been encouraged by what they found, for relations between officers and crews onboard British warships had rarely been worse than during the first few years of the French Revolutionary Wars. Between

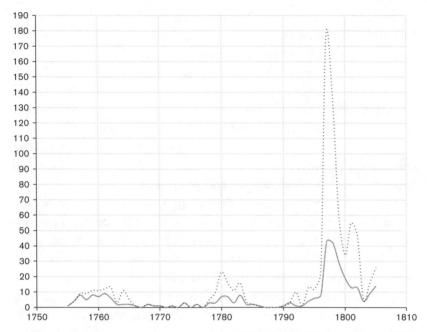

FIGURE 7. Number of courts-martial for mutiny (solid line) and number of men tried for mutiny (dotted line), British Royal Navy, 1755–1805. In order to better illustrate the overall trend, one very unusual mass trial in 1758, which ended in the acquittal of all 45 men accused, has been omitted. Source: "Digest of the Admiralty Records of the Trials by Court-Martial, From the 1st January 1755 to 1st January 1806; Fifty-One Years," TNA (UK) ADM 12/24.

1755 and 1805, the Royal Navy held 311 court-martial trials for mutiny, a far larger number than any other navy. But a significant proportion (64 percent) of these trials involved only a single defendant, and these were mostly cases of individual disobedience that in France, for example, would not have been viewed as mutiny at all, and instead would have been dealt with extrajudicially. However, with each war the Royal Navy fought in this period, the average number of defendants per trial went up, from 1.46 during the Seven Years' War (1756–63) to 2.44 during the War for American Independence (1775–83), and to 3.17 during the French Revolutionary War (1793–1802), suggesting overall a steady increase of collective forms of disobedience throughout the latter half of the century. In absolute terms, the increase was by far the most strongly pronounced during the French Revolutionary Wars, which saw more than twice as many trials (178) and more than three and a half times as many defendants (564) as the Seven Years' War (50/73) and the War for American Independence (34/83) put together.[58]

At the height of the War of Austrian Succession in 1747, the British navy had employed around 48,000 common seamen; twelve years later, in 1759, the number had risen to 77,000 men; and in the final phase of the American War in 1782 to just over 95,000 men. At the conclusion of the French Revolutionary Wars in 1802, the number would reach 118,000, and then go on to climb to over 138,000 in 1812. Finding thousands of new recruits every year became harder and harder, and so the Admiralty concentrated on rationalizing its exploitation of available manpower as much as possible. Most importantly, beginning already in the 1740s, the Board of Admiralty had begun to standardize and centralize all of the navy's operations, aiming to ensure that authority flowed unimpeded from a single center at the top, and that each constituent element within the entire organization became an easily replaceable cog in a vast and smoothly efficient war-making machine.[59]

A first round of reforms targeted the relative autonomy of ship and fleet commanders, primarily by expanding the direct authority of the Board of Admiralty and creating a clearly defined chain of command beneath it. With the passage of the 1749 Navy Bill, orders coming from the Admiralty in London for the first time had to be followed blindly and without question, and failure to do so would be dealt with harshly, regardless of rank. In a second phase that commenced in the 1750s, the Admiralty expanded its direct authority by centralizing the powers of promotion and preferment that previously had resided with individual commanders, and that had allowed them to build up loyal followings on the lower deck. The old system was good for morale and the fighting efficiency of individual ships, but it tied up skilled manpower that was more urgently needed elsewhere. The Admiralty further restricted the autonomy of commanders by standardizing the rules and regulations that governed day-to-day operations at sea, which in turn allowed for the smoother movement of men between different ships. This made it easier to break up and redistribute crews whenever other ships stood in greater need of their skills, or whenever a vessel was temporarily taken out of service.[60]

While these reforms made the Royal Navy a much more efficient fighting force, the impact on the relationship between officers and men onboard the ships was devastating. Previously, officers and crews had served together for the duration of a war, and thus had been able to build relationships during several years of service together. But in the second half of the eighteenth century they often faced each other as strangers who temporarily served together in one ship before being transferred over into another. Officers no longer could rely on their personal prestige or on their powers of patronage to secure the men's obedience and were forced to rely instead on the formal powers vested in their position, which were mostly punitive and violent. In consequence, not only were more men tried for more mutinies in this period, but those convicted suffered increasingly severe consequences. During the Seven Years' War, 13.7 percent of all those accused of mutiny were sentenced to death. During the American War it rose to 30.1 percent, and during the French Revolutionary Wars it rose once again, to 32.4 percent. Nonlethal punishments also became harsher. From the Seven Years' War to the War for American Independence, the average number of lashes per flogging sentence for mutiny jumped from 236 to 403. At the end of the century, it dropped down to 227, but that lowering of the average was largely due to the introduction of light flogging sentences for minor violations that previously had not been punished by courts-martial at all.[61]

In response to this increasing brutality, discontented seamen developed more militant forms of struggle. During the War for American Independence, mutineers on three different ships tried to murder their officers and sail for France, but only those onboard the *Jackall* succeeded. More consequential in the long run, a new strike-like form of mutiny emerged in the early phases of the French Revolutionary Wars. On August 17, 1793, the crew of the *Winchelsea* sent a petition to the Admiralty protesting that "our usage was more like Turks, than of British Seamen. . . . If we are all to go out in the Ship, we shall be under the Obligation of using such means that is unbecoming of British Seamen." They demanded either new officers or that the crew be broken up and distributed among different ships. There was no response, and a month later they sent another petition, emphasizing just how serious they were: "If We get no Redress to this Letter your Lord Ships May Depend that we One and All shall be under the Necessity to free Our Selves." It was apparently clear to them that once again they would get no answer, for only three days later they mutinied. When called to muster in the morning, forty-four men remained below, shouted "one and all," and then barricaded themselves behind their rolled-up hammocks in the bay. Captain Fisher immediately put the marines under arms, and then went below deck to talk to the mutineers. Talk quickly turned into threats and Fisher fired his pistol into one of the hammocks. The mutineers, armed only with a single handspike, took ten minutes to deliberate, and then gave up.[62]

Two weeks after the mutiny, a court-martial sentenced William Price and William Duggan to be flogged around the fleet with 200 lashes each. Both men were beaten nearly to death in front of the assembled Channel fleet—Duggan's punishment was called off after 141 lashes, Price's after 131—but the mutineers were afterwards granted their demands: nine days after the floggings, Captain Fisher, eight petty officers, and eight of his followers on the lower deck were reassigned to other ships. Afraid, perhaps, that tensions between officers and men would escalate out of control, Admiral Sir Peter Parker, commander in chief at Portsmouth, hoped that by imposing a solution painful to both sides he would make clear that the navy's senior leadership would tolerate neither threats from below nor excessive violence from above. But neither side listened. Between 1794 and 1796, the crews of the *Lady Taylor, Squirrel, Bellerophon, Ceres, Amphitrite, Weazle, Nassau, Blanche, Crescent, Shannon, Brunswick, Reunion,* and *Emerald* all sent petitions to the Admiralty protesting the behavior of their officers. On the *Weazle,* wrote its crew in August 1795, Lieutenant McKenley almost daily ordered some of the men to strip, had them tied to the rigging, and then beat them within an inch of their lives. The same month the crew of the *Nassau* complained that they were "realy used worse than dogs," and that they suffered "under the hand of a Tyrant." On the *Shannon,* the crew evoked Jean-Jacques Rousseau's famous opening line in the *Social Contract* by lamenting that "we are born free but now we are slaves."[63]

Lower deck anger at this treatment soon enough exploded into another mutiny. On the evening of November 9, 1794, 300 members of the *Windsor Castle's* crew rose up against two of their officers, Captain William Shield and First Lieutenant George McKinley. Having learned their lesson from the fate of their brothers on the *Winchelsea,* the mutineers immediately armed themselves with all the small arms, tomahawks, cutlasses, boarding pikes, and handspikes they could find. To increase the confusion during the first phase of the mutiny, they fired off a number of pistols to keep loyalists, officers, and marines at bay, and meanwhile ran in four of the great guns and pointed them aft, in the direction of the quarterdeck. Then they unshipped the ladders to make it impossible for any officers to come below.[64]

The morning after the mutiny commenced, Vice Admirals William Hotham, acting commander in chief of the Mediterranean squadron, and Sir Hyde Parker went onboard to investigate the cause of the commotion. Someone from below tossed a letter up on deck, signed "The Company of His Majesty's Ship the Windsor Castle": "No man can go aloft now," the mutineers complained, "But what he is in dread of Being punished for the least frivolous Accident whatever may happen, if not punished with Lashes their wine is stopt and given to another part of the Ships Co. which is quite contrary to the Rules of the Navy." Convinced that their fellow officers would not hesitate to dismiss these charges as ludicrous, the *Windsor Castle*'s captain and first lieutenant immediately applied for a court-martial to contest the allegations. Vice Admiral Hotham, relieved to be able to regularize the conflict, sent word to the mutineers to prepare a list of witnesses. But they refused. They had no interest in such a trial. They just wanted new officers. "We endeavoured by all the arguments we could use," Vice Admiral Parker afterwards reported, "to persuade the men to return to their duty, or to bring forward in a proper manner their complaints, that the officers they complained of might be tried by a Court Martial; but they refused to do either and persisted in declaring that they would not go upon deck nor do any duty until another captain, first lieutenant, and boatswain were appointed."[65]

Since no one was willing to step forward to support the charges made against the officers, the hastily assembled court-martial dismissed them as "malicious, frivolous, and without the smallest foundation of truth." But this made little difference. The mutineers were armed and remained fully in control of the lower deck and all its access points, and by all appearances were determined to do whatever it took to win their demands, even if it involved casualties. Since the mutineers controlled all of the ship's provisions, waiting them out was not an option either. Nor did there appear to be any room for negotiation: "They said that they were determined at every risk to keep their position until the Captain and First Lieutenant were removed, whose treatment they could no longer endure, nor would they fire a Gun against an Enemy until this their request was complied with." Left with no other options, on the fourth day of the mutiny, Captain Shield and Lieutenant McKinley requested from Hotham "to permit them to quit the ship, which I not only approved of, but recommended, as the only method of pacifying the crew and restoring order at this critical juncture." And just like that, the mutineers had won. The two hated officers, cleared by a court-martial of any wrongdoing, were forced out of the ship by the crew, without a single man being punished afterwards.[66]

When less than a year later, on the same station, the crew of the 74-gun *Terrible* mutinied in the exact same way, Captain Campbell was determined to crush the idea that a precedent had been established. "It shall not be," he barked at the crew, "a Windsor Castle's Business." He then ordered the ship's detachment of soldiers from the 30th regiment to assemble around the fore and after hatchways on the main deck, and fire at will on the sailors below. When the smoke cleared, five men rolled around the lower deck, covered in blood, whimpering in pain. Charles Rogers had been shot through both arms, George Everett through one arm and one thigh, William Miles through one of his knees, George Wilkinson through his groin and thigh bone, and Mattio Ciantar through both his shoulders and lungs. Ignoring the carnage, Campbell ordered another five men flogged on the spot, hoping to beat the names of the ringleaders out of them. Afterwards, with five of his men injured from gunshot wounds, five more men flogged, and another twelve standing trial for their lives, five of whom would be sentenced to death, Campbell was careful to claim that the mutineers had been preparing to fire the great guns. But Fifth Lieutenant Clarributt, who was sent below to secure the mutineers' arms, testified that he had found no matches that appear to have been lit, nor did he find any muskets that had been fired, and none that even had been primed. First Lieutenant Charles Patey, Third Lieutenant William Heard, and Fourth Lieutenant John Cramer likewise denied seeing any fire coming from below. Campbell, in other words, had ordered a massacre, and no one made much of an effort to hide it.[67]

The new type of militant strike-like mutiny also appeared at Spithead, the anchorage just off Portsmouth, the navy's largest and most important dockyard. On December 4, 1794, around 10 pm, between forty and fifty members of the *Culloden*'s crew suddenly began running around the lower deck, shouting "Huzzah!", dodging below and between the tightly packed hammocks, overturning a few of them, cutting down others, rolling and hurling shot around the deck, creating complete mayhem. As people staggered to and fro in the darkness, some of the mutineers cut through the chaos and with lightning speed disarmed the marine sentries, and then drove all officers and known loyalists up on deck. "We'll have no Sculkers," they shouted. Others meanwhile raced to the hatchways and unshipped the ladders in order to prevent the marine detachment from coming below, while yet another group began building a "barrocadoe" in the bay, piling up rolled-up hammocks and running in two of the great guns and turning them aft. Someone broke into the magazine and distributed small arms and cutlasses.[68]

The officers present on deck were taken aback by the sudden noise below, but before the mutineers had time to unship the ladders Second Lieutenant John Griffiths managed to get down to see what was happening. He was met with a hail of shot thrown in his direction and was struck on the leg as he dashed back up. He was able to report that the men had shouted "A new ship!" Third Lieutenant Edward Owen also made his way down, but when seeing who he was, the mutineers stopped throwing shot. "I went forward to the Starboard Bay," he later testified, "and attempted to reason with the Men and persuad them to return to their Duty. They answered that the Ship had struck and that they would not go to Sea in her unless overhauled. That if they did go to Sea in her they would not fire a Shot but would be taken by the French." After having clarified just how serious they were, "they then advised me to get upon Deck and began throwing a number of Shot again."[69]

Two weeks before the mutiny, the *Culloden* had been badly battered by violent gale-force winds that had raged across the Channel in mid-November—it ran aground, sprang a leak, and had its rudder smashed to pieces. But the *Culloden*'s new captain, Thomas Troubridge, who was responsible for anchoring in such an exposed position in the first place, nevertheless pressed ahead with preparations for taking the ship to the Mediterranean as ordered, assuring everyone who would listen, and most of all himself, that nothing serious had happened. But his crew did not trust him. Troubridge had arrived in the ship in early November with the record of having already lost a frigate to the French that year, and he now faced the possibility of having done serious damage to one of the fleet's line-of-battleships. Even if it was not his fault, Troubridge, the son of a London baker and thus without connections amongst the navy administration's upper echelons, could not afford to build a reputation as an officer who loses or destroys every ship he commands. He was therefore under pressure to take the *Culloden* to sea, and the crew knew it.[70]

What made matters worse, Troubridge had been quick to give an impression of incompetence. Only three days after assuming command on November 9, Troubridge mishandled a routine maneuver and rammed the *Robust* and carried away its jib boom and foretopgallant mast. And it was just a week later that he anchored the ship right next to a rock that would pierce its bottom once gale-force winds started blowing. Perhaps it was not his fault—he blamed erroneous charts—but these incidents did not exactly inspire confidence in his judgment, especially among those whose lives depended on it. The crew knew perfectly well that in case of catastrophe, two of the ship's three boats were reserved for the officer corps.[71]

Wooden men-of-war only rarely went down, but the *Culloden* crew were among the few who knew exactly what it looked like when a huge vessel like theirs sank. At the end of the battle on the Glorious First of June, they had been one of the first ships to reach the sinking *Vengeur du Peuple,* and while they managed to save over two hundred of its crew, they failed to save hundreds more. What they saw that day, and the sounds they must have heard as scores of men were dragged below fighting and screaming for their lives, was no doubt still fresh in their minds when just six months later they decided that refusing orders was a lesser risk than taking the recently damaged *Culloden* to sea.[72]

While Troubridge on the *Culloden,* his superior Vice-Admiral Bridport on the *Royal William,* Bridport's superior Admiral Parker in Portsmouth, and Parker's superiors at the Admiralty in London all struggled to find a way to end the mutiny without losing face or shedding too much blood, the mutineers prepared themselves for a long, drawn-out struggle. The mutiny was planned and initially carried out by 50 to 60 men, but once it started, it rapidly won the support of about two-thirds of the crew, or just over 250 men. By the second full day of the mutiny, they had organized themselves into nine watches of 27 men each. Each watch was led by one of the original mutineers, but their role appears to have been largely limited to coordinating the necessary tasks that needed to be carried out in order to keep the ship safe. Even so, most men spontaneously took responsibility for various jobs, and the only task that no one seemed very enthusiastic about was emptying the buckets in which they all "relieved" themselves. Several witnesses later testified that no one among the mutineers was really invested with more power than anyone else. One witness emphasized that those who headed the watches were considered "corporals" and not "lieutenants," indicating that they had risen from below on account of their skill and experience but were not considered to be invested with executive authority.[73]

The same day as they made out the watch bill, the mutineers also drafted a formal letter to Vice-Admiral Lord Bridport, the Channel fleet's commanding officer. They began by recalling to his memory their service together during the battle on the First of June, and having thus established their record of "courage and valour," they explained why they did not believe the *Culloden* was "fit for His Majesty's Service without being overhauled or more properly examined." They also registered their objections to the "indifferent usage" they received at the hands of their First Lieutenant, who called them "Cowardly Rascalls" and threatened them "with a small empty Pistol, which is enough to irritate the mildest and couldest tempers in Mankind." They concluded by expressing their hope that "your Lordship will take the trouble of visiting us once more when we will be best able to treat with your Lordship upon what terms we can most Amicable and Honourable settle." The letter was signed: "I am my Lord your very Humble and Obedient Servant, a Delegate."[74]

This was explosive language. Apart from the signature, which carried the unmistakable stench of democracy, words such as "treat ... terms ... [and] settle" belonged to the vocabulary of diplomatic negotiations between enemies and equals, not to that of supplicant children begging to be heard, the usual paternalist register in which petitions were expected to be written at the time. The lower deck's shift in attitude mirrored its change in tactics. Where previously large-scale mutinies had primarily taken the form of unauthorized assemblies and the occasional shipboard riot, the type of mutiny that first appeared on the *Winchelsea,* then on the *Windsor Castle,* and finally in its full maturity on the *Culloden* is best described as an armed strike. Its emergence marked a transformation in the language of inter-class negotiation away from the emphasis on social unity characteristic of eighteenth-century paternalist relationships towards a recognition of the fundamental and permanent opposition that divided officers and crews. As a response to the increased severity of disciplinary violence, no longer did mutineers appeal to their superiors' virtue and generosity. Instead, they stated their demands and then let the ship's weaponry under their control speak for itself. This was class war in a very literal sense.[75]

The *Culloden* mutiny put the authorities into a tight spot. After all, it was perfectly conceivable that the mutineers were correct in their complaints. Most of the crew had spent nearly two years onboard, had crossed the Atlantic twice, and then sailed into battle on the Glorious First of June. Unlike Troubridge, who had been onboard for less than a month, they knew the ship, and they presumably knew when something was wrong with it. Delaying the departure for a few days therefore was an acceptable price for averting a possible catastrophe on the high seas. At the same time, the mutineers' presumptuous arrogance and extreme militancy made it a dangerous proposition to give in to their demands, however reasonable in substance. If the lower deck got it into their heads that orders were up for negotiation if only they were prepared to point loaded guns at their officers, discipline might well collapse throughout the fleet.[76]

Still, faced with only bad options, the Admiralty determined that if the mutineers' complaints proved correct, the ship should be taken for repairs to the dock at Hamoaze. But so as not to vindicate the crew's collective disobedience, they were to be broken up and distributed among different ships afterwards. But the complaints turned out to be wrong. Lord Bridport, along with two other high-ranking officers of the fleet and a number of shipwrights from the yard in Portsmouth, had gone on board and drawn samples of the

Culloden's bilge water: it was pitch black, indicating that its hull was tight and admitted only small amounts of fresh seawater. In that case, the Admiralty informed Parker, he was to send two three-deckers alongside the *Culloden* and use whatever means necessary "to bring the Mutineers on board His Majesty's Ship Culloden to Obedience, and for securing the Ringleaders."[77]

On the *Culloden* the mutineers accepted that their ship was seaworthy after all, but insisted that without guarantee "not to punish any man concerned in the present business or to mention or remember it there after," they would not return to duty. Captains Seymour of the *Leviathan* and Pakenham of the *Invincible,* whom Admiral Parker sent onboard to attempt a negotiated surrender, came back with the news that the mutineers were quite serious in their resolve: the men had told them they were willing to go "down in the Ship rather than come upon Deck on other Terms." Seymour and Pakenham concluded that there was no use "hoping that any thing will avail but Coercion or a General Pardon." This was probably more than just idle posturing on the part of the mutineers. Several witnesses testified that Jeremiah Collins, a forty-year-old able seaman from Cork and one of the most militant men on board, went around cursing that "by the holy St. Jesus before we will go up without coming to honorable Terms I'll blow them to the Bounds of Buggery."[78]

The end of the *Culloden* mutiny became shrouded in controversy. Rough winds delayed the sending of the *Royal George* and the *Royal Sovereign* to lay alongside the *Culloden* and force its crew to surrender, and in the meantime Captain Pakenham was ordered to take another stab at convincing the mutineers to return to duty. And, surprisingly, he succeeded. On December 9, after five days of being barricaded below, the *Culloden* mutineers shuffled up on deck. It is possible that a majority of the men had come to accept defeat and knowing that only the most forward or known troublemakers amongst them were likely to be arrested and made to stand trial, they decided to give up. But that is not what many on the navy's lower deck came to believe. Troubridge, Bridport, Parker, and all the other officers had a strong incentive not to order force against the mutineers, for what if they were disobeyed? What if the crews of the *Royal George* and the *Royal Sovereign* refused to open fire on their comrades? And what if they did obey and then unleashed a broadside or two? And what if the mutineers on the *Culloden* fought back?

The consequences would be just as disagreeable, and potentially very expensive if the three ships managed to inflict any kind of damage upon each other. It is therefore possible, and many thought very likely, that Pakenham was told to deceive the mutineers, and that he lured them up on deck by promising them that a full pardon had been granted.[79]

Troubridge believed that those who initiated the mutiny were "mostly of the lower order of Irish," but the men's efforts to remain anonymous and their extraordinary level of solidarity in the aftermath of the mutiny makes that a difficult claim to evaluate. It is possible, but how would he have known? Having been onboard for just three weeks, he barely knew the men, and during the mutiny they did everything to appear as a united, undifferentiated mass in the eyes of their officers. Soon after the mutiny broke out, they hung hammocks around the hatchways in order to obscure the view from above, and whenever they negotiated, they spoke from behind a screen. Even the letter to Bridport was anonymously handed up on deck attached to a stick. During the court-martial, both the witnesses and the accused continuously sought safety in the anonymous mass, swearing over and over again that no one ever took the lead in anything, that everything happened spontaneously, or that they were too drunk to remember this or that event, and that anyway they slept through the mutiny entirely. The court repeatedly had to remind the men that whatever oath they may have taken during the mutiny—and they did take one, though its content is unclear—it was neither legally nor morally binding. One of the witnesses, Maurice Dunn, was sentenced to three months' solitary confinement in London's Marshalsea prison for gross prevarication.[80]

The Swedish navy's *Krigs-Articlar* (Articles of War) authorized the decimation of a mutinous crew, but the British Royal Navy only recognized crimes committed by individuals, even in the case of mutiny. In practice, courts-martial often prosecuted men more or less at random in order to impose exemplary punishments, but without witnesses that testified to an individual's specific role in the mutiny, there could be no conviction. Of the three men put on trial following the strike on the *Winchelsea,* for example, one had to be acquitted because not a single witness could place him anywhere near the mutiny, and the other two could only be shown to have done nothing to stop it. As for the ten men prosecuted for their part in the *Culloden* mutiny, it appears that some of them were in fact more active than others. Jeremiah Collins, the Irishman who threatened to blow up the ship, was one of them. But it seems that others were simply the only men that

Troubridge could find witnesses against. In the end, eight were sentenced to death by hanging (of whom three were recommended for mercy), and two were acquitted. Troubridge acknowledged that there were another thirty men whom he strongly suspected of having had leading roles in the mutiny, but he could not find or compel anyone to testify against them. The crew knew the value of solidarity.[81]

By refusing to testify, the *Culloden* mutineers also refused to become their shipmates' executioners in a very literal sense. Capital punishment in the British navy was by hanging. The convicted man was taken to stand on the cathead, a large wooden beam that projected outward from the bow of the ship. A rope was then run up through a block attached to the foreyard some twenty feet above, one end with a noose tied around the victim's neck, and the other dropped down along the foremast to the forecastle and from there into the waist, where the crew was forced to assemble and told to grab hold of it. After a short prayer by the chaplain, the master at arms reiterated the sentence—"You are to be hung by the neck under that yard, until you are dead, dead, dead"—and then ordered the crew to pull on the rope until the man's head touched the yard, at which point the rope was tied off and the body left hanging for at least half an hour. Much like running the gauntlet, a punishment common in many other European navies, it was a ritual with roots in Medieval practices of communal redress. But in the context of a rigidly class divided warship, it functioned as a formalized humiliation of the crew instead. Forcing them to murder one of their own, hangings drove home the visceral reality of the crew's complete submission to the captain's will, a lesson especially important for the authorities to underscore in the immediate aftermath of a mutiny.[82]

Many crews refused to learn the lesson. Instead of reinforcing the ship's hierarchy, punitive violence perceived as illegitimate became an important source of the lower deck's sense of solidarity. Just as in the French navy during the struggles that accompanied the introduction of the new *Code Pénal Maritime* in 1790, resistance to the arrest and punishment of shipmates was the single most prominent trigger of mutiny the British navy. It was also the cause of the next major mutiny after the *Culloden*. Following a night of violent rioting onboard the *Defiance,* the crew, including those who until then had remained peaceful, exploded into full-blown mutiny when their officers arrested eight of the most active troublemakers and then attempted to send them into a different ship. But rather than barricade themselves below deck, the crew simply refused to do any duty, and as the first full day of the mutiny came to an end, they informed Captain Home that he had better release the prisoners, for otherwise it surely would be done by force during the dark of night. Home had no choice but to comply.[83]

The original riot had been a chaotic affair, fueled by pent-up frustration and a sense of violated custom. The *Defiance* had just returned from a difficult three-month cruise along the Norwegian coast and the crew was looking forward to spending some time ashore, perhaps with their friends and families, or with the more temporary companions that could be found in the taverns along the Leith waterfront. Their hopes were disappointed: only officers would be allowed off the ship. Captain Home, like many of his colleagues, had learned the lessons of the American war when nearly one in every four men deserted at least once. So he was determined to do whatever it took to minimize the risk of his men getting away, even if it meant, as they put it, that he made them feel "like convicts." To lessen their discomfort and discontent, Home allowed married men to send for their families to join them, but he refused to let the sex workers that otherwise flocked to every ship in harbor come onboard. The young, unmarried men who made up the majority of the crew, and whose only opportunity for sexual relief during the past three months had been with themselves or each other, were not happy. They became even less happy when Captain Home ordered their grog to be watered down. It was the middle of October, the weather was wet, windy, and cold, and the men expected their daily ration of grog to have the customary proportion of one pint rum to three pints water. Even that was barely strong enough to give a man the illusion of warmth, let alone allow him to get drunk. But Captain Home had determined that on the *Defiance* "five-water grog" would be served, "which renders our Grog of no Service to us being thereby spoiled," the mutineers explained.[84]

The crew had legitimate complaints, but they were riven by internal conflicts and lacked the unity, discipline, and mutual trust that was necessary to pull off an organized mutiny as their comrades on the *Culloden* had done. Instead they rioted, broke into the spirit room, threw shots at their officers, randomly fired pistols out of the port holes, and in some cases turned the violence upon each other, using the cloak of chaos to settle some of the scores that had built up over the preceding months. A wiser commander of men than Home perhaps would have recognized these divisions, and by further deepening them solidified his own authority. But his rash decision to seize eight of the most active rioters in the morning had precisely the opposite effect: regardless of their other disagreements, the crew was now largely united in opposing the punishments, and the mutiny soon took a more radical turn. Many of the most experienced and skilled members of the crew had not participated in the riot the night before—some had even attempted to stop it—but these men now emerged as the leaders of the mutiny. And they were determined to seize the moment to fight for better conditions more broadly.[85]

The morning after the prisoners had been freed someone tossed a letter onto the quarterdeck in which "the Ships Co. of H.M. Ship Defiance under your Command (all and singular)" made their position clear. First, their original demands had been for shore leave and stronger grog, and these still stood. "2ndly," they continued, "Here is a quantity of Men upon record who gave in their Names to the Ships Clerk Mr. Thomson as Royalists, these we ordain to go out of the Ship." With "Royalists," they referred to those among the crew who refused to join the mutiny and remained loyal to their officers. The choice of word is significant. The crew adopted the language of revolutionary republicanism to understand and describe the specific conditions of tyranny they lived under onboard ship. If loyalty to the officer corps was denounced as royalism, mutiny in turn was a revolutionary act, not just a corrective intervention to reestablish lost rights and social harmony. Like the emergence of the armed strike as a prominent form of struggle, it is yet more evidence that for a certain number of men in the navy the contest between quarterdeck and forecastle had become an irreconcilable and permanent state of enmity.[86]

It was perhaps not by coincidence that the process of lower deck radicalization had gone furthest in the North Sea fleet, for its ships were filled with men who truly hated the service. It had cost His Majesty's press gangs stationed in the northeast enormous efforts to round up men during the mobilization of 1793–94. Just months before the outbreak of the war, England's North Sea collier fleet—the nursery of some of Britain's toughest and most highly skilled seamen, Captain James Cook among them—was gripped by a militant strike that succeeded in pushing up wage levels in the industry. From October into late November 1792, the strikers brought Tyneside shipping to a complete standstill, interrupting the vital coal deliveries for London's hearths just at the onset of winter. After several weeks of conflict, the shipowners were eventually forced to concede defeat and raise wages from two pounds ten shillings per voyage to three pounds.[87]

When press gangs showed up only a few months later to force the same men to serve in the King's fleet for wages as low as five shillings a week, there was immediate violence. In Whitby, rioters threatened to demolish a press gang's rendezvous, forcing it quickly to abandon the town. In Sunderland they freed captured men from the gang's tender and then laid siege to its rendezvous. In South Shields, hundreds marched behind a banner proclaiming "Liberty For Ever," before ritually humiliating gang members and throwing them out of town. Shortly afterwards they erected a liberty pole in the town's market square, just as the fed-up residents of Boston, New York, Newport, Philadelphia, and other American port cities had done two decades before. In Newcastle, seamen organized in the Magna Carta Club discussed the questionable constitutionality of impressment, while crowds marched through the streets shouting "No King! Tom Paine forever!" One of the city's sons, Thomas Spence, who in 1794 was imprisoned for high treason, published new lyrics to the nation's favorite belligerent anthem:

> When BRITAIN first impelled by pride,
> Usurp'd dominion o'er the main,
> Blest peace, she vainly threw aside,
> And gave her sons the galling chain.
> View Britannia, Britannia view the waves,
> On which thy darling sons are slaves.

The *Defiance* saw the same slide from labor militancy into revolutionary politics. William Handy, who during the mutiny had cleared the quarterdeck of "royalists" with the help of a large wooden burgoo stirrer, proclaimed "with an Oath that the World was nothing without liberty."[88]

Admiral Pringle, commander in chief at Leith, never seriously contemplated giving in to the demands of the mutineers. Though making conciliatory noises, he was determined to break the mutiny by force. Captain William Bligh, late of the *Bounty,* volunteered to lead a detachment of soldiers onboard to restore order, "which," Pringle soon was able to report, "was carried into execution this Morning, but not without some disturbances such as the Men throwing Shot into the Boats, and again loading some of the lower deck Guns." Despite the resistance, which in truth was only minor since the mutineers could not bring themselves to fire the guns, the mutiny rapidly collapsed once Bligh and his troops had gained the deck. The eight original prisoners were re-arrested, and soon joined by nine other men who had taken leading roles in the second phase of the mutiny. The subsequent court-martial, one of the longest in British naval history up to that point, sentenced eight men to death by hanging, four to be flogged round the fleet with 300 lashes each, and three with 100 lashes each. Two men were acquitted. The rest of the crew was broken up, and one hundred of them were sent to serve under the harsh tutelage of Captain William Bligh in the *Director*.[89]

Mariners in each navy reacted differently to the outbreak of the war at sea. In France, where four years of revolutionary struggle to shift authority away from the quarterdeck had brought shipboard discipline close to collapse, ordinary seamen were torn between their commitment to defend the revolutionary republic at sea and their unwillingness to retreat from the ongoing democratization of the navy that such an effort apparently required, at least according to those who held state power. For a brief moment in the spring of 1794, when the republic was at its most radical and at its most imperiled, many of the crews were willing to accept, in the spirit of shared national sacrifice, the return of the old-regime navy's steeply hierarchical and violently enforced structures of authority. But that willingness ended together with the radical Jacobin republic later that summer. Like their counterparts in the revolutionary Batavian fleet, many French seamen after 1794 refused to fight for a republic they no longer recognized as their own.

However, an important difference between the French and Batavian services was the far greater number of foreign-born men onboard the latter's ships. The Dutch traditionally recruited non-native-born labor to fill the majority of berths in its deep-sea industries, primarily German, central European, and Scandinavian migrant workers with no familial ties in the republic. When therefore they mutinied and ran away with the ship or handed it over to the enemy, they did not abandon or betray a physical home, as would have been the case had disaffected seamen in the French navy done the same thing. British warships also carried a substantial proportion of foreign-born men, but nowhere near as many as the Dutch. This in turn may help explain why British mutinies tended to be aimed at improving the conditions of service, whereas discontented seamen on Batavian ships instead tended to just take off, alone or with the whole ship, whenever they reached their breaking point.

The same tendency towards treason was reinforced by the hostility that many career naval men, who in the majority were ethnically Dutch, felt for the revolution. When French forces invaded the United Provinces in the winter of 1794–95, the most disaffected seamen in the Dutch navy simply walked off their ships in the ensuing chaos. Only the men most dedicated to the service stuck around, but far from rewarding their loyalty, the revolutionary government only a few months later destroyed their careers by dismissing the entire commissioned officer corps, thus also cancelling the old navy's patronage system. Some career naval men may very well have been willing to give the new regime the benefit of the doubt—socially they were close to the artisan class which everywhere, including in the Low Countries, were among the staunchest supporters of revolution—but when the financial constraints of the war effort left one promise of improvement after another unfulfilled, they turned on the service and the revolution with a vengeance.

The British navy did not have to cope with the fall-out of a political revolution, nor with the disruption and strains of foreign invasion. But as it once again mobilized for a global war, and once again on a bigger scale than ever before, cumulative changes in the recruitment, deployment, and organization of labor that were intended to maximize the exploitation of available resources ruptured the paternalist bonds between officers and men in ways that were not dissimilar to what happened in both the French and Batavian fleets. But unlike their comrades across the Channel and the North Sea, British tars as a group chose not to run away, but instead to stand together and fight for better conditions onboard ship. Perhaps they realized that as highly skilled mariners they would likely do worse almost anywhere they went, for despite the hardships they suffered onboard the Royal Navy's warships, they were still more powerful, better funded, better supplied, and better officered than any of their rivals. Few of its seamen would have fancied the idea of finding themselves on the receiving end of the Royal Navy's martial violence, but they also knew that its power in large parts derived from their own skill and efficiency at the guns. This in turn gave them confidence in their collective strength whenever they turned those guns on the quarterdeck and commenced negotiations about their working conditions.

Like their comrades in the French Navy, and in contrast to those in the Batavian service, British sailors were largely united behind the war effort during these early stages of the conflict. Their complaints concerned matters they experienced as a violation of the terms and customs they believed to have a right to expect as British seamen, including shore leave, ships that would not break apart in a gale, bread that was not completely infested with weevils, grog that contained the traditional proportion of rum to water, and officers that did not exploit their position to establish a regime of violence and terror. But with each turn in the cycle of mutiny and repression, more and more language began to creep in that integrated their particular grievances into a broader understanding of the situation they found themselves in. Not enough evidence survives from these mutinies to even sketch what that understanding may have looked like. However, that the *Culloden* mutineers asked a "delegate" to write a letter on behalf of the crew, or that the *Defiance* mutineers likened class treason to royalism indicates that at least a few the revolutionary seeds that eventually, in the spring of 1797, would blossom into the "floating republic" at the Nore had already taken root during the first few years of the war.

FOUR

A Revolution in the Fleet

BY EARLY 1797, BRITAIN WAS NO LONGER having a very good war. Republican France, which in 1793 had nearly been crushed by a broad coalition of counter-revolutionary forces, recovered, expelled the invaders, and then pushed far beyond its borders to knock out all of Britain's major continental allies, one by one. The southern Low Countries and the Rhineland were conquered in late 1794, and Prussia withdrew from the war in 1795. Napoleon's army stampeded across northern Italy in 1796 and then battered Austria into submission in early 1797. The United Provinces, since 1787 effectively a joint Anglo-Prussian protectorate, was overrun, switched sides, and in 1795 declared war on Britain. Spain, under French pressure, followed suit in the summer of 1796.[1]

Now it was Britain's turn to fight off a vast European coalition bent on regime change. In December 1796, a French fleet under the command of General Lazare Hoche managed to sail unmolested from Brest and very nearly landed over 14,000 battle-tested troops in Ireland's Bantry Bay. But for a brutal winter storm that shredded the French fleet, destroyed eleven ships, and killed over five thousand men, England's oldest colony might well have become France's youngest sister republic. Two months later, France attacked again, this time landing the so-called Black Legion at Fishguard in southern Wales. Much smaller and less conventional than the forces sent to invade Ireland, the legion consisted of fifteen hundred troublemakers, including ex-royalist prisoners, deserters, and pardoned convicts, who were told to wreak as much havoc as possible in the vain hope that such chaos might trigger a regional insurrection like the violent *Chouannerie* that raged in western France. The chaotic invasion quickly collapsed, but not without first setting off a run on the banks severe enough to force Britain off the gold standard.

Meanwhile, another invasion force was rumored to be assembling at the Texel anchorage in north Holland, to be hurled at England itself, perhaps in coordination with a French fleet sailing simultaneously from Brest. If true, England's only hope for survival was the home command of the Royal Navy. Its heart was the huge fleet that lay at Spithead, and it was here, at the height of the invasion scare in the late spring of 1797, that the "great mutiny" began.[2]

When the fleet mutinies eventually collapsed in early June, unrest had spread from Spithead to engulf almost the entire home command, from the Cork and Plymouth naval stations in the west, all the way to the Nore anchorage and North Sea fleet in the east. Altogether, more than forty thousand men on over a hundred ships rose on their officers and for nearly two months refused to do the work of war. The government, desperate and confused, hoped to blame outside agitators, Irish separatists perhaps, or maybe homegrown radicals of the type that had recently pelted the King's carriage with rocks as he rode through the streets of London. But Aaron Graham, the magistrate dispatched by the Home Office to sniff out evidence of sedition, first at Spithead, then at the Nore, came back emptyhanded both times. He had found nothing to suggest that this was not the work of the seamen themselves. And yet, Graham had no idea how they could have managed to collapse Britain's wooden walls in quite so spectacular a fashion. Lady Spencer, whose husband George was First Lord of the Admiralty at the time, confessed to William Windham, the arch-reactionary head of the War Office, that she found it "most wonderful ... that a mutiny of this extent should have been brewing for three months and not one word of it to have transpired. . . . Surely, surely," she muttered, "it implies a strange want of knowledge amongst the officers."[3]

Fishguard and Bantry Bay had cast some doubt on the navy's ability to keep Britain's island fortress safe, but the great mutiny shook British confidence to the core. The sheer scale of the danger, and the remarkable failure of leadership it suggested, shocked and angered many among Britain's administrative and military elite. One naval officer, who chose to remain anonymous, wrote a blistering open letter in which he heaped scorn on the Admiralty, blaming its members for having first created and then tolerated an environment of corruption and indifference among the Channel fleet's senior officer corps. In particular, he argued, their decision to leave the bulk of the fleet mostly anchored at Spithead in order to protect it against the wear and tear of close blockade duty had allowed several of its major commands to degenerate into short-term sinecures for elderly senior officers. Each of them occupied their position for just a few short weeks before shuffling off into well remunerated retirement after having achieved flag rank. The result of such constant turnover at the top was predictably lax discipline below: many crews onboard the fleet's capital ships were rarely classed, mustered, and exercised, and their disinterested officers, who spent as much time as possible on shore, thus were left ignorant of the character, skills, and rapidly deteriorating morale of the men they were meant to command.[4]

Under the circumstances, this was a comforting explanation. But however much individual failures of command may have contributed to the mutiny, the anonymity between officers and crews, and the growing alienation between them, was in reality a problem that had grown out of the Admiralty's decision to ease the mounting manpower crisis by constantly turning over and redistributing men from ship to ship. Like impressment, it was a calculated sacrifice of stable and harmonious shipboard communities for a more efficient exploitation of available resources. As morale deteriorated, disciplinary violence increased. All of these trade-offs had helped give Britain in the late eighteenth century the most powerful navy in the world, but in the spring of 1797, they also very nearly brought about "a revolution in the fleet."[5]

In December 1796, about four months before the mutiny erupted, Captain Thomas Pakenham, who previously had helped break the *Culloden* mutiny and now commanded the 80-gun *Juste,* wrote to Earl Spencer, First Lord of the Admiralty, with the urgent recommendation to increase the rate of pay for able seamen and petty officers, for he had reason to believe that otherwise they might well lead the rest of the crews into a general, fleet-wide strike. He was not alone in seeing the danger. As early as 1795, Rear-Admiral Philip Patton had published a pamphlet, and sent it to Earl Spencer, as well as to Secretary of State for War Henry Dundas and Prime Minister William Pitt, in which he warned that unless the navy stopped relying on impressment to keep wages artificially low and instead raised the rate of pay of their most highly skilled men to a level commensurate with their labor market value, there was no reason to expect that they "will continue to bear these wrongs indefinitely . . . especially when they have known from experience that possession can be mutinously taken of the largest ships."[6]

According to Admiral Patton's calculations, inflation coupled with rising wage levels in the merchant marine meant that by the mid-1790s "prime seamen" lost about "half the profits of their labour" through impressment. This seemed an obvious injustice, especially when one considered that many of these men would eventually have attained the rank of captain onboard a small merchant ship had their careers not been derailed by prolonged coerced service in the navy. There, it was almost impossible that they would ever advance beyond a position inferior to even the lowest-ranking commissioned officer. Adding insult to injury, instead of paying them what their labor was really worth, the navy turned them into virtual prisoners in order to prevent them from running away and taking employment elsewhere. It was therefore not exactly a surprise, Patton continued, that men thus "detained from their homes, confined onboard a ship, and subjected to martial law during an indefinite term of years" should build up a considerable store of resentment and be "strongly impelled to favour any measures which may have the most distant chance of improving their condition."[7]

Patton was especially worried that the systematic mistreatment and disrespect that Britain's most highly skilled mariners suffered at home would eventually drive them to look for solutions abroad. "The Thirteen Provinces of America have opened an Asylum for the discontented," he wrote, "as they may remain with safety on their shores or be employed in their Ships without danger of their discovery. The language, the customs, the manners, being similar to ours. Even France presents itself under a new aspect to Seamen, it effects to be called a Land of Liberty. The very name fascinates ignorant Men, and may lead them to ruin themselves with their Country." His fears were not unfounded. Exploiting the similarities in language and culture, and the ambiguities of contemporary nationality law, thousands of British seamen throughout the 1790s and into the early 1800s did leave Britain for the United States, where it was relatively easy to claim citizenship and under its protection go to work in the newly independent country's booming merchant marine.[8]

However, only a far smaller number of men left Britain for countries on the continent, where it was harder for them to obscure their original nationality, and the risk of capture as a traitor consequently greater. Still, some British-born mariners decided to take their chances. In September 1799, shortly before the Anglo-Russian invasion of north Holland, almost a dozen men who previously had claimed to be American citizens approached their Dutch officers, revealing that in reality they were all British subjects, mostly from England and Ireland. Some of them had ended up in the Dutch navy as a result of the chaotic forces that in times of war scattered mariners all over the map, but others had clearly steered a more deliberate course. George

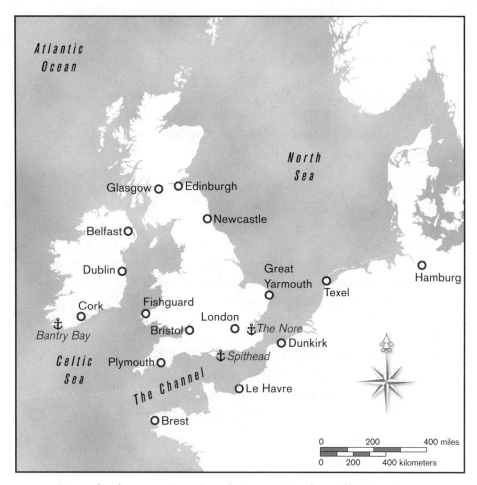

MAP 4. Ports and anchorages on Europe's northwest coast. Map designed by Gerry Krieg.

Watson, a twenty-five-year-old seaman from Whitby in northern England, was originally captured onboard an English merchantman by a French privateer and taken to France. From there he escaped first to Belgium and then to Rotterdam, where he pretended to be an American so that he could take service in the Batavian navy. A few months later, Watson was captured by the British when his ship surrendered together with the rest of the Dutch squadron at Saldanha Bay in late 1796. But he remained undetected and was able to serve in the Royal Navy by pretending to be either Dutch or American, until he deserted a few months later and returned to serve in the Batavian navy once more. Similarly, William Jetking, originally from Linford near the

Thames estuary, deserted from the British army while in the United Provinces, fled to revolutionary France, and then returned to take service in the new Dutch navy after the Batavian Revolution of 1795, travelling together with a group of Polish seamen he had met in France.[9]

Watson and Jetking were rare exceptions, for however bad the working conditions in the British navy, they usually were much worse in rival fleets. Before 1797, the Royal Navy was therefore more likely to attract disgruntled seamen from abroad then lose their own malcontents overseas. For example, the majority of the Dutch, Swedish, Norwegian, Prussian, American, and French sailors who joined the British 74-gun *Monarch* at the Cape of Good Hope in the weeks after the Dutch surrender at Saldanha Bay were still onboard when seven months later the crew decided to join the Spithead mutiny. Others who had been part of the Dutch squadron at Saldanha Bay were sent into ships under Admiral Buckner's command at the Nore just a few months before the mutiny erupted there. Afterwards, there were complaints about French and Dutch "mutinous Republicans" who during the mutiny had taken the lead onboard the sloop *Savage*. Similarly, the eighty Swedish seamen who mutinied onboard the Swedish warship *Brutus* in late 1796, at the time anchoring near Texel in north Holland, and then fled to a British warship cruising just offshore, were probably still onboard that ship when the fleet mutiny erupted just a few months later.[10]

However, as Admirals Pakenham and Patton had predicted, those who initially planned and led the mutiny were almost all British subjects, long-serving, highly skilled able seamen and petty officers who often enjoyed the respect of their superiors and simultaneously exercised considerable authority below deck. Like their counterparts who led many of the mutinies in the French and Dutch fleets, they had a strong sense of corporate identity, rooted in their craft skill and closely tied to the service and its traditions. But unlike them, who defended those traditions against reforms introduced by their respective revolutionary governments, and sometimes did so in the name of political reaction, "prime seamen" in the British navy found themselves in a position of having to challenge a reactionary old-regime state that itself trampled on tradition and the paternalist arrangements that previously had structured life in the service. As Patton argued in his retrospective *Observations on the State of Discipline in the Navy, End of the Year 1797*, where previously there had been at the core of the shipboard social order a close bond between the officer corps and the most highly skilled men on the lower deck, after several decades of reform to make the navy a more efficient, centralized, and authoritarian institution, that close connection had eroded and been trans-formed into an "an open state of hostility" between officers and their prime seamen. As a result, "the natural order of things" had been turned upside down. Instead of trusting in the natural leadership of the lower deck elite, officers increasingly relied on armed marines—by far the least skilled sector of shipboard society—to police the "prime seamen" below deck and ensure the maintenance of proper order onboard ship.[11]

This internal militarization of shipboard society made nonconfronta-tional forms of conflict resolution difficult to pursue and forced lower deck malcontents to contemplate tactics that sometimes were more radical than their actual aims. What the Spithead mutineers really wanted was fair pay-ment and decent treatment in return for their labor, or as one mutineer at the Nore later put it: "Give us our Due at once and no more of it, till we go in search of the Rascals the Enemys of our Country." Given that it had been over 150 years since their last pay raise, and that inflation in the meantime had driven up prices quite considerably, this was hardly an unreasonable demand. Both the army and the militia had been granted a pay raise for that very reason just two years earlier. And yet, whatever the merits of their demands, after the execution of five men following the *Culloden* mutiny in 1794, another five men following the *Terrible* mutiny in 1795, and nine men following the *Defiance* mutiny in 1796, those who planned the Spithead mutiny in 1797 understood that disabling just a single ship did not provide enough leverage to be certain of victory. Nor did it protect them against the retaliation that would inevitably follow.[12]

But there was another way. Admiral Owen believed that some of the Spithead conspirators had participated in the wave of mutinies that swept through Plymouth, Portsmouth, and Sheerness at the end of the American war in 1783, when crews onboard several ships had simultaneously kidnapped their officers and successfully demanded to be demobilized. He also believed that it was no coincidence that the idea to once again coordinate mutinies across multiple ships was first discussed in December 1796, in the immediate aftermath of the French failure to land troops in Ireland. It had reminded everyone of just how important the navy was for keeping England safe, and that was to be the mutineers' leverage.[13]

The conspirators understood the seriousness of holding England's national defense system hostage, and once the mutiny was underway, they did their utmost to contain and de-escalate the conflict in order to avoid its most radi-cal and treasonous implications. They urged the crews to be respectful to their officers, to avoid any irregularity of conduct, and to perform all of their duties with the greatest diligence, except that they were not to weigh anchor, unless—and this qualification they made sure to broadcast far and wide—there were creditable reports of an enemy fleet at sea. In order to underline that their complaints did not concern the behavior of individual officers, but were instead directed at the Admiralty in London, the leading mutineers went out of their way to demonstrate their continued respect for the quarter-deck's authority. In some cases, they even went so far as to ask their captains to select or approve of the men sent from each ship to the central Council of Delegates that met onboard the *Queen Charlotte*. Even though the council during its first meeting issued a formal set of Rules and Orders that included an oath of fidelity for all seamen and marines onboard the mutinous ships, the delegates delayed the swearing of their shipmates in order not to force a premature, fleetwide breach of the established chain of command.[14]

Perhaps mistaking these overt signals of moderation for lack of determination, the Admiralty's first reaction to news of the mutiny, and to the delegates' demand for a long overdue pay raise, was simply a promise that "the subject will have that serious consideration which its importance requires," followed by another order to finally weigh anchor and get the fleet under sail. But far from prompting the mutiny to fizzle out, the Admiralty's failure to respond with paternal grace to the delegates' theater of submission instead triggered the consolidation of their power, and the rapid establishment of an alternative social order in the fleet. Having initially exposed themselves by refusing to organize the mutiny beyond simply a meeting of the delegates, in the hope that such moderation would lead to quick concessions, the delegates now formalized a system of dual power, starting with the previously delayed oath of "fidelity" that asked every seaman and marine to swear "by his maker that the Cause we have Undertaken we Persevere in till Accomplished." Next, while they allowed their officers to keep regular watch on the quarter-deck, the delegates organized in each ship's forecastle a "counter-watch of surveillance" to keep an eye on their activities. Finally, for the duration of the mutiny, they assumed the right to enforce discipline below deck, which by all accounts they did "with a rigour and severity unknown before."[15]

Unfortunately, not much is known about the ways in which the mutineers organized day-to-day decision-making at Spithead, but for the first couple of weeks, at least, it appears that the majority of the crews were happy to follow the lead of the original delegates. Indeed, for as much as the mutiny broke the navy's established chain of command along the line separating the commissioned officer corps from everyone else onboard, it also witnessed the reassertion of the traditional hierarchies of shipboard authority that for centuries had structured life and labor onboard merchantmen and fishing vessels in northwest European waters. Onboard such ships, day-to-day decisions were usually taken without formal consultation by those whose experience and skill had earned them recognized positions of authority, while more consequential questions, including issues that might result in a major change of course, or that potentially carried unusual risks, called for a meeting of all the "people."[16]

A similar system appears to have been followed during early phases of the Spithead mutiny. For example, when after three days of negotiation members of the Board of Admiralty finally agreed to meet the mutineers' demands, the Council of Delegates decided to maintain control of the fleet until an Act of Parliament ratified the Admiralty's concessions and His Majesty the King issued a formal pardon for all those involved. In response, Admiral Gardner first tried to reason with the council onboard the *Queen Charlotte,* hoping to convince them to return to duty immediately, as there was no reason to doubt that the government would fulfil every promise made by the Admiralty. But after an unrecorded comment—perhaps one suggesting that such promises could not be trusted—Gardner lost his composure, grabbed one of the delegates by the collar, threatened the rest, and then ranted "with so much intemperance as led the Delegates to return on board their respective ships, to take the sense of the several Leaders as to the conduct they should pursue." Onboard the *London,* the ship's two delegates in turn decided that "it was now necessary to take the sense of the Ships Company on the proposals made to them," and for that purpose called a meeting below deck, "in order that they might not be influenced by the presence of their officers."[17]

Deference to the tradition of collective decision-making allowed the Council of Delegates to retain the support of the lower deck, even as its members worked hard to contain the emergence of more radical demands, which according to Admiral Owen the delegates feared would undermine "their claim to undiminished loyalty" and thus might threaten their future careers in the navy. Some crews were already muttering about short provisions, others about excessive floggings, yet others about lack of shore leave, and some about the unjust distribution of prize money. But the most insistent and widespread call was for the removal of tyrannical officers, and after Admiral

Colpoys on May 7 opened fire on the mutinous crew of the *London* and killed three men, the crews of over a dozen ships took matters into their own hands and purged their quarterdecks. The captain of the *Marlborough,* the crew explained, battered people so viciously with whatever objects he had at hand that both his spyglass and his trumpet were in constant need of repair. The ship's surgeon was said to accuse sick men of skulking and then have them flogged. The master's mate tore through the lower deck like "a ravenous wolf," threatening anyone who resisted his beatings with cutting their throats and drinking their blood. The captain of marines forced his men to wash their uniforms with seawater and urine, and when the weather was bad, he often ordered a review and took delight in seeing the men's necessaries get blown away. All four officers were summarily thrown off the ship. On the *Pompée,* Lieutenants Baker, Sparks, Humphreys, Bowman, and Snow were sent ashore for being both incompetent and cruel. They had frequently punished men for mistakes that were caused by their own inability to give correct orders. On the *Terrible,* the crew finally got rid of Captain Campbell, whose regime had grown intolerable since he had violently suppressed the mutiny onboard his ship two years before. Altogether, more than a hundred officers were driven from their ships, and the delegates had no choice but to make it part of their "final determination" that, in addition to a pay raise and general royal pardon for everyone involved in the mutiny, the Admiralty would have to accept their expulsion. "Then and not till then shall we be as ready as ever to weigh with the rest of the Fleet."[18]

Meanwhile, following the murder of the three mutineers onboard the *London,* a constitutional debate erupted in the mutinous fleet that made the delegates' attempt to balance respect for the traditions of shipboard popular sovereignty with their own continued loyalty to naval hierarchy difficult to sustain. The source of the debate was a jurisdictional dispute over the question of what body had the proper authority to try Lieutenant Bover and Admiral Colpoys, who in the killing of the three mutineers had been the first to pull the trigger and had given the order to fire, respectively. Militants onboard the *London* and the more radical members on the Council of Delegates both claimed jurisdiction, while their more moderate counterparts hoped to avoid the issue altogether, or at the very least unload the responsibility for it onto someone else.[19]

The delegates from the *Queen Charlotte* and the *Royal George,* who were among the most influential moderate members on the Council of Delegates, went to great lengths to prevent any harm from coming to the two officers, as that would have made it very difficult to continue negotiations with the Admiralty. Initially, they asserted the Council of Delegates' authority over the matter in order to prevent the *London*'s crew from immediately retaliating against the two officers by hanging them from the nearest yardarm. But once that danger was averted, they turned around to support the argument that, as a general principle, each ship's company, speaking through their chosen delegates, had the right to decide what should happen to their officers. The *London*'s two delegates agreed, and without consulting their shipmates decided that Colpoys and Bover should face neither popular justice onboard ship nor be tried by an official court-martial. Instead, they determined, the two officers were to be handed over and tried by the appropriate civil authorities on land.[20]

From the perspective of the majority of the delegates, who hoped to bring the mutiny quickly to a negotiated end, it is easy to see why that may have been an attractive solution. It allowed them to avoid being implicated in any decision over the fate of the two accused officers, while at the same time it confirmed their commitment to both popular sovereignty at sea and to the established legal order on land. But the effect of this stance on the unity of the mutinous fleet proved devastating. As soon as it became clear that the two officers would likely get away, a small but determined group of radicals onboard the *London* turned sharply on the mutiny's moderate leadership, leaving the majority of the crew unsure which of the two sides to support. Similar divisions emerged on other ships, and even spread to the Council of Delegates itself after some of its members, including those from the *Mars,* the *Duke,* and the *Latona,* accused the *London*'s delegates of treachery. On behalf of the crews they represented, they vowed to prevent the extradition of the two officers to the civil authorities on shore. The crew of the *Duke* escalated the war of words still further by threatening to set sail and surrender the ship to the French if the two officers were handed over.[21]

It had been the Admiralty's plan all along to exploit divisions among the mutineers and ideally split them into separate factions, since it was clear from the beginning that neither concessions nor violent threats alone would be enough to reestablish discipline in the fleet and prevent similar insurrections from occurring in the future. Indeed, Admiral Patton in his 1795 pamphlet *Observations on Naval Mutiny* had already put forward a proposal that, he hoped, would serve to reestablish the broken bond between the lower deck elite and their natural allies on the quarterdeck, with the result that "the best Seamen in every Ship will be attached to the Service of their Country, and those very Men who now excite Mutiny, will be most ready to repress it."[22]

Similarly, only three days after the mutiny erupted, Captain Payne, an otherwise obscure commander in the fleet, wrote to Earl Spencer, First Lord of the Admiralty, that this affair "cannot be dealt with like mutinies in individual ships, system and management must be met with the like, nor can anything be executed with success till some apparent disunion is created in the fleet. They are perfectly sensible that their force arises from agreement." Agreement, however, had its limits, and Payne therefore argued that the Admiralty was most likely to succeed if it concentrated its efforts on driving wedges between the different groups of workers that made up the lower deck. Concretely, he recommended that the demand for a wage increase should be granted, but not to all of them equally. That way the issue that united them could be transformed into one over which they became divided. "The increase of wages is so seductive," he wrote, "that they probably cannot [be] divided thereon—though holding out the impropriety of increasing the lowest classes of seamen with the higher ones, would tend to spread difference of opinion, and call on the higher to keep down the claims of the lower orders. Irregularities will be sure to produce schisms."[23]

The Admiralty implemented Payne's recommendations. The navy pay bill that was sent for ratification to Parliament contained a carefully staggered wage increase that especially benefitted experienced seamen, from whose ranks nearly all the delegates were drawn. Able seamen and petty officers saw their monthly wages go up by 33 percent. "Landmen" received only a more modest raise of 20 percent, but their ranks were divided by promoting some of them into the newly established intermediate pay grade of "ordinary seaman," whose wages went up 25.7 percent when compared to their previous pay as landmen.[24]

There is no evidence that anyone took issue with this unequal pay increase, but once it had passed those who were especially favored by it worked hard to bring the mutiny to a rapid end, just as Payne and others had predicted. Following the killing of the three mutineers onboard the *London,* the delegates who led the negotiations with the Admiralty complained repeatedly about the growing influence of radicals on the lower deck, and they were visibly relieved when Admiral Lord Howe finally arrived a week later to announce the royal pardon and together celebrate the resurrection of the established order. Shaken by how close they had come to losing control of the mutiny they had started, many of the delegates, according to Admiral Owen, "became from that time firm supporters of their Officers' authority. Their subsequent good conduct made atonement for their faults, past errors were forgotten, several in the course of time obtained promotion, and were exemplary in their station."[25]

Some of the more radical crews tried to keep the mutiny alive, but the majority of men in the fleet appear to have been happy that it was over, especially as the outcome was a clear victory for the lower deck and signaled a major shift in the power relations that determined day-to-day life onboard the king's ships. For a whole month, ordinary seamen had controlled one of the principal pillars of British imperialism, maintained order and discipline amongst themselves, negotiated as equals with the government, and extracted unprecedented concessions from one of Europe's most entrenched autocracies. Speaking for many members of his class, Lord Collingwood worried that the seamen of the fleet had felt "what power there is in so numerous a body. What is conceded to them is not received as a provision which justice makes them, but as what they have extorted, and they now know how they may extort, what in justice they have not the same claim to."[26]

The seamen onboard the ships that lay at the Nore anchorage at the mouth of the Thames had watched from afar as events unfolded in the Channel fleet throughout April and into early May, and by their understanding of "justice" the navy's lower deck was entitled to "extort" quite a bit more. When they rose on their officers on May 12, they originally had hoped to coordinate their actions with those of their comrades in the Channel fleet at Spithead, but when they found out shortly afterwards that these had returned to duty, and won nothing more than a wage increase, a few additional benefits, and the removal of some fifty disagreeable officers, they sat down to formulate their own far more radical list of demands. Since they did so at a moment of victory, when they believed themselves strong enough to force the concessions they really wanted, it is likely that their list of demands reflected the lower deck's feelings and beliefs much more accurately than did the tamer demands with which the mutiny at Spithead had commenced.

In total, the Nore mutineers eventually put forward ten demands, six of them concerned with pay. First, they wanted assurances that they too, and all other seamen in the navy, were covered by the recent pay raise (which they were). Second, they asked that the marines also receive a modest increase in pay to bring them up to the same level as the seamen with whom they served side by side. Since all other branches of the armed forces had lately received a raise, this was only fair. Third, while the promise of higher pay was all very well, wages were routinely kept in arrears for longer than the navy's own regulations allowed. Since many of the seamen had families who "have no other support than the scanty sum that we can send them out of our own hard-earned wages," the mutineers demanded that the rule of only keeping six months' wages in arrears when a ship goes to sea be rigorously and verifiably observed. With a similar insistence on contractual agreements, they demanded, fourth, that volunteers and those drafted through the Quota Acts of 1795 and 1796 must be paid their bounties in full when signing up. These were, after all, promised to encourage men to enter into the service, and "if Government will break their words with us how can they expect we will keep faith with them—this is only Justice and has a Right to be demanded the same as a Mans Wages." Fifth, while pressed men did not receive a bounty, the mutineers proposed that instead they ought to be given a two-month advance on their wages, and thus be able to furnish themselves with whatever necessities they needed for a long voyage and not be obliged to procure overpriced items from the ship's purser on credit against their future earnings.[27]

Taken individually, none of these demands was especially radical, but taken together they suggested an attempt to counteract the divisive staggered pay raise that Parliament had just passed by demanding benefits for especially those groups that had been awarded a smaller increase, or none at all, such as the marines. However, the Nore mutineers did not just seek to level the differences amongst each other, they also sought to minimize them in relation to the officer corps, as evidenced in their sixth demand for "a more equal distribution of Prize Money." By the terms of the 1708 Convoys and Cruizers Act, the fleet's commander in chief, whether he was present at a capture or not, received one-eighth of the proceeds from every prize taken by one of the ships under his command, the captain was given a quarter, the master, lieutenants, surgeon, and captain of marines together shared an eighth, the warrant officers and petty officers shared another eighth each, and the remaining quarter was distributed among the crew and the marines, which sometimes amounted to several hundred men. In words reminiscent of Colonel Thomas Rainsborough's famous intervention at the 1647 Putney Debates, the last time England's armed forces had collectively negotiated for better treatment and higher pay with the government, the mutineers asked:

What can be more absurd not to say unjust than for an Officer to receive perhaps 200 pounds when at the same time a foremast man who runs as much risk of his life—whose life is as dear to his Wife & Children as that Officers—receive but 12 or 14 shillings[?] What a shameful disproportion[.] Why should not that officers pay be sufficient without having such an enormous share of prize money[?]

Seamen in the North Sea fleet, who soon afterwards joined the mutineers at the Nore and endorsed their demands, added that a more equitable distribution would be for the petty officers, crew, and marines to share three-fifths of all prizes equally among them, and "the remaining 2/5 be divided as His Majesty and the Lords of the Admiralty may think proper to distribute among the other Officers which if Gentlemen worthy of that Appellation or possessed of the least Spark of Justice or Humanity will consider to be as equal a Proportion as honest Men could require or have a right to expect." Such a distribution would still have given each officer a share that on average was at least four times greater than everyone else's onboard.[28]

The mutineers' next demand was for "Liberty," the sailors' traditional word for shore leave. Clearly, however, they also had in mind a broader meaning when they explained that "this invaluable Privilege more particularly inherit to an Englishman, the pride and boast of our Nation and the Natural Right of all, has always been denied us." The reference is to the rights of the freeborn Englishman, and in particular to the famous *habeas corpus* article of Magna Carta: No freeman shall be taken. This right had indeed always been denied to them, for shortly after King John was forced to promulgate the Great Charter in 1215, he issued warrants for a major press, and thus implicitly excluded sailors from its protection. Ever since then, seamen's rights had been systematically violated whenever the country mobilized for war, and never, according to the Nore mutineers, was their lack of "liberty" more painfully real than in the navy's increasingly common practice of pressing seamen straight out of incoming merchantmen:

What can affect the feeling of a Man who has been born into the Enjoyment of Liberty more than after a Voyage of 16 Months to India which he has undertaken probably with the hope of gaining as much as will enable him and perhaps a helpless family to partake of the comfort and enjoyment of his Native home—on his Passage back he is big with hopes of imaginary enjoyment and every day brings him nearer for the much longed for port—But on his coming into that port he is that moment press'd—far from all his hopes immur'd in a ship for 3 4 or perhaps 5 Years without so much as being permitted to see his dear Family or of once treading on his Native Land—What a Disgrace to British Liberty.

In a related demand, the mutineers asked for "a free pardon for all desertions from the navy." After all, the primary reason men ran away, they explained, was their deprivation of "Liberty (which is the principal enjoyment of Life)," and if that was regularly granted, and they were no longer used "the same as a Parcel of Slaves," desertions would be far less frequent.[29]

But to prevent desertions, shore leave alone was not enough. Conditions onboard the ships also had to improve, and in particular the "oppressing and tyrannizing over us according to the caprice and temper of the Officers" had to stop. The mutineers demanded to live in a shipboard society of laws and not of men, and to that end they proposed the abolition of martial law and that only juries composed entirely of seamen and marines, assisted by "able Councellors to explain the Civil Law," be authorized to impose corporal punishments from now on. "This is what has been much wanted," they explained,

> which if adopted long since would have saved humanity a number of Tears[.] For what tender or feeling Man can hear without a pang that an Officer heretofore from private pique—from a conceived offence which was never intended from a man's looks and even from his very thoughts have form'd a crime[—]order'd a wretch'd helpless man into irons[,] sport'd with his feelings for the course of a fortnight 3 weeks a month or often more[,] confined in a torturing Suspense at last he is dragged from his Irons Brought before his Shipmates in a disgraceful manner, strip'd tied up to the gangway hands and feet—his defense not heard but he is entirely left to the caprice and cruelty of the Captain. . . . His flesh is Mangled and torn and his Blood streaming down his back[.] All this for no real cause but that a cruel Lordly Officer conceives that he deserves it.

Trial by jury was another right of the freeborn Englishman that was confirmed by Magna Carta (Articles 14 and 39), but perhaps the mutineers were thinking of more recent examples as they drafted this demand. Both French and Dutch seamen had won the right to be tried by a jury of their peers, and experience had shown that this resulted in fewer and far less bloody convictions, and often in none at all. One French officer deprived of his autocratic powers complained that juries are "too favorable to impunity."[30]

Finally, inspired by the Spithead mutineers' success in forcing the Admiralty to remove fifty of the most objectionable officers from their posts, the Nore mutineers proposed that the crews' veto power be made permanent so that "all Officers turn'd out of a Ship for cruel and oppressive Usage shall never return to the same Ship without the Consent of the Ship's Company." From now on, officers were to serve at the pleasure of their men. As the crew of the *Pompée* had already declared during the final days of the Spithead mutiny, the intention of such a measure was not "of encroaching on the Punishment necessary for the preservation of good order, and discipline so necessary to be observed in his Majesty's Navy, but to crush the Spirit of Tyranny and Oppression so much practiced and delighted in, by Individuals contrary to the Spirit, or Intent of any Laws of our Country." But it would not be enough simply to restrict the officers' powers by issuing new rules and regulations, since "often do we see these statutes trampled upon by the very persons who are appointed to see them enforced." Experiences aboard the *Winchelsea* and other ships had shown that the quarterdeck could not be relied upon to police itself, for one would have to search far and wide for even a single officer willing in a court-martial to condemn one of his peers for excessive brutality, never mind the half dozen officers necessary for a conviction. Shipboard democracy therefore was the only way of preventing tyranny from taking hold on the quarterdeck.[31]

Taken together, the mutineers' ten demands amounted to a sophisticated program of political change that, if implemented, would have begun the transformation of the Royal Navy into a republican fighting force. More remarkable still, while the Admiralty and government pondered how best to meet this presumptuous challenge from below, the mutineers took matters into their own hands and set about creating institutions of self-government that reflected the democratic spirit of their demands. Every new crew that joined the mutiny at the Nore—altogether fifteen ships of the line, nine light and heavy frigates, and thirteen smaller vessels, with a total of approximately 11,000 people onboard—was told that everyone (including women temporarily onboard) must "voluntarily make Oath and Swear that I will be true in the cause we are embarked in." After thus formalizing their entry into the "floating republic," each crew created a number of committees to regulate their internal affairs, including one to determine who would be allowed to go on shore and for how long, which was called the Committee of Liberty. There was also onboard each ship a General Committee, usually comprised of nine seamen, three marines, and a president, which was the ship's primary political forum. This committee collected and sifted through complaints, information, ideas, and proposals from the crew, some of which in turn it passed on to one of the two fleet-wide General Committees, one for internal regulation that met every morning on the *Director,* the other responsible for the overall direction of the mutiny that met onboard the *Sandwich,* called the "parlament ship." Committees reached decisions "according to the form amongst themselves by holding their hands up."[32]

Committee members were surrounded by a tight web of democratic controls, and in particular the delegates who were sent to the General Committee on the *Sandwich* were treated with a fair amount of distrust. For example, the Nore mutineers modified the oath, sworn by their comrades at Spithead to "be true to the Delegates at present assembled," to include the clause "whilst they continue to support the present Cause." Most likely, this was a direct response to the dismay that many at the Nore felt at the role that the Channel fleet delegates had played in bringing the mutiny there to an end against the wishes of some of the more radical crews. At the Nore, in contrast, the mutineers determined in Article 1 of the Rules and Regulations that became the bare-bones constitution for the mutinous fleet, that "we recommend the strictest unanimity as the only means of accomplishing the great object we have in view." To increase oversight and force the delegates to act in unanimous agreement with the constituents they spoke for, the crew of the *Pylades* ("one of the most violent and rebellious ships in the fleet") went so far as to suggest that delegates should not be allowed to hold discussions with Admiralty representatives on shore, as had happened at Spithead, and that each crew as a whole instead should have an ongoing role in the negotiations. Finally, in order to prevent the emergence of a leadership stratum, most crews elected their delegates directly (as opposed to having them chosen by the ship's General Committee) and also instituted a rule that no one person could be both a ship committee member and a fleet delegate at the same time.[33]

Both fleet delegates and ship committeemen were subject to immediate recall if they failed to reflect the interests of their crews, or if they in any way misbehaved. James Robertson and Thomas Sterling, delegates from the *Leopard,* were both ousted from their positions for returning from shore in a state of intoxication. On the *Grampus,* the crew removed and punished their committee's first president, James Smart, who claimed that he had been "a speaker at the London Corresponding Society" and was considered "a scholar" by his shipmates, for neglecting his orders while being on shore. The crew also purged some of the more moderate members from its committee

FIGURE 8. Isaac Cruikshank's cartoon, "The Delegates in Council, or Beggars on Horseback" (1797), attempts to discredit the proletarian government of "the floating republic" by depicting elite opposition figures under the table, secretly steering it. Courtesy of the Royal Museums Greenwich Picture Library.

for advocating what a later generation of revolutionaries would call defeatist positions. On the *Monmouth,* too, the crew replaced about half of its initial General Committee "in consequence of some of the first Committee not being liked by the Ship's Company."[34]

As had already been the case at Spithead, crews that joined the mutiny reeved (i.e., hung) yard ropes, which normally were used to hang people who had been convicted of a capital crime by court-martial. In this case, however, leaving yard ropes on permanent display was meant to symbolize that the ship's company had reconstituted itself as a new polity in accordance with the principles of the "floating republic." It was an act that stood in the same tradition as the widespread erection of gallows in front of the houses of the French rural aristocracy in 1789. Before the Revolution, the display of gallows—in French, *potence,* which derived from the Latin word for power—was a cherished right of the aristocracy, signaling their possession of *jus gladii,* or the right to punish those who have broken the law. At the beginning of the Revolution in the summer 1789, those gallows became targets for angry mobs throughout rural France. Often, they were torn down and immediately resurrected in the same place, a ritualistic enactment of the destitution of the old regime and the constitution of a new order through the people's conquest of *jus gladii.*[35]

Likewise, when sailors onboard the mutinous ships reeved yard ropes, it was more than just a confrontational gesture. Seamen were well aware that their collective security onboard ship, especially when lying so close to shore as they did at the Nore, depended on strict discipline and careful attention to duty. The mutineers therefore took great care to maintain regular and good order amongst themselves, and they created democratically controlled courts to try men for a variety of offences, most commonly for drunkenness and neglect of duty, which violated two of their "most sacred laws, enacted for the Preservation and Unanimity of the Ship's Company." In some cases, punishments were imposed "by the desire of the majority," and in others following the verdict of a jury. The mutinous crews went to great lengths to follow proper procedure when trying a man, formally swearing juries and witnesses to strict impartiality, and providing the accused with a competent councilor who pleaded on his behalf.

The courts were willing to recognize extenuating circumstances, even when they tried those who had tormented them before. The boatswain of the *Proserpine,* for example, argued that he had only followed orders when previously he had abused the crew, and this was enough to sway the court to commute his corporal punishment to ritual humiliation:

> He was disfigured with a large swab tied upon each shoulder, a rope round his neck, and his hands tied behind him: in this state he was placed in a boat, and rowed round the Fleet, with a Drummer by his side, occasionally beating the "Rogue's March"; he was then landed at Sheerness and marched through the Dock Yard and Garrison, guarded by a party of Mutineers; and when they considered him sufficiently punished and degraded, they let him loose, and left him without farther molestation.

Others were not so lucky. Master's mate Edward Dawson of the *Monmouth,* along with the sergeant of marines and a midshipman, was found guilty of conspiring against the ship's company and therefore sentenced to three dozen lashes. But that was still an exceedingly mild sentence when compared to the bloodthirsty and often lethal punishments imposed by regular courts-martial for the equivalent crime of mutiny.[36]

In addition to ritual humiliation and flogging, at both Spithead and the Nore mutineers also punished certain crimes, especially those that endangered the whole ship's company, by tying a yard rope around the transgressor's torso, and then dropping him from aloft and "ducking" him several times into the sea. A ritualized form of drowning, "ducking" dramatically enacted a guilty man's temporary expulsion and subsequent readmittance into the ship's community. This was a form of restorative justice that was common in many northwest European maritime communities, but it was not a punishment sanctioned by either law or custom in the British navy. However, in the context of the mutiny, its adoption further emphasized the lower deck's collective claim to *jus gladii* and the transformation of the ship's judicial system, previously fully under the control of the commissioned officer corps, into an expression of popular sovereignty.[37]

If the reeving of yard ropes symbolized the emergence of a new order in the fleet, the red flags that flew alongside of them were intended to show that it was here to stay, whatever it took. The red flag had several overlapping meanings in the late eighteenth century, but usually the red flag indicated the intention to temporarily suspend peaceful means of conflict resolution in favor of brute force. Authorities on shore often used the red flag to announce martial law, and in the navy the "bloody colours" signified that a ship was prepared to give battle. The latter use of the flag had evolved from the medieval *baucans,* a thirty-yard-long solid red streamer that north European ships flew as they sailed into combat to indicate that no quarter would be given or taken; in other words, that it would be a fight to the death. Pirates during the so-called Golden Age used the "bloody flag" to convey the same meaning, and they ran it up the mast if their prey refused to surrender at the sight of the black Jolly Roger. During the 1775 Liverpool sailors' revolt, lower deck insurgents fought under the red flag as they bombarded the city's Mercantile Exchange. In 1783, dockyard workers rioted in Rotterdam, following behind a red flag as they went from house to house to demand money from the city's wealthy elite. At the outbreak of the Haitian Revolution in 1791, insurgents fought under a "bloody flag" inscribed with the words "death to all whites." In 1797, the red flag reappeared at Spithead, where occasionally it flew from the masts of the mutinous fleet. But at the Nore "the bloody flag of defiance" was there from the beginning and it flew throughout. The mutineers even brought it with them when they held demonstrations on shore.[38]

Unlike its earlier appearances during moments of emergency and struggle, there are signs the mutineers at the Nore positively identified with the red flag as a permanent symbol. One of their communiqués was signed with the slogan "Red For Ever" and an eye witness reported that he had heard some mutineers shouting "huzza for the red flag." It suggests that many leading mutineers no longer believed they were engaged in a narrow struggle for lost rights and paternalist class compromises but instead had begun to develop a consciousness of being engaged in a permanent struggle between two contending classes in which concessions were only ever won by force and never granted freely. Many mutineers also wore red cockades fixed to their hats and caps, bringing together the red flag's combative maritime heritage with the red of the French Revolution, which by the late 1790s had become an international symbol of regicide, class warfare, and social renewal. The mutineers ultimately were so successful in colonizing the meaning of the red flag that the navy dropped it entirely from its official *Signal Book for the Ships of War* in 1799, thus surrendering its powerful symbolism to the global labor movements of the nineteenth and twentieth centuries.[39]

William Gregory of the *Sandwich* gave voice to the peculiar mixture of class-conscious republicanism and maritime militancy that developed at the Nore when he demanded to know from his shipmates: "Is there not many among you here as fit to be our Sovereign as George Rex? He has power and we have the force of gun powder." It is difficult to know just how many such hardline insurrectionists there were in the fleet, but there is evidence of quite a few. Thomas Jephson, fiddle-player onboard the *Sandwich,* for example rejected an officer's order to play "God Save the King" with the explanation that "by Jesus, it's an old state tune and I care nothing about Kings and Queens—Bad luck to the whole of them." Jephson went on to exclaim that "he thought [the mutiny] a glorious thing and that he would be d———d if ever it would end until the head was off of King George and [Prime Minister] Billy Pitt." He further suggested the mutineers should agitate amongst the soldiers at Sheerness, for he was sure they would join them. If in addition the fleet were to stop all shipping going up the Thames to London, they might well trigger a general insurrection: "By Jesus before Saturday night all London will be in an uproar." He also told his comrades that shortly before the mutiny he had been to London and met with revolutionaries who assured him that both the Scots and the Irish were ready to rise up against the government. Similarly at Plymouth, Robert Lee, a private marine whose brother was said to be "an original Member of the Societies of United Irishmen," attempted to lead a violent revolt "to overturn the government" that involved fomenting a mutiny in the naval squadron lying just offshore and at the same time freeing the French prisoners of war held at Mill Prison on land.[40]

Committed revolutionaries like Gregory, Jephson, and Lee probably represented a minority position amongst the mutineers, just as they did in the population at large. However, as often has been the case, whether in the English Civil War of the 1640s or the American War in Vietnam three centuries later, conflicts that pit two fundamentally different social orders against each other tend to radicalize frontline troops on both sides. In a letter to his wife, William Roberts, a mutineer onboard the *Director,* explained that

> wee poor Men ave been fiting against our enemies, and now wee are come hom, wee desire to fite for beter usage: it is a fin thing to bee a Solder or Seler, so it is to walk about Birminghim; . . . wee poor Selers and Solders want nothing more, then to be used well.

William Roberts and many of his fellow mutineers were annoyed to have their patriotism publicly challenged by the government, when they were the ones who suffered more than anyone else for the defense of the country. In an address "to their fellow subjects," the General Committee of Delegates at the Nore angrily demanded to know whether "we who have endured the Toils of a long Disgraceful War [shall] Bear the Shackles of Tyranny and Oppression, Which Vile Gilded Pampered Knaves wallowing in the Lap of Luxury choose to load us with?" George Shave of the *Sandwich* concluded in the same angry spirit "that the Country had been oppressed for these five years, that the war had been too long and now was the time to get themselves righted."[41]

While the mutiny at the Nore raged on, some of those who had participated in the mutiny at Spithead attempted to renew the revolt in the Channel fleet. This time, however, the object would be to force the government to conclude a peace. William Guthrie, a leading conspirator onboard the *Pompée,* one day "pointed his hand through the Port towards France and said it is not our Enemies that live there[,] it is our Friends. He mentioned some words of having left his wife at home with only a shilling." Guthrie added that "the French were willing long ago to make a peace with us but we would not make it with them. He said in case of invasion or if it was necessary for us to go to sea he would go and defend the Country to the utmost." But as things stood, Guthrie and his fellow conspirators thought the greatest danger to the country came not from the French, but from the war-mongering ministry, and they believed only the seamen of the fleet were strong enough to force it into making peace. "Towns and Parishes throughout England had petitioned for it and they could not get it," the conspirators argued, "and if the seamen stood out they were the people who could get it." And then, once there was peace, the people of England could finally fight for "Freedom with Equity" at home.[42]

At the Nore, meanwhile, there were signs that the fleet mutiny had begun to transmit its revolutionary impulse onto shore. In Sheerness, large numbers of people demonstrated with the mutineers' red flag flying high, "inflammatory handbills were published and circulated among the Seamen on board as well as on shore," and rich people evacuated their belongings as the mutiny seemed to be "fast spreading itself into a general rebellion." Encouraging news also reached the fleet from farther afield. J. and M. West wrote to their brother Thomas onboard the *Isis* that even in their hometown of Chertsey in Surrey "the lower Class of People in general wish the Sailors good Success." In Exeter, the general mood of the population was so supportive of the seamen that Thomas Williams, a deserter not connected to the mutiny at the Nore, could score free drinks in several of the town's pubs by pretending to be a travelling delegate on his way back to Sheerness. In London, radical activists began to take an interest in the mutiny. P. F. McCallum, who would later become a transatlantic, anti-imperialist troublemaker, published a democratic newspaper in support of the mutineers, and there were persistent rumors that mysterious persons thought to be active revolutionaries had come down from London to visit with the mutineers at the Nore.[43]

But despite these signs of sympathy for the mutineers within the population at large, there was little to suggest that an actual solidarity movement was taking shape. In late May, the government made it clear that it would not grant a single concession and instead was fully prepared to break the mutiny by force, and the ships now found themselves isolated and surrounded by soldiers who were getting ready for a bombardment with red-hot shot from the shore. Most of the mutineers remained determined to see their grievances redressed, but many grew nervous about the bloodshed that looked ever more likely if they refused to back down. John James of the *Belliqueux* wrote to Susanna Johnson to explain that "we want no more than our Right, and if they do not supply us with Provisions there will be a great deal of Blood spilt I am afraid." R. Mabson of the *Nassau* wrote to reassure his wife that "if you don't hear from me so often don't make yourself so unhappy for I hope no danger will come to us but I am afraid it will be some time before it is settled."

Then he added ominously: "If the Admiralty do not settle this, it will be bad, there is a large fleet here." John Pickering thought the conflict "in all probability can terminate in nothing but Civil War," and John Cox told his wife that "we are afraid of our Lives."[44]

Early on, some mutineers had floated the idea of taking the fleet to sea if their demands were refused, but in the end not nearly enough men were willing to take such a decisive step. The practical problems alone were nearly insurmountable. To begin with, where would they go? William Ross suggested an initial rendezvous at Bantry Bay in Ireland, and his shipmate William Welch proposed France, but to that John Copey objected because "no Enemy shall have our Ship." Instead he advocated sailing for Madeira, "where we will have wood, wine and water." But then what? Someone proposed the "New Colony," which probably referred to New South Wales. They all no doubt remembered that less than a decade before, the crew of the *Bounty* had succeeded in starting a new life beyond the reach of the British Empire somewhere in the South Pacific. But that situation had been very different. The *Bounty* was already in the Pacific when the crew mutinied; they had officers trained in navigation who joined them; and they were well provisioned with both food and water. The ships at the Nore had none of these advantages, and in addition there were large numbers of severely sick men onboard. Even before the mutiny started, virulent fevers had raged on some the ships, and conditions worsened after the government refused to allow anyone to come ashore or be transferred to a hospital ship. The *Nancy*, for example, tried to evacuate seventy of her crew to the *Spanker* hospital ship. The port admiral ordered them all sent back, but not before stuffing their pockets with various proclamations from the Admiralty. The men were too delirious with fever even to notice.[45]

Despite the odds and without a clear destination, on June 9 the General Committee of Delegates signaled for the fleet to put to sea, but not a single ship obeyed. Terrified and insecure, pushed into a corner by the government's confrontational stance, many of the men who had been neither delegates nor committeemen had begun to calculate their chances of escaping the mutiny unharmed to be fairly high. The Admiralty, unable to punish over 10,000 men, most likely would concentrate its wrath only on those who had stood out as especially active. On ship after ship, the committees were pushed aside and the crews surrendered. Mostly, this was a quiet and resigned affair, but on some of the ships it led to violence. On the *Iris*, for example, a shoot-out occurred between the "blue party" and the "bloody party" during which a woman shot a lieutenant through the head who had just cut down her husband with his cutlass.[46]

For some, the end of the mutiny was a heartbreaking experience. At least one of them, William Wallace, chose to shoot himself in the head rather than accept defeat. Others who were convinced they would be executed for their role in the mutiny turned their violence outward instead. James Robertson of the *Leopard* cursed that "he was sure of being hung and he would be damned if he did not do as much mischief as he could." His shipmate Alexander Lawson crawled into the foretop with a musket and opened fire on the officers who now were reclaiming the quarterdeck. But these were acts of desperation. The tide on the lower deck was turning inexorably in the direction of surrender. Some of the very last holdouts considered sacrificing themselves and committing mass murder. William Welch told his remaining comrades "when all comes to all we'll break into the magazine and blow her up." But their resolve faltered, and in the end they and hundreds more like them were overwhelmed by their newly loyalist shipmates and arrested. The last three ships surrendered on June 16, almost exactly two months after the crews of forty-five ships in the Channel fleet had refused to lift anchor and go to war on Easter Sunday, April 15.[47]

Even though the defeat was a painful one, the mutiny was a transformative experience for many of those who had lived through it. Reflecting no doubt the feelings of many onboard the mutinous ships, Alexander Davison wrote to his friend Robert Dunn while the mutiny was still going on to boast and marvel that "all Duty is carried on as well as before we took the Command of her or better for every one does their utmost endeavours in regard to the Duty of the Ship." If only for a few weeks, the seamen of the fleet had created a different way of working together onboard ship, one that replaced the supreme tyranny of His Majesty's officer corps with democratic assemblies below deck and the unrelenting terror of the lash with debate and consent. The mutineers had formed popular institutions of some complexity that reflected some of the most radical political ideals of the revolutionary era. Together they took hundreds of decisions, big and small, that pertained to everything from dirty laundry to negotiating with the king himself. If anyone failed to meet their responsibilities, they were not arbitrarily brutalized as before, but tried by a newly established justice system worthy of the name.[48]

For some of the men, this had not been their first experience of mutiny, and for many more it would not be their last. Matthew Hollister had been one of the leading figures in the *Defiance* revolt just two years before, a disheartening experience that taught him the importance of solidarity, determination, and organization. It is not surprising that he should have volunteered, and been accepted, to go as a delegate from the Nore first to the Channel fleet at Spithead and later to the North Sea fleet at Yarmouth. Isaac Bowstead, "a man of uncommon abilities," was suspected of having been a ringleader of the *Culloden* rising in 1795, and after the final collapse of the Nore mutiny he was arrested in Colchester for behaving "in a very outrageous manner." Bowstead had twice seen the lower deck's organizational capabilities, and he had twice seen the uncompromising repression it encountered. Bitter and disappointed, he "damned his King and Country," and said that "the Town ought to be burned to the ground." Of the more than ten thousand men who had mutinied at the Nore, and of the tens of thousands more who had mutinied elsewhere, how many now felt the same?[49]

Quite a few men left England for good in the weeks following the mutiny. In late July, the Admiralty was informed by one of its agents at Gravesend that a "practice has lately prevailed of many seamen embarking for Hambro' or Embden, but in fact they go to Holland. . . . I don't remember seeing such a number attempting to go out of the Kingdom as there has been for these three weeks or month past." He suspected the Dutch navy was actively recruiting them in London, and perhaps a few of the ex-mutineers actually found the idea of going to war against England quite appealing. Others left for the United States with the aim of joining its recently established navy. Captain Thomas Truxtun of the US frigate *Constellation* complained after having faced down several mutinous assemblies in the early summer months of 1798 that "the Seamen of Great Britain have sat such an Example of Infamy, that the Marine Laws of the United States, England, France, Spain, and Holland, as well as the Rest of the Maritime Powers of Europe, have been, and will still be made more severe in Consequence thereof. It is in the Interest of all Parties at War, to pass Laws, and check such Proceedings, and it has been wise in them to do it." American authorities were not the only ones who worried about the subversive example sailors set in England. In Sweden, as in many other European countries, radical journalists reported enthusiastically on the mutinies, but after they inspired a strike for higher wages in Stockholm's iron carrier corps, the King imposed a complete ban on the publication of any news relating to the seamen in Britain.[50]

In Britain too, there were fears of a wider contagion. Already at Spithead, there had been signs that the insurrectionary impulse was spreading from the navy to the ships that served Britain's carceral archipelago. Less than a week after the outbreak of the mutiny, and just a few days after they had sailed from Spithead, 236 French prisoners of war rose up onboard the *Marquis of Carmathen* transport ship. The guards opened fire and immediately killed ten prisoners and wounded thirty-eight others, three of whom subsequently died. Not long afterwards, members of the New South Wales Corps—among them French prisoners of war, Irish deserters, and German volunteers, who had all come onboard at Spithead during the early days of the mutiny—shouted *"Vive la République"* and then seized control of the Botany Bay–bound convict ship *Lady Shore*. The mutineers held a sea burial ceremony for one of their fallen comrades ("he died," they said, "for liberty") and then proceeded to elect an eight-member "council," which issued new rules and regulations for the ship, and also appointed a new captain and lieutenant. About a month later, they surrendered the ship on behalf of the French Republic to the Spanish authorities in Montevideo. When news reached France several months later, the government praised their efforts and offered citizenship to the foreign-born mutineers in recognition of their services to the French Republic.[51]

In order to contain the risk of the mutiny spreading its influence still further, British officials sought to prevent fugitive ex-mutineers from joining the merchant fleet, and thus they hoped to stop them carrying their experiences "to the distant colonies." The Admiralty suggested that influential members of the merchant community might consider issuing "an immediate public resolution of not employing in their Service any Seamen who after a certain period should have continued in a state of insubordination." Not long afterwards, a powerful "Union of Merchants, Ship Owners, and others interested in Navigation," including Prime Minister William Pitt, the chairman of the East India Company, Hugh Inglis, the governor of the Bank of England, Thomas Raikes, the former chairman of the Society of West Indian Merchants and the London Dock Company, Richard Neaves, and forty-six other men of similar rank and influence, responded with a public proclamation "that no Seaman shall be henceforwards employed in the Service of the Undersigned, who cannot produce a Certificate from his former Commander or Commanders in the Navy, of his orderly and obedient Conduct." They further resolved "to raise a Fund, by Voluntary Subscription . . . for the purposes of detecting and bringing to public justice such lurking Traitors as may have excited and fomented the present mutiny at the Nore."[52]

As the mutiny collapsed into chaos, officers and marines moved quickly to isolate the crews that returned to duty and weed out those most likely to have played leading roles in the mutiny. Of these, 412 were eventually held for trial. Richard Parker, who had been elected president of the "floating republic," was the first to be court-martialed, and to no one's surprise he received a sentence of death. When he was hanged on the last day of June 1797, thousands of people lined the banks of the Medway to watch and mourn his execution in grave-like silence. Parker, only just thirty when he died, had been in and out of the navy for most of his short life, with periods at sea often punctuated by stints in debtor's prison on land. In 1795, he married Ann McHardy, with whom he already had a son, and followed her to Scotland, where they had two more. In the spring of 1797 he was again arrested for debt. To avoid prison, he agreed to sign up as a quota man for the navy, and on March 31, 1797, he went onboard the Leith tender.[53]

When Ann found out, she was beside herself, as she had just lost a son, and now was likely not to see her husband for many years to come, or perhaps ever again. She tried desperately to raise the funds that would see him released, but she was too late. Richard was already on his way to the receiving ships at the Nore, where he arrived at the end of April, only a few days before the mutiny broke out, and two months to the day before his death. When Ann first heard of the mutiny and was told the ringleader was one Richard Parker, she raced to London, where she tried to beg the king for his life, and then on to Rochester, where she desperately tried to find a boatman who would row her out to the fleet. Finally, a market boat from Sheerness took pity on her, but all she managed was a brief glimpse of Richard in the middle distance, moments before his death, and crying out his name she passed out from her grief. She saw, she later said, "nothing but the sea, which appeared to be covered with blood." By the time she came to, Parker was dead, and his body taken away.[54]

Ann Parker was not alone. As the Admiralty's summer of disciplinary terror got underway, hundreds of women were cast adrift, frantically seeking their men's whereabouts, terrified at what might happen to them. Some of them had managed to join their husbands and lovers onboard the mutinous ships. Elizabeth Burk had been onboard the *Lancaster* with her lover Murry, but at the end of the mutiny he was arrested and Elizabeth somehow displaced to the *Inflexible*. A week later, she wrote to her brother, who was still onboard the *Lancaster,* asking him to take care of the clothes she and Murry had left behind, and also letting him know that she thought Murry had been taken to Maidstone Goal, "as I heard there is a great many Men belonging to different Ships there. I am very unhappy at present to think that he is taken. I had not been so uneasy had he got clear, as I am afraid it will go very hard with him. If you hear before me where he is, I hope you will let me know as soon as you can, as I don't know for certainty where he is."[55]

Others managed to stick with their men as they tried to flee abroad amidst the chaos of the collapsing mutiny. Ann Southerland joined a man called Francis and their mutual friend George Rickets as they tried to highjack a fishing smack in order to make it to France. They failed, but others were successful, including the four women who crossed the Channel in a small fishing boat that also carried two fleet committee delegates, nine ship committee members, their president, and five ordinary mutineers from the *Inflexible*. Upon reaching Calais, the fugitives asked the authorities for protection and permission to serve the French Republic at sea, and it is likely they eventually became the crew of the French-licensed privateer *Le Prèsident-Parker* which began hunting for English shipping soon afterwards.[56]

Forty years after the end of the fleet mutinies, the American poet Walt Whitman remembered Ann Parker as a woman whose life had been "involved with the welfare of nations." And indeed, her love for Richard, and the lengths to which she was willing to go to protect him in life as well as death, became an important moment in the long struggle against public executions. Some amongst the upper echelons of the naval officer corps had hoped Parker's corpse would be hung in chains—enclosed, that is, in a metal frame dangling from a gibbet and there left to rot as a warning to others—but the Board of Admiralty ruled against it, suspecting that Parker was remembered too fondly for either seamen or civilians to tolerate such an insult to his honor. And so he was quietly put into the ground in the newly opened naval burial ground at Sheerness. Ann, however, was determined that he should have a decent burial, and, left where he was, she feared his corpse would be dug up by the Company of Surgeons' ghoulish body-snatchers. Together with three other women, Ann secretly disinterred the body only a few hours after it was buried, and then conveyed it to the Hoop and Horseshoe public house in Tower Hill, a London riverside neighborhood densely packed with seafarers and their families. As the "brave Admiral Parker" all but lay in state in a room upstairs, an immense crowd of people gathered outside, prompting fears that rage over his death might trigger an urban insurrection. The angrily mourning mob only dispersed after London's lord mayor personally obtained Ann's permission to have Richard's body buried in the vault of St Mary Matfelon's, the gleaming white chapel in the center of the East End working class community to which the church would eventually give its name. Shaken by the force of opposition to its murderous regime, the government urged the Board of Admiralty to please be more discrete when executing the remaining mutineers, and in particular to adopt such measures as would "prevent the bodies from being exposed to the public view."[57]

British penal logic had already begun to move away from public executions after a mob in 1780 set fire to Newgate Prison, one of London's most prominent symbols of state judicial terror. But the navy, with its insistence on the complete subjugation of the lower deck, was not prepared to abandon the practice just yet. In addition to Parker, at least twenty-five men were executed in front of their assembled comrades throughout July and August, most of them at the Nore and some at Spithead, and at least a further seventeen men had their death sentences publicly and ceremoniously commuted to hard labor from one to seven years. No less than five men were sentenced to being flogged through the fleet with between 40 and 300 lashes each. Hundreds more disappeared into various carceral institutions, including several men who were deported to the newly established penal settlements of New South Wales and Norfolk Island in the South Pacific, not far from where the crew of the *Bounty* had mutinied only a few years before. About three hundred men were held mostly without trial for several months in the *Eagle* prison hulk, but many of them received a pardon in September 1797 and were released just in time for the Battle of Camperdown in early October.[58]

Two dozen men sentenced to solitary confinement, "the principal part of whom appear to be Irish, and convicted of mutiny, sedition and such like dangerous crimes," were sent to the dilapidated Marshalsea prison in the London suburb of Southwark. The prison was notorious for the miserable conditions that prevailed inside. One of the mutineers, John Martin of the *Leopard,* who had been sent there for refusing to give evidence against his shipmates, hanged himself after only a few weeks. The small building, dating from the early fourteenth century, was in such an advanced state of decay that the keeper worried it might not be able to actually hold "such a desperate set of men" for very long. He was right. On September 6, John Broghan,

James Hayes, James O'Neale, David Lamb, and John McEvoy "escaped by breaking through the Prison Wall." Most of the remaining prisoners were quickly transferred to the newly built prison at Coldbath Fields, where they joined several dozen of their comrades who were already incarcerated there.[59]

Coldbath Fields may have been more secure than the Marshalsea, but the conditions inside were even worse. Prisoners sentenced to solitary confinement were held in "dark cells, close confinement, without exercise, without sufficient food, without warmth, without light, without cleanliness, without proper opportunities for their natural occasions, without intelligence given or received, debarred from books, pen, ink, paper, their friends excluded." According to the regulations, each prisoner was to receive about a pound of bread every day, and four days each week about six ounces of bread with some broth, but these provisions were hardly ever issued in full. Most of the prisoners were severely undernourished, and several starved to death, though official records determined their cause of death to be a "visitation of god." There were also at least four suicides between 1797 and 1800.[60]

The prison population was separated into three different wings. One contained vagrants, debtors, and a broad array of convicts, among them smugglers, gamblers, forgers, and libelers. A second wing was reserved for the mutineers. A third one was occupied by state prisoners, which by 1799 included Edward Despard, John Bone, and Thomas Evans, all of them leading figures in the insurrectionary wing of the British democratic movement. Their presence inside the prison, and their militant wives outside of it, disrupted the regime of total isolation on which Governor Aris grounded his rule. Janet Evans, in particular, smuggled out letters from her husband, which she passed on to sympathetic allies in Parliament, who eventually succeeded in establishing a select committee that investigated the conditions inside Coldbath Fields. Evans likewise gave information to her contacts among London's radical book publishers, who used it to whip up popular anger against the English "Bastille." Persistent troublemaking eventually culminated in two riots outside the prison gates, a small one led by John Bone's wife, Elizabeth, in 1798, and a major one in early 1800. Janet Evans also helped connect the state prisoners with the mutineers, who responded enthusiastically to the agitation and hatched a plan to kill both the prison doctor and Governor Aris' son, one of the prison's most hated turnkeys. Their idea was to fake a suicide and in the ensuing chaos murder both men, but one of the conspirators snitched and Aris punished the rest of them with solitary confinement and reduced provisions. It was not long before "the Seamen complained of illness; and in general they had the appearance of men worn out by wretchedness and disease."[61]

The seamen still serving in the fleet did not forget their unfortunate comrades on the inside. As the mutiny was falling apart in the summer of 1797, several crews made agreements that those who escaped punishment would collect money amongst themselves to support their imprisoned friends. And they remained true to their word. In May 1799, Captain James Walker of the *Braakel* reported to the Admiralty with some consternation that he had detected "a new Species of Crime, which the Articles of War do not appear to provide for.... William French and Henry Jordan, Seamen belonging to this Ship and who were both deeply concerned with the Mutiny, the first in the *Polyphemus,* the other in the *Saturn,* have been detected since the Ship was paid in raising a Subscription amongst the Men for the relief of the Mutineers confined in Cold Bath Fields Prison." Upon searching their chests, Walker found letters to and from other crews in the fleet, as well as from a mysterious Mr. Rishiman of Queen Street, London, to whom they intended to send the money.[62]

The crew that collected most money for the Coldbath Fields prisoners was that of the *Saturn.* This was not a coincidence. Having developed a taste for self-government, the crew refused to accept the terms on which the Spithead mutiny ended, and its committee therefore continued to meet regularly below deck in the weeks and months that followed. Subsequently described as "a system of Mutiny of the most extraordinary nature—to render null and void every act of their officers, to divest them of every power," the committee seized control of the ship by gradually taking over the duties that normally were exercised by the highest-ranking officer on watch, eventually sidelining the officer corps completely. They reduced the office of the captain to something akin to an executive branch within their newly constituted shipboard *polis,* before finally pushing him aside as well. Soon after the ship sailed on its first extended cruise following the end of the fleet mutiny, the committee announced that from now on they would oversee the mustering of the crew, an important weekly ritual that reminded every member of the crew of his assigned place within the ship's hierarchy. When one man refused and instead insisted on the officers' continued right to muster him, the committee sent a delegation to the quarterdeck and instructed the captain to have the man flogged, which he obviously refused. After that, the committee simply ignored the captain, and instead managed the ship's day-to-day operations itself. When they returned to Plymouth in late June, the committee decided to give everyone their well-earned shore leave, but they were prevented from going ashore, and eventually they were all arrested. Authorities sentenced eight men to death, and sent three others to Coldbath Fields. One of them, Luke Early, starved to death in his cell just over a year later.[63]

Even though the *Saturn*'s crew was not the only one that remained committed to the principles of the floating republic, most realized that the opportunity for radical reform had passed. Individual lower-deck militants like Colin Brown of the *Phoenix* still occasionally wanted to run away and "have no Government but their own will[,] the sea being wide enough and any Country better than their own." But for the time being, most crews chose to wait and see what kind of disciplinary regime would emerge in the aftermath of the mutinies. For even though they had been defeated, everyone realized that the balance of power between quarterdeck and forecastle had decisively shifted in the latter's favor. On ship after ship, nervous and insecure officers were forced to confront the problem of reestablishing their authority without once again pushing their men over the edge into open revolt. Some were more skillful than others. Captain Worsley turned the *Calypso* into an armed camp, posting marine sentries with drawn swords and loaded pistols everywhere, and giving them orders "to fire at and kill" everyone moving about the ship without permission. He also barred the crew from accessing the main deck without reason, unshipped several ladders, ordered grates laid down, and for long periods of time kept them confined below "as if we were convicts or prisoners." But the crew turned their confinement into a weapon: they simply stayed below indefinitely and refused to do any work until Worsley finally agreed to leave the ship.[64]

Knowing full well that the lower deck was still seething with discontent, many commanders hoped to convince their crews to regularize protests, to speak to them about their grievances before taking action, and to use whatever legal mechanisms were available to see them remedied. Captain Burges of the *Beaulieu,* for instance, appealed to his crew "that should you at any time have just cause of complaint . . . the same laws are open for you to apply to; it is equally in your favour to bring your officers before a court martial, and this I wish to enforce on your minds, doubt not but strict justice would be rendered you without consideration of persons." But most crews, including the *Beaulieu*'s, very much doubted that, and continued to push for a more humane disciplinary regime through direct action instead. Burges was eventually forced to inform the Admiralty that despite his best efforts to reason with the crew, they would not allow him to carry out the executions of four convicted mutineers onboard their ship.[65]

In the home command, mass resistance to punishment continued to trigger eruptions of discontent throughout the summer and into the fall. But the main force of revolt was now moving outward into the Atlantic. On July 1, shortly after news had arrived of the fleet mutinies at home, unrest flared up throughout the small Mediterranean squadron cruising off Cadiz. On the *Almene,* Jens Christian Larsen and George Rankin, the first a Dane, the other an American, and both illegally impressed at Lisbon, tried to free James Davis from his confinement in irons and stir up the rest of the crew to mutiny, but their shipmates were too scared to act. Not so the crew of the *Kingfisher.* After Thomas Leach had been put in irons for drawing a knife on the sloop's master, who had punched him at least a dozen times in the face for refusing an order to pick up a broken bottle, his friend John Sayle in solidarity demanded to be put in irons alongside of him. A short while afterwards, Captain Maitland ordered all hands on deck to witness the two men's punishment—a flogging. When the crew refused to leave the forecastle and commenced cheering instead, Maitland completely lost control. "Damn your bloods, I'll cheer you you Rascalls," he screamed, and then stormed alone into the forecastle with his dagger drawn, stabbed one man to death, and wounded four others, none of whom, he later confessed, had made any resistance beyond hissing at him. The short-lived mutiny quickly collapsed.[66]

More serious trouble erupted the same day on the *Prince Royal.* In the morning, the crew, led by John Anderson and Michael McCann, came to the quarterdeck and presented the officer of the watch with a petition that pled for the life of two of their shipmates, who the day before had been sentenced to death for sodomy. Captain Peard, who at the time was in his cabin, "in the act of shifting myself," sent word that he deeply disapproved of their conduct but nevertheless would forward the petition to Admiral Jervis, one of the most hard-nosed and callous commanders in the navy. His response was not surprising: the two men would be hanged at the appointed hour. "The crime of which they were convicted was of so horrible and detestable a nature, and the times," he drily added, "required summary punishments." The crew reacted angrily to the news, and spent the next hours "whispering" amongst themselves, eventually deciding to rise on the officers that night and take control of the ship. They hoped, Lord Collingwood wrote, "to new model the fleet, *à la Nore,*" but the solidarity below deck was not strong enough to pull it off. A few hours before the planned insurrection, "which involved a great Number of People," a snitch informed Captain Peard of the plan. He immediately doubled all sentinels and ordered the marines and soldiers armed. Next, Captain Peard arrested four of the suspected conspirators and sent them out of the ship. His swift response broke the back of the conspiracy, and the next morning he forced the crew, surrounded by armed soldiers and marines, to hang their two condemned shipmates.[67]

A few days later, the trials of the mutineers got underway. John Anderson, Michael McCann, John Hayes, and James Fitzgerald of the *St. George* were sentenced to death and hanged on July 10. The same day, the trial against Thomas Leach and John Sayle opened, and both were sentenced to receive a punishment beating, Leach with 36 lashes, Sayle with 100 lashes. Two days later, Captain Maitland was tried for murdering one of his men and wounding four others while putting down the mutiny on the *Kingfisher.* In his defense, he cited "the late mutinies in England" and expressed "heartfelt satisfaction" at having prevented something similar onboard his own ship. He was acquitted of all charges. Ten days later, Jens Christian Larsen and George Rankin of the *Almene* were put on trial. Larsen was acquitted; Rankin was executed.[68]

The mutinies in the Mediterranean squadron were stomped out, but a few months later, a series of mutinies erupted in the Cape of Good Hope squadron. Once again, the initial trigger was mass resistance to punishment. On October 7, Captain John Stephens of the *Tremendous* was just about to commence the usual ceremonies that preceded a shipboard flogging when the crew suddenly charged, freed the man, and then scurried up into to the rigging to cheer the other ships of the squadron, who all immediately cheered back. The moment had been well prepared in advance. Ever since the *Rattlesnake* had arrived a few weeks before from the Nore, the sloop's crew had circulated letters to the other ships urging them to rise together in a mutiny, and when the signal finally came the insurrection spread like wildfire through the whole squadron. On all seven ships, the crews immediately set about electing delegates and drawing up lists of grievances, which were later collated and conveyed to Rear-Admiral Pringle on shore. On several ships, the mutineers called their officers one by one to the forecastle, briefly debated their behavior, and then voted on whether to expel them from the ship or not.[69]

The mutiny collapsed after six days, because the majority of the men were fundamentally loyal, even if thoroughly fed up with the chronic shortage of provisions that had plagued the squadron, and the whole colony, for months.

There was, however, a politically motivated minority who took their cue from the Nore and hoped to push for radical change. They had initially provided fuel for the mutiny with accusations of quarterdeck brutality that emphasized the unlawful nature of such behavior. But instead of reacting with violence and repression, which would have served to prove such charges, Rear-Admiral Pringle, neither insulting nor reproaching the men, instead calmly offered a general pardon and pledged to look into all of the mutineers' grievances. If any accusations against officers were found to be justified, he promised to hold them accountable by court-martial. This satisfied the majority of the mutineers and they returned to duty.[70]

The radicals attempted to rekindle the mutiny twice during the next month. They failed both times for lack of support, leaving themselves isolated and vulnerable when the repression finally came. Richard Foot, James Reese, Philip James, and Daniel Chapman were all sentenced to death, Jonathan Scofield to two years' imprisonment, Francis Peacock to eighteen months, and Thomas Kelly to one year. Henry Thomas received fifty lashes, and Andrew Burnett, John Wilson, and Anthony Parker were severely reprimanded. True to his word, Pringle also put two of his officers on trial. Captain Stephens of the *Tremendous* was cleared of all charges, and William Stewart, master of the *Rattlesnake,* convicted of tyranny, oppression, and neglect of duty, was sentenced to be dismissed from the service.[71]

The revolts and repression of 1797 swept away the last vestiges of the old paternalist system that had regulated relations between officers and men for most of the century. By embracing the red flag as their symbol, the mutineers at the Nore signaled their understanding that they were now engaged in a conflict between two sides with fundamentally opposing interests, and that a resolution to this conflict could only come by superior force. The Admiralty accepted the challenge and unleashed an unprecedented campaign of shipboard terror. Week after week, thousands of ex-mutineers were forced to watch as their comrades were dragged up on deck, tortured with the cat, or murdered with the rope. In total that year, the Royal Navy executed at least 59 men for mutiny and related offences and flogged 37 others with as many as 1,000 lashes each. Hundreds were locked up for several months without trial, and dozens more sentenced to several years of solitary confinement and hard labor. A reign of counter-revolutionary terror took the lower deck into its bloody grip.

The scale of the repression matched the threat. Astute observers of French conquests on the continent understood that the success of the republic's armies was not simply due to the genius of its young generals or the better morale of its troops, but because they carried with them a promise of liberation and social renewal that resonated with the common people of the countries they invaded. And thus fell, after just a few hard blows, the governments of the United Provinces, the Republic of Genoa, the Duchy of Modena, and many others. Even in England, despite a long history of popular hostility to all things French, it was clear that "certain classes" found much to admire in French republican views on government. It was therefore necessary, as Admiral Philip Patton admitted, to countenance "at least a possibility of assistance being afforded to an invading army within our own country. If this were to happen to any considerable extent, no army can secure the Government from revolutions."[72]

It was the realization that the navy not only protected Britain from invasion, but quite possibly the established order from social revolution, which had prompted Patton to advocate for extensive naval reform throughout the early years of the war. His proposals fell on deaf ears, but when the fleet mutinies finally erupted, even he seemed surprised at the massive scale of the insurrection, the mutineers' "democratic madness," and the extent to which even the men serving onboard the king's ships had lost "the love for our country" and were willing to countenance outright treason. The intensity of the disciplinary terror that followed the end of the fleet mutinies did little to change their minds.[73]

FIVE

To Clear the Quarterdeck

ON SEPTEMBER 21, 1797, the crew of the British frigate *Hermione*, at the time cruising in the Mona Passage between Hispaniola and Puerto Rico, rose on their officers and killed ten of them. The first to die was Captain Hugh Pigot. "Reminding him of his own severity, and Cruelty," around half a dozen mutineers stabbed and slashed him, "according to the Weapons they were arm'd with (which were various)," and then left him in "a dying state." John Farrell found him, a little later, leaning against the couch in his cabin, soaked in blood but still alive. "You bugger, are you not dead yet?" he cursed, knocking him hard over the head, once again leaving him for dead. Finally, Joseph Mansell, an able seaman from Switzerland, came into the cabin, damned the captain ("You have shewn no Mercy yourself, and therefore deserve none"), ran him through with a bayonet, and then pushed the body out through the cabin window and into the sea.[1]

The next to die was Third Lieutenant Henry Foreshaw, who was beaten and thrown overboard by the twenty-five-year-old Irishman Thomas Nash. Then came the turn of Second Lieutenant Douglas and Midshipman Smith, one of the ship's teenage trainee officers. Midshipman David O'Brien Casey later remembered their deaths: "I perceived Mr. Douglas Second Lieutenant run past my hammock calling out for Mercy and on getting abreast of the Midshipman's Birth saw him seized by several of the Crew . . . those men fell on him and left him apparently Dead on the gratings of the after hold . . . I then saw Mr. Smith the Midshipman put to death in the like manner in the same place." John Place, sergeant of marines, estimated that Douglas had about "twenty Tomahawks, Axes and boarding pikes jagged into him." The mutineers continued stabbing and slashing the corpses even after both men were quite obviously dead.[2]

Meanwhile, a wild celebration erupted throughout the ship. The crew, most of whom so far had not been involved in the mutiny, broke into the spirit room and began looting their officers' possessions. Adrian Paulson, a Dane, was seen wandering around in a frilled shirt, and James Allen, the late Lieutenant Douglas' fourteen-year-old servant helped himself to his master's gold rings, shirts, and boots, telling all who would listen: "He shall not make me jump around the Gun Room any more." Midshipman Casey remembered that "all were more or less inflam'd, and excited by Spirits." Some of the men "were dancing on the Quarter Deck."[3]

Then the mood suddenly shifted. Lawrence Cronin, surgeon's mate from Belfast, climbed onto the gunroom table and "desired all the people to be assembled around the Sky Lights. . . . He read a paper he had got written previous to the Mutiny, purporting [to] the conduct of the Captain and Officers, that he had been a Republican ever since the War, that they were doing a good thing, that all the Officers must be put to death as it was of no use to put [just] one to death." And with that, the mutiny turned into a revolutionary tribunal, its justice merciless and swift. Each of the remaining officers was brought up on deck, his crimes and merits debated, and after a general vote either killed or sent back below. Edward Southcott, the *Hermione*'s master, was among the ship's eight surviving officers: "They brought me on Deck to put me to Death, and . . . they then said that if any body had a Mind to save my life, they should hold up their Hands, the greatest part of the Ship's Company held their hands up, they gave 3 cheers, and I was ordered below." In contrast, Lieutenant Macintosh, "out of his mind in a Fever," lay dying in his cot when four men suddenly came for him, rolled him onto a sheet, and carried him above. After a brief debate and a general vote, the mutineers threw him over the side.[4]

The trials continued into the early morning hours, when most of the crew finally collapsed into their hammocks. The next day, the *Hermione* changed course and headed south, and a week later, the mutineers dropped anchor at La Guaira in the Spanish American province of Caracas. A group of delegates went ashore to negotiate terms with the authorities. In return for surrendering themselves and the ship to the King of Spain, "they asked to be treated as his subjects and not handed over to the English, not even at the conclusion of peace. They also demanded some money." After this had been provisionally granted, the crew came ashore, and soon dispersed.[5]

The mutiny on the *Hermione* marked a turning point in the history of maritime radicalism in the revolutionary Atlantic. Despite the cavalier arrogance with which officers routinely brutalized the crews under their command, violence against officers was rare. Occasionally, there was talk of using the smoke, noise, and chaos of combat as a cloak under which "to clear the Quarter Deck of the Quality," but actual cases of what in the twentieth century would become known as "fragging" appear not to have been common. Officers themselves did not treat it as a serious concern. Some shipboard injuries were undoubtedly intentional—a tackle dropped from aloft onto someone's head, or a shot rolled across the deck to smash an ankle—but this too does not appear to have worried officers very much.

But the *Hermione* was different. The fleet mutineers had shown that a more democratic shipboard order was possible, and their example had spread to ships and squadrons around the world, from the Mediterranean to the Cape of Good Hope, and from the Caribbean Sea to the Indian Ocean. But one by one their attempts to rekindle the floating republic were crushed, until finally the crew of the *Hermione* had had enough. They decided to answer violence with violence, and judicial terror with treason. And once again, the example spread. Armed strikes, which had become the dominant form of mutiny in the Royal Navy during the first few years of the war, disappeared almost entirely from the arsenal of the lower deck, and in their place came a series of violent conspiracies that rejected all forms of negotiation and instead were aimed at seizing control of the ship and taking it to the nearest enemy or neutral port. Within two years of the *Hermione,* there were at least a dozen failed conspiracies in the British Navy, and several more successful attempts in the years that followed.[6]

The *Hermione* under Captain Pigot had not been a happy ship. Sadistic, erratic, and highly irritable, Pigot flogged frequently and without mercy. A week before the mutiny, he appears to have come completely unhinged. First, he took the most irregular step of publicly flogging and demoting one of his midshipmen, David O'Brien Casey, the most popular officer onboard. The grounds were spurious—a minor mistake, an imagined slight—but once Pigot had worked himself into a rage, there was no going back. Casey recalled that Pigot "launch'd out in the most abusive and unofficerlike language, calling me a damn'd lubber, a worthless goodfornothing fellow, that I never did any thing right, and used many other severe expressions." Pigot, Casey later suggested, "appear'd to have drank freely."[7]

A few days later, Pigot exploded again. This time, he decided that some of the topmen aloft were not moving quite fast enough, and so he screamed and shouted, threatening the last man down with a flogging. Three panic-stricken men slipped. They crashed onto the quarterdeck, all three dead. Their comrades aloft froze and stared, and Pigot instantly dispatched two boatswain's mates to beat them all indiscriminately with ropes' ends. The three bodies were unceremoniously dumped overboard. The next morning, "a very severe punishment of several Men, I believe twelve or fourteen, took place in the usual way at the public place of punishment." The men had grumbled at the events of the evening before. Finally, a couple of days later, Pigot had yet another three men punished with the lash, but this time it is not clear why. That night the crew revolted.[8]

Pigot's brutality undoubtedly led to the violence of the mutiny, but the traumatic conditions of war-work in the Caribbean likely played a role as well. Many of the *Hermione* mutineers had first come out to the West Indies between 1793 and 1795. In 1794, they had watched thousands die when yellow fever tore apart their squadron. "In the *Hermione* alone," Midshipman Casey remembered, "we lost in three or four Months, nearly half our Crew; many from apparent good health, dying in a few hours, and such was the malignancy of the prevailing disease, and the extreme rapidity of putrefaction, that we were absolutely obliged to dispose of the Corpse, the moment the person expired." Over 60 percent of all British troops sent to St. Domingue never returned. In the West Indies as a whole, between 1793 and 1801, malaria and yellow fever together killed at least 65,000–70,000 British war-workers, 19,000–24,000 of whom were seamen. Of the two killers, malaria was the more merciful. Death, though painful, came within only hours and days. By contrast, yellow fever dragged on for up to two weeks. After enduring high fever, severe headaches, and nausea, sufferers entering the toxic phase developed jaundice, vomited and defecated congealed blood, bled through the mouth, nose, and eyes, and eventually suffered kidney failure. Then, finally, they died.[9]

For years, the *Hermione* men had lived with the daily fear of—and in closest possible proximity to—death through disease. Out of a shipboard population that usually hovered at just below 180, 134 men died between December 1792 and July 1797, on average one man every ten days or so. On board of the *Hermione,* watching one's closest, most trusted friends quite literally rot to death became an everyday event. Disease, moreover, was not the only horror the West Indies held for the newly arrived warriors from Europe. Slave insurrections broke out on many plantation islands, and these eruptions generated levels of violence that even hardened naval men found difficult to stomach. Nowhere more so than in St. Domingue, where half a million enslaved plantation workers went to war against their masters. Britain hoped to exploit the chaos to capture the colony. It poured thousands of troops into the revolutionary race war that ensued, and all of them became witnesses, victims, and perpetrators of truly horrifying acts of violence. As a young midshipman, David O'Brien Casey witnessed Cap Français falling into the hands of the revolutionaries in 1793: "The scenes which followed were dreadful in the extreme, and impossible for to describe; the Whites were almost indiscriminately murder'd."[10]

As the campaign to reimpose slavery in St. Domingue ground on, the crew of the *Hermione* added their efforts to the mayhem that consumed the colony. They chased enemy privateers around the coast, bombarded rebel positions ashore, burned down villages to terrorize the population, and often took part in amphibious assaults. "In Capturing Port au Prince, the *Hermione* was singly opposed to one of the Batteries for some hours, and in addition to the injury and loss sustained from the Enemy's fire, We suffer'd very severely in Kill'd and Wounded, by the unfortunate bursting of one of our Main Deck Guns. . . . We were also partially engaged at the reduction of St. Marks, Le Arch Leogane, and other fortified places along the Coast, the names of which I do not recollect." The *Hermione*'s duties, Casey concluded, were "distressing in the extreme."[11]

Those who led the mutiny were all veteran war-workers. Indeed, Edward Southcott, the *Hermione*'s master, later claimed that "all the best Men were the Principals of the Mutineers." Most of the thirty or so men who belonged to this original core group were carried on the books as able, a number of them had advanced to become petty officers' mates, and the rest were nearly all topmen, the elite of the lower deck. About a third of them even belonged to a group of twenty-two men who had voluntarily followed Captain Pigot from his previous command onboard the *Success* into the *Hermione* in February 1797. This was a common practice in the navy, and crews sometimes petitioned the Admiralty to be allowed to stay with a popular commander when he was given a new ship. In this case, however, it was Pigot who asked his men to stay with him, and it seems that out of the twenty-five he approached, only three refused. All of them were highly skilled, and Pigot evidently regarded them as critical for making his new command in the *Hermione* a success.[12]

Whatever their reasons for staying with Pigot, it hardly appears to have been a matter of loyalty. But given the horrors of service in the West Indies, and the fact that their old ship was bound for home waters, it is difficult to understand what made them volunteer to stay. Perhaps it was the prospect of further prize money, or the reassuring familiarity of a life they knew, or even a perverse joy in warfare. Perhaps Pigot simply was the devil they knew, and maybe they hoped that despite his sadism he recognized the mutual benefits of the patronage system and eventually would reward their cooperation with promotions. Or maybe it was just their desperation for a few days' worth of drunken revelry in Port Royal's dockside taverns, which Pigot made sure to promise them. Either way, whatever emotional or familial ties might once have bound them to their homelands, after several years of service at sea, these bonds had evidently grown to be relatively weak.

Like most of the navy's crews, the men on the *Hermione* were an extraordinarily diverse lot. Barely half of them had been born in England, while a further fifth came from across the British Empire (Scotland, Wales, the Isle of Man, Canada, Nova Scotia, and the British West Indies). Another fifth hailed from Ireland, and the remaining 10 percent included Prussians, Swedes, Norwegians, Danes, Dutchmen, Portuguese, Italians, Swiss, Americans, and Danish West Indians. At least two of the men were of African descent, but there probably were quite a few more given the ship's long service in the Caribbean. Regardless of their diverse backgrounds, they all ate, drank, toiled, and slept together in cramped conditions for months on end. They earned the same measly wages, they all spent them on the same rum and on the same women, they all chewed on the same tough salt beef, they all suffered from the same diseases, they all were screamed at by the same officers, and they all were ripped to shreds by the same enemy broadsides. They were, quite literally, men in the same boat, and whatever ethnic, racial, national, or religious prejudices may have otherwise divided them, onboard ship they had no choice but to trust each other, whether up in the yards during a gale, below deck during a battle, or indeed when hiding away and plotting a mutiny. Cosmopolitanism, to such men, was not an abstract ideal but a basic reality of life, and it is easy to understand how some of them came to feel, like Florence McCarthy of the *Phoebe,* that "one country was as good to him as another."[13]

News of the failure of the fleet mutinies likely deepened the sense of alienation that many onboard the *Hermione* felt. During their last visit to port, just over a month before the mutiny, Captain Pigot sat on a court-martial which tried six members of the *Thames* crew for uttering words of mutiny and sedition. That crew, in mid-May, had taken part in the last stages of the fleet mutiny at Spithead and had then sailed to Yarmouth, where they arrived just in time for the mutinies in the North Sea squadron on May 26. In early June, they received orders to make sail for the West Indies, but many onboard wanted to stay in England. One of them, John Jenkinson, swore that "he did not like to go to the West Indies and if every man in the Ship was of his mind they would go back to Spithead." Henry Peters agreed, and proposed they cut the weather lanyards, sending the masts overboard, and making any sailing to the West Indies, or elsewhere, impossible. The *Thames*'s officers grew nervous from all this muttering, and they made a point of carrying their small arms. This angered the crew. John Chrystall suggested that maybe one ought to teach them a lesson on the relative balance of power onboard by turning some of the great guns aft and blowing "the Quarter Deck to Hell." George Delmar threatened to use a cannon ball to bash the boatswain's brains out. John Daley, finally, questioned the officers' right to beat people, grumbling that "it was a pity we were not like the French, to have no flogging at all."[14]

These were the unruly men who brought news of the "floating republic" to the future mutineers on the *Hermione,* and before going out on their final cruise, they were forced to witness their punishments. The court-martial that included Captain Pigot sentenced one of them to 50 lashes, and two to be flogged round the fleet with 300 lashes each, simply for having uttered words that were deemed seditious. In light of their own mutiny a few weeks later, it is interesting to consider what conclusions the men on the *Hermione* may have drawn from watching such brutal punishments right after hearing of the great but defeated upsurge of lower deck militancy on the other side of the Atlantic earlier that summer. One thing at least must have seemed certain: the lines were hardening, and the time for putting forward petitions and demands had passed. The lower deck had struck with unprecedented force, yet the Admiralty had swept aside most of their demands and instituted a policy of repression instead. The sailors onboard the *Hermione* were no doubt especially disappointed to hear that no mechanism for replacing tyrannous officers would be forthcoming any time soon. They were stuck with Captain Pigot and his lash.[15]

At the time of the mutiny, there were around 160 men on the *Hermione*'s lower deck. Only one of them afterwards surrendered to British authorities. Thirty-five others were captured between 1797 and 1806, of whom fifteen were hanged and gibbeted, nine were hanged, two were transported to New South Wales for life, one was recommended for mercy, two were admitted King's evidence, and six were acquitted. All others got away. Based on rumors and the testimonies of those who were caught, it appears that many stayed put in Caracas, and those who had learned a trade before entering the navy took it up again. Among them was Lawrence Cronin, the Belfast republican.

Others became day laborers, and quite a large number were allowed to enlist in the Spanish army. The ship's only identifiable black men, Thomas Diamond and John Jackson, together joined the local coasting trade.[16]

After the mutiny, most of the professional seafarers among the mutineers melted back into the international maritime labor market from whence they had originally come. Sometimes they went back onboard warships, and in a small number of cases there are suggestions that former *Hermione* men participated in mutinies onboard other ships. John Pearce, one of the troublemakers on the *Malta,* had been a marine on the *Hermione,* and it seems that one of the *Danae* mutineers might also have been onboard at the time of the mutiny. There were even two cases of unrest in the young US Navy that centered on men who might have come from the *Hermione.*[17]

But most of the fugitives avoided further naval service and went aboard Danish, Dutch, American, Spanish, French, Swedish, or British merchantmen instead, and in these they continued working the Caribbean, going up the North American seaboard, and crossing the Atlantic to Europe and Africa. John Duncan signed on with the Danish *Eagle* and cruised the Caribbean for a while, but he told his shipmates who he was, and somehow the governor of Saint-Croix came to hear about it. Duncan was put into confinement, sent to Saint-Thomas, and from there to Copenhagen, where King Christian VII instructed his foreign minister to present him as a gift to the British consul. Duncan was hanged soon afterwards in Portsmouth Harbor. More adventurous types joined French privateers and in these waged commercial war on Britain. This promised higher wages and better conditions of service than most merchantmen, but the dangers were greater too. John Mason, Antonio Marco, John Elliott, Joseph Mansell, and Pierre D'Orlanie were only on board the *Magecienne* for a few weeks before the British warship *Valiant* made her a prize. Isaac Stoutenling and Thomas Charlton held out slightly longer, but they, too, fell into British hands onboard a captured French privateer. Like almost all of those who got caught, they simply could not keep their mouths shut. They bragged about the mutiny, and someone told on them.[18]

Christmas 1797 was not a merry one onboard the British 38-gun *Amelia.* The newly commissioned frigate had already spent four months riding at anchor off Plymouth and Captain Herbert was still trying to scrape together a crew large enough to get underway. It was not for lack of trying. The navy's traditional reservoirs of manpower had long since been exhausted, and the attempt in 1795 and 1796 to make new populations subject to coerced naval recruitment through the Quota Acts had only temporarily eased the crisis. Herbert was desperate and willing to take almost anyone, including over twenty men who had been involved in the violent conspiracies onboard the *Saturn* earlier that summer. Another dozen men came from the *Artois,* a ship virtually identical to the *Amelia* that had recently struck submerged rocks and sunk off the Brittany coast. The survivors, without even being given shore leave to recover, were simply assigned to the first captain who asked for them, which turned out to be Captain Herbert. He added further to the *Amelia*'s ragtag crew by dispatching press gangs to snatch recruits off the streets in Plymouth. On Christmas Eve, they brought back Robert Larkin, beaten black and blue. Larkin, a twenty-eight-year-old Dubliner, had only just come back from the West Indies, where he had been discharged from the navy as an invalid, and he had a sick ticket to prove it. But the *Amelia*'s press gang did not care, nor did Captain Herbert. Officially invalided or not, Larkin was an able seaman of prime working age. Nothing else mattered.[19]

It did not take long for the combustible human flotsam on the *Amelia*'s lower deck to ignite. On Boxing Day, only his second day onboard the ship, Larkin riled up an angry, mutinous mob of about twenty men with bitter tirades about their "rights," raging against "the Buggers" on the quarterdeck and pledging that they would free themselves from "bondage" soon enough. In a rant that must have gone down especially well with the men from the *Saturn,* Larkin cursed "the cowardly Buggers at Spithead" on whose failure to push the Admiralty into genuine concessions he blamed their continued "slavery." Normally, such a disturbance of the ship's order would have been enough for at least a flogging, but Captain Herbert chose to let it pass, recognizing perhaps that Boxing Day traditionally belonged to the servant class, and why not let the men blow off some steam before they finally got underway? Knowing that their upcoming duties would include the lucrative hunt for French privateers, Herbert might have calculated that once the first shares of prize money began trickling down onto the lower deck, whatever discontent was agitating his men was likely soon to dissipate. But instead it got worse. When the *Amelia* returned to port in early February, Larkin again led an angry, drunken assembly, and this time they promised that "they would kill every Bugger of an Officer in the Ship—and the Ship might go to Hell for they cared nothing about her." And as Larkin raged on, two dozen voices shouted "I am for the same. I am for the same," and then they roared "For the New Act."[20]

This was not the first time Larkin and his comrades had threatened their officers. Even during the troubles in December, they had repeatedly invoked what they called the "New Act," and they appear to have remained deliberately vague about its meaning. Sometimes it sounded like an insistence on the right to expel unpopular officers from the ship, a right some believed the lower deck had won as a result of the fleet mutinies. At other times, the "New Act" appeared to refer to the literal heaving overboard of hated officers, the murderous "New Act" that had been pioneered onboard the *Hermione* just a few months before, perhaps not coincidentally on the very same station on which Larkin had previously served. Captain Herbert, in any case, decided not to take any more chances. He asked for eighteen men to be removed from the ship, and then arrested Larkin and four of his comrades, three of whom were eventually tried and convicted by court-martial for holding mutinous assemblies and encouraging the murder of officers. Evidence revealed that the threats had not just been drunken boasting: after the *Amelia* had sailed from Plymouth in late December, small groups of men, many of them former *Saturn* mutineers, had formed "clubs" that met regularly to discuss the murder of officers and the freeing of themselves from "bondage" and "slavery." Ominously, whenever there was a risk of being overheard, they had switched to speaking Irish among themselves.[21]

The appearance of Irish radicalism, however chaotic, was the last thing the British navy needed in the winter of 1797–98. In October, France had pushed Austria out of the war, and with that had defeated or terrified into neutrality every significant power in continental Europe. The First Coalition was crushed, and France was now free to turn its full military might on Britain. The British victories at Cape St. Vincent in February and especially at Camperdown in October had prevented the launch of a full-scale invasion attempt in 1797, but both the Spanish and the Dutch navy remained capable of putting further forces to sea; likewise the French Atlantic fleet, which had stayed safely anchored at Brest for most of the year. In Ireland, meanwhile, the long-simmering independence struggle was quickly heating up as British forces reacted to the failed French invasion of 1796 with an ugly counterinsurgency campaign that turned large parts of rural Ireland into a war zone. All that prevented the Irish insurrectionary leadership from launching a full-scale rebellion in response was the hope that if only they waited just a little bit longer, the French navy might well slip past the British blockade a second time and finally deliver the military aid they so desperately needed to challenge Britain's imperial might.[22]

Ironically, the Royal Navy relied quite heavily on the labor of Irish seamen to prevent that aid from reaching Ireland. Forty percent of the *Amelia*'s crew, for example, were Irish-born, more or less average for the Channel fleet's western squadron, which were the ships primarily responsible for keeping the south Celtic Sea free of French shipping. Most of these men had either been impressed or were driven by poverty and despair to volunteer for the service, and as such they were no different than mariners born in Britain, its colonies, continental Europe, or elsewhere overseas. But what set the Irish apart was that up to several thousand of them had ended up in the navy because of a British scheme to use coercive naval recruitment as a tool of counterinsurgency warfare. At first, this was a spontaneous measure developed during Lord Carhampton's campaign to stomp out rural unrest in Connacht, when in collusion with local magistrates he simply forced nearly 1,300 suspected revolutionaries without trial into the navy in late 1795. In early 1796, however, the government retroactively legalized Carhampton's mass kidnapping with the Indemnity Act, and then regularized the practice with the Insurrection Act soon afterwards. In addition, naval press gangs snatched up anyone who local magistrates along the coasts pointed out as a suspected rebel. Other mechanisms were also available. Political prisoners against whom there was insufficient evidence might simply be declared vagabonds and bundled off into the navy, as happened to several suspected United Irishmen allegedly involved in a conspiracy to assassinate Carhampton in the spring of 1797.[23]

Even though no aggregate numbers exist for the various schemes that drove suspected radicals into the fleet, the Royal Navy's lower deck was clearly home to a fair number of Irish rebels who might be willing to rise on their officers in support of a French-backed anti-British insurrection. Indeed, Theobald Wolfe Tone, leader of the Society of United Irishmen, proclaimed it a virtual certainty as early as 1796, as did his fellow United Irish emissaries Edward Fitzgerald and Arthur O'Connor, who assured French officials that there was no reason to fear that French naval support for an Irish war of liberation would run into any kind of trouble with the Royal Navy, for they had "well-founded hopes" that in the event of a rebellion a large part of the British fleet would fall into their hands.[24]

The French were no doubt happy to hear these assurances, but the failed invasion attempt of December 1796 had already cost them nearly five thousand men and eleven ships damaged beyond repair. That fiasco had been followed in short order by the defeat first of their Spanish allies off Cape St. Vincent in February 1797 and then of their Dutch allies off Camperdown in

October later that same year. The Directory therefore was not enthusiastic about the idea of sending yet another fleet which it barely could afford into the British-controlled Celtic Sea, simply in the hope that discontented Irishmen might mutiny and allow it to slip through. It did not help matters that despite their demographic weight, and despite the confident pronouncements of Tone and others, Irish seamen had not made their numbers count during the mutinies at either Spithead or the Nore. Except for just a few crews, and individual seamen here and there, the fleet mutineers in the end had remained loyal to the British state, while their delegates, including many Irishmen, had pledged repeatedly to go out and fight any enemy fleet that put to sea.[25]

It was clear to the leadership of the United Irish that if France were to be persuaded to provide meaningful military support, the Irishmen would first have to make a serious effort to infiltrate and subvert the Channel fleet, and especially its western squadron, which was responsible for blockading Brest. At first, relatively few members of the United Irish had been caught up in the various counterinsurgency dragnets that swept Irish political prisoners into the navy, but after the Bantry Bay fiasco made the organization a primary target for government repression, their numbers began to creep up. And once the fleet mutinies erupted, and the stunning potential for crippling Britain's maritime defenses became apparent, they suddenly exploded. Already in April, when the Spithead mutiny was barely two weeks old, there were reports from Belfast that "United rebels" sentenced to service in the fleet were barely able to contain their joy, "for they would be of more service to *the cause* on board a man-of-war than they could be at present on land." In June, John Connelly, a United Irish poet from Dublin, got himself sentenced to service in the fleet on purpose, so that he might find a receptive audience for the songs he had composed about the fleet mutinies. There were many more like them, hundreds more. By July, a mere month after the final collapse of the mutiny at the Nore, there were up to one thousand new United men in the navy.[26]

Government and naval authorities were aware of and worried about this sudden influx. Until then, the majority of Irish political prisoners who had been funneled into the navy were Defenders, a mostly proletarian, ultra-militant revolutionary organization, which however was dismissed as relatively harmless, since its members were "of the Catholic persuasion, and in general deluded and ignorant men." But with the rise in the number of

United men had come what many imperial elites in their almost comical class arrogance considered a far more dangerous breed of Irishman, one that looked very much like themselves: Protestant or Dissenting, often well-educated, and a member of "the higher classes," who somehow or other had fallen victim to political enthusiasm. When the uptick in the number of United rebels entering the navy had first become apparent, Edward Newenham, a reformist member of the Irish ruling class, wrote to Earl Spencer, First Lord of the Admiralty, to warn against allowing any of these people to come onboard ship, for a single such fanatic, armed only with a stack of issues "of that rebellious newspaper, the *Northern Star*," was capable of "poisoning the minds" of a whole ship's crew. But the navy took the risk, unwilling to forego even such a toxic pool of desperately needed manpower, and instead they tried to manage and surveil suspicious men as best they could. The United poet, for instance, was sent into a gunboat, a tiny vessel onboard which his songs could do but little harm and put under a captain who had proven himself reliably authoritarian by acting decisively against the Spithead mutineers. In other cases, the Admiralty tried to funnel suspects into small vessels bound for overseas stations, where they would be either far removed from the central theaters of war or in the midst of a murderous disease environment, preferably both. But the number of suspects was simply too large, and the urgent need for manpower to strengthen the home command too great for all of them to be shoved to the periphery, especially during the tense winter of 1797–98, when all of England stared across the Channel in fear of yet another French invasion attempt, this one rumored to be led by that master of republican warfare, General Napoleon Bonaparte.[27]

Some of those who stared back from the other side were well aware of the opportunities that the Royal Navy's heavy reliance on Irish seamen presented. Among them were Léonard Bourdon, a former Jacobin hardliner now working as an intelligence agent attached to the French embassy in Hamburg, and his secretary William Duckett, an illustrious Irish subversive whose enthusiasm for sowing anarchy and chaos onboard the ships of the Royal Navy was unrivalled among French covert operators. In February 1798, at the exact same moment that unrest onboard the *Amelia* was driving towards its peak, Duckett and Bourdon were poking around Hamburg's busy waterfront, interviewing British mariners and itinerant Irish radicals to see what they might learn about the mood on the Royal Navy's lower deck in the aftermath of the fleet mutinies. Their discoveries, summarized in a report to the Directory, were startling. Most importantly, they claimed, following the fleet mutinies the Admiralty had not really succeeded in resurrecting the authority of its officer corps, and indeed the wave of punitive violence that ripped through the fleet in retaliation for the Nore mutiny had only "made more vivid the resentment of the rest of the crews." More promising still, among the large numbers of Irish seamen, outrage against the naval officer corps was increasingly joined by a growing hatred for Britain's heavy-handed counterinsurgency in Ireland, which together, they claimed, had led to a truly explosive, even revolutionary level of discontent on the lower deck. Veteran fleet mutineers and furious Irishmen together were like "a volcano continuously ready to erupt."[28]

Duckett and Bourdon's report was not completely fanciful. For example, the sentencing of eight men to death for mutiny on the *Saturn* in the late summer of 1797, and the removal and dispersal of another twenty men from the same ship, only drove the remaining crew deeper into violent, vengeful disaffection. They pledged "to have Revenge for their Shipmates now under sentence of Death, whom they consider as having fallen a Sacrifice for the common Cause, and the Prosecutor and Officers who appeared as evidences against them will be the first Objects." Hearing this, Captain Douglas asked for several dozen more men to be taken out of his ship, and it was some of those who in turn ended up on the *Amelia,* where shortly afterwards they started plotting mutiny and murder. The trouble on that ship, moreover, suggests that the intermingling of maritime and Irish radicalisms may indeed have produced a spirit even more militant and uncompromising than that which had animated the fleet mutineers. For unlike them, who ultimately had only sought more or less radical improvements in the conditions of war-work, Larkin and his fellow malcontents onboard the *Amelia* denounced those conditions without qualification as "slavery," "bondage," and "kidnapping," language that left little room for a negotiated settlement of grievances.[29]

Duckett and Bourdon were not naïve about the lower deck's chances in going up against the might of the British officer corps. They argued that without foreign aid disaffected British seamen, however revolutionary they may be, were likely to just keep repeating the pattern of starting "movements of rebellion and insubordination that deliver their leaders to the hangman and end up redoubling the weight of their chains," which is exactly what happened to Larkin and his comrades onboard the *Amelia*. Duckett and Bourdon therefore emphasized in their report the importance of getting word to potential mutineers in the British navy that France would welcome them as allies, and that if they were to meet with French warships at sea there would be no fighting, other than alongside each other for "the freedom and independence of their country, and for the destruction of that infamous Government that they abhor." Drawing on Duckett's sprawling network of cosmopolitan subversives, he and Bourdon had in fact already put together a plan for two Irishmen to travel from Hamburg to Cork, "carrying with them a very short, very energetic text that lays out all the English and Irish subjects of complaint, and assurances of the French government's position, on which [the sailors] can depend completely." Once arrived at Cork, the two secret agents were to pass on the address to a recently promoted naval lieutenant, identified only as "B," who was known to be a friend of Irish freedom and who would be able to smuggle the text onboard the ships anchoring in the roadstead.[30]

What came of Bourdon and Duckett's plan is unknown, but someone clearly managed to get a similar message through to the British warships at Plymouth, where three months later a major conspiracy was underway that at its height involved several hundred men on at least half a dozen ships. The conspiracy appears to have been triggered in mid-May when Bartholomew Duff, a thirty-three-year-old Dubliner serving onboard the 80-gun *Caesar,* "received letters from Ireland enclosing Letters from France, which Letters inform'd him that any assistance they should want they should have from France . . . and that they should do their best Endeavours to take the Ship to France." The letters also contained specific instructions on how to be recognized as a friendly vessel when it came time to sail into Brest. Duff, who most likely was sent into the navy the previous fall as a United Irish emissary, soon afterwards began swearing a rapidly growing number of his shipmates into the Society of United Irishmen. As was the usual practice in recruiting new members, he made them take two oaths, the first a general one promising "On the cross, to be United Irishmen, equal to their Brothers in Ireland, and to have nothing to do with the King and his Government," and the second "To take the Caesar into France or any other enemy's port." Eventually forty-five seamen and eleven marines swore the oaths, approximately 9 percent of the crew. Duff and his fellow conspirators then reached out to the crews of ships anchoring nearby. On the 74-gun *Defiance,* which already had both United Irishmen and Defenders onboard, their appeal was especially resonant, and here too somewhere between forty and fifty men were soon sworn in, though with a slightly different oath that included the promise "to kill every Officer and Man that shall hinder us except the Master, and to hoist a Green Ensign with a Harp in it, and afterwards to kill and destroy the Protestants." The conspiracy also spread to the massive 98-gun *Glory,* onboard which all Irish seamen and marines first issued a formal statement of loyalty to king, country, and constitution, before up to sixty of them went on to hatch a secret plot to save their liquor allowance over several days, then get all the English sailors drunk at once, lock them below deck, murder the officers, and sail for Brest. Similar plots, more or less developed, were afoot on a number of other ships, including the *Atlas,* the *Queen Charlotte,* and the *Captain.*[31]

The rapid spread of the conspiracy was testament to the United Irishmen's successful work of subversion that had preceded it. As on the *Amelia,* the primary organizational form this work took was in the creation of "Irish clubs," which met regularly below deck and gave likeminded men the opportunity to talk politics (for example, about "the affairs of Ireland and France," or how "the Government of England had no right to the possession of Ireland," as well as "on the subject of the United Irishmen in Ireland and in the Fleet"). Like the Jacobin and many other clubs in France, their sister societies throughout western Europe, the Democratic-Republican Societies in North America, the various corresponding societies in Britain, or indeed the Society of United Irishmen itself before it was pushed into illegality, the clubs onboard ship made it a particular point of emphasis to correspond with each other, busily sending letters back and forth in which they exchanged news about the growing number of members on each ship, and on the various procedures each club adopted in carrying on its business. The clubs took guidance on these questions from pamphlets that had been smuggled onboard in multiple copies and were surreptitiously passed from hand to hand, from club to club, and from ship to ship. On the *Defiance,* there were several copies of a "book or pamphlet" that spoke about "the Affairs of Ireland and the French[,] what strength they had there, the Rules of the United Irishmen, and the Obligations and Instructions for them on board the Ship." Following these instructions, and the example of the Society of United Irishmen itself, the clubs on some of the ships eventually evolved into a secret organization, with several sworn cells on each ship overseen by an "inspecting committee" that handled the lateral correspondence with their counterparts on other ships, as well as with contacts on shore, which represented the next higher level within the wider United Irish command structure.[32]

By the time the 1798 Rebellion erupted in late May, the United Irish thus had managed to establish a significant organizational presence onboard several ships of the western squadron. But of course, by then it no longer made much difference. The French Directory had decided as early as February—just as Duckett and Bourdon were putting pen to paper—that its limited amphibious resources were better spent on Napoleon's attempted conquest of the far eastern Mediterranean, which if successful would have forced Britain to stretch its military capacities even more thinly across the globe in order to protect its possessions in the East Indies. While the United Irish leadership therefore waited throughout the spring to trigger the rebellion in the hope that a French fleet would eventually come sailing over the horizon, the French military withdrew most of its forces and supplies from the Atlantic coast and sent them south to Toulon, where a massive invasion fleet gathered and finally sailed for Egypt in May. The French government was then taken aback when news arrived that a rebellion had erupted in Ireland at the very same time and scrambled to scrape together as much military aid as it could spare, which in the end amounted to just a couple of thousand soldiers who sailed after the rebellion had effectively already been defeated. In the meantime, Duckett was told to activate his British and Irish contacts to stoke as much naval unrest as possible, and several thousand incendiary pamphlets were distributed to British seamen in neutral ports to encourage the same.[33]

But it was all for naught: on not a single British warship did conspiracy erupt into mutiny. Instead, when they began to be discovered in late July, the most fully matured conspiracies, those onboard the *Caesar,* the *Defiance,* and the *Glory,* had plateaued at around fifty men, which onboard a frigate like the *Hermione* would have been more than sufficient, but onboard second- and third-rate warships represented less than 10 percent of the crew and was simply not enough to seize and hold the ship for as long as it would take to sail to France. Attempts to recruit additional men had proven difficult and often ended with threats of violence to ensure the silence of those who did not wish to join the conspiracy. Lawrence Carroll, for instance, rejected Nicholas Ryan's overtures by telling him that he hoped the Irish rebellion would be defeated. That in turn sent Ryan into a rage, cursing Carroll for not being a real Irishman and threatening him with murder.[34]

However, while outright opponents of the Rebellion were probably in the minority, so too unfortunately, were those willing to risk their life in its support. Wolfe Tone, despite the confident assurances he gave the French government at the time, had in fact already recognized the problem of only lukewarm support for a rebellion in his 1796 address *To the Irishmen Now Serving Aboard the British Navy,* copies of which were circulating in the western squadron in 1798. In the pamphlet, which was originally meant to be distributed after the successful French landing at Bantry Bay, Tone tripped lightly past the patriotic glories of fighting for a free and independent Ireland, and instead devoted considerable attention to the monetary advantages to be gained by those involved in seizing control of British warships and turning them into Irish privateers. But in 1798, there was never really a point at which it looked like the Rebellion might succeed, and as the bodies of dead rebels piled higher and higher during the summer, the attempt to create an Irish privateering fleet at best seemed likely to end in French exile, and at worst with a trial for mutiny or treason. Some were still willing to take the gamble. John Bryan, for instance, told his comrades that "he had served in the French Navy this war and he was a Republican." Another man agreed that in France "the people lived very happy since the present mode of Government." To many, however, there was no point in becoming a martyr, losing many years' worth of back wages, and forever abandoning friends and family back home in Ireland, or elsewhere in the British Isles.[35]

Still, in the end it was not the lack of support from fellow Irishmen that led to the discovery of the conspirators, but betrayal by some of their English-born shipmates. In late July, a group of them onboard the *Caesar*—terrified, they claimed, by all the murderous muttering coming from the Irish seamen—went aft and reported the existence of a plot to their officers. To help explain why it had taken them several weeks to speak up, John Nicholls later testified that a lot of the men had been aware for some time that something was afoot amongst the Irish, but they had simply been too afraid to either confront or report them. His and others' testimonies described how sectarian tensions divided the lower deck, and how an unholy brew of Catholic fanaticism and aggressive Irish separatism had made them fear for their lives. Multiple witnesses described how one of the central conspirators on the *Caesar,* Michael Butler, had taken great delight in telling everyone that "he would support the Roman cause up to the Arm in blood," that "he should never die easy till he swum in English blood," and finally that "he would think no more of putting a protestant to death than he would a mad dog." As conspiracies were uncovered across the squadron, a similar picture began to emerge on most of the other ships. Joseph Harben of the *Glory* told the court that Lawrence Dowd had sought to kill him simply for having criticized the Rebellion. His shipmate James Quickly testified that he believed the purpose of the "Irish club" had been to plan the murder of all the Scottish and English seamen onboard. That, he claimed, was the shared fear of almost everyone below deck, though he also conceded that no one really knew for sure since the conspirators had mostly spoken Irish among themselves.[36]

Not everyone agreed that sectarian divisions really were that deeply entrenched on the lower deck, and some questioned the motives of those who testified otherwise. John Mahoney accused a key witness in the *Caesar* trial, on whose evidence six men were eventually hanged, of having invented a "Roman" plot simply to improve his own standing with the ship's captain, as "he expects to get to be a Nob in the Navy by his Informations." Still, whether wholly invented or just embellished, testimony that emphasized ethno-religious divisions below deck was welcomed by naval authorities, as it helped provide a comforting explanation for the widespread disciplinary rot that apparently still infected Britain's wooden walls, even a year after the end of fleet mutinies. Feeding off a well-established British narrative about savage and sectarian Irish violence, such testimony created the illusion of a clear line dividing the loyal British tar from the rebellious Irish rabble, which in turn meant the poison of political subversion was contained and could easily be removed from the navy's body politic. In reality, that line was nowhere near as clear. For example, on the *Defiance,* conspirators swore "to kill and destroy the Protestants," but according to Daniel Lynch, several of those who took that oath were "Jacobin Protestants," including Lynch himself. Complicating matters still further, many treated "Irish" and "Catholic" as synonymous ways of describing the conspirators, even though they also included several Frenchmen and, on the *Defiance* and the *Captain,* even some Englishmen. Indeed, it was two English-born seamen, James Goodman and Samuel Rodden, who spread the conspiracy from the one ship to the other. Conversely, on the *Caesar,* "protestant" was used interchangeably with "nob," a slang term for members of the upper classes (i.e., the "nobility") which onboard ship was also used to refer to the officer corps, whose all-powerful minority position mirrored that of the tiny Protestant landed elite in Ireland.[37]

All this was language strongly reminiscent of Defenderism, a militant political tendency that had merged its loose organizational structures with those of the United Irish during the latter's embrace of insurrectionism in 1795–96. Originally forged in the violent class warfare that raged in late eighteenth-century rural Ireland, where property ownership and Protestantism were virtually synonymous, and where Catholicism had long served as the legal basis for the political exclusion of the indigenous Irish, Defenderism developed an understanding of class that was articulated in the language of ethnic and religious difference, which is why Defenders can appear as mostly sectarian in their political orientation. And yet, once transported into the very different social world of the ship, a place where class divisions were very sharply defined and sectarian ones hardly at all, the language of ethnic and religious difference that dominated Defender political discourse in rural Ireland lost much of its original meaning and came to be used primarily to describe class and political solidarities instead. Aiding the slippage from one to the other was the easy compatibility between elements of Defender political ideology and the traditions of maritime radicalism encountered onboard ship, most of all the degree to which both tendencies reacted to the experience of extreme social and political inequality with a strong commitment to egalitarianism as both means and end of revolutionary struggle. The common ground the two traditions fought on was already evident onboard the *Amelia* in the way in which Larkin and his friends unleashed accusations of "slavery," "bondage," and "kidnapping" to amplify their critique of both coerced naval servitude and of British colonial rule in Ireland, and it was repeated onboard the *Defiance,* where one conspirator explained with the same telling ambiguity that their shared desire "to get free of Slavery and Confinement" united them all, Irish Catholic rebel and British Protestant seaman.[38]

The two traditions also overlapped in their shared predilection for violent direct action. In preparation for the expected revolt on the *Defiance,* conspirators hid handspikes throughout the ship, sturdy wooden sticks designed for the backbreaking labor of turning the capstan, which in moments of mutiny were often used as clubs. Below deck on the *Defiance,* the conspirators referred to them as "trees of liberty," which was a nicely concise way of articulating the idea of physical force republicanism, one of the most important long-term ideological legacies of the 1798 Irish Rebellion. However, while physical force republicanism eventually came to be associated with sectarian violence against Protestants, unionists, and British imperial personnel, the tree of liberty as a political symbol in late eighteenth-century Ireland was closely identified with the cosmopolitan republicanism of the United Irish, who used it in a famous catechism to teach the rise and progress of revolutionary liberty across the Atlantic world:

What is that in your hand? It is a branch.
Of what? Of the tree of liberty.
Where did it first grow? In America.
Where did it bloom? In France.
Where did the seeds fall? In Ireland.

Fittingly, for a symbol representing the transatlantic movement of revolution, many of the first so-called liberty trees in the port cities of British North America were actually ships' masts that had been transformed into liberty poles on land, their great height more suitable than ordinary trees for flying signaling flags that would be visible at a great distance. It was therefore particularly meaningful that the *Defiance* conspirators also identified their "trees of liberty" as a repurposed part of the ship: handspikes that were transformed from tiny spokes in the vast imperial war machine into head-cracking weapons of anti-colonial resistance.[39]

William Davis of the *Lowestoff* brought the tradition full circle when in early 1799 he had a vision of the ship's mainmast and yards as a tree of liberty, "and its branches extended thro' all the British Navy." But in reality, that dream had already been achieved and defeated early in the cycle of struggle that stretched from the eruption of the Spithead fleet mutiny in April 1797 to the crushing of the western squadron conspiracies in the late summer of 1798. What began as an extraordinary show of solidarity across the entirety of the Channel fleet, and in a matter of weeks expanded to involve the vast majority of men serving in the home command, already showed signs of strain from the beginning of the Nore mutiny in mid-May, and then was shattered at its collapse in early June. Even as the mutinous impulse spread outward to naval stations from Nova Scotia all the way to Ceylon, in the home command, where it all started, the lower deck was left bitter, demoralized, and divided. Most ex-mutineers accepted the return of the quarterdeck's authority, some grudgingly, others eagerly. But as Duckett and Bourdon were soon to understand, a sizeable minority remained unyielding, seething with rage radiating in all directions.[40]

The influx of Irish radicals in the months that followed gave that rage a focus and greater strength, but the transformation of the lower deck's struggle for better working conditions into an insurrectionary, anti-colonial movement sheared off even more men from what once had been the common cause. And yet, even though there clearly were those who on principle opposed the broader political project of Irish independence and others who worried about the intensity of the conspirators' sectarian language, what is most striking was the silence that all of them maintained, even as dozens of their shipmates spent weeks plotting mayhem and murder in their midst. It was only after the Irish Rebellion was effectively defeated, and the French still were showing little sign of sending significant support, that small groups of men began coming forward with information for their officers, telling tales of widespread sectarian violence and intimidation, often in the hope of explaining away why it taken them quite so long to speak up.

It was certainly true that some in the Irish independence movement, on shore as well as at sea, interpreted the meaning of revolution as Catholic revenge and therefore took the oath "to kill and destroy the Protestants" seriously. It was equally true, however, that retrospectively amplifying their voices had the effect of delegitimizing lower deck political radicalism by associating it with a belligerent ethnic other, a move that became an important strategy for dealing with the upsurge in violent insurrectionism that swept through the British navy after 1797. For example, coinciding with the spread of conspiracies in the western squadron in the summer of 1798, there was a plan to trigger a multi-ship mutiny in the Mediterranean fleet that was primarily concerned with fighting back against Admiral Earl St. Vincent's extreme and violent system of discipline. But when the conspiracy was uncovered, St. Vincent blamed the whole affair on the nefarious activities of the United Irishmen, even though their influence was secondary at best.[41]

The flagship's resident clergyman, the Reverend Robert Baynes, repeated the same charge in a sermon he preached to accompany the execution of three of the conspirators on July 10. Standing on the quarterdeck, surrounded by the ship's officers and detachment of marines, Baynes began by lecturing the assembled crew that "we cannot all be in the most desirable situation . . . we cannot all be kings, rulers, and judges—we cannot all be powerful and wealthy; but we may all be sober, honest, and industrious—we may live in peace and harmony with one another, and be content with our several lots." And of course, the majority of British seamen understood that, Baynes maintained, but there was "a set of murmuring and discontented wretches, the very pests of society who have, by some means or other, crept into the British navy—some of them, I believe, as the chosen emissaries of the seditious, or enemies to their country, on shore." Having defined those on the lower deck unwilling to accept the inequalities that governed British life as irredeemably evil, and as alien both to the navy and the nation, Baynes went on to offer absolution to the rest, those "good, obedient, and sober men" whose simple minds had been poisoned by those who from now on they must shun "as you would do a pestilence."[42]

It is unlikely that the men who had been called on deck to witness the executions shared Baynes's grim enthusiasm for the old regime's class relations. But that did not really matter, for beside him stood three Irishmen convicted of having challenged the social order he celebrated, and whose lives would now be snuffed out, just as soon as he finished speaking. And that, in the end, was all the argument he needed. But this was not just a crude and intentionally humiliating demonstration of power. It was also an invitation to national reconciliation, to be consecrated through the ritualistic killing of a hostile ethnic other. Baynes's use of epidemiological language—likening Irish anti-colonial radicals to a "pestilence"—rhetorically created an organic unity among the ethnically British part of the ship's community, a very literal imagination of a miniature national body politic that was under threat from a foreign-borne disease. Consequently, any measure, even severe bloodletting, was justified in purging and restoring that body's naturally healthy and balanced constitution, an effort that every single member of the national community who had not been diseased beyond recovery ought to have an obvious self-interest in supporting. Indeed, Baynes concluded his sermon by dwelling on the moral duty of British seamen to prioritize their national subjecthood over other solidarities, to break with the lower deck's tradition of expansive fraternal solidarity, to realign their loyalties vertically towards the quarterdeck, and in future to report any and all mutinous talk or conduct immediately to their officers.[43]

Similar attempts at ethno-national bonding followed the courts-martial that were held during the late summer and fall of 1798 in the western squadron; though in line with post-Rebellion government policy in Ireland and in recognition of the continued indispensability of Irish labor in the home command, the rhetoric here was more conciliatory and inclusive than Baynes's viciously xenophobic authoritarianism. But the unusual savagery of the punishments spoke a different language, one that echoed Baynes's more unforgiving attitude to Irish subversion. Even though not a single ship experienced a mutiny, a total of twenty-five men were sentenced to death, eight to transportation, and over twenty to floggings around the fleet. The executions began with the hanging of six men from the *Caesar* on August 30, followed by eleven men from the *Defiance* a few weeks later, and finally another eight men from the *Glory* some weeks after that. Then there were the punishment beatings, beginning on August 25 with two men from the *Caesar* who both had been sentenced to 500 lashes each. The first round of floggings was interrupted after 76 and 71 lashes, respectively, "which were as many as they were able to undergo at one time." A week later, on September 2, the floggings continued, and this time both men received 48 lashes, and a marine from the *Neptune* the first 35 of 150 lashes. And so it continued throughout the fall, week after week, over a dozen men repeatedly flogged to the brink of death, nursed back to relative health, and then flogged some more. November 12 was especially bloody: on that day, the two *Caesar* men each received 50 lashes, the marine from the *Neptune* 41 lashes, a man from the *Niger* and one from the *Druid* 50 lashes each, and two men from the *Queen Charlotte* a horrifying 275 and 225 lashes each.[44]

Under the onslaught of punitive violence, the back of lower deck insurrectionism broke. Scrambling to dissociate themselves from the radicals, most crewmen in the home command kept their heads down throughout the fall and winter of 1798–99, anxiously hoping their spooked officers found no reason to notice them, for at the least sign of political subversion, courts-martial now routinely handed out staggeringly disproportionate punishments. Four marines onboard the *St. George* were given 300 lashes each with the cat-o'-nine-tails simply because one of them, when drunk, had wished success to the United Irish and raised a toast to the tree of liberty, and his three comrades had failed to report him. Given such extreme reactions to dissent, or even just careless provocation, it is perhaps understandable that some Irish tars sought to shield themselves against suspicion with absurd public declarations of loyalty to "our present mild and happy Constitution," even as they were forced to watch their shipmates being tortured to death right in front of their eyes. Only a tiny number of hardliners carried on fighting, but they were often isolated and driven to desperate acts of terror. On the *Diomede,* there was talk of setting fire to the powder room and blowing up the ship, but it does not appear the attempt was actually made in the end. In contrast, Robert Nelson of the *Belliqueux* was caught trying to cut the tackles of the main deck guns during a storm in early November, which had he been successful could easily have destabilized and sunk the ship, killing all four hundred men onboard.[45]

The surge of treasonous conspiracies from below was not restricted to the British navy. In January 1798, just a few months after the *Hermione* mutiny, nine men onboard the Batavian sloop *Havick*, five of them Dutch, one Ottoman, two Germans, and one American, were discovered as they plotted to kill their officers, steal the ship, and then sail with it to the British-controlled colony of Demerara. Some months after that, trouble was brewing onboard the 64-gunship *Utrecht*. Eventually, thirty-six men, including a small handful of native-born Dutchmen, a scattering of Prussians, Saxons, Bohemians, Hungarians, Galicians, Poles, Ottomans, Russians, and Swedes, conspired to kill the ship's officers and then sail to either England or Hamburg, depending on the winds. The following year, a group of Swedish, Danish, Dutch, Alsatian, Flemish, and Prussian conspirators planned to kill the *Vernieler* gunboat's officers, but they too were arrested before they could act.[46]

Despite the extraordinarily diverse range of men involved in the conspiracies onboard the Dutch warships, naval authorities did not make xenophobic distinctions when prosecuting troublemakers. In France, by contrast, where far fewer foreign-born men served than in the Dutch navy, authorities reacted with severe repression to the least sign or suspicion of their involvement in oppositional activities. Lorens Revers, for instance, was sentenced to death in the summer of 1794 on the ludicrous charge of being "an emissary of a foreign power" intent on overthrowing the French government. Born around 1760 in Stockholm, Revers had worked on merchantmen sailing out of London in the late 1770s and was captured by the French onboard a British ship somewhere in the West Indies. But since he was not a British subject, instead of becoming a prisoner of war he was allowed to join the multinational Irish Brigade of the French army. He remained with his regiment throughout the 1780s, even though he tried to desert three times (once in North America, a second time in the Caribbean, and a third time in South Asia). By 1790, he somehow had made it onboard a ship that sailed from Cap Français to Bordeaux, where he went ashore and then spent the winter drifting around France, first to Nantes and Vannes, and eventually on to Paris. He then returned to England, but in 1793 was once again captured onboard a British ship by the French. Once again, he took up the offer to work for the French military as an alternative to imprisonment, this time onboard a warship. But he soon tried to get his fellow POW-workers to go on strike, and for that, finally, he was dragged in front of the Revolutionary Tribunal, and quickly executed.[47]

As the war continued, its centrifugal forces threw off more and more men like Revers—drifters whose cosmopolitan biographies made it difficult to determine whether they were neutral, friend, or foe, and whose loyalties seemed flexible at best, non-existent at worst. In response, the French government announced that it would treat seamen from neutral or allied countries caught serving onboard enemy ships no longer as potential recruits, nor even as prisoners of war, but instead would prosecute them as pirates, or unlawful combatants. Spain enacted a similar policy of criminalizing cross-border employment in 1797, and Britain briefly considered retaliating in kind.[48]

Ethnic and national lines of exclusion were hardening in many places around the Atlantic in the late 1790s, including even North America, where mariners of diverse backgrounds had long been able to find safe havens. But by the time Thomas Nash washed ashore in Charleston, South Carolina, the reception had become a good deal more hostile. After a shipmate denounced him as one of the *Hermione* mutineers to the local justice of the peace, Nash was immediately arrested, thrown in jail, and British authorities notified. They quickly sent Lieutenant John Forbes, a former midshipman on the *Hermione,* and he immediately recognized the Irishman Nash as "a seaman on board the Hermione British frigate," and "one of the principals in the commission of the said acts of murder and piracy, whose conduct in that transaction has become known to this deponent by depositions made, and testimony given in courts-martial, where some of the said crew have been tried." The British asked for his extradition under Article 27 of the controversial 1794 Anglo-American Treaty of Amity, Commerce, and Navigation (also known as the Jay Treaty), the first time in US history that such a request was successfully made.[49]

It was unfortunate for Nash that he arrived in the United States in the midst of a blistering xenophobic scare that was especially severe in the immediate aftermath of the outbreak of the Quasi-War with France in the summer of 1798. Taking advantage of the belligerent fervor that ripped through the country during those months, the Federalist majority in Congress pushed through the infamous Alien and Sedition Acts, a repressive suite of laws that among other things made every noncitizen liable for deportation at the president's pleasure. The acts were justified as necessary for preventing the radical currents of the revolutionary Atlantic from undermining the constitutional settlement of 1789, but in reality, they were meant primarily to intimate and neutralize immigrant political activists, who overwhelmingly supported the Republican opposition. The Irish, who streamed into the country by the tens of thousands in the 1790s, were a particular target, for their virulent Anglophobia, intolerance of privilege, and insurrectionary experience made them into natural enemies of the reactionary Federalist party, one of whose members railed hysterically on the floor of the House that "I feel every disposition to respect those honest and industrious people who have become citizens . . . but I do not wish to invite hordes of wild Irishmen, nor the turbulent and disorderly of all parts of the world, to come here with a view to disturb our tranquility, after having succeeded in the overthrow of their own Governments."[50]

Nash himself was evidently aware of the disadvantage of being Irish, for shortly before he was to be handed over to the British, he suddenly produced a seaman's protection certificate made out in the name of Jonathan Robbins, native of Danbury, Connecticut. He went on to claim "that about two years ago he was pressed from on board the brig Betsey of New-York, commanded by capt. White, and bound for St. Nichola Mole, by the crew of the British frigate Hermione, [at that time] commanded by captain Wilkinson, and was detained there contrary to his will, in the service of the British nation, until the said vessel was captured by those of her crew who took her into a Spanish port by force; and that he gave no assistance in such capture."[51]

This, of course, was entirely plausible. The Royal Navy impressed thousands of Americans during the 1790s, and US newspapers were full of stories similar to the one told by Nash. The British claimed to press only their own subjects, thousands of whom actually did work in the booming American merchant marine. But it was virtually impossible to tell an American citizen from one of His Majesty's subjects, and faced with both an acute and chronic shortage of manpower, many of the Royal Navy's press gangs did not try very hard to make the distinction. They picked their way through hundreds of American merchant ships and simply pressed any skilled mariner who reasonably could be suspected of being British, with tolerable command of English often being considered sufficient proof.[52]

In order to strengthen their mariners' claim to American citizenship, the US Congress in 1796 passed "An act for the relief and protection of American seamen" which, among other things, officially regularized the vocationally specific proto-passports that seafarers had begun carrying after the revolution. Under the act, seafarers who produced proof of US citizenship and a witness, and paid a small fee, would be issued with a "seaman protection certificate" that contained the man's name, age, birthplace or date and place of naturalization, as well as any distinguishing physical marks, such as height, complexion, scars, injuries, or tattoos. But the descriptions were often vague, and that quickly created a market for certificates below deck. It was easy enough for US mariners to obtain one and then sell it to a non-US shipmate for a few dollars or a drink, before simply getting a new one next time they were in port. The real Jonathan Robbins most likely was one of these men. His certificate, issued in 1795, the year before they were standardized, simply described him as "five feet six inches high, and aged about twenty-three years." Nash, according to the *Hermione*'s muster book, was twenty-eight in 1795, and in a British government pamphlet listing the most sought-after mutineers, he was described as "5 feet 10 inches high." The fit was close enough, or at least Nash must have hoped so.[53]

But Judge Bee, the man presiding over Nash's case, was not convinced. For one thing, he wondered why an American named Jonathan Robbins would pretend to be an Irishman called Thomas Nash when being pressed into service onboard a British warship, and then, when arrested in the United States and threatened with extradition, remain in jail for several months without making any mention of this or producing the certificate that allegedly proved his US citizenship? However, even if it was true, and Judge Bee was perfectly willing to grant that possibility, it did not really matter, for by the terms of the treaty with Great Britain, which President Adams himself had asked him to apply, the man's real name, his country of citizenship, and whether or not he was pressed into service were issues "altogether immaterial" to the question at hand. Even if Nash had been the most "respectable citizen of the U. States," given the same circumstances, Bee still would have had to deliver him up to the British. And so he did. Nash was quickly taken to the Jamaica naval station, sentenced to death, and hanged. His corpse was left rotting in a gibbet at the entrance of Port Royal harbor as a brutal reminder that His Majesty's reach was long, and His vengeance terrible.[54]

The Republican opposition in the United States was outraged by the precedent that had been set by the extradition and subsequent execution. It was bad enough, they believed, that the Jay Treaty had failed to bring impressment to an end—that issue, among others, had caused riots up and down the Atlantic seaboard when details of the treaty were first made public in 1795—but no one had thought that the inconspicuous extradition article, which at the time barely received mention, would four years later end up turning the American government itself into a collaborator of the Royal Navy's thuggish press gangs. In a series of anonymous open letters, South Carolina senator Charles Pinckney argued that Jonathan Robbins's extradition under Article 27 of the treaty meant that no American seaman, or any other citizen travelling abroad, would henceforth be safe from impressment, for the British would know that if anyone dared to resist by force, the American government would not step in to protect, aid, or assist them. This seemed very much like a renunciation of American independence. One scandalized newspaper demanded to know "Why did we overthrow the government of good old George?" while another asked: "Spirit of Seventy-Six, whither have ye flown?"[55]

Others wondered where that of Sixty-Nine had gone, for in that year, as a young Boston lawyer, John Adams had been prepared to defend the killing of a British press ganger from the *Rose* as a case of perfectly legal self-defense. But now, thirty years on, the same John Adams as president of the United States was ordering the removal of a man who stood accused of essentially the same crime, to be tried by a British military court. One newspaper accused the president of acting like the hapless Captain Isaac Phillips of the 20-gun *Baltimore,* who the year before had allowed a British officer to board his ship and remove fifty-five men with barely so much as a protest, let alone any form of material resistance. It seemed shocking for a lowly commander to treat his country's sovereignty with such contempt, but for the captain of the good ship United States it was beyond intolerable. He had to be replaced: "The crew of the Federal ship will shortly be piped on deck to choose a new commander," the *Centinel of Freedom* reminded its readers, but the article's author promised that he "would not [be] holding up his hand for John Adams, our present commander." The attacks on Adams eventually peaked with a censure motion in Congress in early 1800, but the attempt was defeated after Representative John Marshall offered a brilliant defense of the president, a feat that fast-tracked Marshall's appointment first to the position of Secretary of State and then to the Supreme Court later that year.[56]

In order to amplify the enormity of the government's crime, the opposition enthusiastically embraced the idea of "the unfortunate Jonathan Robbins," a young American mariner guiltlessly wronged, but like Melville's Billy Budd, unfailingly virtuous even under the most trying circumstances. Robbins was portrayed by Republican journalists as bearing impressment and injustice without complaint, patiently enduring beastly sufferings until finally he struck back with decisive force against his cruel British oppressor. To underscore his role as republican hero and slayer of royalist tyrants, opposition writers outdid each other in describing Captain Pigot's depraved rule onboard the *Hermione* in lurid and obscene detail. *The Times* claimed to know that Pigot, "one of the most cruel monsters that ever disgraced the human form," habitually had two boatswain's mates simultaneously flog the men, that he had the boatswain flog the mates, and that he finally flogged the boatswain, all at the same time. Not to be outdone, *The Democrat* breathlessly recounted that when Pigot's wife asked for a divorce, he, "enraged, accompanied by a part of his crew, seized upon the defenceless fair, carried her on board his ship, and—horrible to relate! stripped her naked, tied her down upon her back, and with a cat o'nine tails in his own hands, compelled every man on board the vessel to offer some indignity to his wife, thus placed!"[57]

Other newspapers began to exaggerate the number of impressed Americans onboard the *Hermione,* and the mutiny soon morphed into a miniature American Revolution. Claiming that between sixty and seventy US seamen participated in the mutiny, the *Otsego Herald; or, Western Advertiser* went on to describe the executions of the officers onboard in grisly detail, and then concluded with the caustic observation that "the cruelty of tyrants sometimes recoils on their heads." A writer for the *Aurora General Advertiser* reported that around two-thirds of the *Hermione*'s crew were impressed Americans, and then confessed that when he had "first heard of the extirpation of the officers of this execrable corsair, he felt that intense satisfaction which every man must feel, who wishes for the liberty of American seamen."[58]

During the late 1790s and early 1800s, the struggle against Britain's continued impressment of American seamen played an important role in articulating the larger meaning of American independence, but also of the racialized nature of American citizenship. In Britain itself, anti-impressment activism was closely intertwined with the growing abolitionist movement—Granville Sharpe, for instance, was among the leaders of both campaigns—but in America the comparison between slavery and impressment was obviously a more delicate matter. And yet, US citizens hurled around condemnations of slavery with surprising ease when it came to the impressment of their fellow citizens, though often they were careful to specify that the comparison they made was with slavery in North Africa, which threatened every American mariner who sailed into the Mediterranean. Many white Americans considered this far worse than their own southern slave system, in part because the idea of being enslaved by a Muslim master was particularly abhorrent to many North American Christians. But more importantly, as slavery in the United States was beginning to be justified with reference to pseudo-scientific theories of racial difference, it seemed perverse that North Africans would enslave people with complete disregard for their color, and even stoop so low as to enslave white people.[59]

Since the American critique of impressment similarly turned on the fact that the British seized whomever they pleased without regard for national citizenship—like race, a category with much purchase in the post-revolutionary United States—it was easy for nationalists in the early republic to harness the growing moral weight of antislavery and conflate British press gangs with Barbary corsairs, and by extension the plight of impressed Americans with that of slaves in general. But the insistence on similarities only went so far, for in contrast to the imagined docility of African-descended slaves in the United States, America's tars were portrayed as almost constitutionally averse to tyranny. Yet such claims only served the purpose of racializing the characteristics required for republican citizenship if, like the imaginary Jonathan Robbins, impressed American seamen were white and native-born, but that was often not the case. When in 1806, for instance, the British *Leopard* famously opened fire on the USS *Chesapeake* to force the surrender of four deserters, three of whom were native-born Americans, it was an inconvenient and therefore frequently unreported fact that two of them—David Martin and William Ware—were African Americans.[60]

Martin and Ware, along with the real Thomas Nash, were in fact typical of the men who labored onboard America's ocean-going ships. Like them, many of those who carried the Stars and Stripes across the oceans were either excluded from US citizenship altogether or they belonged to groups that were marginalized from the community of genuine national citizens, who increasingly were defined as racially white and ideally of "Anglo-Saxon" descent. An 1808 census found that around 60 percent of the US navy's personnel was foreign-born, and that the vast majority of them were Irishmen. Likewise, in the early nineteenth-century American merchant marine, a large and growing proportion of men below deck were foreign-born, and the New England whaling fleet was particularly dependent on the skill and muscle-power of foreign-born and Native American hands. Finally, in both the navy and civilian shipping, African Americans accounted for around 20 percent of most crews.[61]

There was a fair amount of unease amongst the American naval officer corps about the many foreign-born and nonwhite men who served onboard their ships, for it was impossible to know who they were, where they had been, or what kind of ideas and past experiences they might be carrying with them onto the lower deck. It was a distressing thought, for instance, that black sailors who had witnessed or participated in the slave revolts that rocked the Caribbean would find their way onboard US warships, where they might sabotage the nation's seaborne defenses in support of an invasion attempt by "ten thousand blacks and people of color," armed in the French Caribbean and prepared to start a revolutionary race war in America's slave-holding southern states. Such paranoid fears in part explain why time and again orders were issued to exclude nonwhites from the service altogether. In March 1798, Secretary of War James McHenry informed the lieutenant of marines onboard the *Constellation* that "no Negro, Mulatto, or Indian [is] to be enlisted nor any Description of Men except Natives of fair Conduct or Foreigners of unequivocal Characters for Sobriety and Fidelity." A month later, Captain Thomas Truxtun of the *Constellation* urged his lieutenant to "pay particular attention in examining the men you enter, So that none but hale hearty men compose the Crew of this Ship, and the more real Natives you can procure the better." In August of the same year, Benjamin Stoddert, the newly minted Secretary of the Navy, repeated the order that "no Negroes or Mulatoes are to be admitted, and as far as you can judge, you must be cautious to exclude all Persons whose Characters are suspicious."[62]

There is no evidence to indicate that black or foreign-born seamen serving in the US navy actually were any more likely to cause trouble than their white native-born shipmates, and if anything, it might well have been the reverse. White American-born seamen had very high expectations of what a post-revolutionary, republican navy was supposed to be like, and inevitably there was disappointment when it turned out that conditions were not so very different than in the old world's royal navies. The US navy's Articles of War in fact were closely modeled on those that governed Britain's Royal Navy, and they too authorized brutal punishment beatings for minor mistakes. Some of the fleet's early officers, most notably Captain Thomas Truxtun, tried to limit the application of corporal punishments to cases of willful disobedience and mutiny, and when inexperience or simple human error were to blame for a mistake, they frequently granted pardons. But many of the less charismatic or skilled commanders made no such distinctions, and hundreds of men working on American warships were viciously beaten over trivialities.[63]

John Rea, a proudly republican seaman on the USS *George Washington,* was stunned by the brutality that was allowed to exist onboard the ships of the US navy. After he left the service in 1802, Rea published an open letter in which he denounced the dismal conditions he had found onboard, including the constant punishment beatings:

Who could believe that on board of an *American* Ship, carrying but one hundred men, exclusive of officers, in a nine months voyage, upwards of fifty men should be put in irons—upwards of forty *flogged at the gang-way;* amongst whom, *three hundred and sixty-five lashes* were distributed—exclusive of innumerable *rope's-ending's, sword beatings, etc. etc. etc.* And all this, except in one solitary instance (for *theft*) for *eating, drinking, sleeping, missing of muster,* or some other trifling fault, which all men are subject to, and which no *gentleman,* or *humane Officer,* could think of punishing!!

For Rea, the violence itself was not the worst of it. It was the feeling of degradation. And like many seamen at the time, Rea found it particularly unbearable to be brutalized by the *George Washington*'s midshipmen, trainee officers who could be as young as twelve or thirteen years old. "How preposterous does it appear," he cursed, "to have brats of boys, twelve or fifteen years old, who six months before had not even seen salt water, strutting in livery, about a Ship's decks, damning and flashing old experienced sailors!"[64]

Rea's anger at the horrific conditions he encountered in the navy served to invigorate the strength of his republican convictions. To his mind, the American Revolution's outstanding achievement was to have secured the equality of all men, and he therefore was outraged by the class arrogance he found among the officers onboard. As someone whose "family contributed their part in the Revolution," he expected to be treated with the dignity and respect due to a fellow citizen, and not to be beaten up by upper-class children or, as a "freeman," to be ordered around and brutalized by a captain so violent he was "unfit for having command in a Negro-Quarter!" While in response to the tyranny he discovered onboard the *George Washington,* Rea invoked "the main deck of America, where 'all men are equally free,'" his own racial consciousness, and his attempt to appeal to the privileges he imagined were due to his native-born whiteness, gave the lie to that comparison. William Ray, in contrast, who sailed under the same captain as Rea a few years later, emphasized in his autobiography that in his globetrotting experience it did not much matter who you were or where you went—the deck of an American warship, the prisons of North Africa, or even the United States itself—as a poor man of whatever race you were likely to have to fight against tyranny and abject slavery everywhere.[65]

If Rea was inspired by the segregated "main deck of America," Ray's cosmopolitan radicalism was forged on the lower deck, a place far offshore where America's promise of equality perhaps was most fully realized, for here, at least, all races, ethnicities, and nationalities were brutalized with equal vigor. A generation before, that same experience, and the cooperative resistance it engendered, had carried seamen from around the Atlantic world into the port cities of North America to stoke the fires of revolution. But already then, the emerging American ruling class had experienced their participation as profoundly threatening, and processes of distortion and exclusion, through racist public discourse and discriminatory legislation, commenced almost immediately. After the constitutional settlement of 1789 these processes accelerated. Crispus Attucks, famously the first victim of the American Revolution, was remembered, if at all, as white and respectable by the early republican mythmakers of the Revolution, and not for what he really was: a runaway slave and Atlantic sailor of both African and Native American descent.[66]

It is ironic that John Adams, the man who ordered Thomas Nash to be extradited, also defended Crispus Attucks's killers in court almost thirty years before, and to the extent that the Nash-Robbins affair contributed to his defeat in the 1800 presidential election, it may be considered a small token of revenge for the revolutionary Atlantic. But it changed little, for the majority of those who attacked the Adams administration did so in defense of a nationalist fantasy, and by embracing the imaginary Jonathan Robbins, white republican Connecticut tar, they reinforced the vicious xenophobia that made possible the delivery of the real Thomas Nash into the hands of his executioners in the first place. One US newspaper sympathetic to the cause of Irish freedom cursed after the whole affair was over that "the law formerly of the British in Ireland, that killing *a mere Irishman was not murder*," now applied to the United States as well.[67]

The failure of the fleet mutinies to significantly improve the conditions of service, combined with the intensifying counterinsurgency in Ireland and the coerced recruitment of ever more foreign-born workers almost inevitably produced the cycle of treasonous, retributive conspiracies that began with the *Hermione* in September 1797. In 1798, the lower deck's raging discontent briefly found a focus in the movement to secure an Irish republic, but after its failure and yet another intense round of punitive violence, this time accompanied by explicitly xenophobic repression and surveillance, the lower deck's ability to mount large-scale collective resistance collapsed for good. Cowed and terrified by the quarterdeck's superior capacity to inflict violence, and increasingly deprived of safe and welcoming harbors around the Atlantic rim, lower deck malcontents tried to keep their mouths shut and their heads down. They were not always successful. Acts of individual provocation and violence increased after 1797–98, often as a result of alcohol-fueled desperation. In 1800 and 1801, a few, mostly small, vessels with disproportionately large numbers of foreign-born men onboard were successfully seized by their crews and taken into enemy ports, but these too were desperate acts of escape, with no trace of the sophisticated, transnational radicalism that had flourished below deck in 1797–98.[68]

Conclusion: The Marine Republic

In civilizations without boats, dreams dry up,
espionage takes the place of adventure,
and the police take the place of pirates.

—MICHEL FOUCAULT,
"Of Other Spaces" (1986)

IN 1794, THOMAS SPENCE, who had just been released from prison on a charge of high treason, published "The Marine Republic," a short allegorical origin story about an island he called Spensonia, a place where property was held in common, the political structure democratic, and the population prosperous, tolerant, and cosmopolitan. One day, the story went, an old man called together his sons and gave them a "gallant ship," not to one of them, or to just a select few, but to all of them, to own and sail as common property. They were to elect officers from amongst themselves and replace them whenever necessary. Every man who worked onboard the ship was to be paid regularly and fairly "according to station and agreement," and all profits remaining after wages and expenses had been subtracted were to be shared equally among the crew. The sons lived by these principles and prospered. But England's monarchical government weighed heavily on their minds, and together with their families they decided to sail for America in the hope of finding a more egalitarian and equitable form of government there. They never made it. Their ship, somewhere out in the Atlantic, sailed into a storm, was tossed about and eventually wrecked on an uninhabited island, which turned out to have "luxurious soil and agreeable climate." They decided to stay. They broke up their ship to build houses, and they began to cultivate the land. And they adopted the "Marine Constitution," declaring "the property of the island to be the property of them all collectively in the same manner as the ship had been, and that they ought to share the profits thereof in the same way. The island they named Spensonia, after the name of the ship which their father had given them."[1]

Spence was one of the most radical members of the English democratic movement, and one of the founding members of the modern communist tradition. The great concern of his life was the realization of his "land plan," a plan for the expropriation of all landlords and the reestablishment of the commons. So why then did he choose to speak about a marine republic? Why a story about ships and islands when he dreamed of a global confederation of democratic, agrarian, parish communes? Genre is part of the answer. Spence read widely in the history of political thought, a history in which maritime imagery crops up repeatedly, from Plato and Aristotle in ancient Greece, Horace in Augustan Rome, to James Harrington and John Locke in early modern England. As political philosophers who came from societies intimately connected to the sea, but who often had no experience of seafaring themselves, the appeal of such imagery was its intuitive simplicity. It was easy to deploy ships as metaphors for purely political societies, in which the existence of captain and crew seemed determined by the requirements of the physical environment itself, and not by a history of struggle between contending social classes. Self-contained and isolated, apparently devoid of productive activity, ships were a perfect canvas on which to project theories of government that presupposed as natural the existence of ruler and ruled.[2]

But Spence knew better. He knew, in contrast to the political philosophers, that social relations onboard ship were not purely political, but were produced by a history of expropriation and struggle. He understood that common seamen had once shared in the ownership of the ship, and only when they lost that share and had become wage-dependent drudges did they acquire "the desperate, careless, and reprobate character" which was essentialized into the degrading stereotype of jolly Jack Tar in England, Jan Maat in the Low Countries, and Jean Matelot in France. Spence knew all of this, because he had spent his life around sailors. He was born in Newcastle, home to the fiercely combative sailors of the North Sea collier fleet, where he remained until the age of thirty-eight. In 1788, he moved to London, where thousands of sailors from all the world's seagoing nations clogged the streets of the neighborhoods in which Spence set up shop as a bookseller. In his writings, he returned again and again to the plight of common seamen, but also to the world-transformative promise of their struggles. In early 1795, as press gangs tore through London's sailortown and were met with rioting crowds nearly everywhere they went, Spence published a treatise that likened the condition of naval war-workers to that of enslaved Africans and argued for the legality and moral justice of armed resistance. The same year, he serialized a history of the 1647 Neapolitan Revolution led by Masaniello, a simple fisherman. In 1797, he supported the fleet mutineers and later compared their struggle to the great revolutions in America and France.[3]

The comparison was not absurd. The 1790s were the Atlantic's great age of mutiny, a period of such widespread lower deck unrest that it would remain unrivalled in significance and political sophistication until the great sailor revolts at Kiel, Kronstadt, and Sevastopol in the era of communist revolution more than century later. In France, where the lower deck's insurrectionary movement began, unrest was initially slow to jump from shore to ship. But in early December 1789, when the central state's authority collapsed in the war-port of Toulon, mutiny rapidly whipped through and destabilized the network of warships, squadrons, fleets, and naval stations that upheld French imperial authority overseas.

What began as a chaotic eruption of stored-up discontent quickly developed into a set of sophisticated political ideas and practices that might be called revolutionary maritime republicanism. For example, when in April 1793 the crews of the frigates *Melpomene* and *Minerve* demanded to be given shore leave in Toulon, their protest no longer took the form of unruly assemblies or groveling petitions. Instead, they wrote round robins, a type of petition with disputed origins, but which by the late eighteenth century had come to be strongly associated with the oppositional culture of deep-sea mariners. On round robin petitions, signatures were not added in columns, but in a large circle that made it impossible to determine who had signed first and who had come last. This was an especially useful erasure of hierarchy onboard warships, for depending on a captain's whim, collective petitioning could be treated as a form of mutiny and punished with the death penalty. However, most navies' judicial systems were unwilling to recognize and therefore unable to prosecute a collective subject, and it was therefore always of the utmost importance to identify and isolate individual ringleaders. Round robins were a pragmatic form of self-defense against that effort. But considering that individual signatures were not really necessary at all, its particular form also expressed a confident solidarity that reflected the experience of individual courage, mutual dependence, and collective strength that was, and always had been, a foundational element of maritime working-class culture.[4]

Reflecting the extent to which that culture after 1789 had come to be integrated with ideas drawn from contemporary revolutionary republican-

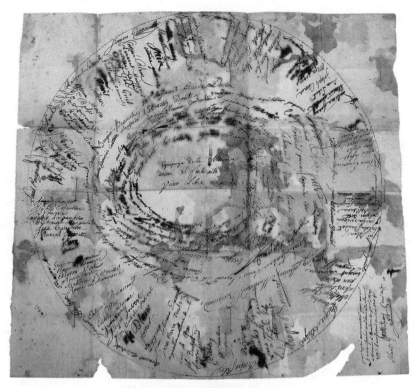

FIGURE 9. The *Minerve* crew's round robin petition. Source: Service Historique de la Défense (Marine), Toulon, Institutions de répression, Cour martial maritime, Procédures et interrogatoires, 1792-An II, 4O1. Photograph by Phil Deloole.

ism, the crew of the *Melpomene* addressed their round robin to "citizens, brothers, and friends," and matter-of-factly referred to themselves as "the *sans-culottes* composing the crew of the Melpomene." Like their comrades onboard the *Minerve,* they also decorated their round robin with the slogans "Union and Fraternity" and "Live Free or Die," which expressed values that were dear to revolutionary republican and seaman alike. The repeated invocation of fraternity, first in the address, then in the slogan, is especially significant. Along with liberty and equality, it was one of the core values of the broader revolutionary movement, which, despite the gendered nature of the language, expressed solidarity with the entire human race as a first step in realizing the dream of a universal republic. But it was also a value that resonated in particular with seamen who—torn from home, scattered across the world, and thrown together in close confinement with men from many nations—frequently emphasized their shared occupational identity by referring to each other as "brother tars." But in contrast to the landed revolutionaries' often only principled embrace of fraternity, the "brotherhood of the sea" was a lived experience that embraced the whole community of seafarers and enabled men to easily crisscross linguistic, national, and imperial boundaries as they moved between different ships and navies. On the level of individual ships, it expressed itself in the creation of "fictive kinship" networks that were especially strong if a crew had gone through combat together. These bonds were invaluable before, during, and after a mutiny when the strength of a crew's solidarity might mean the difference between life and death.[5]

Liberty was another revolutionary demand that resonated especially strongly with sailors. For them, liberty meant shore leave, the brief moments when they escaped from coercion, constant supervision, twenty-four-hour work cycles, and the terroristic discipline of the lash. When revolutionaries spoke of tyranny, the horrors of slavery, and the blessings of liberty, sailors knew better than most what they were talking about. The denial of shore leave, the lack of liberty that kept hundreds of malnourished, overworked, and bored men cooped up in a tiny space for months and years was also one of the most important reasons why epidemic disease repeatedly tore through the lower deck and left thousands of victims in its wake. When the crews of the *Minerve* and the *Melpomene* therefore proclaimed "Liberty or Death," it was not just a threat, but also a simple statement of fact.

The ever-present danger of death, and perhaps in equal measure the likely prospect of inflicting it upon others, contributed to the enthusiasm with which naval seamen embraced the ideas of consent and popular sovereignty. Crews in the Batavian navy, perhaps because they were all volunteers and to a large part made up of long-distance migrant workers, of whom many had previously served under different flags and would eventually go on to serve under yet others, were especially prone to justify mutiny by arguing that the post-revolutionary change of flags had invalidated their prior agreement of service. They had not given their consent to serving the Batavian Republic, and therefore would not consider themselves bound by the Articles of War, the bare-bones constitutional framework derived from martial law that governed life at sea.[6]

A similar attitude emerged among seamen in the British navy, especially in the second half of the decade when large numbers of formerly Dutch-employed sailors flooded onto its ships. During the mutiny at the Nore, the swearing of individual oaths became a critical constitutional ritual that formally marked a crew's entry into the floating republic. After witnessing the importance that Nore mutineers placed on the swearing of these public oaths, Admiral Lord Keith, who was formally in command of the ships at the Nore, suggested that from now on all seamen, before receiving their pay, should be forced to sign an oath of allegiance to the king. "This I recommend," he wrote, "upon the suggestion that many of the Mutineers seem to feel the Impression of the illegal Oath they had taken to be true to the Mutineers' Cause, but none had ever been tendered to them on the part of the King or His Majesty's Government, and this Class of Men are in general too ill-informed to understand that all Subjects owe Allegiance from their birth."[7]

It is entirely possible that Lord Keith may really have found the ideas of popular sovereignty and consent to be too absurd to comprehend, but the lower deck was not under any kind of misapprehension as to whom they owed allegiance and why. First and foremost, they were true to each other, but increasingly, first in the French navy, then in the British, they also developed a sense of collectively acting on behalf of the nation, which to them was embodied not by the sovereign but by the people as a whole. They understood that the control of fire power not only gave them strength to pursue their own interests but also imposed a responsibility to act with care on behalf of the people on shore, and that responsibility they treated with obvious respect. In the British navy, mutineers at both Spithead and the Nore repeatedly issued long explanations of their actions "to their fellow subjects on shore," but never to their commanders, the Admiralty, or the king, to whom they only ever issued demands. Similarly, French seamen repeatedly overrode orders if they thought them not in accordance with the wishes of the French people, even when such orders served the sailors' own immediate interests.

The reorientation towards new collective sources of political authority on land was accompanied by the final decline of authoritarian paternalism at sea. After half a century of increasing militarization that tended to reduce everyone onboard to their formal function, personal dependency relations that previously had fostered a sense of vertical crew cohesion were replaced by a deepening division of shipboard society into two sharply defined and opposing classes that found its most striking expression in the adoption of the red flag as a symbol of permanent struggle between them. But class war never replaced the war between nations. Outright anti-war mutinies were exceedingly rare, and there were only few instances of crews refusing to enter combat. That ought not to be surprising. Most navies authorized officers to execute men on the spot who refused to fight, and once cannonballs started to fly it would have been suicide not to fire back. Moreover, among the native-born members of a crew, which in the French navy was the overwhelming majority and in the British navy usually around half of a ship's company, many were willing to fight both against their own officer corps and against their nation's enemies, especially if, as in the case of French and British mariners, a century of near-incessant conflict had created a culture of enmity that was passed down from generation to generation within their respective communities.

It probably was not a coincidence that only in the Batavian navy, with its huge number of foreign-born men, did officers have persistent problems getting their men to fight. In 1796, the squadron sent to secure the Cape of Good Hope colony surrendered to the British navy without firing a single shot after violent mutinies had broken out on several of the ships and the officer corps had become convinced that their men were as likely to fire on them as on the enemy if the order to prepare for combat was given. Across the Atlantic, on the Surinam station, another squadron collapsed as low morale, miserable conditions, and high-handed, arrogant leadership triggered one mass escape after another, and also several murder plots. In the home command, things looked much the same. In 1799, yet another fleet surrendered to the British amidst a violent, chaotic mass mutiny near the Texel anchorage. It marked the final collapse of Batavian naval power.

In the French navy, where the revolution wreaked most of its havoc before the war even started, lower deck unrest did not have quite so direct an impact on the war effort. Even so, it remains significant that the only battle in which the French republican fleet distinguished itself—the Battle of 13 Prairial in Year II, or as it became known in Great Britain, the Glorious First of June, 1794—was waged at a time when the lower deck's political aspirations were most closely aligned with those of the central government. Notwithstanding the profound disagreements between Jacobin authoritarianism and the decentralized democratic aspirations of French lower deck republicanism, adherents of both were genuinely dedicated to the defense of the revolutionary republic and agreed on the importance of confronting the Royal Navy, the seaborne battering ram of the European counter-revolution. Even the names of the ships that met that day signaled the revolutionary nature of the conflict: while the British sent into battle the *Caesar,* the *Queen,* the *Royal George,* the *Royal Sovereign,* the *Majestic,* and the *Queen Charlotte,* the French met them with the *Tyrannicide,* the *Jacobin,* the *Patriote,* the *Republicain,* the *Montagne,* the *America,* the *Juste,* and, most famous of all, the *Vengeur du Peuple.*

Despite crippling material constraints that made defeat in the battle almost inevitable, an overwhelming majority of French seamen were willing to sacrifice themselves for the good of the republic in 1794. But that was a fleeting moment, and as the French republic decayed into a new empire, the lower deck's willingness to suffer and kill on its behalf went into steep decline. So did its appetite for collective action. Ever since December 1789, French lower deck unrest had been oriented towards the state, part of the broad struggle to rebuild the French Atlantic empire on a new constitutional foundation, republican and ideally democratic. After the fall of the Jacobin republic brought that effort to an end, lower deck malcontents apparently no longer saw much political use in mutiny and returned, with force and *en masse,* to the age-old remedy of desertion instead. While the privateering fleet soaked up some of the revolutionary fervor that drained from the navy after 1794, especially in the Lesser Antilles where Victor Hugues oversaw a ferocious squadron of privateers crewed in large parts by recently liberated slaves, for the remainder of the war French seamen mostly disappeared from the Atlantic as a significant political or military force. It would take another eleven years before French naval power was crushed for good at Battle of Trafalgar in October 1805, but that was only a delayed confirmation of a collapse that had begun long before.[8]

In contrast to their demoralized counterparts across the Channel, British lower deck insurgents never struggled over the state and the nature of its power at sea, but instead waged a campaign for better working conditions that initially remained within, but eventually pointed beyond the established order, both in England and abroad. With this came a cycle of increasingly hostile and violent conflicts with the state and its local representatives onboard ship, but it never seriously threatened the fleet's capacity to carry out major operations. By the time the war drew to a temporary close in fall of 1801, officers and crews had fought each other to a lopsided stalemate.

On the one hand, when news of peace triggered the usual mutinies to demand the rapid demobilization of crews, courts-martial reacted with severe violence. Following a failed and explicitly peaceful conspiracy to seize the *Syren* and sail home to England in early 1802, seven men were sentenced to death, and four to be flogged around the fleet with three hundred lashes each. Some months later, the crew of the *Gibraltar* got together in a disorderly assembly and "said they wanted to go home. They had been a long while out, and it was now twelve months since the peace had been concluded." For that, two men were sentenced to death, and the captain was relieved of his com-

FIGURE 10. British political cartoon, "The Balance of Justice" (1802), depicts the imbalance of class justice: one dead governor weighs as much as thirteen dead sailors. Courtesy of The Trustees of the British Museum.

mand for not having secured more ringleaders to prosecute. More dramatically still, after crews onboard several ships anchored in Bantry Bay refused to sail to the West Indies in December 1801, and also began to put in place some of the self-governing institutions that had flourished at the Nore, fourteen men were arrested, and six of them promptly hanged.[9]

On the other hand, just five days after the Bantry Bay mutineers were executed at Spithead, the former acting governor of Gorée Island, Joseph Wall, stood trial at the Old Bailey on a charge of having imposed, in 1782, an unlawful punishment for mutiny that led to a man being beaten to death with eight hundred lashes. The timing of the trial was a coincidence, but popular anger at the killing of the Bantry Bay mutineers nonetheless made it impossible to engineer a pardon for Wall after he was convicted of murder. And so he hanged as well. It undoubtedly represented a shift in the balance of class forces that members of the imperial elite now considered it necessary to sacrifice one of their own to counterbalance the killing of six commoners. But at the same time, it also established in the minds of many a brutal exchange rate that officially fixed the death of one officer convicted of murder as the equivalent value of half a dozen dead mutineers whose only crime had been the demand to return home after almost a decade of coerced service at sea. After so many years of struggle for decent conditions and respect, this was an ambiguous victory at best.[10]

Thomas Spence was unable to participate in the popular agitation surrounding the executions of Governor Wall and the Bantry Bay mutineers, for he was back in prison on a sentence of seditious libel after the House of Commons' Committee of Secrecy had accused him of agitating for "a beautiful and powerful new republic . . . to be effected by a general Insurrection of the People, for which the Revolutionary Outrages in France, and the Mutiny in our own Fleet, were held out as laudable Examples." In reality, Spence had gone even further than that. Admonishing the people of England to "talk no more of impossibilities," he proclaimed the fleet mutinies to be not just an example but a model of popular insurrection for them to follow. What especially had impressed him was the ability of the mutineers to turn social relations completely on their head simply by making the collective decision to ignore their officers' authority. Once that decision had been made, all of their power vanished, and that without any of the violence that had accompanied the revolution in France. Spence thought that given the relative number of officers onboard ship, and the terrifying powers of discipline lodged in their hands, a "mutiny on land" should be even easier to accomplish, since landlords were far fewer in number and did not enjoy the luxury of martial law to prop up their rule.[11]

For Spence, a true revolution meant "the restoration of society to its natural state," the reclamation of lost rights and liberties, and the reestablishment of the commons. And that is what he saw when he looked out into the revolutionary, mutinous Atlantic. From the hesitant struggles in the French fleet during the first few months of the revolution to the "floating republic" at the Nore, naval mutineers in 1790s drew on traditions of maritime egalitarianism that were centuries old, that had survived often deeply submerged and only as memories of what once had been. And yet, the world of the 1790s was far from the one envisioned by Spence. Those who were fed up with Europe's tyrannical governments could no longer hope for asylum in America, as the extradition of Thomas Nash, the Alien and Sedition Acts, and the blistering xenophobia and racism of the early republic made clear. Nor could they hope to be castaway on an uninhabited Atlantic island, as Spence's "marine republicans" had been, for most those were covered in plantations worked by enslaved Africans. Even the South Pacific, where the *Bounty* mutineers so recently had found a refuge, was rapidly turning into Britain's very own carceral archipelago. With symbolism that hardly could have been more dispiriting, less than a decade after the mutiny on the *Bounty,* naval mutineers were among the first convicts to be sent to the penal colony in New South Wales.[12]

The solidarity of the men below deck remained strong, but their inability to escape from under the lash and the unrestrained violence of the quarterdeck also kept them on the defensive. At the end of the revolutionary 1790s, the back of lower deck insurrectionism had been broken. Individuals could run away, and they did so in large numbers. But wherever they went, they were likely to find conditions that were as dismal and repressive as those they had left behind. Mutinies continued to erupt now and again for the remainder of the war, but not until the era of communist revolution did sailors once again feel strong enough to seize control of whole fleets, run up the red flag, and force their rulers to confront the mutinous spirit of the marine republic.

ABBREVIATIONS

AN (F)	Archives Nationales, Paris, France
KrA (S)	Krigsarkivet, Stockholm, Sweden
LMA (UK)	London Metropolitan Archives, United Kingdom
NA (NL)	Nationaal Archief, The Hague, The Netherlands
NA (I)	National Archives, Dublin, Ireland
NMM (UK)	National Maritime Museum, Greenwich, United Kingdom
RA (DK)	Rigsarkivet, Copenhagen, Denmark
SHM-T (F)	Service Historique de la Défense (Marine), Toulon, France
SHM-V (F)	Service Historique de la Défense (Marine), Vincennes, France
TNA (UK)	The National Archives, Kew, United Kingdom

NOTES

INTRODUCTION: LIKE A SHIP ON FIRE

1. On the Royal Navy outkilling its enemies, see Adam Nicolson, *Men of Honour: Trafalgar and the Making of an English Hero* (London: HarperCollins, 2005), 20. For a description of Camperdown, see William James, *The Naval History of Great Britain, from the Declaration of War by France, in February 1793; to the Accession of George IV, in January 1820* (London: Baldwin, Cradock, and Joy, 1822), 2:75–89; and Christopher Lloyd, *St. Vincent and Camperdown* (New York: Macmillan, 1963), 133–157.

2. For the Saldanha Bay surrender, see Conclusions of the council of war, 16 August 1796, NA (NL), Hoge Militaire Rechtspraak, 1795–1813 (1818), 2.01.11, inv. nr. 221. For Dutch mutineers fighting on the British side at Camperdown, see Letter, Capt. Lieut. Ruijsch to Vice-Admiral de Winter, 12 July 1797, NA (NL), Departement van Marine, 1795–1813, 2.01.29.01, inv. nr. 236.

3. For the British spy report, see Letter, John Mitchell, Hamburg, 19 May 1797, TNA (UK) ADM 1/4172. For the *Hector,* see Letter, Vice-Admiral Raders to the Committee for Naval Affairs, Texel, 9 October 1797, NA (NL), Departement van Marine, 1795–1813, 2.01.29.01, inv. nr. 237. For the *Vrijheid* and *Kortenaar,* see Report, Vice-Admiral de Winter, 4 October 1797, NA (NL), Departement van Marine, 1795–1813, 2.01.29.01, inv. nr. 236.

4. The most up-to-date overview of the fleet mutinies is Ann Veronica Coats and Philip MacDougall, eds., *The Naval Mutinies of 1797: Unity and Perseverance* (Woodbridge: Boydell Press, 2011). For British mutineers fleeing to the Batavian Republic and joining the Dutch navy, see Extract from a letter from Gravesend, 26 July 1797, forwarded to Evan Nepean, TNA (UK) ADM 1/4173; and Report, Vice-Admiral de Winter, 4 October 1797, NA (NL), Departement van Marine, 1795–1813, 2.01.29.01, inv. nr. 236.

5. For the cultural politics surrounding the celebrations after Camperdown, see Timothy Jenks, *Naval Engagements: Patriotism, Cultural Politics, and the Royal Navy, 1793–1815* (New York: Oxford University Press, 2006), 109–123; Holger

Hoock, *Empires of the Imagination: Politics, War, and the Arts in the British World, 1750–1850* (London: Profile, 2010), 132–161; and J. E. Cookson, *The British Armed Nation, 1793–1815* (Oxford: Clarendon Press, 1997), 214–222.

6. For Plato's comment and the trope of the ship of state, see Plato, *The Republic* (Cambridge: Cambridge University Press, 2000), 191–192; and David Keyt, "Plato and the Ship of State," in *The Blackwell Guide to Plato's Republic,* ed. Gerasimos Santas (Malden, MA: Blackwell, 2006), 189–213. For broad surveys of the use of the trope, see Eckart Schäfer, "Das Staatsschiff. Zur Präzision eines Topos," in *Toposforschung: Eine Dokumentation,* ed. Peter Jehn (Frankfurt: Athenäum, 1972), 259–292; and Helmut Quaritsch, "Das Schiff als Gleichnis," in *Recht über See: Festschrift. Rolf Stödter zum 70. Geburtstag am 22. April 1979,* ed. Hans Peter Ipsen and Karl-Hartmann Necker (Heidelberg: R.v. Decker's Verlag, G. Schenk, 1979), 2702–2772.

7. Frans Michael Franzén, "En blick på det adertonde seklet. Vid magister-promotionen i Åbo, 1798," in *Skaldestycken* (Örebro: M. N. Lindh, 1828), 2:161; my translation of the poem is based on David Kirby, *The Baltic World 1772–1993: Europe's Northern Periphery in an Age of Change* (New York: Routledge, 1999), 29–30; for background on Franzén's travels, see Juha Manninen, "Frans Michael Franzén och franska revolutionen," *Historisk tidskrift för Finland* 74, no. 1 (1989): 31–64. For Herder, see Bernhard Suphan, ed., *Herders Sämmtliche Werke* (Berlin: Weidmannsche Buchhandlung, 1883), 18:315. See also Hans Blumenberg, *Shipwreck with Spectator: Paradigm of a Metaphor for Existence* (Cambridge, MA: MIT Press, 1997), 44–47.

8. Plato, *The Laws,* ed. Malcolm Schofield (Cambridge: Cambridge University Press, 2016), 140–141; Yves Charbit, "The Platonic City: History and Utopia," *Populations* 57, no. 2 (2002): 219–212, 227–228; Aristotle, *The Politics and The Constitution of Athens,* ed. Stephen Everson (Cambridge: Cambridge University Press, 1996), 174–175. On the egalitarian culture of European maritime communities, see Karel Davids, "Seamen's Organization and Social Protest in Europe, c. 1300–1825," *International Review of Social History* 39, 52 (1994): 145–169.

9. On the reemergence of Aristotelian thinking in regard to the sea in early modern Europe, see Jonathan Scott, *When the Waves Ruled Britannia: Geography and Political Identities, 1500–1800* (New York: Cambridge University Press, 2011).

10. On maritime radicalism in the American Revolution, see Peter Linebaugh and Marcus Rediker, *The Many-Headed Hydra: Slaves, Sailors, Commoners, and the Hidden History of the Revolutionary Atlantic* (Boston: Beacon, 2000), 211–248. For the role of port cities specifically in the American Revolution, see Benjamin Carp, *Rebels Rising: Cities and the American Revolution* (New York: Oxford University Press, 2009). On the role of anti-impressment resistance in the coming of the American Revolution, see Christopher P. Magra, *Poseidon's Curse: British Naval Impressment and the Atlantic Origins of the American Revolution* (New York: Cambridge University Press, 2016).

11. Herman Melville, *Billy Budd, Sailor, and Other Stories* (Harmondsworth: Penguin, 1970), 333.

1. Johan Schedvin, "Den 26. nov," in "Journal förd om bord på kongliga svenska fregatten Eurydice. Under en sjöresa 1793," Sjöhistoriska Museet, Stockholm, SE/SSHM/SME/75; *The Annual Register, or a View of the History, Politics, and Literature, for the Year 1793. A New Edition* (London: Baldwin, Cradock, and Joy, 1821), chronicle, 54; Paul Cottin, *Toulon et les Anglais en 1793, d'après des documents inédits* (Paris: Paul Ollendorff, 1898), 178–179.

2. Schedvin, "Den 26. nov,"; *Annual Register,* chronicle, 54–55.

3. On warships, see Nicholas Blake, *Steering for Glory: A Day in the Life of a Ship of the Line* (London: Chatham, 2005), 8; and Noel Mostert, *The Line Upon the Wind: The Great War at Sea, 1793–1815* (New York: W.W. Norton, 2007), 64. On the *Boyne* and *Queen Charlotte,* see John Knox Laughton, ed., *Journal of Rear-Admiral Bartholomew James, 1752–1828* (London: Navy Records Society, 1896), 273–274; and William O.S. Gilly, *Narratives of Shipwrecks of the Royal Navy: Between 1793 and 1849,* 2nd ed. (London: John W. Parker, 1851), 2, 36–40.

4. Cottin, *Toulon et les Anglais,* 168–178.

5. "Genoa, Oct. 9," in *Evening Mail* issue 734 (November 4–6, 1793); Laurent Lautard, *Esquisses historiques: Marseille depuis 1789 jusqu'en 1815* (Marseille: Marius Olive, 1844), 357–358; National Convention, session of 25 Frimaire Year II/15 December 1793, in Jérôme Mavidal et al., eds., *Archives parlementaires de 1787 à 1860 recueil complet des débats législatifs et politiques des chambres françaises* (Paris: Librairie administrative de P. Dupont, 1862), 81:514–515.

6. Schedvin, "Juldagen" and "Den 27 dec."

7. On the causes of the war against Russia, see Göran Rydstad, "1788: Varför krig? Något om bakgrund och 'orsaker' till Gustav III:s ryska krig," in *Gustav III:s ryska krig,* ed. Gunnar Artéus (Stockholm: Probus, 1992), 9-22; for the course of the war, see Claes Bernes, *Segelfartygens tid* (Stockholm: Medströms Bokförlag, 2008), 80-117.

8. Schedvin, "Den 30. Aug."

9. Jan Glete, *Navies and Nations: Warships, Navies and State Building in Europe and America, 1500–1860* (Stockholm: Almqvist and Wiksell, 1993), 2:311; Martine Acerra and Jean Meyer, *Marines et révolution* (Rennes: Éditions Ouest-France, 1988), 55–93; Jean Meyer, "Forces navales et puissances économiques," in *Seamen in Society/Gens de mer en société,* ed. Paul Adam (Perthes: Commission internationale d'histoire maritime, 1980), section 2:78.

10. On Dutch manning problems, see Jaap R. Bruijn, *The Dutch Navy of the Seventeenth and Eighteenth Centuries* (Columbia: University of South Carolina Press, 1993), 195–196. On French and British shortages, see Meyer, "Forces navales," section 2:78–79.

11. For an overview of the North Atlantic's early modern maritime labor market, see Paul C. van Royen, Jaap R. Bruijn, and Jan Lucassen, eds., *"Those Emblems of Hell?" European Sailors and the Maritime Labour Market, 1570–1870 (Research in*

Maritime History No. 13) (St. John's, Newfoundland: International Maritime Economic History Association, 1997).

12. Denver Brunsman, *The Evil Necessity: British Naval Impressment in the Eighteenth-Century Atlantic World* (Charlottesville: University of Virginia Press, 2013). Schedvin, "Den 28. augusti."

13. On anti-impressment resistance, see Nicholas Rogers, *The Press Gang: Naval Impressment and Its Opponents in Georgian Britain* (London: Continuum, 2007), 37–58. On the role of broadly shared anti-impressment sentiment in the coming of the American Revolution, see Christopher P. Magra, *Poseidon's Curse: British Naval Impressment and the Atlantic Origins of the American Revolution* (New York: Cambridge University Press, 2016). On Britain's long-term strategic plan, see Daniel A. Baugh, "Withdrawing from Europe: Anglo-French Maritime Geopolitics, 1750–1800," *The International History Review* 20, no. 1 (1998): 1–32. For Richardson and the town of Shields, see Spencer Childers, ed., *A Mariner of England: An Account of the Career of William Richardson from Cabin Boy in the Merchant Service to Warrant Officer in the Royal Navy, as Told by Himself* (London: John Murray, 1908), 121.

14. For the legal context of foreign seamen in Britain, see Sara Caputo, "Alien Seamen in the British Navy, British Law, and the British State, c. 1793–1815," *The Historical Journal* 62, no. 3 (2019): 685–707. On the *Hermione* crew, see *Hermione* muster book, April to July 1797, TNA (UK) ADM 36/12011; *Adventure* muster book, January to February 1797, TNA (UK) ADM 36/12931; *Success* muster book, December 1796 to September 1797, TNA (UK) ADM 36/14745. For the average proportion of foreign-born men in the British navy, see N. A. M. Rodger, "Shipboard Life in the Old Navy: The Decline of the Old Order?," in *The North Sea: Twelve Essays on the Social History of Maritime Labour,* ed. Lewis R. Fischer, Harald Hamre, Poul Holm, and Jaap R. Bruijn (Stavanger: Stavanger Maritime Museum/The Association of North Sea Societies, 1992), 29–30. On crew composition in the Dutch navy, see Karel Davids, "Maritime Labour in the Netherlands, 1570–1870," in *"Those Emblems of Hell?,"* ed. Royen, Bruijn, and Lucassen, 49–50.

15. On *zielverkopers,* see Hugo Landheer, "Een maandceelhouder en zijn klanten: De Amsterdamse logementhouder Hendrik Klaver," *Holland: Historisch Tijdschrift* 45, nos. 3–4 (2013): 137–145; and Christian van Bochove and Ton van Velzen, "Loans to Salaried Employees: The Case of the Dutch East India Company, 1602–1794," *European Review of Economic History* 18, no. 1 (2014): 19–38.

16. On migration patterns, see Jelle van Lottum, "Some Thoughts about Migration of Maritime Workers in the Eighteenth-Century North Sea Region," *International Journal of Maritime History* 27, no. 4 (2015): 647–661. On declining conditions in the Dutch navy, see Bruijn, *The Dutch Navy,* 120–126, 170–183. On the *Kortenaar,* see Letter from Captain van Grootenray to Admiral de Winter, 14 July 1799, NA (NL), 2.01.29.01, inv. nr. 236.

17. On Dutch recruitment of foreign labor, see Jelle van Lottum, Jan Lucassen and Lex Heerma van Voss, "Sailors, National and International Labour Markets and National Identity, 1600–1850," in *Shipping and Economic Growth,* ed. Richard W. Unger (Leiden: Brill, 2011), 321–323. On "lascars," see Aaron Jaffer, *Lascars and*

Indian Ocean Seafaring, 1780–1860: Shipboard Life, Unrest, and Mutiny (Woodbridge: Boydell Press, 2015); and Michael H. Fisher, "Working across the Seas: Indian Maritime Labourers in India, Britain, and in Between, 1600–1857," *International Review of Social History* 51, S14 (2006), 21–45. On "black jacks" in the Royal Navy, see Charles R. Foy, "The Royal Navy's Employment of Black Mariners and Maritime Workers, 1754–1783," *International Journal of Maritime History* 28, no. 1 (2016): 6–35. For a broader overview, see W. Jeffrey Bolster, *Black Jacks: African American Seamen in the Age of Sail* (Cambridge, MA: Harvard University Press, 1997).

18. On naval service as a path to freedom, see Charles R. Foy, "'Unkle Sommerset's' Freedom: Liberty in England for Black Sailors," *Journal for Maritime Research* 13, no. 1 (2011): 21–36. More broadly, on the sea and African American freedom struggles, see Julius S. Scott, *The Common Wind: Afro-American Currents in the Age of the Haitian Revolution* (Brooklyn, NY: Verso, 2018).

19. Schedvin, "Den 27. aug."

20. For the *système des classes,* see Terry Crowdy, *French Warship Crews, 1789–1805: From the French Revolution to Trafalgar* (Botley: Osprey, 2005), 10–11; Eugene L. Asher, *The Resistance to the Maritime Classes: The Survival of Feudalism in the France of Colbert* (Berkeley: University of California Press, 1960), 9–15.

21. On the benefits awarded to classed seamen, see Asher, *Resistance,* 11–13. On punishments, see Etienne Taillemite, *Histoire ignorée de la Marine française* (Paris: Perrin, 2003), 95–100; on "galley slavery," see André Zysberg, "Les gens de mer et l'état: La mobilisation navale en Europe," in *The Sea in History: The Early Modern World,* ed. Christian Buchet and Gérard Le Bouëdec (Woodbridge: Boydell Press, 2017), 827–829.

22. On maritime borderlands populations, see T.J.A. Le Goff, "Problèmes de recrutement de la Marine française pendant la Guerre de Sept Ans," *Revue Historique* 283, no. 2 (574) (1990): 208–209; and "Les gens de mer devant le système de classes (1755–1763): Resistance ou passivité?" *Revue du Nord,* special series, no. 1 (1986): 463–479. Henri Lauvergne, *Choléra-Morbus en Provence* (Toulon: Aurel, 1836), 17, 22.

23. Maurice Loir, *La Marine royale en 1789* (Paris: Armand Colin, 1892), 33–41.

24. On resistance to conscription, see Le Goff, "Les gens de mer," 466–472.

25. On the composition of French crews, see T.J.A. Le Goff, "Les origines sociales des gens de mer français au XVIIIe siècle," in *La France d'Ancien Régime: Études réunies en l'honneur de Pierre Goubert* (Toulouse: Privat, 1984), 367–380. On the transformation of deep-sea shipping, see T.J.A. Le Goff, "Offre et productivité de la main d'œuvre dans les armaments français au 18éme siècle," in *Seamen in Society,* 104–105; Jari Ojala, Jaakko Pehkonen, and Jari Eloranta, "Deskilling and Decline in Skill Premium during the Age of Sail: Swedish and Finnish Seamen, 1751–1913," *Explorations in Economic History* 61 (2016): 85–94. Despite the relative decline in skill levels, deep-sea shipping was comparatively a high-skill industry: see Jelle van Lottum and Jan Luiten van Zanden, "Labour Productivity and Human Capital in the European Maritime Sector of the Eighteenth Century," *Explorations in Economic History* 53, Supplement C (2014): 83–100.

26. On the growth of warships, see Meyer, "Forces navales," 80. On the *Scipio*, see C. G. Evertsen to the committee for naval affairs, 30 July 1797, NA (NL), Departement van Marine, 1795–1813, 2.01.29.01, inv. nr. 236. On landsmen in the British navy, see J. S. Bromley, "The British Navy and its Seamen: Notes for an Unwritten History," in Adam, *Seamen in Society,* 40; Larry Neal, "The Cost of Impressment during the Seven Years War," *Mariner's Mirror* 64, no. 1 (1978), 25.

27. Patrik Höij, "Båtsmännen vid skärgårdsflottan: Tjänstgöringsförhållanden och social förankring i lokalsamhället," in *Skärgårdsflottan: Uppbygnad, militär användning och förankring i det svenska samhället 1700–1824,* ed. Hans Norman (Lund: Historiska Media, 2000), 241–260; Lars Ericson, *Svenska knektar: Indelta soldater, ryttare och båtsmän i krig och fred,* 2nd ed. (Lund: Historiska Media, 2004), 29–45; Kent Zetterberg, "The Organization of the Army and the Navy in Sweden," in *The Army and the Navy in Spain and Sweden in a Period of Change (1750–1870),* ed. Enrique Martínez Ruiz, Magdalena del Pazzis Pi Corrales, and Juan Torrejón (Cádiz and San Fernando: Fundación Berndt Wistedt, Universidad de Cádiz, and Fundación Municipal de Cultura Ayuntamiento de San Fernando, 2001), 23–24.

28. Höij, "Båtsmännen," 251; "Art. 72," in *Sveriges Rikes Sjö-Articlar* (Stockholm: Kongl. Tryckeriet, 1755), 39–40.

29. On pauper children, see Roland Pietsch, "Ships' Boys and Youth Culture in Eighteenth-Century Britain: The Navy Recruits of the London Marine Society," *The Northern Mariner/Le marin du nord* 14, no. 4 (2004): 11–24; Brunsman, *Evil Necessity,* 42–43; Bruijn, *The Dutch Navy,* 183; Valentina K. Tikoff, "Adolescence in the Atlantic: Charity Boys as Seamen in the Spanish Maritime World," *Journal of Early Modern History* 14, no. 1 (2010): 45–73. On landless European peasants, see Davids, "Maritime Labour," 62–5; Le Goff, "The Labour Market," in *"Those Emblems of Hell?,"* ed. Royen, Bruijn, and Lucassen, 300–301; Martin Rheinheimer, *Arme, Bettler und Vagranten: Überleben in der Not, 1450–1850* (Frankfurt a. M.: Fischer, 2000), 14–54; Arnošt Klíma, "Agrarian Class Structure and Economic Development in Pre-Industrial Bohemia," *Past and Present* 85 (1979), 54; for the number of Bohemians in the Dutch navy, see various muster books in NA (NL), Departement van Marine: Monsterrollen, 1795–1810, 2.01.30.

30. The classic statement on the operation of this sector is Marcus Rediker, *Between the Devil and the Deep Blue Sea: Merchant Seamen, Pirates, and the Anglo-American Maritime World, 1700–1750* (Cambridge: Cambridge University Press, 1987).

31. Daniel Vickers, *Farmers and Fishermen: Two Centuries of Work in Essex County, Massachusetts, 1630–1850* (Chapel Hill: University of North Carolina Press, 1994). See also Daniel Vickers (with Vince Walsh), *Young Men and the Sea: Yankee Seafarers in the Age of Sail* (New Haven, CT: Yale University Press, 2005).

32. For the longer-term transition from one sector to the other, see Richard P. Jackson, "From Profit-Sailing to Wage-Sailing: Mediterranean Owner-Captains and Their Crews during the Medieval Commercial Revolution," *The Journal of European Economic History* 18, no. 3 (1989): 605–628; and Heide Gerstenberger, "On Maritime Labour and Maritime Labour Markets in Germany, 1700–1900," in *Maritime Labour: Contributions to the History of Work at Sea, 1500–2000,* ed.

Richard Gorski (Amsterdam: Amsterdam University Press, 2008), 43–59. For the growing specialization of maritime labor in the eighteenth century, see Karel Davids, "Local and Global: Seafaring Communities in the North Sea Area, c. 1600–2000," *International Journal of Maritime History* 27, no. 4 (2015): 629–646.

33. Voltaire, "Man," in *A Philosophical Dictionary* (London: W. Dugdale, 1843), 2:188; Schedvin, "Den 22. okt."

34. On the comparison between ships and factories, see Rediker, *Between the Devil and the Deep Blue Sea,* 77–115. On ships as "total institutions," see Vilhelm Aubert, *The Hidden Society* (Totowa, NJ: Bedminster, 1965); for a critique, see Heide Gerstenberger, "Men Apart: The Concept of 'Total Institution' and the Analysis of Seafaring," *International Journal of Maritime History* 8, no. 1 (1996): 173–182.

35. N. A. M. Rodger, *The Wooden World: An Anatomy of the Georgian Navy* (New York: W. W. Norton, 1996), 15–29; Crowdy, *French Warship Crews,* 16–19.

36. John Harland, *Seamanship in the Age of Sail* (Annapolis, MD: Naval Institute Press, 1985), 91–94; Brian Lavery, *Nelson's Navy: The Ships, Men and Organization, 1793–1815* (Annapolis, MD: Naval Institute Press, 1989), 194–199. On the watch system in the French navy, see Pierre Prétou and Denis Roland, "L'enfermement du large: Les officiers au temps de la marine à voile," in *Fureur et cruauté des capitaines en mer,* ed. Pierre Prétou and Denis Roland (Rennes: Presses Universitaires de Rennes, 2012), 44–45.

37. On the introduction of divisions in the British navy, see G. J. Marcus, *Heart of Oak: A Survey of British Sea Power in the Georgian Era* (New York: Oxford University Press, 1975), 117; and John Knox Laughton, ed., *Letters and Papers of Charles, Lord Barham, Admiral of the Red Squadron, 1758–1813, Volume 1* (London: Navy Records Society, 1907), 304–308. For the Swedish navy, see Otto Emil Lybeck, *Svenska flottans historia, andra bandet, tredje perioden: Från frihetstidens slut till freden i Kiel* (Malmö: A.-B. Allhems, 1945), 434.

38. On holystoning, see William Robinson, *Jack Nastyface: Memoirs of an English Seaman* (Annapolis, MD: Naval Institute Press, 1973), 32; and A British Seaman, *Life On Board a Man-of-War* (Glasgow, 1829), 28–29.

39. Lieut. Thomas Hodgskin, RN, *An Essay on Naval Discipline* (London, 1813), 44.

40. Robinson, *Nastyface,* 31–38; Lavery, *Nelson's Navy,* 200–203.

41. Samuel Leech, *A Voice from the Main Deck: Being a Record of the Thirty Years Adventures of Samuel Leech* (London: Chatham, 1999), 141–142.

42. A British Seaman, *Life,* 142.

43. For the vision of shipboard society as a machine, see A Captain in the Royal Navy, *Observations and Instructions for the Use of the Commissioned, the Junior, and other Officers of the Royal Navy* (London, 1804), 36, and Leech, *A Voice,* 22. On the importance of terror, see Hodgskin, *Essay,* ix. For the "flesh carpenters," see A British Seaman, *Life,* 35.

44. On the range of available punishments, see William Falconer, *An Universal Dictionary of the Marine,* 5th ed., corrected (London, 1784), no pagination; Lybeck, *Svenska flottans historia,* 436; G. Bent Pürschel, "Træk af flådens retsvæsen," in

Flåden gennem 450 år, ed. R. Steen Steensen, 2nd ed. (Copenhagen: Martins Forlag, 1970), 308–317; "Décret concernant le code pénal maritime (16, 19 et 21 Août 1790)," in *Recueil,* 1:122–140; Robinson, *Nastyface,* 138–151. On punishments ordered by British courts-martial, see "Digest of the Admiralty Records of Trials by Court-Martial, From the 1st January 1755 to 1st January 1806," TNA (UK) ADM 12/24; for the Dutch navy, see various trial records in NA (NL), Hoge Krijgsraad en Zeekrijgs-sraden, 1607–1794, 1.01.45; and NA (NL), Hoge Militaire Rechtspraak, 1795–1813 (1818), 2.01.11.

45. Schedvin, "Den 16. sept."

46. Leech, *A Voice,* 43, 60. Court-martial of Johan Baptist Ernaúw, 7 February 1789, NA (NL), Hoge Krijgsraad en Zeekrijgsraden, 1607–1794, 1.01.45, inv. nr. 376. See also Roland Pietsch, "Hearts of Oak and Jolly Tars? Heroism and Insanity in the Georgian Navy," *Journal for Maritime Research* 15, no. 1 (2013): 69–82.

47. "An Account shewing the number of lunatic Seamen and Marines received into Hoxton House each Year from the 1st January 1794 to the 15th August 1818, with those who have died or been discharged, also the number re-entered in each year during the same period" and "State of the Lunatics in the Asylum at the Royal Hospital at Haslar in September 1824," TNA (UK) ADM 105/28.

48. Louis Garneray, *The Floating Prison: The Remarkable Account of Nine Years' Captivity on the British Prison Hulks during the Napoleonic Wars* (London: Conway Maritime Press, 2003), 16–17. Other sources also describe POWs addicted to gambling: see "Report, B. S. Rowley, Ambrose Serle, and John Harness, Rochester 23d May 1801," TNA (UK) ADM 105/44. For the traditional view of hulks as floating tombs, see Philippe Masson, *Les sépulcres flottants: Prisonniers français en Angleterre sous l'Empire* (Rennes: Éditions Óuest-France, 1987); for a recent revisionist take, see Tim Leunig, Jelle van Lottum, and Bo Poulsen, "Surprisingly Gentle Confinement: British Treatment of Danish and Norwegian Prisoners of War during the Napoleonic Wars," *Scandinavian Economic History Review* 66, no. 3 (2018): 282–297.

49. Crosbie Garstin, ed., *Samuel Kelly: An Eighteenth-Century Seaman* (New York: Frederick A. Stokes and Co., 1925), 138. Ned Ward, *The Wooden World Dissected,* 7th ed. (London, 1756), 78.

50. On eighteenth-century deep-sea mariners' culture and worldview, see also Rediker, *Between the Devil and the Deep Blue Sea,* 153–204. On middle class incomprehension of lower deck culture, see Nigel Penn, "The Voyage Out: Peter Kolb and VOC Voyages to the Cape," in *Many Middle Passages: Forced Migration and the Making of the Modern World,* ed. Emma Christopher, Cassandra Pybus, and Marcus Rediker (Berkeley: University of California Press, 2007), 72–91.

51. James R. Durand, *The Life and Adventures of James R. Durand* (Bridgeport: Stiles, Nichols and Son, 1817), 54. John Edsall, *Incidents in the Life of John Edsall* (Catskill, 1831), 93.

52. William Oliver, "A Letter of Dr William Oliver, F.R.S. Concerning a Calenture," *Philosophical Transactions* 24 (1704–05), 1562–1564. A. D. Macleod, "Calenture—Missing at Sea?" *British Journal of Medical Psychology* 56 (1983): 347–350. Macleod disagrees with Oliver, arguing that calenture never occurs at

night. Schedvin, "Den 13. okt." The *Eurydice's* muster book reported Sven Snäll's death as due to edema, which has symptoms similar to those of tuberculosis and scurvy combined. "Fregatten Euridices Munster Rulla, 1793," KrA (S), Flottans Arkiv, Sjöexpeditioner, Skeppsmönsterrullor, 1793:1. Thomas Trotter, *Observations on the Scurvy: With a Review of the Theories Lately Advanced on that Disease; and the Opinions of Dr Milman* (Edinburgh, 1786), 25–28.

53. Schedvin, "Den 30. okt"; "Fregatten Euridices Munster Rulla, 1793," KrA (S), Flottans Arkiv, Sjöexpeditioner, Skeppsmönsterrullor, 1793:1.

54. Schedvin, "Den 5. mars" to "Den 12. juni"; "Raport utaf Örlogsfregatten Euridice til ankars på Helsingörs Redd den 14. Junii 1794," KrA (S), 1794 års kommitté för örlogsflottan, Övriga inkomna handlingar, Serie EII, Volym 2, Nummer 531.

55. H. Arnold Barton, *Scandinavia in the Revolutionary Era, 1760–1815* (Minneapolis: University of Minnesota Press, 1986), 226–227; Bernes, *Segelfartygens tid*, 128.

56. "Raport utaf Örlogsfregatten Euridice til ankars på Helsingörs Redd den 14. Junii 1794," KrA (S), 1794 års kommitté för örlogsflottan, Övriga inkomna handlingar, Serie EII, Volym 2, Nummer 531; Letter, Vice-Admiral Clas Wachtmeister to the Royal Committee, n.p., n.d., KrA (S), 1794 års kommitté för örlogsflottan, Övriga inkomna handlingar, Serie EII, Volym 2, Nummer 601; "Raport utaf Örlogsfregatten Euridice til ankars vid Köpenhamn d: 25 Junii 1794," KrA (S), 1794 års kommitté för örlogsflottan, Övriga inkomna handlingar, Serie EII, Volym 2, Nummer 618; Letter, Vice-Admiral Clas Wachtmeister to the Royal Committee, n.p., n.d., KrA (S), 1794 års kommitté för örlogsflottan, Övriga inkomna handlingar, Serie EII, Volym 3, Nummer 888.

57. For the Dutch maritime industries, see C.H.F. Simons, *Marine justitie* (Assen: Van Gorcum, 1974), 47–48; Matthias van Rossum, "'Amok!': Mutinies and Slaves on Dutch East Indiamen in the 1780s," in *Mutiny and Maritime Radicalism in the Age of Revolution: A Global Survey*, ed. Clare Anderson et al. (Cambridge: Cambridge University Press, 2014), 109–130; Jaap R. Bruijn and E.S. van Eyck van Heslinga, eds., *Muiterij: Oproer en berechting op schepen van de VOC* (Haarlem: De Boer Maritiem, 1980). For French shipping, see Alain Cabantous, *La Vergue et les fers: Mutins et déserteurs dans la Marine de l'ancienne France (XVIIe–XVIIIe s.)* (Paris: Tallandier, 1984), 13, 20; Le Goff, "Les gens de mer," 472. For British shipping, see Rediker, *Between the Devil and the Deep Blue Sea*, 227; and A.N. Gilbert, "The Nature of Mutiny in the British Navy in the Eighteenth Century," in *Naval History: The Sixth Symposium of the U.S. Naval Academy*, ed. D.M. Masterson (Wilmington: Scholarly Resources, 1987), 113.

58. Rodger, "Shipboard Life," 32.

59. For a description of paternalist modes of social control onboard ship, see Rodger, *The Wooden World*, 205–211; for comprehensive studies of the modes of social control onboard warships, see AnnaSara Hammar, *Mellan kaos och kontroll: Social ordning i svenska flottan, 1670–1716* (Stockholm: Nordic Academic Press, 2014); and Thomas Malcomson, *Order and Disorder in the British Navy, 1793–1815: Control, Resistance, Flogging and Hanging* (Woodbridge: Boydell Press, 2016).

60. On disincentives to mutiny, see Cabantous, *La Vergue et les fers,* 22–25.

61. On the number of desertions in the British navy, see Christopher Lloyd, *The British Seaman, 1200–1860: A Social Survey* (Rutherford: Fairleigh Dickinson University Press, 1970), 265. On desertions from the Batavian fleet, see Thea Roodhuyzen, *In woelig vaarwater: Marineofficieren in de jaren 1779–1802* (Amsterdam: De Bataafse Leeuw, 1998), 138–165; on desertion in the French navy, see Memorandum on insufficient punishments of naval deserters, SHM-V (F), CC/3/1471, Personnel, Troupes et équipages, Mémoirs sur les jurys militaires etc.; Letter from Captain D'Auvergne, Prince of Bouillon to Secretary Dundas, Jersey, 31 May 1797, TNA (UK) ADM 1/4172; Vice-Admiral Morard de Galles to the Minister of the Navy and Colonies, Brest, 14 Nivôse Year VII [3 January 1799], SHM-V (F), BB/3/153, Service Général, Correspondance, Brest, 1799; Manning levels during Germinal, Year 7 [March-April 1799], SHM-V (F), BB/3/158, Service Général, Correspondance, Toulon, 1799; Substance of the last information which has reached me directly from my correspondents in the sea ports, Brest, 20 Floréal Year V [9 May 1797], TNA (UK) ADM 1/4172.

62. Bent Blüdnikow, "Folkelig uro i København 1789–1820," *Fortid og Nutid* 33 (1986): 14–17; "Om Hovedtrækkene af Dagens Historie," *Minerva, et Maanedskrivt* 31 (Januar, Februar, og Marts 1793), 274–276; Henrik Horstbøll and Uffe Østergård, "Reform and Revolution: The French Revolution and the Case of Denmark," *Scandinavian Journal of History* 15, no. 3 (1990): 167; Edit Rasmussen, "Tømrerstrejken i København 1794 og dens omfang," *Hisstoriske Meddelser om København* (1984): 69–85.

63. Bernes, *Segelfartygens tid,* 129–130.

64. Schedvin, "Den 31. mars," "Den 6. maj," and "Den 26. maj." On the colonial origin of revolutionary Europe, see Pierre Serna, "Every Revolution Is a War for Independence," in *The French Revolution in Global Perspective,* ed. Suzanne Desan, Lynn Hunt, and William Max Nelson (Ithaca, NY: Cornell University Press, 2013), 165–82.

65. For examples of seamen comparing their lot to slavery, see Court-Martial against James Anderson of the Perdrix, 1 June 1798, TNA (UK) ADM 1/5345; and Report of Captain Adjoint A. J. Knok, NA (NL) 2.01.11, inv. nr. 221. Hugh Crow, *Memoirs of the Late Captain Hugh Crow of Liverpool* (London: Longman, Rees, Orme, Brown, and Green, 1830), 22.

CHAPTER TWO: WHO WILL COMMAND THIS EMPIRE?

1. William S. Cormack, *Revolution and Political Conflict in the French Navy, 1789–1794* (Cambridge: Cambridge University Press, 1995), 18–23; Etienne Taillemaite, *Histoire ignorée de la Marine française* (Paris: Perrin, 2003), 177–199; Martine Acerra and Jean Meyer, *Marines et révolution* (Rennes: Éditions Ouest-France, 1988), 58.

2. On Malouet's career, see Contre-amiral Ducasse, "Pierre-Victor Malouet au service de la Marine (1740–1814)," *Revue Historique des Armées,* no. 4 (1990): 86–97; and Abel Poitrineau, "L'État et l'avenir des colonies françaises de plantation à la fin

de l'Ancien Régime, selon P. V. Malouet," *Revue d'Auvergne* 104, nos. 1–2 (1990): 41–54. On reforms in the dockyard, see Malcolm Crook, *Toulon in War and Revolution: From the Ancien Régime to the Restoration, 1750–1820* (Manchester: Manchester University Press, 1991), 47; Acerra and Meyer, *Marines,* 88.

3. On Toulon's dockyard workers, see Julian Saint-Roman, "La précarité des ouvriers de l'arsenal de Toulon à travers leurs mobilités: Fin XVIIIe siècle–début XIXe siècle," *MEFRIM* 123, no. 1 (2011): 103–113, and "La démocratie turbulente des ouvriers de l'arsenal de Toulon, 1789–1793," in *Peuples en révolution: D'aujourd'hui à 1789,* ed. Cyril Belmonte and Christine Peyrard (Aix-en-Provence: Presses universitaires de Provence, 2014), 125–138. On 1789 unrest, see Cormack, *Revolution and Political Conflict,* 49–77; Crook, *Toulon,* 78–99.

4. Comte d'Albert de Rions, *Mémoire historique et justicatif de M. le Comte d'Albert de Rions, sur l'Affaire de Toulon* (Paris, 1790), 64–108.

5. On French port cities and economic growth, see Richard Drayton, "The Globalization of France: Provincial Cities and French Expansion c. 1500–1800," *History of European Ideas* 34, no. 4 (2008): 424–430; Paul Cheney, *Cul de Sac: Patrimony, Capitalism, and Slavery in French Saint-Domingue* (Chicago: University of Chicago Press, 2017), 15–41. On the accumulation of colonial capital in the metropolis, see Allan Potofsky, "Paris-on-the-Atlantic from the Old Regime to the Revolution," *French History* 25, no. 1 (2011): 89–107. Rochefort officers quoted in Cormack, *Revolution and Political Conflict,* 74.

6. National Assembly, Monday, 7 December 1789, Evening session, in Jérôme Mavidal et al., eds., *Archives parlementaires de 1787 à 1860 recueil complet des débats législatifs et politiques des chambres françaises* (Paris: Librairie administrative de P. Dupont, 1862), 10:418–419. On Malouet's background and career, see Ducasse, "Pierre-Victor Malouet," and Pointrineau, "L'État et l'avenir."

7. National Assembly, Monday, 7 December 1789, Evening session, in Mavidal et al., *Archives parlementaires,* 10:418–419.

8. Letter from M. de la Gallissonnière, Port-au-Prince, 1 January 1790, SHM-V (F), BB/4/3, Vol. 3, ff. 103–104.

9. On the speed of news spreading throughout the empire, see Kenneth J. Banks, *Chasing Empire across the Sea: Communications and the State in the French Atlantic, 1713–1763* (Montreal and Kingston: McGill-Queen's University Press, 2002), 76–77; on Saint-Domingue's trade, see Thomas M. Doerflinger, "The Antilles Trade of the Old Regime: A Statistical Overview," *Journal of Interdisciplinary History* 6, no. 3 (1976), 410–411.

10. On Gallissonnière's mounting anxiety, see his letter, Port-au-Prince, 12 June 1790, SHM-V (F), BB/4/3, Vol. 3, ff. 113–114; on disorder in Brest during the first year of the revolution, see Phillippe Henwood and Edmond Monage, *Brest: Un port en révolution, 1789–1799* (Rennes: Éditions Ouest-France, 1989), 55–82.

11. For general overviews of these developments, see Laurent Dubois, *Avengers of the New World: The Story of the Haitian Revolution* (Cambridge, MA.: Harvard University Press, 2004), 76–85, and C. L. R. James, *The Black Jacobins: Toussaint L'Ouverture and the San Domingo Revolution* (London: Penguin, 1980), 50–59.

12. On the economic weight of Saint-Domingue, see Dubois, *Avengers*, 21. On the importance of American slavery and Atlantic trade to European capitalism, see Robin Blackburn, *The American Crucible: Slavery, Emancipation, and Human Rights* (London: Verso, 2011), 99–120.

13. "Décret," National Assembly, session of March 8, 1790, in Mavidal et al., *Archives parlementaires*, 12:72–73; on the evolving legal status of the colonies within the empire, see Miranda Spieler, "The Legal Structure of Colonial Rule during the Revolution," *The William and Mary Quarterly*, 3rd ser., 66, no. 2 (April 1, 2009): 365–408.

14. "Instructions Addressed by the National Assembly to the Colony of Saint-Domingue," in *Slave Revolution in the Caribbean, 1789–1804: A Brief History with Documents,* ed. Laurent Dubois and John D. Garrigus (Boston: Bedford/St. Martin's, 2006), 71–72; on the Assembly's reaction, see Pamphile de Lacroix, *Mémoires pour servir à l'histoire de la révolution de Saint-Domingue* (Paris: Pillet Ainé, 1819), 1:32, 1:34–37.

15. Lacroix, *Mémoires,* 1:41–42; Letter from M. de la Gallissonnière, Port-au-Prince, August 2, 1790, SHM-V (F), BB/4/3, Vol. 3, f. 119.

16. Letter from M. de la Gallissonnière, Port-au-Prince, 1 January 1790, SHM-V (F), BB/4/3, Vol. 3, f. 104.

17. Letter from M. de la Gallissonnière, Port-au-Prince, August 2, 1790, SHM-V (F), BB/4/3, Vol. 3, ff. 119–121.

18. Letter from M. de la Gallissonnière, Port-au-Prince, August 2, 1790, SHM-V (F), BB/4/3, Vol. 3, ff. 121–122; "Déposition de M. de France, Lieut. de Vaisseau," SHM-V (F), BB/4/3, Vol. 3, f. 158.

19. Lacroix, *Mémoires,* 1:42–44; "Copie de la lettre de l'équipage du vaisseau reçu le 30 juillet 1790," SHM-V (F), BB/4/3, Vol. 3, f. 129.

20. On medieval maritime law codes, see Edda Frankot, "Medieval Maritime Law from Oléron to Wisby: Jurisdictions in the Law of the Sea," in *Communities in European History: Representations, Jurisdictions, Conflicts,* ed. Juan Pan-Montojo and Frederik Pedersen (Pisa: Pisa University Press, 2007), 151–172; and Robin Ward, *The World of the Medieval Shipmaster: Law, Business and the Sea c. 1350–c. 1450* (Woodbridge: Boydell Press, 2009). On the 1614 sea regulation, see Ulrich Welke, *Der Kapitän: Die Erfindung einer Herrschaftsform* (Münster: Westfälisches Dampfboot, 1997), 29.

21. Letter from M. de la Gallissonnière, Port-au-Prince, August 2, 1790, SHM-V (F), BB/4/3, Vol. 3, ff. 124–125.

22. For Gallissonnière's report on the mutiny, see M. de la Gallissonnière, Port-au-Prince, August 2, 1790, SHM-V (F), BB/4/3, Vol. 3, ff. 124–127.

23. For a recent study that overemphasizes the crew's racism, see Jeremy P. Popkin, "Sailors and Revolution: Naval Mutineers in Saint-Domingue, 1790–93," *French History* 26, no. 4 (2012): 464–468; for the *Léopard*'s name change, see "Expédition du Procés Verbal fait à bord du vaisseau le Léopard surnommé le Sauveur des Français en rade à Saint Marc, 6 août 1790," SHM-V (F), BB/4/3, Vol. 3, ff. 150–152. On Governor de Peinier's assessment, see Letter from M. de la Gallissonnière, Port-au-Prince, August 2, 1790, SHM-V (F), BB/4/3, Vol. 3, f. 125.

24. For the order to prepare red-hot shot, see Lacroix, *Mémoires,* 1:48; on taking the ship's officers hostage, see "Copie de la lettre de M. de Santo Domingo, reçu le 30 juillet 1790," SHM-V (F), BB/4/3, Vol. 3, ff. 129–130; for the Saint-Marc assembly's appeal, see Lacroix, *Mémoires,* 1:45.

25. On the crew's refusal to fight on behalf of the assembly, see Thomas Madiou, *Histoire d'Haiti* (Port-au-Prince: JH Courtois, 1847), 1:46; on the crew's arrival in Brest, see Letter, Redon de Beaupréau, Brest, September 14, 1790, SHM-V (F), BB/3/2, 1790, f. 130.

26. On the creation of the *Comité de Marine,* see Cormack, *Revolution and Political Conflict,* 79, and "Décret concernant le code pénal maritime (16, 19, et 21 Août 1790)," in *Recueil,* 1:122; on the committee's early work, see Norman Hampson, "The 'Comité de Marine' of the Constituent Assembly," *The Historical Journal* 2, no. 2 (1959): 134–136.

27. *Rapport sur les peines à infliger dans l'Armée Navale, et dans les ports et arsénaux, fait au nom du Comité de la Marine, dans la séance du 16 Août 1790* (Paris, 1790), 4–7. For parallel reforms in the French revolutionary army, see Charles H. Hammond, Jr., "The French Revolution and the Enlightening of Military Justice," *Proceedings of the Western Society for French History* 34 (2006): 134–146.

28. "Décret concernant le code pénal maritime (16, 19, et 21 Août 1790)," in *Recueil,* 1:123–126; *Rapport sur les Peines,* 8.

29. "Décret concernant le code pénal maritime (16, 19, et 21 Août 1790)," in *Recueil,* 1:129–130; *Rapport sur les Peines,* 10.

30. "Décret concernant le code pénal maritime (16, 19, et 21 Août 1790)," in *Recueil,* 1:130–139; *Rapport sur les Peines,* 10–12.

31. On the evolution of imperial legal geographies during the age of revolution, see Lauren Benton, *A Search for Sovereignty: Law and Geography in European Empires, 1400–1900* (New York: Cambridge University Press, 2010), 162–221; Miranda Spieler, *Empire and Underworld: Captivity in French Guyana* (Cambridge, MA: Harvard University Press, 2012).

32. On the background of committee members, see Hampson, "Comité de Marine," 132–133, 135–136; on the Brest mutiny, see "Lettre de M. de la Luzerne, en date du 13 septembre," National Assembly, session of 13 September 1790, in Mavidal et al., *Archives parlementaires,* 18:729; "Rapport sur l'insurrection arrivée à Brest," National Assembly, session of 15 September 1790, in Mavidal et al., *Archives parlementaires,* 18:766; "8 septembre 1790," in *Brest pendant la Révolution (documents inédits): Correspondance de la municipalité avec les députés de la Sénéchaussée de Brest aux États Généraux et à l'Assemblée Constituante, 1789–1791,* ed. L. Esquieu and L. Delourmel (Brest: Soc. Anon. de l'Union Républicaine du Finistère, 1909), 196; "Affaire de Brest," *Révolutions de Paris* 63 (18–25 September 1790), 525.

33. On the seamen's complaints, see "8 septembre 1790," in *Brest pendant la Révolution,* 197–198.

34. "8 septembre 1790," in *Brest pendant la Révolution,* 197–198. On galley slavery, see André Zysberg, "Les gens de mer et l'état: La mobilisation navale en Europe," in *The Sea in History: The Early Modern World,* ed. Christian Buchet and Gérard Le

Bouëdec (Woodbridge: Boydell Press, 2017), 826–829. I owe the image of slavery as a "dreadful horizon" to Vincent Brown.

35. "8 septembre 1790," in *Brest pendant la Révolution,* 198.

36. "Décret," National Assembly, session of 15 September 1790, in Mavidal et al., *Archives parlementaires,* 18:767.

37. "Rapport sur l'insurrection arrivée à Brest," National Assembly, session of 15 September 1790, in Mavidal et al., *Archives parlementaires,* 18:766; "Décret," National Assembly, session of 15 September 1790, in Mavidal et al., *Archives parlementaires,* 18:767.

38. Henwood and Monage, *Brest,* 12–30.

39. "Nouvelles de Provinces: Brest," *Révolutions de Paris* 57 (7–14 August 1790), 244.

40. Alan Forrest, *Conscripts and Deserters: The Army and French Society during the Revolution and Empire* (New York: Oxford University Press, 1989), 16; Georges Lefebvre, *The French Revolution: From its Origins to 1793* (London: Routledge, 2001), 136–139; Jean-Paul Marat quoted in Albert Soboul, *The French Revolution, 1787–1799: From the Storming of the Bastille to Napoleon* (London: Unwin Hyman, 1989), 174.

41. "Affaire de Brest," *Révolutions de Paris* 63 (18–25 September 1790), 529; *Rapport sur les Peines,* 10.

42. On the *Ferme* mutiny, see "Copie d'une lettre écrite à M. d'Albert par M. Redon, le 11 septembre 1790," SHM-V (F), BB/3/2, f. 128; on the municipality's reaction, see "13 septembre 1790," in *Brest pendant la Révolution,* 201; on the arrival of the *Léopard,* see Intendant Redon, Brest, 13 September 1790, SHM-V (F), BB/3/2, f. 127.

43. "L'équipage du *Léopard* cherche de justifier sa conduite," Brest, 13 September 1790, SHM-V (F), BB/4/3, Vol. 3, f. 185.

44. Intendant Redon, Brest, 14 September 1790, SHM-V (F), BB/3/2, f. 130. "17 septembre 1790," in *Brest pendant la Révolution,* 206–207; "Affaire de Brest," *Révolutions de Paris* 63 (18–25 September 1790), 527.

45. On the rumors about events in Saint-Domingue, see "15 septembre 1790," in *Brest pendant la Révolution,* 203; on the erection of gallows in de Marigny's front yard, see "Affaire de Brest," *Révolutions de Paris* 63 (18–25 September 1790), 527; on the municipality's reaction, see "22 septembre 1790," in *Brest pendant la Révolution,* 210.

46. For the officers' letter, see "Copie de la lettre écrite par MM. les officiers de la marine réunis à Brest, à M. de la Luzerne," in *Recueil,* 1:165–166; on the *Patriote* mutiny, see Albert de Rions, Brest, 16 September 1790, in *Recueil,* 1:163, and "Affaire de Brest," *Révolutions de Paris* 63 (18–25 September 1790), 527.

47. Albert de Rions, Brest, 16 September 1790, in *Recueil,* 1:163–165.

48. For the municipality's letter, see "20 septembre 1790," in *Brest pendant la Révolution,* 208; for Souillac's complaint, see M. de Souillac, Brest, 18 October 1790, SHM-V (F), BB/4/1, Vol. 1, f. 90.

49. "Décret qui ordonne la poursuite des auteurs de l'insurrection qui a eu lieu à bord du vaisseau le *Léopard,* et de l'insulte faite à M. de Marigny, etc.," in *Recueil,* 1:168–169; Henwood and Monange, *Brest,* 115–116; "Adresse de la Société des Amis

de la Constitution, établie à Brest, aux Citoyens composant les Equipages de l'Armée Navale," SHM-V (F), BB/4/1, Vol. 1, f. 94.

50. "Adresse de la Société des Amis de la Constitution, établie à Brest, aux Citoyens composant les Equipages de l'Armée Navale," SHM-V (F), BB/4/1, Vol. 1, f. 94.

51. Ibid.

52. "20 octobre 1790," in *Brest pendant la Révolution,* 220; "Rapport et extrait d'une lettre des commissaires envoyés à Brest," in *Recueil,* 1:181.

53. "Copie d'un lettre ecrite par M. de Souillac à MM. Bori et Gandon, Commissaires du Roy, en date de Brest le 23 octobre 1790," SHM-V (F), BB/4/1, Vol. 1, ff. 101–102.

54. "27 octobre 1790," in *Brest pendant la Révolution,* 223; *Adresse de l'equipage du vaisseau Le Superbe, en rade de Brest, à la Société des Amis de la Constitution. Séance du 4 Novembre 1790. Imprimée par ordre de l'Assemblée Nationale* (Paris, 1790). See also Cormack, *Revolution and Political Conflict,* 104–105.

55. M. de Bougainville, Brest, 10 November 1790, SHM-V (F), BB/4/1, Vol. 1, f. 52; M. de Bougainville, Brest, 12 November 1790, SHM-V (F), BB/4/1, Vol. 1, f. 54.

56. M. de Bougainville, Brest, 17 November 1790, SHM-V (F), BB/4/1, Vol. 1, f. 56; M. de Bougainville, Brest, 19 November 1790, SHM-V (F), BB/4/1, Vol. 1, f. 57; "Ordre Général, No. 25," SHM-V (F), BB/4/1, Vol. 1, f. 59; "Ordre Général, No. 26," SHM-V (F), BB/4/1, Vol. 1, f. 62.

57. M. de Bougainville, Brest, 26 November 1790, SHM-V (F), BB/4/1, Vol. 1, f. 63; M. de Bougainville, Brest, 8 December 1790, SHM-V (F), BB/4/1, Vol. 1, f. 70; M. de Bougainville, Brest, 10 December 1790, SHM-V (F), BB/4/1, Vol. 1, ff. 71–72.

58. For the standard provisions onboard a French warship, see Terry Crowdy, *French Warship Crews, 1789–1805: From the French Revolution to Trafalgar* (Botley: Osprey, 2005), 23; M. de Bougainville, Brest, 10 December 1790, SHM-V (F), BB/4/1, Vol. 1, f. 71; M. de Bougainville, Brest, 22 December 1790, SHM-V (F), BB/4/1, Vol. 1, f. 76–77; "Ordre du 26 decembre," SHM-V (F), BB/4/1, Vol. 1, f. 80.

59. M. de Bougainville, Brest, 1 December 1790, SHM-V (F), BB/4/1, Vol. 1, f. 64; M. de Bougainville, Brest, 10 December 1790, SHM-V (F), BB/4/1, Vol. 1, f. 72; M. de Bougainville, Brest, 1 December 1790, SHM-V (F), BB/4/1, Vol. 1, f. 64; M. de Bougainville, Brest, 8 December 1790, SHM-V (F), BB/4/1, Vol. 1, f. 70; for the Brest epidemic of 1793–94, see Taillemaite, *Histoire ignorée,* 284; for an overview of common ailments, see Antoine Poissonnier-Desperrières, *Traité des maladies des gens de mer* (Paris: Lacombe, 1767).

60. "Ordre du 26 decembre," SHM-V (F), BB/4/1, Vol. 1, f. 80; "6 novembre 1790," in *Brest pendant la Révolution,* 226–227; see also William S. Cormack, "Legitimate Authority in Revolution and War: The French Navy in the West Indies, 1789–1793," *International History Review* 18, no. 1 (1996): 5–6, 8.

61. Cormack, "Legitimate Authority," 4–6, 8–9. See also Thomas H. Le Duc, "A Yankee Trader Views the French Revolution in Martinique," *The New England Quarterly* 11, no. 4 (1938): 802–807.

62. M. de Rivière, "Extrait du Journal de ma Station aux Isles du Vent," SHM-V (F), BB/4/5, Vol. 2, ff. 42–57; "Discours prononcé au nom de MM. les Commissaires

du roi par M. de Montdenoix, aux gens de Mer qui composent les équipages du vaisseau la Ferme, commandé par M. de Rivière chef de division et la frégate l'Embuscade, commandée par M. d'Orleans. Fort-Royal, à bord du vaisseau la Ferme, le 3 juin 1791," SHM-V (F), BB/4/5, Vol. 2, ff. 70–71; Cormack, "Legitimate Authority," 4–5, 9–10.

63. M. de Rivière, on board the *Ferme,* 17 June 1791, SHM-V (F), BB/4/5, Vol. 2, f. 68; National Assembly, session of 18 September 1790, in Mavidal, *Archives parlementaires,* 19:48; M. de Rivière, "Extrait du Journal de ma Station aux Isles du Vent," SHM-V (F), BB/4/5, Vol. 2, ff. 44, 46, 48, 52–54. On the distribution of prize money, see M. Merlin, *Répertoire universel et raisonné de jurisprudence,* 3rd ed. (Paris: Garnery, 1808), 9:782–786.

64. R. P. Crowhurst, "Profitability in French Privateering, 1793–1815," *Business History* 24, no. 1 (1982): 48–60.

65. M. de Rivière, "Extrait du Journal de ma Station aux Isles du Vent," SHM-V (F), BB/4/5, Vol. 2, ff. 54–56.

66. For the worsening conditions onboard the *Ferme,* see "Le Vaisseau du Roy La Ferme, commandé par M. de Riviere, chef de division. Etat de situation d'Equipage à l'epoque du 14 juin 1791," SHM-V (F), BB/4/5, Vol. 2, f. 74; "Le Vaisseau du Roy La Ferme, commandé par M. de Riviere, chef de division. Etat de situation d'Equipage à l'epoque du 9 Nov 1791," SHM-V (F), BB/4/5, Vol. 2, f. 90; and "Le Vaisseau La Ferme, Commandé par M. de Riviere, Chef de Division. Etat de situation d'Equipage à l'epoque du 13 Juin 1792," SHM-V (F), BB/4/12, Vol. 5, f. 21. For the *Embuscade* mutiny, see "Copie d'une lettre de M. d'Orléans, capitaine de la frégate l'Embuscade, en rade de l'ile de Ré," National Assembly, session of 23 November 1791, in Mavidal et al., *Archives parlementaires,* 35:317.

67. "Extrait du procès-verbal des délibérations de l'équipage l'Embuscade," National Assembly, session of 23 November 1791, in Mavidal et al., *Archives parlementaires,* 35:318; "Copie d'une lettre de M. d'Orléans, capitaine de la frégate l'Embuscade, en rade de l'ile de Ré," National Assembly, session of 23 November 1791, in Mavidal et al., *Archives parlementaires,* 35:318; M. de Rivière, Fort-Royal, 9 November 1791, SHM-V (F), BB/4/5, Vol. 2, f. 86; National Assembly, session of 17 December 1791, in Mavidal et al., *Archives parlementaires,* 36:203–204; M. Bertrand, minister of the marine, National Assembly, session of 20 December 1791, in Mavidal et al., *Archives parlementaires,* 36:272–273; Cormack, "Legitimate Authority," 12–13.

68. "Jugement Rendu par le Conseil Martial, Assemblé à bord du Vaisseau La Ferme, Mouillé en rade du Fort-Royal, Isle Martinique," SHM-V (F), BB/4/12, Vol. 5, f. 10; M. de Rivière, Martinique, 17 June 1792, SHM-V (F), BB/4/12, Vol. 5, f. 19; "Jugement Rendu par le Conseil de Guerre tenu à bord du Vaisseau La Ferme, le 17 Octobre 1792," SHM-V (F), BB/4/12, Vol. 5, f. 47.

69. M. A. Lacour, *Histoire de la Guadeloupe* (Basse-Terre: Imprimerie du Gouvernement, 1857), 2:98–101; Cormack, "Legitimate Authority," 14–15.

70. Lacour, *Histoire,* 2:99–101.

71. Lacour, *Histoire,* 2:99–103; Jean-François Landolphe, *Mémoires du Capitaine Landolphe* (Paris: A. Bertrand and Pillet Aîné, 1823), 2:126–136.

72. National Convention, session of 8 November 1792, in Mavidal et al., *Archives parlementaires,* 53:314–315; Cormack, "Legitimate Authority," 16; "Copie du Journal de la Calipso, du 29. 7bre au 15. 8bre 1792," SHM-V (F), BB/4/12, Vol. 5, ff. 62–70; "Copie du procès verbal de la prise de possession de la Gabare la Bienvenue," SHM-V (F), BB/4/12, Vol. 5, f. 70; Lacour, *Histoire,* 108–116; "Compte rendu à ses concitoyens par le Capitaine Lacrosse, commandant la frégate de la République, La Félicité, de sa mission aux Isles-du-Vent de l'Amérique, pendant les années 1792 à 1793," National Convention, session of the 22nd day of the first month of Year II (13 October 1793), in Mavidal et al., *Archives parlementaires,* 76:510.

73. Lacour, *Histoire,* 2:118–120.

74. Lacour, *Histoire,* 2:121–131; Landolphe, *Mémoires,* 2:137–149; "Compte rendu à ses concitoyens par le Capitaine Lacrosse, commandant la frégate de la République, La Félicité, de sa mission aux Isles-du-Vent de l'Amérique, pendant les années 1792 à 1793," National Convention, session of the 22nd day of the first month of Year II (13 October 1793), in Mavidal et al., *Archives parlementaires,* 76:510–511; Kieran Russell Kleczewski, "Martinique and the British Occupation, 1794–1802" (PhD diss., Georgetown University, 1988), 73.

75. "Compte rendu à ses concitoyens par le Capitaine Lacrosse, commandant la frégate de la République, La Félicité, de sa mission aux Isles-du-Vent de l'Amérique, pendant les années 1792 à 1793," National Convention, session of the 22nd day of the first month of Year II (13 October 1793), in Mavidal et al., *Archives parlementaires,* 76:521; Lacour, *Histoire,* 2:123; Cormack, "Legitimate Authority," 22.

76. Kleczewski, "Martinique," 77–82, 88–91.

77. "Procès-verbal qui prouve la nécessité dans laquelle La Crosse se trouvé d'abandoner les colonies du Vent et repasser en France," National Convention, session of the 22nd day of the first month of Year II (13 October 1793), in Mavidal at al., *Archives parlementaires,* 76:532–533.

78. "Procès-verbal qui prouve la nécessité," in Mavidal et al., *Archives parlementaires,* 76:532–533. On the small whites, see Anne Pérotin-Dumon, "Ambiguous Revolution in the Caribbean: The White Jacobins, 1789–1800," *Historical Reflections/Réflexions historiques* 13, nos. 2–3 (1986): 499–515.

79. "Procès-verbal qui prouve la nécessité," in Mavidal et al., *Archives parlementaires,* 76:532–533.

80. Article 2 of the decree on the constitutional principles of the navy, National Assembly, session of June 26, 1790, in Mavidal et al., *Archives parlementaires,* 16:469.

81. On the political culture of urban workers in various locales, see Albert Soboul, *The Sans Culottes: The Popular Movement and Revolutionary Government, 1793–1794* (New York: Anchor, 1972), esp. 95–134; Eric Foner, *Tom Paine and Revolutionary America,* updated edition (New York: Oxford University Press, 2005); and E. P. Thompson, *The Making of the English Working Class* (Harmondsworth: Penguin, 1963), esp. 19–203.

82. On fraternity among the *sans-culottes,* for example, see Soboul, *The Sans Culottes,* 153–157; on fraternity onboard ship, see Rediker, *Between the Devil and the Deep Blue Sea,* 243–244; Margaret S. Creighton, "Fraternity in the American

Forecastle," *The New England Quarterly* 63, no. 4 (1990): 531–557; Brian J. Rouleau, "Dead Men Do Tell Tales: Folklore, Fraternity, and the Forecastle," *Early American Studies* 5, no. 1 (2007), 30–62; W. Jeffrey Bolster, *Black Jacks: African American Seamen in the Age of Sail* (Cambridge, MA: Harvard University Press, 1997), 75.

83. On the preservation of Saint-Domingue, see Letter, Lieutenant de Santo Domingo, Brest, 13 September 1790, SHM-V (F), BB/4/3, Service Général, Campagnes (1790–1913), 1790, vol. 3, f. 184. On the Cap Français insurrection, see Jeremy Popkin, *You Are All Free: The Haitian Revolution and the Abolition of Slavery* (New York: Cambridge University Press, 2010), esp. 189–245. On the *America* mutiny, see "Proces verbal, 23 juilliet 1793," AN(F), D/XXV/54.

CHAPTER THREE: DEMONS DANCING
IN A FURNACE

1. Moreau de Jonnès, *Adventures in the Revolution and under the Consulate* (London: Peter Davies, 1969), 53.

2. De Jonnès, *Adventures,* 63–65; Louis Garneray, *Voyages, avontures et combats: Souvenirs de ma vie maritime* (Brussels: Alphonse Lebègue, 1851), 162.

3. Crosbie Garstin, ed., *Samuel Kelly: An Eighteenth Century Seaman* (New York: Frederick A. Stokes and Co., 1925), 195; John Hoxse, *The Yankee Tar* (Northampton, 1840), 108; William Spavens, *The Seaman's Narrative* (London, 1796), 33.

4. For deaths in the Royal Navy, see Peter Kemp, *The British Sailor: A Social History of the Lower Deck* (London: J. M. Dent and Sons, 1970), 139; Dudley Pope, *Life in Nelson's Navy* (London: Unwin Hyman, 1981), 131; and Michael Duffy, *Soldiers, Sugar, and Seapower: The British Expeditions to the West Indies and the War against Revolutionary France* (Oxford: Clarendon, 1987), 334. For deaths in the French navy, see Etienne Taillemite, *Histoire ignorée de la Marine française* (Paris: Perrin, 2003), 284.

5. C. H. F. Simons, *Marine justitie* (Assen: Van Gorcum, 1974), 122–125.

6. On the Toulon surrender and the Quiberon Bay mutiny, see William S. Cormack, *Revolution and Political Conflict in the French Navy, 1789–1794* (Cambridge: Cambridge University Press, 1995), 173–241.

7. Strikes: "M. Kéon, Brest, le 15. Juin 1792, l'an 4.e de la liberté," SHM-V (F), BB/3/9, 1792; and "Copie de la lettre du Citoyen Savary Capitaine de la Capricieuse, en rade de l'Isle d'Aix, le 23. mai 1793, an 2 de la République, au Commandant des Armes," SHM-V (F), BB/3/27, 1793. Arson: "M. Kéon, Brest, le 6. Fevrier 1792," SHM-V (F), BB/3/9, 1792; and "De Secqville, à L'Orient, le 22. Avril 1793, L'an 2 de la République française," SHM-V (F), BB/3/24, 1793. Attacks on officers: "M. Kéon, Brest, le 27. Juin 1792, l'an 4.e de la liberté," SHM-V (F), BB/3/9, 1792; "Un refus général: De Secqville, à L'Orient, le 1.er Juillet 1793, L'an 2 de la République française," SHM-V (F), BB/3/24, 1793. On the *Engageante,* see "Mémoire sur ce qui s'est passé à bord de la frégate de la République L'Engagéante. Le 15. Mai 1793. L'an 2 de la République," SHM-V (F), BB/3/24, 1793.

8. Healthy fear: "Le Commandant des Armes au Ministre de la Marine, Brest, le 14. Juin 1793, l'an 2 de la République," SHM-V (F), BB/3/22, 1793.

9. "Observations et projet de décret sur les classes de la marine," in Mavidal et al., *Archives parlementaires,* 13:117–120; "(No. 180) Extrait du rapport et décret sur les classes des gens de mer," *Recueil,* 1:215–217. See also Norman Hampson, "The 'Comité de Marine' of the Constituent Assembly," *The Historical Journal* 2, no. 2 (1959), 134–135.

10. "Observations et projet de décret sur les classes de la marine," in Mavidal et al., *Archives parlementaires,* 13:117–120.

11. Hampson, "Comité de Marine," 134–135.

12. Alan Forrest, *Conscripts and Deserters: The Army and French Society during the Revolution and Empire* (New York: Oxford University Press, 1989), 26–34.

13. Marie-Cécile Thoral, *From Valmy to Waterloo: France at War, 1792–1815* (New York: Palgrave Macmillan, 2011), 48–51; Jean-Clément Martin, "The Vendée, *Chouannerie,* and the State, 1791–99," in *A Companion to the French Revolution,* ed. Peter McPhee (Malden, MA: Wiley-Blackwell, 2013), 246–259.

14. Jean-Bon Saint-André, *Collection des arrêtes* (Brest: Gauchlet, An II [1793–94]), 24–36.

15. Saint-André, *Collection des arrêtes,* 24–36, 46–47, 149–153. The disciplining and subordination of the French officer corps during Year II mirrored that which had already taken place in the British navy at mid-century. See Sarah Kinkel, *Disciplining the Empire: Politics, Governance, and the Rise of the British Navy* (Cambridge, MA: Harvard University Press, 2018).

16. Saint-André, *Collection des arrêtes,* 24–36, 37–42.

17. On the *America* mutiny and trial, see "Extrait des Registres du Greffe du Tribunal Criminel du Département du Finistère, du 24 Nivôse, an second de la République Française" SHM-V (F), BB/3/51, 1794; and Cormack, *Revolution and Political Conflict,* 252–253; Phillippe Henwood and Edmond Monage, *Brest: Un port en révolution, 1789–1799* (Rennes: Éditions Ouest-France, 1989), 212–214; Léon Lévy-Schneider, *Le conventionnel Jeanbon Saint-André, membre du comit de salut public, organisateur de la Marine de la Terreur, 1749–1813* (Paris: F. Alcan, 1901), 652–653. On the *America's* previous history, see chapter 2.

18. Henwood and Monage, *Brest,* 212. On the old-regime navy's forms of corporal punishment, see Alain Berbouche, *Marine et justice: La justice criminelle de la Marine française sous l'Ancien Régime* (Rennes: Presses Universitaires de Rennes, 2010), 89–92.

19. On Grard, see "Jugement rendu par le tribunal révolutionnaire, etabli à Brest à l'instar de celui de Paris, qui condamne François Grard à la peine de mort. Du premier thermidor, l'an second de la république Française, une et indivisble," AN (F), W545, Juridictions Extraordinaire, Tribunal révolutionnaire de Brest. On deserters escaping to the Vendée, see "De Secqville, à L'Orient, le 25. Mars 1793, L'an 2 de la République française," SHM-V (F), BB/3/24, Service Général, Correspondance, Lorient, 1793.

20. "Jugement rendu par le tribunal révolutionnaire, etabli à Brest à l'instar de celui de Paris, qui condamne Jean-Joesph Algant, charpentier, âgé de trente ans, demeurant

à Pournich, à la peine de mort. Du premier Floréal, l'an deux de la république Française, une et indivisible" and "Jugement rendu par le tribunal révolutionnaire, etabli à Brest à l'instar de celui de Paris, qui condamne François Legouy à la peine de mort. Du vingt-six ventôse, l'an deux de la république Française, une et indivisible," AN (F), W544, Juridictions Extraordinaire, Tribunal révolutionnaire de Brest.

21. Levée: "Jugement rendu par le tribunal révolutionnaire, etabli à Brest à l'instar de celui de Paris, qui condamne Jean-Jacques-François Levée à la peine de mort. Du premier Floréal, l'an second de la république Française, une et indivisible," AN (F), W544, Juridictions Extraordinaire, Tribunal révolutionnaire de Brest.

22. A. T. Mahan, *The Influence of Sea Power Upon the French Revolution and Empire, 1793–1812* (London: Sampson Low, Marston, and Co., 1892), 1:140–144.

23. On the collapse of French naval power and the return of the old regime's institutional structures after 1794, see Olivier Chaline, "Révolution et Marine française: Quelques remarques sur l'exercice de l'autorité," *Revue d'Histoire Maritime* 4 (2005): 173–176. On the garrisoning of troops, see "Arrêté du comité de salut public, portant des mesures pour faire rejoinder les marins fuyards ou déserteurs. Du 3 Floréal, an III [22 April 1795]," in *Recueil,* 5:266–270. On the *colonnes mobiles,* see "Substance of the last information which has reached me directly from my Correspondents in the Sea Ports, Brest 20 floral/9th May 1797," TNA (UK) WO 1/922. On mass desertions in Toulon, see "Le Comité du Salut Public aux Represetants du peuple Niou et Brunél, delégués près l'armee navale, du 7 Prairial l'an 3 [26 May 1795]," SMH-V (F) BB/4/80, Service Général, Campagnes 1795, Vol. 17.

24. On the use of soldiers onboard ship, see Thoral, *From Valmy to Waterloo,* 52. On the different disciplinary trajectory of the French republican army, see Annie Crépin, "The Army of the Republic: New Warfare and a New Army," in *Republics at War, 1776–1840: Revolutions, Conflicts, and Geopolitics in Europe and the Atlantic World,* ed. Pierre Serna, Antonino de Francesco, and Judith A. Miller (New York: Palgrave Macmillian, 2013), 131–148.

25. Thea Roodhuyzen, *In woelig vaarwater: Marineofficieren in de jaren 1779–1802* (Amsterdam: De Bataafse Leeuw, 1998), 120–121.

26. "Schepen welke in de maand Febr. 1795 nog in dienst waren" and "Rapport van 's Lands Scheepen en Vaartuijgen liggende te Vlissingen, 8 Maart 1795," NA (NL), Departement van Marine, 1795–1813, 2.01.29.01, inv. nr. 227.

27. Simon Schama, *Patriots and Liberators: Revolution in the Netherlands, 1780–1813* (New York: Vintage, 1977), 201–207; R. R. Palmer, "Much in Little: The Dutch Revolution of 1795," *The Journal of Modern History* 26, no. 1 (1954), 23; J. C. de Jonge, *Geschiedenis van het Nederlandsche zeewezen,* 2nd ed. (Haarlem: A. C. Kruseman, 1862), 5:201–202.

28. De Jonge, *Geschiedenis,* 5:209–218.

29. Roodhuyzen, *In woelig vaarwater,* 138–139. Court-martial against Jan van der Pot, November 9, 1795, and court-martial against Hendrik van der Hoer, October 10, 1795, NA (NL), Hoge Militaire Rechtspraak, 1795–1813 (1818), 2.01.11, inv. nr. 210.

30. Taco Hayo Milo, *De geheime onderhandelingen tusschen de Bataafsche en Fransche Republieken van 1795 tot 1797, in verband met de expeditie van schout bij*

nacht E. Lucas naar de Kaap de Goede Hoop (Den Helder: De Boer, 1942), 1–2; "Extract uit de Resolutien van de Heeren Staaten van Holland en Westfriesland, genomen in haar Edele Groot Mog. Vergadering op Woensdag den 10 Maart 1779," NA (NL), Admiraliteitscolleges XXXII Van Bleiswijk, 1690–1787, 1.01.47.22, inv. nr. 18; "Recueil van Resolutien Placaten 1795–1798," NA (NL), Inventaries Marine 1795–1813: Aanhangsel I, 2.01.29.02, inv. nr. 36; Jaap R. Bruijn, *The Dutch Navy in the Seventeenth and Eighteenth Centuries* (Columbia: University of South Carolina Press, 1993), 201–202; C. R. Boxer, *The Dutch Seaborne Empire 1600–1800* (Harmondsworth: Penguin, 1973), 60–93; Karel Davids, "Maritime Labour in the Netherlands, 1570–1870," *Research in Maritime History*, no. 13 (1997): 41–71.

31. Roodhuyzen, *In woelig vaarwater*, 138–140; de Jonge, *Geschiedenis*, 5:229–231; Schama, *Patriots and Liberators*, 201–207; Jonathan I. Israel, *The Dutch Republic: Its Rise, Greatness, and Fall, 1477–1806* (Oxford: Clarendon, 1998), 1127; A. P. Fortanier, *Geschiedenis van het ontstaan en de ontwikkeling der Nederlandsche koloniën* (Amsterdam: G. L. Funke, 1869), 41–42, 64–65.

32. Milo, *Geheime onderhandelingen*, 52–75; de Jonge, *Geschiedenis*, 5:237–238; Captain Gerardus Donckum's second report, NA (NL), Inventaries van de Archieven van het Departement van Marine, 1795–1813, 2.01.29.01, inv. nr. 451.

33. Captain Gerardus Donckum's second report, NA (NL), Inventaries van de Archieven van het Departement van Marine, 1795–1813, 2.01.29.01, inv. nr. 451. The official name for the United East Indies Company was Vereenigde Oostindische Compagnie, or VOC.

34. "Relaas van de Ondergeteckende gecommandeert hebbende 't Bataafse Fregatt van Oorlog Jazon, wegens de overwelding en Aflopen daarvan door de Equipage op den 4e Junij 1796 geschied, omtrent op de Noordenbreidte van 53 Graden en 357 Graden 30 minuten Lengte, en vervolgens het Opbrengen van gen: Fregatt in een Vijandelijke haven aan de Westkust van Schotland gelegen," NA (NL), Inventaries van de Archieven van het Departement van Marine, 1795–1813, 2.01.29.01, inv. nr. 451; court-martial of Jacob Hillebrand, NA (NL), Hoge Militaire Rechtspraak, 1795–1813 (1818), 2.01.11, inv. nr. 220; Transport Office, Letters to the Admiralty, June 21, 1796, and February 2, 1797, TNA (UK) ADM 98/107; Prisoners of War register, Edinburgh (and Greenock), 1796–1801, TNA (UK) ADM 103/111.

35. "Relaas" and second report, NA (NL), Inventaries van de Archieven van het Departement van Marine, 1795–1813, 2.01.29.01, inv. nr. 451.

36. Court-martial of Klaas Scheepmakers, 25 December 1795, and court-martial of Jan Christian Ludeman, 26 February 1797, NA (NL), Hoge Militaire Rechtspraak, 1795–1813 (1818), 2.01.11, inv. nr. 210; Report of first clerk Hendrik Cramer of the *Kortenaar*, 28 August 1797, Departement van Marine, 1795–1813, 2.01.29.01, inv. nr. 236; courts-martial of Jacob Cramer, Anthony Stam, Gideon Lotterij, Adrianus Keijzer, Bartholomeus Bruijn, and Gerben Gooijtjes, 4 July 1796, NA (NL), Hoge Militaire Rechtspraak, 1795–1813 (1818), 2.01.11, inv. nr. 210; courts-martial of Willem Rikkert, Johannes Breytenbach, Abram Mulder, Daniel Coens, Pieter van der End, Arij van Heusten, Arij Zuijderveld, Pieter Temperman, Klaas de Kok, Gerret Vinjer, Guiliaum Vijnands, Simon van Sluijsdam, Claas Roels, Jan Reinard,

Pieter Elling, Arno ldus Hoijel, and Arnold Homan, 8–14 November 1796, NA (NL), Hoge Militaire Rechtspraak, 1795–1813 (1818), 2.01.11, inv. nr. 210; various papers relating to the investigation of the unrest on the *Monikkendam,* NA (NL), Hoge Militaire Rechtspraak, 1795–1813 (1818), 2.01.11, inv. nr. 212. On the importance and interpretation of seamen's tattoos, see Ira Dye, "The Tattoos of Early American Seafarers, 1796–1818," *Proceedings of the American Philosophical Society* 133, no. 4 (1989): 520–554, and Simon P. Newman, "Reading the Bodies of Early American Seafarers," *William and Mary Quarterly,* 3rd series, 55, no. 1 (1998): 59–82.

37. Roodhuyzen, *In woelig vaarwater,* 123–124; de Jonge, *Geschiedenis,* 5:209–210.

38. "Relaas," NA (NL), Inventaries van de Archieven van het Departement van Marine, 1795–1813, 2.01.29.01, inv. nr. 451.

39. Letter, Captain P. Hartsinck, Surinam, 30 May 1797, NA (NL), West-Indisch Comitté, 1795–1800, 2.01.28.01, inv. nr. 128.

40. Petition, 30 May 1797, NA (NL), West-Indisch Comitté, 1795–1800, 2.01.28.01, inv. nr. 128.

41. Letter, Captain P. Hartsinck, Surinam, 30 May 1797, NA (NL), West-Indisch Comitté, 1795–1800, 2.01.28.01, inv. nr. 128.

42. Richard Price, "Dialogical Encounters in a Space of Death," in *New World Orders: Violence, Sanction, and Authority in the Colonial Americas,* ed. John Smolenski and Thomas J. Humphrey (Philadelphia: University of Pennsylvania Press, 2005), 47–65; Voltaire, *Candide, or Optimism* (London: Penguin, 1947), 85–86; J. G. Stedman, *Narrative of a Five Years' Expedition against the Revolted Negroes of Surinam, in Guiana on the Wild Coast of South America, from the Year 1772 to 1777* (London: J. Johnson and J. Edwards, 1796); Cornelis Ch. Goslinga, *The Dutch in the Caribbean and in the Guianas 1680–1791* (Dover, NH: Van Gorcum, 1985), 522–524.

43. Report, S. A. van Overfelt, 14 August 1794 to 14 May 1796, NA (NL), Departement van Marine, 1795–1813, 2.01.29.01, inv. nr. 459; Letter, P. Hartsinck, Surinam, 26 October 1796, NA (NL), West-Indisch Comitté, 1795–1800, 2.01.28.01, inv. nr. 127A; Weekly reports on state of the squadron in Surinam, NA (NL), West-Indisch Comitté, 1795–1800, 2.01.28.01, inv. nr. 127A.

44. Report, S. A. van Overfelt, 14 August 1794 to 14 May 1796, NA (NL), Departement van Marine, 1795–1813, 2.01.29.01, inv. nr. 459; "Verzameling van Zee-Orders voor de Zeemagt van het Koninkrijk der Nederlanden 1738–1829," NA (NL), Inventaries Marine 1795–1813: Aanhangsel II, 2.01.29.03, inv. nr. 2; Michael Craton, *Testing the Chains: Resistance to Slavery in the British West Indies* (Ithaca: Cornell University Press, 1982), 270–273; Cornelis Ch. Goslinga, *The Dutch in the Caribbean and in Surinam 1791/5–1942* (Assen: Van Gorcum, 1990), 1–20. For mechanism of social control in Paramaribo, see Pepijn Brandon, "Between the Plantation and the Port: Racialization and Social Control in Eighteenth-Century Paramaribo," *International Review of Social History* 64, Special Issue 27 (2019): 95–124.

45. Letter, P. Hartsinck, Surinam, 5 and 6 May 1797, NA (NL), West-Indisch Comitté, 1795–180, 2.01.28.01, inv. nr. 127A. For French West Indian privateering,

see Laurent Dubois, *A Colony of Citizens: Revolution and Slave Emancipation in the French Caribbean, 1787–1804* (Chapel Hill: University of North Carolina Press, 2004), 241–246; William S. Cormack, *Patriots, Royalists, and Terrorists in the West Indies: The French Revolution in Martinique and Guadeloupe, 1789–1802* (Toronto: University of Toronto Press, 2019), 201–210; and Edgardo Pérez Morales, *No Limits to Their Sway: Cartagena's Privateers and the Masterless Caribbean in the Age of Revolutions* (Nashville, TN: Vanderbilt University Press, 2018), 28–39.

46. "Pétition à la Convention Nationale, par les Patriotes, Citoyens de Couleur, Déportés par les Anglais et débarqués à Rochefort, après s'être rendus maîtres des Transports No. 34 et 42 par le 41me degré de latitude Nord," SHM-V (F), AA2 51, Actes du Pouvoir Souerain, Pluviose-Fructidor an II.

47. De Jonnès, *Adventures*, 219–224.

48. Letter, P. Hartsinck, Surinam, 2 and 4 October 1797, NA (NL), West-Indisch Comitté, 1795–1800, 2.01.28.01, inv. nr. 127A. For cooperation between sailors and slaves in the Greater Caribbean during the revolutionary 1790s, see Julius S. Scott, *The Common Wind: Afro-American Currents in the Age of the Haitian Revolution* (London: Verso, 2018).

49. Goslinga, *The Dutch in the Caribbean and in Surinam,* 164; courts-martial of Jan le Clerk, Gerriet Hutte, Jan Wax, and Isaac Hutte, 19 January 1798, NA (NL), West Indisch Comitté, 2.01.28.01, inv, nr. 128.

50. Weekly reports on state of the squadron in Surinam, NA (NL), West-Indisch Comitté, 1795–1800, 2.01.28.01, inv. nr. 127A; Report on the conspiracy on the *Havick,* NA (NL), West-Indisch Comitté, 1795–1800, 2.01.28.01, inv. nr. 128.

51. March 28 and May 13, 1796, Vice-Admiral Engelbertus Lucas' dispatches; the strength of the squadron at Gran Canaria, NA (NL), Hoge Militaire Rechtspraak, 1795–1813 (1818), 2.01.11, inv. nr. 221.

52. May 13, 1796, Vice-Admiral Engelbertus Lucas' dispatches; "Relatie van mijne Reise naar Indien in 1796, op het Esquader van den Schout bij Nacht Lucas"; and *Nationaale Bataafse Courant,* 31 May 1797, NA (NL), Hoge Militaire Rechtspraak, 1795–1813 (1818), 2.01.11, inv. nr. 221.

53. August 20, 1796, Vice-Admiral Engelbertus Lucas's dispatches; Statement of the *Trompe*'s officers; *Nationaale Bataafse Courant,* 31 May 1797, NA (NL), Hoge Militaire Rechtspraak, 1795–1813 (1818), 2.01.11, inv. nr. 221. The ship's name *Havick* is spelled *Havik* in these sources, at variance with its spelling in sources for note 50 above.

54. August 20, 1796, Vice-Admiral Engelbertus Lucas's dispatches; Statement of the *Castor*'s officers; Statement of the *Revolutie*'s officers; and *Nationaale Bataafse Courant,* 31 May 1797, NA (NL), Hoge Militaire Rechtspraak, 1795–1813 (1818), 2.01.11, inv. nr. 221.

55. *Nationaale Bataafse Courant,* 31 May 1797; Report of Captain Adjoint A. J. Knok, NA (NL), Hoge Militaire Rechtspraak, 1795–1813 (1818), 2.01.11, inv. nr. 221.

56. August 20, 1796, Vice-Admiral Engelbertus Lucas's dispatches; conclusions of the council of war, 16 August 1796; August 20, 1796, Vice-Admiral Engelbertus Lucas's dispatches; and "Relatie," NA (NL), Hoge Militaire Rechtspraak, 1795–1813 (1818), 2.01.11, inv. nr. 221.

57. Report of Captain Adjoint A. J. Knok, NA (NL), Hoge Militaire Rechtspraak, 1795–1813 (1818), 2.01.11, inv. nr. 221; Admiral Elphinstone, terms of the capitulation and letter to the Admiralty, 30 August 1796, TNA (UK) ADM 1/55; September 22 and December 7, 1796, Vice-Admiral Engelbertus Lucas's dispatches, NA (NL), Hoge Militaire Rechtspraak, 1795–1813 (1818), 2.01.11, inv. nr. 221; Letter, Admiral Elphinstone to the Admiralty, 1 November 1796, TNA (UK) 1/55.

58. "Digest of the Admiralty Records of Trials by Court-Martial, From the 1st January 1755 to 1st January 1806; Fifty-One Years," TNA (UK) ADM 12/24. In order to better illustrate the overall trend, I have removed from the analysis one very atypical 1758 trial that involved forty-five defendants and ended in acquittal. No similar mass trial for mutiny occurred throughout the period.

59. For the number of men in the Royal Navy, see N. A. M. Rodger, *The Command of the Ocean: A Naval History of Britain, 1649–1815* (New York: W. W. Norton, 2004), 638–639.

60. For the mid-century naval reform movement, see Kinkel, *Disciplining the Empire,* esp. chs. 3 and 4. For changes to the impressment system, see Denver Brunsman, *The Evil Necessity: British Naval Impressment in the Eighteenth-Century Atlantic World* (Charlottesville: University of Virginia Press, 2013), 69–71.

61. "Digest of the Admiralty Records of Trials by Court-Martial, From the 1st January 1755 to 1st January 1806; Fifty-One Years," TNA (UK) ADM 12/24. For a broader analysis of increasing disciplinary violence in this period, see Patrick Underwood, Steven Pfaff, and Michael Hechter, "Threat, Deterrence, and Penal Severity: An Analysis of Flogging in the Royal Navy, 1740–1820," *Social Science History* 42, no. 3 (2018): 411–439.

62. "Winchelsea Crew," 17 August 1793, Petitions 1793–1797, TNA (UK) ADM 1/5125; "Winchelsea Crew," 14 September 1793, Petitions 1793–1797, TNA (UK) ADM 1/5125; court-martial of William Price, William Duggan, and Robert Field of the *Winchelsea,* 30 September to 2 October 1793, TNA (UK) ADM 1/5330.

63. Court-martial of William Price et al., TNA (UK) ADM 1/5330. For petitions sent to the Admiralty between 1793–1797, see TNA (UK) ADM 1/5125. Rousseau opens Book I, Chapter I of *The Social Contract* with "Man is born free, and everywhere he is in chains." Jean-Jacques Rousseau, *The Social Contract and Other Later Political Writings,* ed. Victor Gourevitch (Cambridge: Cambridge University Press, 1997), 41.

64. Court-martial of William Shield and George McKinley of the *Windsor Castle,* 11 November 1794, TNA (UK) ADM 1/5331; Letter, William Hotham to the Admiralty, Britannica, St. Fiorenzo Bay, 10 November 1794, TNA (UK) ADM 1/392.

65. Court-martial of William Shield and George McKinley of the *Windsor Castle,* 11 November 1794, TNA (UK) ADM 1/5331; Letter, William Hotham to the Admiralty, Britannica, St. Fiorenzo Bay, 10 November 1794, TNA (UK) ADM 1/392; Hyde Parker to William Hotham, St. Fiorenzo Bay, 10 November 1794, TNA (UK) ADM 1/392.

66. Letter, William Hotham to the Admiralty, Britannica, St. Fiorenzo Bay, 10 November 1794, TNA (UK) ADM 1/392; Letter, William Hotham to the Admiralty, Britannica, St. Fiorenzo Bay, 12 November 1794, TNA (UK) ADM 1/392.

67. Court-martial of Hugh Irwin et al., 25 September to 3 October 1795, TNA (UK) ADM 1/5331.

68. The events of the mutiny are reconstructed from the minutes of the court-martial trial against Francis Watts, James Johnson (the 2nd), Cornelius Sullivan, Joseph Curtain, David Hyman, Jeremiah Collins, Samuel Triggs, James Leader, John Morrish, and James Bartlett of the *Culloden,* 15 to 20 December 1794, TNA (UK) ADM 1/5331; the correspondence contained in Letters from the Commander-in-Chief, Portsmouth, 1794, TNA (UK) ADM 1/1008; *Culloden,* Captain's log, 9 November 1794 to 8 November 1795, TNA (UK) ADM 51/1130; *Culloden,* Master's log, 29 December 1793 to 29 December 1794, TNA (UK) ADM 52/3014.

69. Court-martial of Francis Watts et al., TNA (UK) ADM 1/5331.

70. *Culloden,* Captain's log, 9 November 1794 to 8 November 1795, TNA (UK) ADM 51/1130; Jonathan Neale, *The Cutlass and the Lash: Mutiny and Discipline in Nelson's Navy* (London: Pluto, 1985), 68–71; P. K. Crimmin, "Troubridge, Sir Thomas, first baronet (c. 1758–1807)," in *Oxford Dictionary of National Biography* (Oxford: Oxford University Press, 2004), 55:435–440.

71. *Culloden,* Captain's log, 9 November 1794 to 8 November 1795, TNA (UK) ADM 51/1130; Neale, *The Cutlass and the Lash,* 68–71, 75–76.

72. William James, *The Naval History of Great Britain, from the Declaration of War by France, in February 1793; to the Accession of George IV, in January 1820* (London: Baldwin, Cradock, and Joy, 1822), 1:234.

73. During the initial confusion, 82 men opposed to the mutiny fled or were driven up on deck and, according to Troubridge, another 46 remained stuck below against their will. There is no indication that they tried to interfere with the mutiny in any way. Court-martial of Francis Watts et al., TNA (UK) ADM 1/5331; Letter, Thomas Troubridge to Admiral Peter Parker, Culloden, Spithead, 6 December 1794, TNA (UK) ADM 1/1008; court-martial of Francis Watts et al., TNA (UK) ADM 1/5331.

74. "Attachments," court-martial of Francis Watts et al., TNA (UK) ADM 1/5331.

75. Neale, *The Cutlass and the Lash,* 85; Marcus Rediker, *Between the Devil and the Deep Blue Sea: Merchant Seamen, Pirates, and the Anglo-American Maritime World, 1700–1750* (Cambridge: Cambridge University Press, 1987), 233.

76. Neale, *The Cutlass and the Lash,* 71–72, 76.

77. Letter, Admiral Parker to the Lords of the Admiralty, Royal William, Spithead, December 7, 1794, TNA (UK) ADM 1/1008; letter, Captains Seymour and Pakenham to Admiral Parker, Leviathan, Spithead, December 7, 1794, TNA (UK) ADM 1/1008; letter, Admiral Parker to the Lords of the Admiralty, Royal William, Spithead, December 9, 1794, TNA (UK) ADM 1/1008.

78. "Attachments," court-martial of Francis Watts et al., TNA (UK) ADM 1/5331; Letter, Captains Seymour and Pakenham to Admiral Parker, Leviathan,

Spithead, 7 December 1794, TNA (UK) ADM 1/1008; court-martial of Francis Watts et al., TNA (UK) ADM 1/5331; *Culloden* muster book, October 1 to November 8, 1794, TNA (UK) ADM 36/12169.

79. James Dugan, *The Great Mutiny* (New York: G. P. Putnam's Sons, 1965), 107–108.

80. Letter, Thomas Troubridge to Admiral Peter Parker, Culloden, Spithead, 6 December 1794, TNA (UK) ADM 1/1008; court-martial of Francis Watts et al., TNA (UK) ADM 1/5331.

81. *Kongl. Maj:ts Krigs-Articlar för des krigsmagt til lands och siös, gifne Stockholms Slott den 31 Martii 1798* (Stockholm: Kongl. Tryckeriet, 1798), ch. 5, §14; for the operation, in theory and practice, of the British naval court-martial, see John D. Byrn, Jr., *Crime and Punishment in the Royal Navy: Discipline on the Leeward Islands Station, 1784–1812* (Aldershot: Scolar Press, 1989). See also Marcus Eder, *Crime and Punishment in the Royal Navy of the Seven Years' War, 1755–1763* (Aldershot: Ashgate, 2004); court-martial of William Price et al., TNA (UK) ADM 1/5330; court-martial of Francis Watts et al., TNA (UK) ADM 1/5331; Neale, *The Cutlass and the Lash,* 95–97.

82. For a discussion of court-martial proceedings as a site of counterinsurgency and resistance, see David Featherstone, "Counter-Insurgency, Subalternity and Spatial Relations: Interrogating Court-Martial Narratives of the Nore Mutiny of 1797," *South African Historical Journal* 61, no. 4 (2009): 766–787. For the description of a hanging, see Joshua Davis, *A Narrative of Joshua Davis* (Boston, 1811), 66.

83. Court-martial of William Parker (1st) et al., January 20 to February 11, 1796, TNA (UK) ADM 1/5334.

84. Kemp, *The British Sailor,* 139; Court-martial of William Parker (1st) et al., TNA (UK) ADM 1/5334. Many naval historians continue to deny the existence of homosexuality on the lower deck despite ample evidence to the contrary, including in the court-martial minutes of the *Defiance* trial. Court-martial of William Parker (1st) et al., TNA (UK) ADM 1/5334; and Neale, *The Cutlass and the Lash,* 161–162. See also B. R. Burg, *Boys at Sea: Sodomy, Indecency, and Courts Martial in Nelson's Navy* (New York: Palgrave Macmillan, 2007). "Copy of Petition from the Defiance," TNA (UK) ADM 1/522.

85. Court-martial of William Parker (1st) et al., TNA (UK) ADM 1/5334.

86. "Copy of Letter thrown on the Quarter Deck of the Defiance. Writer not known," TNA (UK) ADM 1/522.

87. Norman McCord and David E. Brewster, "Some Labour Troubles of the 1790s in North East England," *International Review of Social History* 13, no. 3 (1968): 366–383.

88. Nicholas Rogers, *The Press Gang: Naval impressment and its Opponents in Georgian Britain* (London: Continuum, 2007), 106–107; "A Song. Tune—Rule Britannia," in Thomas Spence, *One Pennyworth of Pig's Meat; or, Lessons for the Swinish Multitude* (London, 1793–95), 2:67; court-martial of William Parker (1st) et al., TNA (UK) ADM 1/5334.

89. Letter, Admiral Pringle to the Lords of the Admiralty, on board the *Asia,* October 19, 1795, TNA (UK) ADM 1/522; Gavin Kennedy, "Bligh and the *Defiance* Mutiny," *Mariner's Mirror* 65, no. 1 (1979): 65–68; court-martial of William Parker (1st) et al., TNA (UK) ADM 1/5334; Neale, *The Cutlass and the Lash,* 159.

CHAPTER FOUR: A REVOLUTION IN THE FLEET

1. For an overview of Britain's troubles during the mid-1790s, see Roger Knight, *Britain Against Napoleon: The Organization of Victory, 1793–1815* (London: Penguin, 2014), 61–94.

2. For a survey of France's invasion plans, see Sylvie Kleinman, "Initiating Insurgencies Abroad: French Plans to 'Chouannise' Britain and Ireland, 1793–1798," *Small Wars and Insurgencies* 25, no. 4 (2014): 784–799.

3. For Graham's findings, see "Aaron Graham to John King, Esq., Portsmouth, 22 May 1797," TNA (UK) ADM 1/4172; for Lady Spencer's muttering, see "Lady Spencer to William Windham, Wimbledon, April 20, 1797," in William Windham, *The Windham Papers, Volume II* (Boston: Small, Maynard and Co., 1913), 48–49.

4. "16th June 1797, Letter on the Subject of the Fleet," NMM (UK) WYN/109/7.

5. "Captain Payne to Spencer, George Inn, 18th April, 1797," in *Private Papers of George, second Earl Spencer, First Lord of the Admiralty, 1794–1801,* ed. Julian S. Corbett (London: Navy Records Society, 1914), 2:113.

6. For Pakenham's exchange with Earl Spencer, see Ann Veronica Coats, "'Launched into Eternity': Admiralty Retribution or the Restoration of Discipline?," in *The Naval Mutinies of 1797: Unity and Perseverance,* ed. Ann Veronica Coats and Philip MacDougall (Woodbridge: Boydell Press, 2011), 212–213. For Patton's warning, see Philip Patton, *Observations on Naval Mutiny* (1795), 5.

7. Patton, *Observations on Naval Mutiny,* 5; Philip Patton, "Observations on the State of Discipline in the Navy, End of the Year 1797. In a Letter to a Friend," in *The Natural Defense of an Insular Empire, Earnestly Recommended; with A Sketch of a Plan, to Attach Real Seamen to the Service of Their Country* (Southampton: T. Skelton, 1810), 8, 13–14.

8. Patton, *Observations on Naval Mutiny,* 6–7. For deserters to the United States and efforts to better regulate the issuing of US citizenship certificates, see Nathan Perl-Rosenthal, *Citizen Sailors: Becoming American in the Age of Revolution* (Cambridge, MA: Belknap Press of Harvard University Press, 2015).

9. For Watson and Jetking, see "Interrogation of George Watson of the Oldenbarneveld" and "Interrogation of William Jetking," NA (NL), Hoge Militaire Rechtspraak, 1795–1813 (1818), 2.01.11, inv. nr. 238.

10. For the crew of the *Monarch,* see Monarch muster book, 1797, TNA (UK) ADM 36/11752. For formerly Dutch sailors sent to the Nore, see Minutes, Sick and Hurt Board, 1796, TNA (UK) ADM 99/266. For the *Savage,* see Letter, Overijssel, Downs, 19th June 1797, TNA (UK) ADM 1/668. For the mutiny on the *Brutus,* see *Stockholms Post-Tidningar,* January 30, 1797.

11. For the background and status of the leading mutineers at Spithead, see William Manwaring and Bonamy Dobree, *The Floating Republic: An Account of the Mutinies at Spithead and the Nore in 1797* (Barnsley: Pen and Sword, 2004), 262–263. Philip Patton, *Observations on the State of Discipline in the Navy, End of the Year 1797. In a Letter to a Friend* (n.p., n.d.), 15. For the demographic background of the marines, see Britt Zerbe, *The Birth of the Royal Marines, 1664–1802* (Woodbridge: Boydell Press, 2013), 87–100.

12. For the Nore mutineer, see "No. 29" (Note, Henry Long to the Lords Commissioners of the Board of the Admiralty, onboard the *Champion,* n.d.), Papers found onboard the *Repulse,* 12 June 1797, TNA (UK) ADM 1/727 C370.

13. Owen, "Recollections," NMM (UK) COO/2/A. For the 1783 mutinies, see John Barrow, *The Life of Richard Earl Howe, K.G., Admiral of the Fleet, and General of Marines* (London: John Murray, 1838), 165–168.

14. For the conciliatory behavior of the delegates, see Owen, "Recollections," NMM (UK) COO/2/A. For the mutineers' rules and orders, see Ann Veronica Coats, "Spithead Mutiny: Introduction," in *The Naval Mutinies of 1797*, ed. Coats and MacDougall, 24–25.

15. For the Admiralty's lackluster response, see Conrad Gill, *The Naval Mutinies of 1797* (Manchester: Manchester University Press, 1913), 24–25. For the internal structures of self-government set up by the mutineers, see Owen, "Recollections," NMM (UK) COO/2/A; and Philip Patton, "An Account of the First Mutinous Combination among the Seamen, which took place at Spithead on the 13th April 1797, with Observations," NMM (UK) TUN/212. For "dual power," see Leon Trotsky, *History of the Russian Revolution* (Chicago: Haymarket, 2008), 149–155.

16. For traditional practices of shipboard authority, see Cheryl Fury, *Tides in the Affairs of Men: The Social History of Elizabethan Seamen, 1580–1603* (Westport, CT: Greenwood, 2002), 45–84; Robin Ward, *The World of the Medieval Shipmaster: Law, Business and the Sea c. 1350–c. 1450* (Woodbridge: Boydell Press, 2009), 100–113.

17. On the Gardner incident, see Owen, "Recollections," NMM (UK) COO/2/A. See also David W. London, "What Really Happened On Board HMS *London?*" in *The Naval Mutinies of 1797*, ed. Coats and MacDougall, 61–78.

18. Owen, "Recollections," NMM (UK) COO/2/A. Declarations of the crews and marines of the *Marlborough,* the *Pompée,* the *Terrible,* and the *Ramillies,* TNA (UK) ADM 1/4172.

19. Owen, "Recollections," NMM (UK) COO/2/A.

20. Ibid.

21. Ibid.

22. Patton, *Observations on Naval Mutiny*, 17.

23. "Captain Payne to Spencer, George Inn, 18th April, 1797," in Corbett, *Private Papers of George, Second Earl Spencer*, 2:112–113.

24. *Address to the Nation, by the Seamen at St. Helen's* (Edinburgh, 1797), 3–4.

25. Owen, "Recollections," NMM (UK) COO/2/A.

26. "To Dr. Alexander Carlyle, *Excellent*, off Cadiz, June 3, 1797," in *The Private Correspondence of Admiral Lord Collingwood*, ed. Edward Hughes (London: Naval Records Society, 1957), 82–83.

27. "Address from the British Seamen and Marines at the Nore to their Brethren and Fellow Subjects on shore," Papers found onboard the *Repulse*, 12 June 1797, TNA (UK) ADM 1/727 C370.

28. On the division of prize money, see Dudley Pope, *Life in Nelson's Navy* (London: Unwin Hyman, 1981), 234. On criticism against that division, see "Address from the British Seamen and Marines at the Nore to their Brethren and Fellow Subjects on shore," Papers found onboard the *Repulse*, 12 June 1797, TNA (UK) ADM 1/727 C370. On the North Sea fleet's suggestions, see "Articles demanded by the North Sea Fleet in addition to those demanded by the Fleet at the Nore," Papers found onboard the *Repulse*, 12 June 1797, TNA (UK) ADM 1/727 C370.

29. "Address from the British Seamen and Marines at the Nore to their Brethren and Fellow Subjects on shore," Papers found onboard the *Repulse*, 12 June 1797, TNA (UK) ADM 1/727 C370. On impressment and Magna Carta, see J. R. Hutchinson, *The Press-Gang Afloat and Ashore* (New York: E. P. Dutton and Co., 1914), 5, 7.

30. "Articles demanded by the North Sea Fleet in addition to those demanded by the Fleet at the Nore," Papers found onboard the *Repulse*, 12 June 1797, TNA (UK) ADM 1/727 C370. For the French officer's complaint, see "Aux Représentans du Peuple composant la commission nommée par le conseil des cinq cens pour le code penal maritime," SHM-V (F), CC/3/1650, Personnel, Troupes et équipages (1792–1913), Lettres reçue se rapportant à diverses questions de justice maritime.

31. "Address from the British Seamen and Marines at the Nore to their Brethren and Fellow Subjects on shore," Papers found onboard the *Repulse*, 12 June 1797, TNA (UK) ADM 1/727 C370; Declarations of the crew of the *Pompée*, TNA (UK) ADM 1/4172; Declarations of the crew of the *Marlborough*, TNA (UK) ADM 1/4172.

32. For a list of the ships that participated at the Nore, see James Dugan, *The Great Mutiny* (New York: G. P. Putnam's Sons, 1965), 476–478. For a copy of the full oath, see "No. 7," Papers found onboard the *Repulse*, 12 June 1797, TNA (UK) ADM 1/727 C370. On the importance of oaths to "subaltern political activity" during the 1790s, see David Featherstone, *Resistance, Space and Political Identities: The Making of Counter-Global Networks* (Chichester: Wiley-Blackwell, 2008), 110–114. On women being sworn, most of them presumably visiting wives, girlfriends, and sex workers, see court-martial of John Burrows et al., 22–25 August 1797, TNA (UK) ADM 1/5341. For the use of "floating republic" among the mutineers, see *Memoirs of Richard Parker, the Mutineer* (London, 1797), 18. On the committee of liberty, see "No. 8," Papers found onboard the *Repulse*, 12 June 1797, TNA (UK) ADM 1/727 C370. On the composition of general ship committees, see court-martial of Richard Brown et al., 29 July–5 August 1797, TNA (UK) ADM 1/5340. On fleet-wide committees, see Charles Cunningham, *A Narrative of Occurrences That Took Place during the Mutiny at the Nore* (Chatham, 1829), 15; and T. K. King to Jenny King, Sheerness, June 1, 1797, TNA (UK) PC 1/38/122. On committee

voting, see court-martial of William Gregory et al., 6–19 July 1797, TNA (UK) ADM 1/5340.

33. For the modified oath, see "No. 7," Papers found onboard the *Repulse,* 12 June 1797, TNA (UK) ADM 1/727 C370. For the Rules and Regulations, see No. 40 ("Orders and Regulations to be observed on board the different ships in the fleet, May 13 1797"), Papers found onboard the *Repulse,* 12 June 1797, TNA (UK) ADM 1/727 C370. For the *Pylades,* see "No. 6," Report and results of the papers found on board the *Inflexible,* TNA (UK) ADM 3/137. For the prohibition on dual office holding, see court-martial of Richard Brown et al., TNA (UK) ADM 1/5340.

34. For the *Leopard,* see court-martial of Dennis Sullivan et al., 28 June-4 July 1797, TNA (UK) ADM 1/5339; for the *Grampus,* see court-martial of James Smart et al., 10–12 July 1797, TNA (UK) ADM 1/5340; for the *Monmouth,* see court-martial of Richard Brown et al., TNA (UK) ADM 1/5340.

35. On the tearing down of gallows, see John Markoff, *The Abolition of Feudal-ism: Peasants, Lords, and Legislators in the French Revolution* (University Park: The Pennsylvania State University Press, 1996), 224–225. On the concepts of destituent and constituent power, see Raffaele Laudani, *Disobedience in Western Political Thought: A Genealogy* (New York: Cambridge University Press, 2013). On the symbolic function of gallows, see Joris Coolen, "Places of Justice and Awe: The Topography of Gibbets and Gallows in Medieval and Early Modern North-Western and Central Europe," *World Archeology* 45, no. 5 (2013): 762–779.

36. For the "sacred laws," see "No. 12," Papers found onboard the *Repulse,* June 12, 1797, TNA (UK) ADM 1/727 C370; for the use of juries, see court-martial of Dennis Sullivan et al., TNA (UK) ADM 1/5339; for the provision of councilors, see "No. 9" and "No. 11," Papers found onboard the *Repulse,* June 12, 1797, TNA (UK) ADM 1/727 C370; for the *Proserpine,* see Cunningham, *Narrative,* 13–14; for the *Monmouth,* see court-martial of Richard Brown et al., TNA (UK) ADM 1/5340.

37. Patton, "An Account of the First Mutinous Combination," NMM (UK) TUN/212. On ducking, see John H. Dacam, "'Wanton and Torturing Punishments': Patterns of Discipline and Punishment in the Royal Navy, 1783–1815" (PhD diss., University of Hull, 2009), 102.

38. W. G. Perrin, *British Flags: Their Early History, and their Development at Sea; With an Account of the Origin of the Flag as a National Device* (Cambridge: Cambridge University Press, 1922), 160–161; Marcus Rediker, *Villains of All Nations: Atlantic Pirates in the Golden Age* (Boston: Beacon Press, 2004), 83; R. B. Rose, "A Liverpool Sailors' Strike in the Eighteenth Century," *Transactions of the Lancashire and Cheshire Antiquarian Society,* 68 (1958): 85; for the Rotterdam riot, see NA (NL), 1.01.47.21 (Admiraliteitscolleges XXXI Bisdom, 1525–1793), inv. nr. 163; "Philadelphia General Advertiser: Reports from the Insurrection, October-November 1791," in *Slave Revolution in the Caribbean, 1789–1804: A Brief History with Documents,* ed. Laurent Dubois and John D. Garrigus (Boston: Bedford/St. Martin's, 2006), 98; Cunningham, *Narrative,* 8; *The Whole Trial and Defense of Richard Parker, President of the Delegates for Mutiny, etc.* (London, 1797), 4, 12, 34–35; court-martial against the men from the fleet at the Nore, TNA (UK) ADM 1/5339.

39. "The Delegates of the Different Ships at the Nore Assembled in Council—to their fellow Subjects," Petitions 1793–1797, TNA (UK) ADM 1/5125; Anne Hawkins and Helen Watt, "'Now Is Our Time, the Ship Is Our Own, Huzza for the Red Flag': Mutiny on the Inspector, 1797," *Mariner's Mirror*, 93, no. 2 (2007): 156; court-martial against the men from the fleet at the Nore, TNA (UK) ADM 1/5339; court-martial against the men from the *Sandwich*, TNA (UK) ADM 1/5340; Perrin, *British Flags*, 175.

40. For Gregory, see court-martial of William Gregory et al., TNA (UK) ADM 1/5340; for Jephson, see court-martial of Thomas Jephson of the *Sandwich*, 27 July 1797, TNA (UK) ADM 1/5340; for Lee, see courts-martial of Robert Lee, 23 June 1797, Daniel Coffey, 24 June 1797, and John McGinness, 26 June 1797, Plymouth, TNA (UK) ADM 1/5491; Letter to Charles Grenville, Dublin Castle, 4 July 1797, TNA (UK) HO 100/70; see also Thomas L. Haughton, "The Execution of Three Royal Marines on Plymouth Hoe in 1797," *Irish Sword* 11, no. 45 (1974): 246–247.

41. For Roberts, see William Roberts to Elizabeth Roberts, *Director*, 2 June 1797, TNA (UK) PC 1/38/122; for the delegates' address, see "The Delegates of the Different Ships at the Nore Assembled in Council—to their fellow subjects," included in court-martial of William Gregory et al., TNA (UK) ADM 1/5340; for Shave, see court-martial of Dennis Sullivan et al., TNA (UK) ADM 1/5339.

42. Court-martial of William Guthrie et al., 20–23 July 1797, TNA (UK) ADM 1/5339.

43. For demonstrations at Sheerness, see Cunningham, *Narrative*, 12, 17, 70; for the Wests' letter, see J. and M. West to Thomas West, Chertsey, 5 June 1797, TNA (UK) HO 42/212; for Williams, see court-martial of Thomas Williams, 24 June 1797, TNA (UK) ADM 1/5339; on connections to London radicals, see James Epstein, "The Radical Underworld Goes Colonial: P. F. McCallum's *Travels in Trinidad*," in *Unrespectable Radicals? Popular Politics in the Age of Reform*, ed. Michael T. Davis and Paul A. Pickering (Aldergate: Ashgate, 2008), 148; court-martial of William Gregory et al., TNA (UK) ADM 1/5340; court-martial of Thomas Jephson, TNA (UK) ADM 1/5340; Cunningham, *Narrative*, 97–100.

44. John James to Susanna Johnson, *Belliqueux*, 1 June 1797, TNA (UK) PC 1/38/122; Letter, R. Mabson to Mrs Mabson, *Nassau*, 2 June 1797, TNA (UK) PC 1/38/122; John Pickering to James Pickering, Yarmouth, 29 May 1797, TNA (UK) PC 1/38/122; John Cox to Mrs John Cox Galston, Nore, 31 May 1797, TNA (UK) PC 1/38/122.

45. For Bantry Bay and Madeira, see court-martial of Dennis Sullivan et al., TNA (UK) ADM 1/5339; for the "new colony," see "No. 57," Report and results of the papers found on board the *Inflexible*, TNA (UK) ADM 3/137; for illness onboard the *Sandwich*, see Surgeon William Snipe to Captain James Robert Mosse of the *Sandwich*, 22 March 1797, TNA (UK) ADM 1/727; for the refusal to accept sick mutineers, see Cunningham, *Narrative*, 70.

46. *Memoirs of Richard Parker*, 20.

47. For Wallace, see Cunningham, *Narrative*, 82; on the *Leopard*, see court-martial of Dennis Sullivan et al., TNA (UK) ADM 1/5339.

48. Alexander Davison to Robert Dunn, *Sandwich,* 2 June 1797, TNA (UK) PC 1/38/122.

49. For Matthew Hollister, see court-martial of William Parker (1st) et al., 20 January–11 February 1796, TNA (UK) ADM 1/5334; Gill, *Naval Mutinies,* 171; for Isaac Bowstead, see William Mason to the Duke of Portland, Colchester, 25 June 1797, TNA (UK) ADM 1/4172.

50. On mutineers heading to the Low Countries, see "Extract from a letter from Gravesend, 26 July 1797, forwarded to Evan Nepean," TNA (UK) ADM 1/4173; to the United States, see Moreau de Jonnès, *Adventures in the Revolution and under the Consulate* (London: Peter Davies, 1969), 157; "Captain Truxtun concerning mutinous assemblies on board U.S. Frigate *Constellation,* 2 July 1798," in *Naval Documents Related to the Quasi-War between the United States and France* (Washington, DC: Government Printing Office, 1935), 1:157. For Sweden, Rolf Karlbom, *Hungeruplopp och strejker 1793–1867: En studie i den svenska arbetarrörelsens uppkomst* (Lund: Gleerup, 1967), 41–42. For similar examples from the Danish press, see *Minerva, et Maanedskrivt* 48 (April, May, and June 1797), 121–124, 250–251, 388–392.

51. On the *Marquis of Carmathen,* see "Capt. Thomas Middleton to Evan Nepean, Comet, Lynn Roads, 15th May 1797," TNA (UK) ADM 1/2133. On the *Lady Shore,* see "Mutiny on the Lady Shore, 28 May 1798," in *Historical Records of New South Wales. Volume III—Hunter. 1796–1799,* ed. F. M. Bladen (Sydney: Charles Potter, 1895), 392–395; John Black, *An Authentic Narrative of the Mutiny Aboard the Ship Lady Shore* (Ipswich, n.d.); James George Semple Lisle, *The Life of Major J. G. Semple Lisle* (London, 1799), 181–182; "Rapport au Directoire exécutif, par le ministre des relations extérieures, sur les prisonniers français qui se sont rendus maîtres du bâtiment anglais sur lequel ils étaient conduits à Botany-bay. Du 1.er Germinal an VI. [21 March 1798]," in *Recueil,* 8:399–406.

52. On fears that the mutiny might spread, see "Captain Payne to Spencer, George Inn, 18th April, 1797," in Corbett, *Private Papers of George, Second Earl Spencer,* 2:113; Cunningham, *Narrative,* x. On the idea of blacklisting, see Stow to Evan Nepean, 27 May 1797, TNA (UK) ADM 1/727 C341. For the resolution, see "At a Numerous and Respectable Meeting of Merchants, Ship-Owners, and Insurers, and other Inhabitants of London, concerned in Commerce and Navigation, etc.," TNA (UK) ADM 3/137.

53. Ann Veronica Coats, "Parker, Richard (1767–1797)," *Oxford Dictionary of National Biography,* Oxford University Press, 2004; online, January 2008 at http://www.oxforddnb.com/view/article/21333, accessed 9 Aug 2017.

54. Camden Pelham, *The Chronicles of Crime; or, The New Newgate Calendar, Vol. 1* (London: Thomas Tegg, 1841), 356–358.; *Epochs and Episodes of History: Memorable Days and Notable Events* (London: Ward, Lock, and Co., 1882), 386.

55. "Eliz. Burk to Barth. Burk, Inflexible, June 23, 1797," TNA (UK) HO 42/212.

56. "Examination taken by the JPs of the Borough and Town of Deal of mutineers trying to escape to France, 15 June 1797," TNA (UK) ADM 1/4172; for the *Inflexible* fugitives, see "Affaire des matelots anglais de l'Inflexible," AN (F)

F/7/7264, Dossier 9686, and "Aux Representants du Directoire Executif, 16 Juin 1797/28 prairial an V," AN (F) AF III 58 plaq. 2 (I am grateful to Nathan Perl-Rosenthal and Matthieu Ferradou respectively for these references); for mention of the *Le Président-Parker* privateer, see Morard de Galles to the Minister of Marine, Brest, 11 frimaire year VI/1 December 1797, SHM-V (F), BB/3/114, f. 207.

57. Walt Whitman, "Richard Parker's Widow," in *The Early Poems and the Fiction*, ed. Thomas L. Brasher (New York: New York University Press, 1963), 296; on Parker's disinterment and funeral, see Gill, *The Naval Mutinies*, 247–249, and Pelham, *The Chronicles of Crime*, 356–358; on the importance of capital punishment to the eighteenth-century British state and economy, see Peter Linebaugh, *The London Hanged: Crime and Civil Society in the Eighteenth Century* (Cambridge: Cambridge University Press, 1992); for the government's advice to the Admiralty, see John King to Evan Nepean, Whitehall, 4 July 1797, TNA (UK) ADM 1/4173.

58. For the attack on Newgate Prison, see Linebaugh, *The London Hanged*, 333–370; due to the incomplete and sometimes unclear documentation, historians disagree about the exact number of men sentenced and executed, though all estimates are within a similar range. For a compilation of estimates, see Dugan, *The Great Mutiny*, 389–390. My own figures are based on the partially incomplete "List of the Mutineers," TNA (UK) ADM 3/137; on mutineers sent to New South Wales, see "Convicts transported, 1787–1809," TNA (UK) HO 11/1. See also Bryan Gandevia, "Redfern, William (1774/5-1833), convict surgeon and pastoralist in Australia," *Oxford Dictionary of National Biography* (New York: Oxford University Press, 2004); online, September 23, 2004 at https://doi-org.pitt.idm.oclc .org/10.1093/ref:odnb/52448, accessed December 13, 2019; on the *Eagle*, see Dugan, *The Great Mutiny*, 390.

59. William Cruchley to the Duke of Portland, 27 July 1797, TNA (UK) PC 1/44/156; Entry book for Admiralty prisoners, 1773–1799, TNA (UK) PRIS 11/15; List of pardoned mutineers sent to Coldbath Fields prison in preparation of their being sent to the hulks, TNA (UK) ADM 1/4173. See also Jerry White, "Pain and Degradation in Georgian London: Life in the Marshalsea Prison," *History Workshop Journal* 68 (2009): 69–98.

60. On general conditions, see Francis Burdett, *Cold Bath Fields Prison, by some called the English Bastille!* (London, 1799), 11; for the description of the cells, see Affidavit by Joseph Burks, LMA (UK) MJ/SP/1799/FEB/054/1–4; for victuals, see *Impartial Statement of the Cruelties Discovered in the Coldbath-Fields Prison, by the Grand and Traverse Juries for the County of Middlesex, and Reported in the House of Commons, on Friday the 11th of June, 1800* (London: J.S. Jordan, 1800), 15; for the condition of the prisoners, see "Register of the Deaths of Prisoners in the House of Correction for the County of Middlesex; and of what Diseases or Complaint they died," LMA (UK) MA/G/CBF/417.

61. On Janet Evans and Elizabeth Bone, see Iain MacCalman, *Radical Underworld: Prophets, Revolutionaries and Pornographers in London, 1795–1840* (Cambridge: Cambridge University Press, 1988), 16; J. Ann Hone, *For the Cause of Truth: Radicalism in London, 1796–1821* (Oxford: Clarendon Press, 1982), 121–128. For

Catherine Despard's anti-prison activism, see Peter Linebaugh, *Red Round Globe Hot Burning: A Tale at the Crossroads of Commons and Closure, of Love and Terror, of Race and Class, and of Kate and Ned Despard* (Oakland: University of California Press, 2019), 355-373. For Janet Evans's role as go-between, see "Statement of Thomas Aris" and "Second examination of Thomas Aris, 14 January 1799," Middlesex— Proceedings of the General Quarter Sessions in the Month of January 1799 respecting several Matters relating to the House of Correction for the said County and certain Prisoners confined in that Prison, LMA (UK) MA/G/GEN/450. For the failed insurrection plot, see *Impartial Statement*, 10.

62. Richard Smith to John Roguin Smith, *Eagle* prison ship, 18 July 1797, TNA (UK) HO 42/212; James Walker to Evan Nepean, Nore, 21 May 1799, TNA (UK) ADM 1/731.

63. Court-martial of John Goody (alias Gooday) et al., 19–27 July 1797, TNA (UK) ADM 1/5340; "Letter from members of the court-martial to R. King, *Cambridge* in Hamoaze, 27th July 1797" and "Letter from Captain Douglas to R. King, *Saturn,* Plymouth Sound, August 1, 1797," TNA (UK) ADM 1/812. For the importance of mustering and exercise for the maintenance of order onboard, see Thomas Malcomson, *Order and Disorder in the British Navy, 1793–1815: Control, Resistance, Flogging and Hanging* (Woodbridge: Boydell Press, 2016), 74–86. For Luke Early, see *Further Account (Being Part II.) of the Cruelties Discovered in Coldbath-Fields Prison, as Reported in the House of Commons, on Tuesday, the 22d July, 1800, etc.* (London: J. S. Jordan, 1800), 10.

64. For Colin Brown, see Court-martial of Colin Brown et al., 3 to 7 July 1797, TNA (UK) ADM 1/5340. For the *Calypso,* see Court-martial against Joseph Wells et al., 14 July 1797, TNA (UK) ADM 1/5340; and "Letter from the Ship's Company of the Calypso" TNA (UK) ADM 1/812.

65. Court-martial of Abraham Nelson et al., 6–17 July 1797, TNA (UK) ADM 1/5340.

66. For further unrest in the home command, see Court-martial of Joseph Wells et al., 14 July 1797, TNA (UK) ADM 1/5340; Court-martial of William Lee and Thomas Preston, 28–29 August 1797, TNA (UK) ADM 1/5341; Court-martial of John Lloyd (alias Lydd), 4 August 1797, TNA (UK) ADM 1/5341; Court-martial of Michael Collins, 24–26 August 1797, TNA (UK) ADM 1/5341; Court-martial of John Burn, 13–14 December 1797, TNA (UK) ADM 1/5342; Court-martial of John Grover and John Brown (3rd), 15–16 December 1797, TNA (UK) ADM 1/5342; for the *Almene,* see Court-martial of John Anderson (alias Jens Christian Larsen) and George Rankin, 22–24 July 1797, TNA (UK) ADM 1/5340; for the *Kingfisher,* see Court-martial of Thomas Leach and John Sayle, 10–11 July 1797, TNA (UK) ADM 1/5340.

67. Court-martial of John Benson and Philip Francis, 30 June 1797, TNA (UK) ADM 1/5340; Captain Peard to Admiral Jervis, *St. George,* 5 July 1797, TNA (UK) ADM 1/396; Admiral Jervis to Evan Nepean, *Ville de Paris,* 3 July 1797, TNA (UK) ADM 1/396; "To his sister, *Excellent,* off Cadiz, August 7, 1797," in Hughes, *Private Correspondence of Admiral Lord Collingwood,* 85.

68. Court-martial of John Anderson et al., 7–8 July 1797, TNA (UK) ADM 1/5340; Court-martial of Thomas Leach and John Sayle, 10–11 July 1797, TNA (UK) ADM 1/5340; Court-martial of Captain John Maitland, 12 July 1797, TNA (UK) ADM 1/5340; Court-martial of John Anderson (alias Jens Christian Larsen) and George Rankin, 22–24 July 1797, TNA (UK) ADM 1/5340.

69. Rear-Admiral Thomas Pringle to Evan Nepean, *Tremendous,* Cape of Good Hope, 13 October 1797, TNA (UK) ADM 1/56; Court-martial of Captain George Hopewell Stephens, 6–14 November 1797, TNA (UK) ADM 1/5342. See also Nicole Ulrich, "International Radicalism, Local Solidarities: The 1797 British Naval Mutinies in Southern African Waters," in *Mutiny and Maritime Radicalism in the Age of Revolution: A Global Survey,* ed. Clare Anderson et al. (Cambridge: Cambridge University Press, 2014), 61–85.

70. Rear-Admiral Pringle to Evan Nepean, *Tremendous,* 17 August 1797, TNA (UK) ADM 1/56; Address of the *Rattlesnake*'s crew, TNA (UK) ADM 1/56; Rear-Admiral Pringle to Evan Nepean, *Tremendous,* 9 October 1797, TNA (UK) ADM 1/56.

71. Court-martial of Philip James et al., 17–23 November 1797, TNA (UK) ADM 1/5342; Court-martial of Andrew Burnet et al., 30 November-5 December 1797, TNA (UK) ADM 1/5488; Court-martial of Thomas Kelly, 9 December 1797, TNA (UK) ADM 1/5487; Court-martial of George Hopewell Stephens, TNA (UK) ADM 1/5342; Court-martial of William Stewart, 7–8 December 1797, TNA (UK) ADM 1/5487.

72. Anon. [Philip Patton], *Strictures on Naval Discipline, and the Conduct of a Ship of War. Intended to Produce an Uniformity of Opinion Among Sea-Officers* (Edinburgh: Murray and Cochrane, 1810), 4–5.

73. Anon. [Philip Patton], *Strictures,* 4–5.

CHAPTER FIVE: TO CLEAR THE QUARTERDECK

1. "Statement of service," NMM (UK) BGR/12; Court-martial of James Irwin et al., 23 May 1798, TNA (UK) ADM 1/5344; Joseph Mansell's confession, TNA (UK) ADM 1/248.

2. On Foreshaw, see Court-martial of James Irwin et al., 23 May 1798, TNA (UK) ADM 1/5344. On Douglas and Smith, see Court-martial of John Williams et al., 13–15 March 1799, TNA (UK) ADM 1/5348; and Court-martial of John Watson and James Allen, 31 July 1800, TNA (UK) ADM 1/5353.

3. Court-martial of John Pearce, 25 August 1801, TNA (UK) ADM 1/5357; Court-martial of John Watson and James Allen, 31 July 1800, TNA (UK) ADM 1/5353; "Statement of service," NMM (UK) BGR/12.

4. Court-martial of John Pearce, 25 August 1801, TNA (UK) ADM 1/5357; Court-martial of John Watson and James Allen, 31 July 1800, TNA (UK) ADM 1/5353; Court-martial of John Williams et al., 13–15 March 1799, TNA (UK) ADM 1/5348; "Statement of service," NMM (UK) BGR/12.

5. "Statement of service," NMM (UK) BGR/12; Court-martial of James Irwin et al., 23 May 1798, TNA (UK) ADM 1/5344; "John Slenison's confession," TNA (UK) ADM 1/397; "Statement, Don Ysidro Ornez," TNA (UK) ADM 1/397.

6. On "fragging," see A British Seaman, *Life On Board a Man-of-War* (Glasgow, 1829), 128; Court-martial John Wright and George Tomms, 29–30 October 1798, TNA (UK) ADM 1/5347; Sir Robert Steele, *The Marine Officer, or, Sketches of Service* (London: Henry Colburn, 1840), 142–143, 205–206. On less lethal anti-officer violence, see Joshua Davis, *A Narrative of Joshua Davis, an American Citizen, who was Pressed and Served On Board Six Ships of the British Navy* (Boston, 1811), 71; John C. Dann, ed., *The Nagle Journal: A Diary of the Life of Jacob Nagle, Sailor, from the Year 1775 to 1841* (New York: Weidenfeld and Nicolson, 1988), 76. On treasonous conspiracies, see "Digest of the Admiralty Records of Trials by Court-Martial, From the 1st January 1755 to 1st January 1806; Fifty-one Years. Volume Fourth," TNA (UK) ADM 12/24.

7. "Statement of service, 1789–1839, of Lt. David O'Brien Casey (1779–1853)," NMM (UK) BGR/12.

8. "Statement of service," NMM (UK) BGR/12; John Mason's confession, TNA (UK) ADM 1/248. Emphasis in the original.

9. "Statement of service," NMM (UK) BGR/12; David Patrick Geggus, *Slavery, War, and Revolution: The British Occupation of Saint Domingue 1793–1798* (Oxford: Clarendon, 1982), 275; Michael Duffy, *Soldiers, Sugar, and Seapower: The British Expeditions to the West Indies and the War against Revolutionary France* (Oxford: Clarendon, 1987), 333–334.

10. *Hermione* muster book, April-July 1797, TNA (UK) ADM 36/12011; "Statement of service," NMM (UK) BGR/12. See also Jeremy D. Popkin, *Facing Racial Revolution: Eyewitness Accounts of the Haitian Insurrection* (Chicago: University of Chicago Press, 2007), 180–232.

11. "Statement of service," NMM (UK) BGR/12.

12. Court-martial of William Johnson and Adiel Powelson, alias Henry Poulson, 2 July 1801, TNA (UK) ADM 1/5357; *Hermione* muster book, April-July 1797, TNA (UK) ADM 36/12011; *Success* muster book, December 1796–September 1797, TNA (UK) ADM 36/14745; court-martial of John Williams et al., 13–15 March 1799, TNA (UK) ADM 1/5348.

13. The last surviving muster book, ending in July 1797, contains 168 names. For about half of these (85) it is possible to establish a place of origin. *Hermione* muster book, April-July 1797, TNA (UK) ADM 36/12011; *Adventure* muster book, January-February 1797, TNA (UK) ADM 36/12931; *Success* muster book, December 1796-September 1797, TNA (UK) ADM 36/14745; court-martial of Florence McCarty and William Grace, 7 April 1800, TNA (UK) ADM 1/5352.

14. Court-martial of John Chrystall et al., 14–15 August 1797, TNA (UK) ADM 1/5341; *Thames* logbook, 12 December 1796 to 31 December 1798, TNA (UK) ADM 51/1227.

15. Court-martial of John Chrystall et al., 14–15 August 1797, TNA (UK) ADM 1/5341.

16. *Mutineers of the Hermione* (Antigua, 1798); Joseph Mansell's confession, TNA (UK) ADM 1/248; court-martial of John Brown et al., 5 May 1798, TNA (UK) ADM 1/5344; for African-Atlantic coasting, see W. Jeffrey Bolster, *Black Jacks: African American Seamen in the Age of Sail* (Cambridge, MA: Harvard University Press, 1997), esp. ch. 2, and David S. Cecelski, *The Waterman's Song: Slavery and Freedom in Maritime North Carolina* (Chapel Hill: University of North Carolina Press, 2001).

17. Letter, Alan Gardner, Cawsand Bay, 26 March 1800, TNA (UK) ADM 1/115; *The New Hampshire Gazette,* August 12, 1800; Letter, Milbank, Spithead, 11 August 1801, TNA (UK) ADM 1/1048; "Extract from Captain Thomas Truxtun's journal, U.S. Frigate *Constellation,* at Hampton Roads, 31 August 1798, Friday" in *Naval Documents Related to the Quasi-War between the United States and France* (Washington, DC: Government Printing Office, 1935), 1:312, 1:365; W. M. P. Dunne, "The *Constellation* and the *Hermione,*" *Mariner's Mirror* 70, no. 1 (1984): 82–85; Eugene S. Ferguson, *Truxtun of the Constellation: The Life of Commodore Thomas Truxtun, U.S. Navy, 1755–1822* (Baltimore, MD: Johns Hopkins University Press, 1956), 146–147; James E. Valle, *Rocks and Shoals: Order and Discipline in the Old Navy, 1800–1861* (Annapolis, MD: Naval Institute Press, 1980), 110–111.

18. For Duncan's fate, see John Duncan's confession, TNA (UK) ADM 1/731; Letter, Robert Stephen Fitzgerald, Copenhagen, 10 December 1798, TNA (UK) FO 22/32; RA (DK) 0008, Marineministeriet, Skibsjournaler 1650–1969, Iris Fregat 1797–1798, Nummer 689A-1–689A-3; RA (DK) 515, Holmens chef (søetaten), Vagtrapporter fra Gammel- og Nyholms Hovedvagt, 1798–1800, Nummer 12; Letter, Halifax, 13 September 1798, TNA (UK) ADM 1/494. The *Magecienne* yielded quite a haul. Along with five from the *Hermione,* there were three deserters from the *Aquilon,* and two suspected mutineers from the *Grampus* on board; the latter two were let go for lack of evidence, however. See Letter, Admiral Parker, Saint Nicholas Mole, 12 March 1798, TNA (UK) ADM 1/248; court-martial of Anthony Mark (alias Antonio Marco) et al., 17 March 1798, TNA (UK) ADM 1/5343; court-martial of John Percy et al., 17 May 1798, TNA (UK) ADM 1/5344. For Stoutenling and Charlton, see Letter, Halifax, 13 September 1798, TNA (UK) ADM 1/494.

19. For the crew of the *Amelia,* see *Amelia* muster book, 1 Sept. 1797–31 Aug. 1798, TNA (UK) ADM 36/12492; for the mutiny on the *Saturn,* see chapter 4; on the subsequent disposal of suspected *Saturn* conspirators, see "R. King to Evan Nepean, Cambridge at Hamoaze, 5 August 1797" and "R. King to Evan Nepean, Cambridge at Hamoaze, 27 August 1797," TNA (UK) ADM 1/812; on the wrecking of the *Artois,* see "Sir Edmund Nagle to Warren, Sylph, at sea, 31 July 1797," in *The Channel Fleet and the Blockade of Brest, 1793–1801,* ed. Roger Morriss (Aldershot: Ashgate for the Navy Records Society, 2001), 261–262; for details of Larkin's impressment, see Court-martial against Robert Larkin, Dennis Broughal, and William Hayes, 8–9 March 1798, TNA (UK) ADM 1/5343.

20. Court-martial against Robert Larkin, Dennis Broughal, and William Hayes, 8–9 March 1798, TNA (UK) ADM 1/5343.

21. Ibid.; "Charles Herbert to R. King, HMS Amelia, Bourne Coast, 1 March 1798," TNA (UK) ADM 1/813.

22. Marianne Elliott, *Partners in Revolution: The United Irishmen and France* (New Haven: Yale University Press, 1982).

23. For an estimate of the number of Irishmen in the navy, see N. A. M. Rodger, "Mutiny or Subversion? Spithead and the Nore," in *1798: A Bicentenary Perspective,* ed. Thomas Bartlett, David Dickson, Dáire Keogh, and Kevin Whelan (Dublin: Four Courts Press, 2003), 562; on Carhampton's pacification of Connacht, see Thomas Bartlett, "Defence, Counter-insurgency and Rebellion: Ireland 1793–1803," in *A Military History of Ireland,* ed. Thomas Bartlett and Keith Jeffery (Cambridge: Cambridge University Press, 1996), 259–265; Marianne Elliott, *Wolfe Tone,* 2nd ed. (Liverpool: Liverpool University Press, 2012), 289–290; Jim Smyth, *The Men of No Property: Irish Radicals and Popular Politics in the Late Eighteenth Century* (London: Macmillan, 1998), 110–111; for the political use of press gangs, see "Lord Aldborough to Edward Cooke, Belfast, 9 August 1796," NA (I) Rebellion Papers 620/24/97 (I am grateful to Tim Murtagh for sharing a transcript of this source with me); for the sending of "vagabonds" into the fleet, see "Earl Camden to the Duke of Portland, Dublin Castle, 30 May 1797," TNA (UK) HO 100/69.

24. Theobald Wolfe Tone, *An Address to the People of Ireland on the Present Important Crisis* (Belfast, 1796), 21; "Balthazard Barthélémy to the Directory, Basle, 18 messidor year IV (6 July 1796)," AN (F) AF III 186B doss. 858, p. 35 (Mathieu Ferradou generously shared a transcript of Barthélémy's letter with me).

25. On the failure of the Bantry Bay expedition, see Marianne Elliott, *Wolfe Tone,* 312–322; on the evolution of French policy towards Ireland, see Marianne Elliott, "The Role of Ireland in French War Strategy, 1796–1798," in *Ireland and the French Revolution,* ed. Hugh Gough and David Dickson (Dublin: Irish Academic Press, 1990), 202–219, and Sylvie Kleinman, "Initiating Insurgencies Abroad: French Plans to 'Chouannise' Britain and Ireland, 1793–1798," *Small Wars and Insurgencies* 25, no. 4 (2014): 784–799.

26. On the happy "United rebels," see "Edward Newenham to Earl Spencer, 28 April 1797," in *Private Papers of George, Second Earl Spencer, First Lord of the Admiralty, 1794–1801,* ed. Julian S. Corbett (London: Navy Records Society, 1914), 2:119–120; on the United Irish poet, see "R. King to Evan Nepean, Cambridge at Hamoaze, 7 June 1797," TNA (UK) ADM 1/812; on the numbers of new United men in the navy, see Elliott, *Partners in Revolution,* 142; for the overall role of the United Irish in the mutinies of 1797, see W. Benjamin Kennedy, "The United Irishmen and the Great Naval Mutiny of 1797," *Eire-Ireland* 25, no. 3 (1990): 7–18.

27. On the different perception of Defenders and United Irishmen, see "Mr. Cooke to C. Grenville, Dublin, 21 June 1797," TNA (UK) ADM 1/4172; on the disposal of the United poet, see "Evan Nepean to R. King, 9 June 1797," TNA (UK) ADM 1/812; on the dangers of allowing United men into the navy, see "Edward Newenham to Earl Spencer, 28 April 1797," in Corbett, *Private Papers of George, Second Earl Spencer,* 119–120; for the practice of sending suspects to foreign stations, see for example "Charles Tarrant to Edward Cooke, 5 June 1797," NA (I) Rebellion

Papers 620/31/37 (I am grateful to Tim Murtagh for sharing a transcript of this source with me), "Evan Nepean to John Barneby Jr., 26 July 1798," TNA (UK) ADM 1/669, and "R. King to Evan Nepean, Cambridge in Hamoaze, 2 September 1798," TNA (UK) ADM 1/813.

28. "Léonard Bourdon to the Directory, 9 ventôse year 6 (27 February 1798)," AN (F) AF III 57 doss. 225, p. 3 (I am grateful to Mathieu Ferradou for sharing a transcript of this source with me); on Bourdon and his mission in Hamburg, see Michael J. Sydenham, *Léonard Bourdon: The Career of a Revolutionary, 1754–1807* (Waterloo, ON: Wilfrid Laurier University Press, 1999), 285–307; on Hamburg and Irish radical networks, see Paul Weber, *On the Road to Rebellion: The United Irishmen and Hamburg, 1796–1803* (Dublin: Four Courts Press, 1997); on William Duckett, see Joseph O. Baylen and Norbert J. Gossman, eds., *Biographical Dictionary of Modern British Radicals, Volume 1: 1770–1830* (Hassocks: Harvester Press, 1979), s.v. "Duckett, William (1768–1841)."

29. On the plans for revenge onboard the *Saturn,* see "Captain Douglas to R. King, Saturn, Plymouth Sound, 1 August 1797," TNA (UK) ADM 1/812; on the further dispersal of *Saturn* troublemakers, see Court-martial against Patrick Little, 31 May 1798, TNA (UK) ADM 1/5344; on the language of slavery onboard the *Amelia,* see Court-martial against Robert Larkin et al., 8–9 March 1798, TNA (UK) ADM 1/5343.

30. On Bourdon and Duckett's scheming, see "Léonard Bourdon to the Directory, 9 ventôse year 6 (27 February 1798)," AN (F), AF III 57 doss. 225, p. 3; on the covert networks that connected French agents, Irish radicals, and British naval mutineers, see Elliott, *Partners in Revolution,* 134–144.

31. On the *Caesar* conspiracy, see Court-martial against Bartholomew Duff, et al., 16–23 August 1798, TNA (UK) ADM 1/5346; on the *Defiance* conspiracy, see Court-martial against John Brady et al., 8–14 September 1798, TNA (UK) ADM 1/5346; on the *Glory* and *Atlas* conspiracies, see Court-martial against William Regan et al., 1–9 October 1798, TNA (UK) ADM 1/5347; on the *Queen Charlotte* conspiracy, see Court-martial against Charles O'Neil and Patrick Malloy, 9 November 1798, TNA (UK) ADM 1/5347; on the *Captain* conspiracy, see Court-martial against Thomas Grumley et al., 5–8 December 1798, TNA (UK) ADM 1/5347; on the importance of oath-swearing to the United Irish, see Michael Durey, "Loyalty in an Age of Conspiracy: The Oath-Filled Civil War in Ireland 1795–1799," in *Unrespectable Radicals? Popular Politics in the Age of Reform,* ed. Michael T. Davis and Paul A. Pickering (Abingdon: Ashgate, 2013), 71–89.

32. On the Franco-British history of revolutionary clubs, see Micah Alpaugh, "The British Origins of the French Jacobins: Radical Sociability and the Development of Political Club Networks," *European History Quarterly* 44, no. 4 (2014): 593–619; on the spread of French revolutionary clubs across Europe, see Jacques Godechot, *La grande nation: L'expansion révolutionnaire de la France dans le monde de 1789 à 1799,* 2nd ed. (Paris: Flammarion, 1983), 261–291; on Democratic-Republican societies in the United States, see Alfred F. Young, *The Democratic Republicans of New York: The Origins, 1763–1797* (Chapel Hill: University of North Carolina Press,

1967), 392–412; on the criminalization of popular societies in Britain and Ireland, see Albert Goodwin, *The Friends of Liberty: The English Democratic Movement in the Age of the French Revolution* (Cambridge, MA: Harvard University Press, 1979), 359–450, and Roger Wells, *Insurrection: The British Experience, 1795–1803* (Gloucester: Allan Sutton, 1983), 44–63; on the correspondence between shipboard clubs, see Court-martial against Thomas Grumley et al., TNA (UK) ADM 1/5347; on the circulation of pamphlets and evolution of a hierarchical cellular structure, see Court-martial against John Brady et al., TNA (UK) ADM 1/5346.

33. Elliott, *Partners in Revolution,* 214–40.

34. For Lawrence Carroll and Nicholas Ryan, see Court-martial against John Brady et al., TNA (UK) ADM 1/5346.

35. Theobald Wolfe Tone, "To the Irishmen Now Serving Aboard the British Navy," in *Life of Theobald Wolfe Tone, Founder of the United Irish Society, and Adjutant General and Chef de Brigade in the Service of the French and Batavian Republics, Vol. II,* ed. William Theobald Wolfe Tone (Washington: Gales and Seaton, 1826), 326–328; for John Bryan, see Court-martial against John Bryan and William Whiley, 14 July 1798, TNA (UK) ADM 1/5345; for the praise of the French government, see Court-martial against William Timings and James Cormick, 9 July 1798, TNA (UK) ADM 1/5345; for the fear of losing back wages during a related conspiracy, see Court-martial against John MacDonald et al., 20 March 1798, TNA (UK) ADM 1/5343.

36. For John Nicholls and Michael Butler, see Court-martial against Bartholomew Duff et al., TNA (UK) ADM 1/5346; for Dowd and Quickly, see Court-martial against William Regan, et al., TNA (UK) ADM 1/5347.

37. For accusations of made-up evidence during the *Caesar* trial, see Court-martial against John Mahoney, 23 July 1799, TNA (UK) ADM 1/5350; on the history of British fears of Irish violence, see James Kelly, "'We Were All to Have Been Massacred': Irish Protestants and the Experience of Rebellion," in *1798: A Bicentenary Perspective,* ed. David Dickson et al. (Dublin: Four Courts Press, 2003), 312–330; on the *Defiance,* see Court-martial against John Brady, et al., TNA (UK) ADM 1/5346; on the *Captain,* see Court-martial against Thomas Grumley et al., TNA (UK) ADM 1/5347; on the *Caesar,* see Court-martial against Bartholomew Duff et al., TNA (UK) ADM 1/5346.

38. For the history of the Defenders and their social context, see Smyth, *The Men of No Property;* on the centrality of egalitarianism in the Irish democratic movement, see Ultán Gillen, "Constructing Democratic Thought in Ireland in the Age of Revolution, 1775–1800," in *Re-imagining Democracy in the Age of Revolution: America, France, Britain, Ireland 1750–1850,* ed. Joanna Innes and Mark Philp (Oxford: Oxford University Press, 2013), 149–161; on the language of slavery onboard the *Amelia,* see Court-martial against Robert Larkin et al., TNA (UK) ADM 1/5343; on the language of slavery onboard the *Defiance,* see Court-martial against John Brady et al., TNA (UK) ADM 1/5346.

39. On the history of the tree of liberty as a contested revolutionary symbol, see Alfred F. Young, "Liberty Tree: Made in America, Lost in America," in *Liberty Tree: Ordinary People and the American Revolution* (New York: New York University

Press, 2006), 325–394; on the United Irish catechism and its context, see Philip Pettit, "The Tree of Liberty: Republicanism: American, French, and Irish," *Field Day Review* 1 (2005): 29–41.

40. Court-martial against William Davis, 24 January 1799, TNA (UK) ADM 1/5348.

41. On the conspiracy in the Mediterranean fleet, see Court-martial against Michael Connell et al., 2–3 July 1798, Court-martial against Richard Jones, 5 July 1798, and Court-martial against Thomas Boyd, 6 July 1798, TNA (UK) ADM 1/5345; for Admiral Earl St. Vincent's claim that the United Irish were behind it, see "St. Vincent to Admiral Sir H. Nelson, HMS Ville de Paris, 5th July 1798," in *Memoirs of Admiral The Right Honorable the Earl of St. Vincent, G.C.B., etc.,* ed. Jedediah Stephens Tucker (London: Richard Bentley, 1844), 1:338.

42. Rev. Robert Baynes, *A Discourse on Mutiny, Preached Onboard His Majesty's Ship Prince, 98 Guns, off Cadiz, July the 10th, 1798, on the Occasion of the Execution of the Three Mutineers of the Princess Royal* (London, 1807).

43. Priscilla Wald has proposed the notion of "imagined immunities" as an elaboration of Benedict Anderson's concept of "imagined communities," see her *Contagious: Cultures, Carriers, and the Outbreak Narrative* (Durham, NC: Duke University Press, 2008).

44. For the sentences against the conspirators, see Court-martial against Bartholomew Duff, et al. and Court-martial against John Brady, et al., TNA (UK) ADM 1/5346, and Court-martial against William Regan, et al. and Court-martial against Thomas Grumley, et al., TNA (UK) ADM 1/5347; for the transportation of eight *Defiance* conspirators to New South Wales, see "Convicts transported in the *Nile, Minorca,* and *Canada* (June 1801)," TNA (UK) HO 11/1; for the carrying out of flogging sentences in installments, see "R. King to Evan Nepean, Cambridge in Hamoaze, 25 August 1798," "R. King to Evan Nepean, Cambridge in Hamoaze, 2 September 1798," and "R. King to Evan Nepean, Cambridge in Hamoaze, 12 November 1798," TNA (UK) ADM 1/813.

45. For a series of reports from western squadron commanders on the mood onboard their ship in the late summer of 1798, see TNA (UK) ADM 1/813; for the punishment of the four marines, see Court-martial against Patrick Townsend, James Reilley, Hugh McGinnis, and John Marshall, 15 January 1799, TNA (UK) ADM 1/5348; for a declaration of loyalty signed by forty-nine Irish seamen onboard the *Romney* on September 3, 1798, see TNA (UK) ADM 1/669; for the discussion of blowing up the *Diomede,* see Court-martial against John Wright and George Tomms, 29–30 October 1798, TNA (UK) ADM 1/5347; for Nelson's sabotage attempt, see Court-martial against Robert Nelson, 24–29 January 1799, TNA (UK) ADM 1/5348; Nelson later twice escaped from prison, and was twice retaken. See "Marshalsea entry book Admiralty prisoners," TNA (UK) PRIS 11/15.

46. *Havick:* NA (NL), West-Indisch Comitté, 1795–1800, 2.01.28.01, inv. nr. 128. *Utrecht:* NA (NL), Hoge Militaire Rechtspraak, 1795–1813 (1818), 2.01.11, inv. nr. 234. *Vernieler:* NA (NL), Hoge Militaire Rechtspraak, 1795–1813 (1818), 2.01.11, inv. nr. 218.

47. "Arrêté du comité de salut public, concernant l'enrôlement des marins étrangers. Du 25 Prairial an III [13 June 1795]," *Recueil,* 5:337–340; Christelle Breccia, "Les matelots embarqués à Toulon au XVIIIème siècle. D'après les rôles d'équipage du *Guerrier,* de la *Provence* et du *Héros*" (master's thesis, Université de Provence–Centre d'Aix, 2003), 60–62. For the file on Lorens Revers, see AN (F), W543, Jurisdictions Extraordinaire, Tribunal révolutionnaire de Brest.

48. On French criminalization of cross-border employment, see "Arrêté du Directoire exécutif, portant que les individus natifs de pays alliés ou neutres, qui feraient partie des équipages de bâtimens ennemis, seront traités comme pirates. Du 8 Brumaire an VII [29 October 1798]," in *Recueil,* 9:35–36. On Spanish criminalization and the British response, see Henry Dundas to Lords Commissioners of the Admiralty, 2 November 1797, TNA (UK) ADM 1/4174.

49. William Portlock's and John Forbes's affidavits are reprinted in Charles Pinckney, *Three Letters, Written and Originally Published, under the Signature of a South Carolina Planter* (Philadelphia: Aurora Office, 1799), 5–6; Court-martial of Jonathan (or Nathan) Robbins (alias Thomas Nash), 15 August 1799, TNA (UK) ADM 1/5350; on the legal and political context of the case, see Ruth Wedgwood, "The Revolutionary Martyrdom of Jonathan Robbins," *The Yale Law Journal* 100, no. 2 (1990): 229–368; Christopher H. Pyle, *Extradition, Politics, and Human Rights* (Philadelphia: Temple University Press, 2001), 8–47; and A. Roger Ekirch, *American Sanctuary: Mutiny, Martyrdom, and National Identity in the Age of Revolution* (New York: Pantheon, 2017).

50. James Morton Smith, *Freedom's Fetters: The Alien and Sedition Laws and American Civil Liberties* (Ithaca, NY: Cornell University Press, 1956), 3–34; Samuel Eliot Morison, *The Life and Letters of Harrison Gray Otis, Federalist, 1765–1848* (Boston: Houghton Mifflin Co., 1913), 1:108. See also on Irish immigrant radicalism David A. Wilson, *United Irishmen, United States: Immigrant Radicals in the Early Republic* (Ithaca, NY: Cornell University Press, 1998).

51. On Nash/Robbins suddenly claiming American citizenship, see Pinckney, *Three Letters,* 7–8.

52. For the impressment of American seamen, see George Selement, "Impressment and the American Merchant Marine, 1782–1812," *Mariner's Mirror* 59, no. 4 (1973): 409–418; James Fulton Zimmerman, *Impressment of American Seamen* (Port Washington, NY: Kennikat, 1925), esp. 11–90; and Paul A. Gilje, *Free Trade and Sailors' Rights in the War of 1812* (New York: Cambridge University Press, 2013), 99–109; for a contemporary critique of the British custom of using language to determine nationality, see Pinckney, *Three Letters,* 18.

53. On the creation of the seamen's protection bureaucracy, see Nathan Perl-Rosenthal, *Citizen Sailors: Becoming American in the Age of Revolution* (Cambridge, MA: Belknap Press of Harvard University Press, 2015); see also Simon P. Newman, "Reading the Bodies of Early American Seafarers," *The William and Mary Quarterly,* 3rd series, 55, no. 1 (1998): 60; and Zimmerman, *Impressment,* 29–61. On British seamen fraudulently acquiring documents proving US citizenship, see "Admiral Hyde Parker to Lords of Admiralty, Cape Nicholas Mole, 19 June 1797," TNA (UK)

ADM 1/4173. Though likely never to be resolved, most of the available evidence suggests that the man arrested in Charleston was Thomas Nash, not Jonathan Robbins. See Wedgwood, "The Revolutionary Martyrdom of Jonathan Robbins," 310–311. For an opposing view suggesting the likelihood of Nash/Robbins being, as he claimed, a native-born American citizen, see Larry D. Cress, "The Jonathan Robbins Incident: Extradition and the Separation of Powers in the Adams Administration," *Essex Institute Historical Collections* 111, no. 2 (1975): 99–121. Robbins's protection certificate is reprinted in Francis Wharton, *State Trials of the United States during the Administrations of Washington and Adams* (Philadelphia: Carey and Hart, 1849), 394; *Hermione* muster book, April 7 to July 7, 1797, TNA (UK) ADM 36/12011; "*Mutineers of the Hermione* (Antigua, 1798)," in TNA (UK) ADM 1/2316.

54. Pinckney, *Three Letters,* 8–9; "British Frigate Hermione," *The Philadelphia Gazette and Universal Advertiser,* August 12, 1799; Wedgwood, "Jonathan Robbins," 299–305; Ekirch, *American Sanctuary,* 90–110.

55. Todd Estes, *The Jay Treaty Debate, Public Opinion, and the Evolution of Early American Political Culture* (Amherst: University of Massachusetts Press, 2006), 71–103; Pinckney, *Three Letters,* 8–9; "Jonathan Robbins!" *The Constitutional Telegraph,* October 16, 1799; "From the (Phila.) Aurora," *Independent Chronicle and Universal Advertiser,* September 2, 1799.

56. For the HMS *Rose* case, see Jesse Lemisch, *Jack Tar vs. John Bull: The Role of New York's Seamen in Precipitating the Revolution* (New York: Garland, 1997), 34; and Christopher P. Magra, *Poseidon's Curse: British Naval Impressment and the Atlantic Origins of the American Revolution* (New York: Cambridge University Press, 2016), 223–225. On the *Baltimore,* see John F. Campbell, "The Havana Incident," *American Neptune* 22 (1962): 264–276; and Gilje, *Free Trade and Sailors' Rights,* 115–116. For a representative newspaper reaction to the incident, see "British Aggression," *Columbian Centinel,* January 12, 1799. The *Centinel of Freedom* is quoted in Wedgwood, "The Revolutionary Martyrdom of Jonathan Robbins," 360. For the attempt to censure Adams, see *Mr Livingston's Motion, 20th February 1800* (Philadelphia, 1800); *Speech of the Hon. John Marshall, Delivered in the House of Representatives, of the United States, on the Resolution of the Hon. Edward Livingston. Relative to Thomas Nash, alias Jonathan Robbins* (Philadelphia: Printed at the Office of the "True American," 1800). See also R. Kent Newmyer, *John Marshall and the Heroic Age of the Supreme Court* (Baton Rouge: Louisiana State University Press, 2001), 136–142.

57. *The Times; and District of Columbia Daily Advertiser,* October 10, 1799; *The Democrat,* May 21, 1806.

58. *Otsego Herald; or, Western Advertiser,* December 27, 1797; "From a Correspondent," *Aurora General Advertiser,* March 16, 1798.

59. On seamen and early US nationalism, see Paul A. Gilje, *Liberty on the Waterfront: American Maritime Culture in the Age of Revolution* (Philadelphia: University of Pennsylvania Press, 2004), 155–162; see also his *Free Trade and Sailors' Rights,* 85–98. For the intersection of the anti-impressment and anti-slavery movements, see Denver Brunsman, "The Evil Necessity: British Naval Impressment in the Eighteenth-Century Atlantic World" (PhD diss., Princeton, 2004), 319–323. For a

comparison of British impressment to "Algerine slavery," see "On the British Naval Mutiny Business," *The Time Piece, and Literary Companion,* June 21, 1797. For outrage against color-blind North African slavery, see Frederick C. Leiner, *The End of Barbary Terror: America's 1815 War Against the Pirates of North Africa* (Oxford: Oxford University Pres, 2004), 16–17.

60. For the conflation of impressment, Barbary captivity, and American slavery, see Matthew Mason, "The Battle of the Slaveholding Liberators: Great Britain, the United States, and Slavery in the Early Nineteenth Century," *William and Mary Quarterly,* 3rd series, 59, no. 3 (2002): 665–696. On the racial politics of the Chesapeake-Leopard affair, see Robert E. Cray, Jr., "Remembering the USS Chesapeake: The Politics of Maritime Death and Impressment," *Journal of the Early Republic* 25, no. 3 (2005): 456–458, 463–465.

61. On the diversity of US naval crews, see Christopher McKee, "Foreign Seamen in the United States Navy: A Census of 1808," *William and Mary Quarterly,* 3rd series, 42, no. 3 (1985): 386–388; on merchant shipping crews, see Gilje, *Liberty on the Waterfront,* 24–25; and Daniel Vickers (with Vince Walsh), *Young Men and the Sea: Yankee Seafarers in the Age of Sail* (New Haven: Yale University Press, 2005), 174–178; on whaling crews, see James Farr, "A Slow Boat to Nowhere: The Multi-Racial Crews of the American Whaling Industry," *Journal of Negro History* 68, no 2 (1983): 159–170; and Nancy Shoemaker, *Native American Whalemen and their World: Indigenous Encounters and the Contingency of Race* (Chapel Hill: University of North Carolina Press, 2015), 13–14, 201. For African-American mariners, see Bolster, *Black Jacks,* 6; and Ira Dye, "Early American Merchant Seafarers," *Proceedings of the American Philosophical Society* 120, no. 5 (1976): 348–353. Some recent works have downplayed the diversity of US crews. See Perl-Rosenthal, *Citizen Sailors;* and Brian Rouleau, *With Sails Whitening Every Sea: Mariners and the Making of an American Maritime Empire* (Ithaca, NY: Cornell University Press, 2014).

62. Harold L. Langley, "The Negro in the Navy and Merchant Service, 1789–1860," *Journal of Negro History* 52, no. 4 (1967): 275–276; "To the President of the United States from H. Knox, Boston, 26th June 1798," in *Naval Documents,* 1:139–140; "To Lieutenant of Marines, Frigate *Constellation,* from Secretary of War, 16 March 1798," in *Naval Documents,* 1:41; "To Lieutenant John Rodgers, U.S. Navy, from Captain Thomas Truxtun, U.S. Navy," in *Naval Documents,* 1:50; "To Lieutenant Henry Kenyon from Secretary of Navy," in *Naval Documents,* 1:281.

63. On the US Articles of War, see Valle, *Rocks and Shoals,* 43; on punishments, see "To Captain Thomas Tingey, U.S. Navy, from Captain Thomas Truxtun, U.S. Navy, 1st December 1800," in *Naval Documents,* 7:1–3.

64. John Rea, *A Letter to William Bainbridge Esqr., Formerly of the United States Ship George Washington; Relating to Some Transactions Onboard Said Ship, during a Voyage to Algiers, Constantinople, etc.* (Philadelphia, 1802), 13, 16. Emphasis in the original.

65. Rea, *A Letter,* 3–4, 14, 23; William Ray, *Horrors of Slavery, or, The American Tars in Tripoli,* ed. Hester Blum (New Brunswick, NJ: Rutgers University Press, 2008).

66. On the role of seamen in the conflicts leading up to the revolution, see Jesse Lemisch, "Jack Tar in the Streets: Merchant Seamen in the Politics of Revolutionary America," *William and Mary Quarterly,* 3rd series, 25, no. 3 (1968): 371–407; Peter Linebaugh and Marcus Rediker, *The Many-Headed Hydra: Sailors, Slaves, Commoners, and the Hidden History of the Revolutionary Atlantic* (Boston: Beacon, 2000), 211–247; on Attucks, see Marcus Rediker, "The Revenge of Crispus Attucks; or, The Atlantic Challenge to American Labor History," *Labor: Studies in the Working-Class History of the Americas* 1, no. 4 (2004): 35–45; Mitch Kachun, "From Forgotten Founder to Indispensable Icon: Crispus Attucks, Black Citizenship, and Collective Memory, 1770–1865," *Journal of the Early Republic* 29, no. 2 (2009): 249–286.

67. On the Nash-Robbins affair during the election of 1800, see Ekirch, *American Sanctuary,* 168–200. *The Times; and District of Columbia Advertiser,* February 18, 1800 (emphasis in the original).

68. "Digest of the Admiralty Records of Trials by Court-Martial, From the 1st January 1755 to 1st January 1806; Fifty-one Years. Volume Fourth," TNA (UK) ADM 12/24.

CONCLUSION: THE MARINE REPUBLIC

1. Thomas Spence, "The Marine Republic," in *One Pennyworth of Pig's Meat; or, Lessons for the Swinish Multitude* (London, 1793–95), 2:68–72.

2. Pierre Prétou and Denis Roland, "Le pouvoir extraordinaire: Les fondements culturels de l'autorité à bord," in *Fureur et cruauté des capitaines en mer,* ed. Pierre Prétou and Denis Roland (Rennes: Presses Universitaires de Rennes, 2012), 14–33.

3. On Spence's background see P. M. Ashraf, *The Life and Times of Thomas Spence* (Newcastle upon Tyne: Frank Graham, 1983). See also Matilde Cazzola, "'All Shall Be Happy by Land and by Sea': Thomas Spence as an Atlantic Thinker," *Atlantic Studies/Global Currents* 15, no. 4 (2018): 431–450. Thomas Spence, "The Restorer of Society to Its Natural State," in *The Political Works of Thomas Spence,* ed. H. T. Dickinson (Newcastle upon Tyne: Avero, 1983), 78, 83. Spence, "The Seaman's Friend," in *One Pennyworth of Pigs' Meat; or, Lessons for the Swinish Multitude,* 3:8–21. Spence, "The Remarkable History of the Rise and Fall of Masaniello, the Fisherman of Naples," in *Pigs' Meat; or, Lessons for the Swinish Multitude,* 3:22–56, 67–97, 123–136, 152–164, 172–178, 197–213; "Masaniello" is an abbreviation of the name Tommaso Aniello.

4. For the *Melpomene* round robin, see "Minerve—Melpomene," SHM-T (F) 4O1, Institutions de répression, Cour martial maritime, Procédures et interrogatoires, 1792-An II. On the disputed origins of the round robin, see *Notes and Queries: A Medium of Intercommunication for Literary Men, General Readers, etc., Eighth Series, Volume Tenth, July–December 1896* (London: John C. Francis, 1896), 391–392. The analysis of the round robin in this paragraph builds on Marcus Rediker, *Between the Devil and the Deep Blue Sea: Merchant Seamen, Pirates, and the*

Anglo-American Maritime World, 1700–1750 (Cambridge: Cambridge University Press, 1987), 234–235. The Swedish navy was one of the few whose articles of war had a provision that allowed for the decimation of a mutinous crew by lot. See *Kongl. Maj:ts Krigs-Articlar för des krigsmagt til lands och siös, gifne Stockholms Slott den 31 Martii 1798* (Stockholm: Kongl. Tryckeriet, 1798), ch. 5, §14.

5. The emergence of exceptionally strong group cohesion among warriors is a well-known phenomenon. See Richard Holmes, *Acts of War: The Behavior of Men in Battle* (New York: Free Press, 1985), 31–73.

6. On the fear of killing, see Dave Grossman, *On Killing: The Psychological Cost of Learning to Kill in War and Society* (New York: Back Bay Books, 1995).

7. Admiral Lord Keith to Henry Dundas, London, 27 June 1797, TNA (UK) ADM 1/4172.

8. Martine Acerra and Jean Meyer emphasize "structural weaknesses," but also consider the period between 1795 and 1798 as a slow collapse and the 1798 Battle of Aboukir Bay as the French navy's decisive defeat. See their *Marines et révolution* (Rennes: Éditions Ouest-France, 1988), 97–99.

9. *Syren:* Court-martial of Henry Ross et al., 23–25 February 1802, Court-marital of Seton Ross, 27 February—1 March 1802, and Court-martial of Richard Croft, 4–5 March 1802, TNA (UK) ADM 1/5360. *Gibraltar:* Court-martial of Thomas Bean and James Silk, 1–3 November 1802 and Court-martial of Captain William Hancock Kelly, 3–8 March 1803, TNA (UK) ADM 1/5363. Bantry Bay: "Naval Court Martial for the Trial of the Mutineers Late of His Majesty's Ship Temeraire; held on board His Majesty's Ship Gladiator, in Portsmouth Harbour, Wednesday, Jan. 6, 1802," *The Times* (London) (January 13, 1802) and "Execution of the Mutineers." *The Times* (London) (January 18, 1802).

10. David Dean, "Joseph Wall of Goree Island," *African Affairs* 57, no. 229 (1958): 295–301. Don Manuel Alvarez Espriella, *Letters from England, Vol. I* (London: Longman, Hurst, Rees and Orme, 1808), 103–104; James Davey and Richard Johns, *Broadsides: Caricature and the Navy, 1756–1815* (Barnsley: Seaforth, 2012), 61.

11. *Reports from Committees of the House of Commons, Vol. X, Miscellaneous Subjects: 1785–1801* (London, 1803), 830–831. Spence, "The Restorer of Society to Its Natural State," 78.

12. Convicts transported, 1787–1809, TNA (UK) HO 11/1.

BIBLIOGRAPHY

ARCHIVES

Archives Nationales, Paris, France
Krigsarkivet, Stockholm, Sweden
London Metropolitan Archives, London, United Kingdom
Nationaal Archief, The Hague, The Netherlands
National Archives, Dublin, Ireland
The National Archives, Kew, United Kingdom
National Maritime Museum, Greenwich, United Kingdom
Rigsarkivet, Copenhagen, Denmark
Service Historique de la Défense (Marine), Toulon, France
Service Historique de la Défense (Marine), Vincennes, France
Sjöhistoriska Museet, Stockholm, Sweden

Newspapers

Aurora General Advertiser
Columbian Centinel
The Constitutional Telegraph
The Democrat
Evening Mail
Independent Chronicle and Universal Advertiser
Minerva, et Maanedskrivt
The New Hampshire Gazette
Otsego Herald; or, Western Advertiser
The Philadelphia Gazette and Universal Advertiser
Révolutions de Paris
Stockholms Post-Tidningar
The Time Piece, and Literary Companion

The Times; and District of Columbia Daily Advertiser
The Times (London)

SOURCES

A British Seaman. *Life On Board a Man-of-War; Including a Full Account of the Battle of Navarino*. Glasgow, 1829.

A Captain in the Royal Navy. *Observations and Instructions for the Use of the Commissioned, the Junior, and Other Officers of the Royal Navy*. London, 1804.

Acerra, Martine, and Jean Meyer. *Marines et révolution*. Rennes: Éditions Ouest-France, 1988.

Adam, Paul, ed. *Seamen in Society/Gens de mer en société*. Perthes: Commission internationale d'histoire maritime, 1980.

Address to the Nation, by the Seamen at St. Helen's. 2nd ed. Edinburgh, 1797.

Adresse de l'equipage du vaisseau Le Superbe, en rade de Brest, à la Société des Amis de la Constitution. Séance du 4 Novembre 1790. Imprimée par ordre de l'Assemblée Nationale. Paris, 1790.

Alpaugh, Micah. "The British Origins of the French Jacobins: Radical Sociability and the Development of Political Club Networks." *European History Quarterly* 44, no. 4 (2014): 593–619.

Alvarez Espriella, Manuel. *Letters from England, Vol. I*. London: Longman, Hurst, Rees, and Orme, 1808.

Anderson, Clare, Niklas Frykman, Lex Heerma van Voss, and Marcus Rediker, eds. *Mutiny and Maritime Radicalism in the Age of Revolution: A Global Survey (International Review of Social History Special Issue 21)*. Cambridge: Cambridge University Press, 2014.

The Annual Register, or a View of the History, Politics, and Literature, for the Year 1793. A New Edition. London: Baldwin, Cradock, and Joy, 1821.

Aristotle. *The Politics and the Constitution of Athens*. Edited by Stephen Everson. Cambridge: Cambridge University Press, 1996.

Asher, Eugene L. *The Resistance to the Maritime Classes: The Survival of Feudalism in the France of Colbert*. Berkeley: University of California Press, 1960.

Ashraf, P.M. *The Life and Times of Thomas Spence*. Newcastle upon Tyne: Frank Graham, 1983.

Aubert, Vilhelm. *The Hidden Society*. Totowa, NJ: Bedminster, 1965.

Banks, Kenneth J. *Chasing Empire across the Sea: Communications and the State in the French Atlantic, 1713–1763*. Montreal and Kingston: McGill-Queen's University Press, 2002.

Barrow, John. *The Life of Richard Earl Howe, K.G., Admiral of the Fleet, and General of Marines*. London: John Murray, 1838.

Bartlett, Thomas. "Defence, Counter-Insurgency and Rebellion: Ireland 1793–1803." In *A Military History of Ireland*, edited by Thomas Bartlett and Keith Jeffery, 259–265. Cambridge: Cambridge University Press, 1996.

Barton, H. Arnold. *Scandinavia in the Revolutionary Era, 1760–1815*. Minneapolis: University of Minnesota Press, 1986.

———. "Sweden and the War for American Independence." *William and Mary Quarterly*, 3rd series, 23, no. 3 (1966): 408–430.

Baugh, Daniel A. "Withdrawing from Europe: Anglo-French Maritime Geopolitics, 1750–1800." *The International History Review* 20, no. 1 (1998): 1–32.

Baylen, Joseph O., and Norbert J. Gossman. *Biographical Dictionary of Modern British Radicals, Volume 1: 1770–1830*. Hassocks: Harvester Press, 1979.

Baynes, Robert. *A Discourse on Mutiny, Preached Onboard His Majesty's Ship Prince, 98 Guns, off Cadiz, July the 10th, 1798, on the Occasion of the Execution of the Three Mutineers of the Princess Royal*. London, 1807.

Benton, Lauren. *A Search for Sovereignty: Law and Geography in European Empires, 1400–1900*. New York: Cambridge University Press, 2010.

Berbouche, Alain. *Marine et justice: La justice criminelle de la Marine française sous l'Ancien Régime*. Rennes: Presses Universitaires de Rennes, 2010.

Berg, Lars Otto. "The Swedish Navy, 1780–1820." In *Between Imperial Eagles: Sweden's Armed Forces during the Revolutionary and Napoleonic Wars, 1780–1820*, edited by Fred Sandstedt, 77–107. Stockholm: Armémuseet, 2000.

Bernes, Claes. *Segelfartygens tid*. Stockholm: Medströms Bokförlag, 2008.

Black, John. *An Authentic Narrative of the Mutiny Aboard the Ship Lady Shore*. Ipswich, n.d.

Blackburn, Robin. *The American Crucible: Slavery, Emancipation, and Human Rights*. London: Verso, 2011.

Bladen, F. M., ed. *Historical Records of New South Wales. Volume III—Hunter. 1796–1799*. Sydney: Charles Potter, 1895.

Blake, Nicholas. *Steering to Glory: A Day in the Life of a Ship-Of-The-Line*. Chatham, 2005.

Blüdnikow, Bent. "Folkelig uro i København 1789–1820." *Fortid og Nutid,* no. 33 (1986): 1–54.

Blumenberg, Hans. *Shipwreck with Spectator: Paradigm of a Metaphor for Existence*. Cambridge, MA: MIT Press, 1997.

Bolster, W. Jeffrey. *Black Jacks: African American Seamen in the Age of Sail*. Cambridge, MA: Harvard University Press, 1997.

Boxer, C. R. *The Dutch Seaborne Empire, 1600–1800*. Harmondsworth: Penguin, 1973.

Brandon, Pepijn. "Between the Plantation and the Port: Racialization and Social Control in Eighteenth-Century Paramaribo." *International Review of Social History* 64, Special Issue 27 (2019): 95–124.

Breccia, Christelle. "Les matelots embarqués à Toulon au XVIIIème siècle. D'après les rôles d'équipage du *Guerrier,* de la *Provence* et du *Héros*." Master's thesis, Université de Provence—Centre d'Aix, 2003.

Bromley, J. S. "The British Navy and Its Seamen: Notes for an Unwritten History." In *Seamen in Society/Gens de mer en société,* edited by Paul Adam, 36–47. Perthes: Commission internationale d'histoire maritime, 1980.

Bruijn, Jaap R. *The Dutch Navy of the Seventeenth and Eighteenth Centuries.* Columbia: University of South Carolina Press, 1993.

Bruijn, Jaap R., and E. S. van Eyck van Heslinga, eds. *Muiterij: Oproer en berechting op schepen van de VOC.* Haarlem: De Boer Maritiem, 1980.

Brunsman, Denver. *The Evil Necessity: British Naval Impressment in the Eighteenth-Century Atlantic World.* Charlottesville: University of Virginia Press, 2013.

———. "The Evil Necessity: British Naval Impressment in the Eighteenth-Century Atlantic World," 319–323. PhD diss., Princeton, 2004.

Burdett, Francis. *Cold Bath Fields Prison, by Some Called the English Bastille!* London, 1799.

Burg, B. R. *Boys at Sea: Sodomy, Indecency, and Courts Martial in Nelson's Navy.* New York: Palgrave Macmillan, 2007.

Byrn, John D., Jr. *Crime and Punishment in the Royal Navy: Discipline on the Leeward Islands Station, 1784–1812.* Aldershot: Scolar Press, 1989.

Cabantous, Alain. *La vergue et les fers: Mutins et déserteurs dans la Marine de l'ancienne France (XVIIe–XVIIIe s.).* Paris: Tallandier, 1984.

Campbell, John F. "The Havana Incident." *American Neptune,* no. 22 (1962): 264–276.

Caputo, Sara. "Alien Seamen in the British Navy, British Law, and the British State, c. 1793–1815." *The Historical Journal* 62, no. 3 (2019): 685–707.

Carp, Benjamin. *Rebels Rising: Cities and the American Revolution.* New York: Oxford University Press, 2009.

Cazzola, Matilde. "'All Shall Be Happy by Land and by Sea': Thomas Spence as an Atlantic Thinker." *Atlantic Studies/Global Currents* 15, no. 4 (2018): 431–450.

Cecelski, David S. *The Waterman's Song: Slavery and Freedom in Maritime North Carolina.* Chapel Hill: University of North Carolina Press, 2001.

Chaline, Olivier. "Révolution et Marine française: Quelques remarques sur l'exercice de l'autorité." *Revue d'Histoire Maritime* 4 (2005): 147–179.

Charbit, Yves. "The Platonic City: History and Utopia." *Populations* 57, no. 2 (2002): 207–235.

Cheney, Paul. *Cul de Sac: Patrimony, Capitalism, and Slavery in French Saint-Domingue.* Chicago: University of Chicago Press, 2017.

Childers, Spencer, ed. *A Mariner of England: An Account of the Career of William Richardson from Cabin Boy in the Merchant Service to Warrant Officer in the Royal Navy, as Told by Himself.* London: John Murray, 1908.

Coats, Ann Veronica, and Philip MacDougall, eds. *The Naval Mutinies of 1797: Unity and Perseverance.* Woodbridge: Boydell Press, 2011.

Cookson, J. E. *The British Armed Nation, 1793–1815.* Oxford: Clarendon Press, 1997.

Coolen, Joris. "Places of Justice and Awe: The Topography of Gibbets and Gallows in Medieval and Early Modern North-Western and Central Europe." *World Archaeology* 45, no. 5 (2013): 762–779.

Corbett, Julian S., ed. *Private Papers of George, Second Earl Spencer, First Lord of the Admiralty, 1794–1801.* 2 vols. London: Navy Records Society, 1914.

Cormack, William S. "Legitimate Authority in Revolution and War: The French Navy in the West Indies, 1789–1793." *International History Review* 18, no. 1 (1996): 1–27.

———. *Patriots, Royalists, and Terrorists in the West Indies: The French Revolution in Martinique and Guadeloupe, 1789–1802.* Toronto: University of Toronto Press, 2019.

———. *Revolution and Political Conflict in the French Navy, 1789–1794.* Cambridge: Cambridge University Press, 1995.

Cottin, Paul. *Toulon et les Anglais en 1793, d'àpres des documents inédits.* Paris: Paul Ollendorff, 1898.

Craton, Michael. *Testing the Chains: Resistance to Slavery in the British West Indies.* Ithaca: Cornell University Press, 1982.

Cray, Robert E., Jr. "Remembering the USS Chesapeake: The Politics of Maritime Death and Impressment." *Journal of the Early Republic* 25, no. 3 (2005): 445–474.

Creighton, Margaret S. "Fraternity in the American Forecastle." *The New England Quarterly* 63, no. 4 (1990): 531–557.

Crépin, Annie. "The Army of the New Republic: New Warfare and a New Army." In *Republics at War, 1776–1840: Revolutions, Conflicts, and Geopolitics in Europe and the Atlantic World,* edited by Pierre Serna, Antonino De Francesco, and Judith A. Miller, 131–148. New York: Palgrave Macmillan, 2013.

Cress, Larry D. "The Jonathan Robbins Incident: Extradition and the Separation of Powers in the Adams Administration." *Essex Institute Historical Collections* 111, no. 2 (1975): 99–121.

Crook, Malcolm. *Toulon in War and Revolution: From the Ancien Régime to the Restoration, 1750–1820.* Manchester: Manchester University Press, 1991.

Crow, Hugh. *Memoirs of the Late Captain Hugh Crow of Liverpool; Comprising A Narrative of His Life, Together with Descriptive Sketches of the Western Coast of Africa; Particularly of Bonny; The Manners and Customs of the Inhabitants, the Productions of the Soil, and the Trade of the Country. To Which Are Added, Anecdotes and Observations, Illustrative of the Negro Character.* London: Longman, Rees, Orme, Brown, and Green, 1830.

Crowdy, Terry. *French Warship Crews, 1789–1805: From the French Revolution to Trafalgar.* Botley: Osprey, 2005.

Crowhurst, R. P. "Profitability in French Privateering, 1793–1815." *Business History* 24, no. 1 (March 1982): 48–60.

Cunningham, Charles. *A Narrative of Occurrences That Took Place during the Mutiny at the Nore, in the Months of May and June, 1797; with a Few Observations upon Impressment of Seamen, and the Advantages of Those Who Are Employed in His Majesty's Service; Also on the Necessity and Useful Operations of the Articles of War.* Chatham, 1829.

Dacam, John H. "'Wanton and Torturing Punishments': Patterns of Discipline and Punishment in the Royal Navy, 1783–1815." PhD diss., University of Hull, 2009.

Dancy, J. Ross. *The Myth of the Press Gang: Volunteers, Impressment, and the Naval Manpower Problem in the Late Eighteenth Century.* Woodbridge: Boydell Press, 2015.

Dann, John C., ed. *The Nagle Journal: A Diary of the Life of Jacob Nagle, Sailor, from the Year 1775 to 1841.* New York: Weidenfeld and Nicolson, 1988.

Davey, James, and Richard Johns. *Broadsides: Caricature and the Navy, 1756–1815.* Barnsley: Seaforth, 2012.

Davids, Karel. "Local and Global: Seafaring Communities in the North Sea Area, c. 1600–2000." *International Journal of Maritime History* 27, no. 4 (2015): 629–646.

———. "Maritime Labour in the Netherlands, 1570–1870." *Research in Maritime History,* no. 13 (1997): 41–71.

———. "Seamen's Organization and Social Protest in Europe, c. 1300–1825." *International Review of Social History* 39, 52 (1994): 145–169.

Davis, Joshua. *A Narrative of Joshua Davis, an American Citizen, Who Was Pressed and Served On Board Six Ships of the British Navy.* Boston, 1811.

Dean, David. "Joseph Wall of Goree Island." *African Affairs* 57, no. 229 (1958): 295–301.

Dickinson, H. T., ed. *The Political Works of Thomas Spence.* Newcastle upon Tyne: Avero, 1983.

Dickson, David, Kevin Whelan, Thomas Bartlett, and Dáire Keogh, eds. *1798: A Bicentenary Perspective.* Dublin: Four Courts Press, 2003.

Doerflinger, Thomas M. "The Antilles Trade of the Old Regime: A Statistical Overview." *Journal of Interdisciplinary History* 6, no. 3 (1976): 397–415.

Drayton, Richard. "The Globalisation of France: Provincial Cities and French Expansion c. 1500–1800." *History of European Ideas* 34, no. 4 (2008): 424–430.

Dubois, Laurent. *A Colony of Citizens: Revolution and Slave Emancipation in the French Caribbean, 1787–1804.* Chapel Hill: University of North Carolina Press, 2004.

———. *Avengers of the New World: The Story of the Haitian Revolution.* Cambridge, MA: Harvard University Press, 2004.

Dubois, Laurent, and John D. Garrigus, eds. *Slave Revolution in the Caribbean, 1789–1804: A Brief History with Documents.* Boston: Bedford/St. Martin's, 2006.

Ducasse, Contre-amiral. "Pierre-Victor Malouet au service de la Marine (1740–1814)." *Revue Historique des Armées,* no. 4 (1990): 86–97.

Duffy, Michael. *Soldiers, Sugar, and Seapower: The British Expeditions to the West Indies and the War against Revolutionary France.* Oxford: Clarendon Press, 1987.

Dugan, James. *The Great Mutiny.* New York: G. P. Putnam's Sons, 1965.

Dunne, W. M. P. "The Constellation and the Hermione." *Mariner's Mirror* 70, no. 1 (1984): 82–85.

Durand, James R. *The Life and Adventures of James R. Durand, from the Year One Thousand Eight Hundred and One, until the Year One Thousand Eight Hundred and Sixteen. Written by Himself. His First Leaving His Parents: How He Was Cast Away, and the Hardships He Underwent; His Entering the American Service; Together with the Particulars of His Impressment and Service on Board a British*

Man of War, Seven Years and 1 Month, until 1816. Bridgeport: Stiles, Nichols and Son, 1817.

Durey, Michael. "Loyalty in an Age of Conspiracy: The Oath-Filled Civil War in Ireland 1795–1799." In *Unrespectable Radicals? Popular Politics in the Age of Reform,* edited by Michael T. Davis and Paul A. Pickering, 71–89. Abingdon: Ashgate, 2013.

Dye, Ira. "Early American Merchant Seafarers." *Proceedings of the American Philosophical Society* 120, no. 5 (1976), 331–360.

———. "The Tattoos of Early American Seafarers, 1796–1818." *Proceedings of the American Philosophical Society* 133, no. 4 (1989): 520–554.

Eder, Marcus. *Crime and Punishment in the Royal Navy of the Seven Years' War, 1755–1763.* Aldershot: Ashgate, 2004.

Edsall, John. *Incidents in the Life of John Edsall.* Catskill, 1831.

Ekirch, A. Roger. *American Sanctuary: Mutiny, Martyrdom, and National Identity in the Age of Revolution.* New York: Pantheon, 2017.

Elliott, Marianne. *Partners in Revolution: The United Irishmen and France.* New Haven: Yale University Press, 1982.

———. "The Role of Ireland in French War Strategy, 1796–1798." In *Ireland and the French Revolution,* edited by Hugh Gough and David Dickson, 202–219. Dublin: Irish Academic Press, 1990.

———. *Wolfe Tone.* 2nd ed. Liverpool: Liverpool University Press, 2012.

Epochs and Episodes of History: Memorable Days and Notable Events. London: Ward, Lock and Co., 1882.

Epstein, James. "The Radical Underworld Goes Colonial: P. F. McCallum's Travels in Trinidad." In *Unrespectable Radicals? Popular Politics in the Age of Reform,* edited by Michael T. Davis and Paul A. Pickering, 147–165. Aldergate: Ashgate, 2008.

Ericson, Lars. *Svenska knektar: Indelta soldater, ryttare och båtsmän i krig och fred.* 2nd ed. Lund: Historiska Media, 2004.

Esquieu, L., and L. Delourmel, eds. *Brest pendant la Révolution (documents inédits): Correspondance de la municipalité avec les députés de la Sénéchaussée de Brest aux États Généraux et à l'Assemblée Constituante, 1789–1791.* Brest: Soc. Anon. de l'Union Républicaine du Finistère, 1909.

Estes, Todd. *The Jay Treaty Debate, Public Opinion, and the Evolution of Early American Political Culture.* Amherst: University of Massachusetts Press, 2006.

Falconer, William. *An Universal Dictionary of the Marine.* 5th ed., corrected. London, 1784.

Farr, James. "A Slow Boat to Nowhere: The Multi-Racial Crews of the American Whaling Industry." *Journal of Negro History* 68, no. 2 (1983): 159–170.

Featherstone, David. "Counter-Insurgency, Subalternity and Spatial Relations: Interrogating Court-Martial Narratives of the Nore Mutiny of 1797." *South African Historical Journal* 61, no. 4 (2009): 766–787.

———. *Resistance, Space and Political Identities: The Making of Counter-Global Networks.* Chichester: Wiley-Blackwell, 2008.

Ferguson, Eugene S. *Truxtun of the Constellation: The Life of Commodore Thomas Truxtun, U.S. Navy, 1755–1822.* Baltimore: Johns Hopkins University Press, 1956.

Fisher, Michael H. "Working across the Seas: Indian Maritime Labourers in India, Britain, and in Between, 1600–1857." *International Review of Social History* 51, no. S14 (2006): 21–45.

Foner, Eric. *Tom Paine and Revolutionary America.* Updated ed. New York: Oxford University Press, 2005.

Forester, C. S. *The Adventures of John Wetherell.* London: Michael Joseph, 1954.

Forrest, Alan. *Conscripts and Deserters: The Army and French Society during the Revolution and Empire.* New York: Oxford University Press, 1989.

Fortanier, A. P. *Geschiedenis van het ontstaan en de ontwikkeling der Nederlandsche koloniën.* Amsterdam: G. L. Funke, 1869.

Foucault, Michel. "Of Other Spaces." *Diacritics* 16, no. 1 (1986): 22–27.

Foy, Charles R. "The Royal Navy's Employment of Black Mariners and Maritime Workers, 1754–1783." *International Journal of Maritime History* 28, no. 1 (2016): 6–35.

———. "'Unkle Sommerset's' Freedom: Liberty in England for Black Sailors." *Journal for Maritime Research* 13, no. 1 (2011): 21–36.

Frankot, Edda. "Medieval Maritime Law from Oléron to Wisby: Jurisdictions in the Law of the Sea." In *Communities in European History: Representations, Jurisdictions, Conflicts,* edited by Juan Pan-Montojo and Frederik Pedersen, 151–172. Pisa: Pisa University Press, 2007.

Franzén, Frans Michael. "En blick på det adertonde seklet. Vid magister-promotionen i Åbo, 1798." In *Skaldestycken,* 2:161. Örebro: M. N. Lindh, 1828.

Further Account (Being Part II.) of the Cruelties Discovered in Coldbath-Fields Prison, as Reported in the House of Commons, on Tuesday, the 22d July, 1800, Etc. London: J. S. Jordan, 1800.

Fury, Cheryl A. *Tides in the Affairs of Men: The Social History of Elizabethan Seamen, 1580–1603.* Westport, CT: Greenwood, 2002.

Garneray, Louis. *The Floating Prison: The Remarkable Account of Nine Years' Captivity on the British Prison Hulks during the Napoleonic Wars.* London: Conway Maritime Press, 2003.

———. *Voyages, aventures et combats: Souvenirs de ma vie maritime.* Brussels: Alphonse Lebègue, 1851.

Garstin, Crosbie, ed. *Samuel Kelly: An Eighteenth Century Seaman, Whose Days Have Been Few and Evil, to Which Is Added Remarks, Etc., on Places He Visited during His Pilgrimage in This Wilderness.* New York: Frederick A. Stokes Co., 1925.

Geggus, David. *Slavery, War, and Revolution: The British Occupation of Saint Domingue 1793–1798.* Oxford: Clarendon Press, 1982.

Gelder, Roelof. *Het Oost-Indisch avontuur: Duitsers in dienst van de VOC (1600–1800).* Nijmegen: SUN, 1997.

Gerstenberger, Heide. "Men Apart: The Concept of 'Total Institution' and the Analysis of Seafaring." *International Journal of Maritime History* 8, no. 1 (1996): 173–182.

———. "On Maritime Labour and Maritime Labour Markets in Germany, 1700–1900." In *Maritime Labour: Contributions to the History of Work at Sea, 1500–2000*, edited by Richard Gorski, 43–59. Amsterdam: Amsterdam University Press, 2008.

Gilbert, Arthur N. "The Nature of Mutiny in the British Navy in the Eighteenth Century." In *Naval History: The Sixth Symposium of the US Naval Academy*, edited by Daniel M. Masterson, 111–120. Wilmington: Scholarly Resources, 1987.

Gilje, Paul A. *Free Trade and Sailors' Rights in the War of 1812*. New York: Cambridge University Press, 2013.

———. *Liberty on the Waterfront: American Maritime Culture in the Age of Revolution*. Philadelphia: University of Pennsylvania Press, 2004.

Gill, Conrad. *The Naval Mutinies of 1797*. Manchester: Manchester University Press, 1913.

Gillen, Ultán. "Constructing Democratic Thought in Ireland in the Age of Revolution, 1775–1800." In *Re-Imagining Democracy in the Age of Revolution: America, France, Britain, Ireland 1750–1850*, edited by Joanna Innes and Mark Philp, 149–161. Oxford: Oxford University Press, 2013.

Gilly, William O. S. *Narratives of Shipwrecks of the Royal Navy: Between 1793 and 1849*. 2nd ed. London: John W. Parker, 1851.

Glete, Jan. *Navies and Nations: Warships, Navies and State Building in Europe, 1500–1860*. 2 vols. Stockholm: Almqvist and Wiksell, 1993.

———. *Warfare at Sea, 1500–1650: Maritime Conflicts and the Transformation of Europe*. New York: Routledge, 2000.

Godechot, Jacques. *La grande nation: L'expansion révolutionnaire de la France dans le monde de 1789 à 1799*. 2nd ed. Paris: Flammarion, 1983.

Goodwin, Albert. *The Friends of Liberty: The English Democratic Movement in the Age of the French Revolution*. Cambridge, MA: Harvard University Press, 1979.

Goslinga, Cornelis Ch. *The Dutch in the Caribbean and in the Guianas 1680–1791*. Dover, NH: Van Gorcum, 1985.

———. *The Dutch in the Caribbean and in Surinam 1791/5–1942*. Assen: Van Gorcum, 1990.

Grossman, Dave. *On Killing: The Psychological Cost of Learning to Kill in War and Society*. New York: Back Bay Books, 1995.

Hammar, AnnaSara. *Mellan kaos och kontroll: Social ordning i svenska flottan, 1670–1716*. Stockholm: Nordic Academic Press, 2014.

Hammond, Charles H., Jr. "The French Revolution and the Enlightening of Military Justice." *Proceedings of the Western Society for French History*, no. 34 (2006): 134–146.

Hampson, Norman. "The 'Comité de Marine' of the Constituent Assembly." *The Historical Journal* 2, no. 2 (1959): 130–148.

Harland, John. *Seamanship in the Age of Sail*. Annapolis, MD: Naval Institute Press, 1985.

Haughton, Thomas L. "The Execution of Three Royal Marines on Plymouth Hoe in 1797." *Irish Sword* 11, no. 45 (1974): 246–247.

Hauterive, Borel d'. *Annuaire de la noblesse de France et des maisons souveraines de l'Europe*. Paris, 1862.

Hawkins, Anne, and Helen Watt. "'Now Is Our Time, the Ship Is Our Own, Huzza for the Red Flag': Mutiny on the Inspector, 1797." *Mariner's Mirror* 93, no. 2 (2007): 156–179.

Henwood, Phillippe, and Edmond Monage. *Brest: Un port en révolution, 1789–1799*. Rennes: Éditions Ouest-France, 1989.

Hodgskin, Thomas, Lieut., RN. *An Essay on Naval Discipline*. London, 1813.

Höij, Patrik. "Båtsmännen vid skärgårdsflottan: Tjänstgöringsförhållanden och social förankring i lokalsamhället." In *Skärgårdsflottan: Uppbygnad, militär användning och förankring i det svenska samhället 1700–1824*, edited by Hans Norman, 241–260. Lund: Historiska Media, 2000.

Holmes, Richard. *Acts of War: The Behavior of Men in Battle*. New York: Free Press, 1985.

Hone, J. Ann. *For the Cause of Truth: Radicalism in London, 1796–1821*. Oxford: Clarendon Press, 1982.

Hoock, Holger. *Empires of the Imagination: Politics, War, and the Arts in the British World, 1750–1850*. London: Profile, 2010.

Horace. *The Complete Odes and Epodes*. Oxford: Oxford University Press, 1997.

Horstbøll, Henrik, and Uffe Østergård. "Reform and Revolution: The French Revolution and the Case of Denmark." *Scandinavian Journal of History* 15, no. 3 (1990): 155–179.

Hoxse, John. *The Yankee Tar. An Authentic Narrative of the Voyages and Hardships of John Hoxse, and the Cruises of the US Frigate Constellation, and Her Engagement with the French Frigates Le Insurgente and Le Vengeance, in the Latter of Which the Author Loses His Right Arm, and Is Severely Wounded in the Side*. Northampton, 1840.

Hughes, Edward, ed. *The Private Correspondence of Admiral Lord Collingwood*. London: Navy Records Society, 1957.

Hutchinson, J. R. *The Press-Gang Afloat and Ashore*. New York: E. P. Dutton and Co., 1914.

Impartial Statement of the Cruelties Discovered in the Coldbath-Fields Prison, by the Grand and Traverse Juries for the County of Middlesex, and Reported in the House of Commons, on Friday the 11th of June, 1800. London: J. S. Jordan, 1800.

Israel, Jonathan I. *The Dutch Republic: Its Rise, Greatness, and Fall, 1477–1806*. Oxford: Clarendon, 1998.

Jackson, Richard P. "From Profit-Sailing to Wage-Sailing: Mediterranean Owner-Captains and Their Crews during the Medieval Commercial Revolution." *The Journal of European Economic History* 18, no. 3 (1989): 605–628.

Jaffer, Aaron. *Lascars and Indian Ocean Seafaring, 1780–1860: Shipboard Life, Unrest, and Mutiny*. Woodbridge: Boydell Press, 2015.

James, C. L. R. *The Black Jacobins: Toussaint L'Ouverture and the San Domingo Revolution.* London: Penguin, 1980.

James, William. *The Naval History of Great Britain, from the Declaration of War by France, in February 1793; to the Accession of George IV, in January 1820.* Vol. 1. 5 vols. London: Baldwin, Cradock, and Joy, 1822.

Jenks, Timothy. *Naval Engagements: Patriotism, Cultural Politics, and the Royal Navy, 1793–1815.* New York: Oxford University Press, 2006.

Jonge, J. C. de. *Geschiedenis van het Nederlandsche zeewezen.* Vol. 5. 6 vols. Haarlem: A. C. Kruseman, 1862.

Jonnès, Moureau de. *Adventures in the Revolution and under the Consulate.* London: Peter Davies, 1969.

Kachun, Mitch. "From Forgotten Founder to Indispensable Icon: Crispus Attucks, Black Citizenship, and Collective Memory, 1770–1865." *Journal of the Early Republic* 29, no. 2 (2009): 249–286.

Karlbom, Rolf. *Hungeruplopp och strejker 1793–1867: En studie i den svenska arbetar-rörelsens uppkomst.* Lund: Gleerup, 1967.

Kemp, Peter. *The British Sailor: A Social History of the Lower Deck.* London: J. M. Dent and Sons Ltd., 1970.

Kennedy, Gavin. "Bligh and the Defiance Mutiny." *Mariner's Mirror* 65, no. 1 (1979): 65–68.

Kennedy, W. Benjamin. "The United Irishmen and the Great Mutiny of 1797." *Eire-Ireland* 25, no. 3 (1990): 7–18.

Keyt, David. "Plato and the Ship of State." In *The Blackwell Guide to Plato's Republic,* edited by Gerasimos Santas, 189–213. Malden, MA: Blackwell, 2006.

Kinkel, Sarah. *Disciplining the Empire: Politics, Governance, and the Rise of the British Navy.* Cambridge, MA: Harvard University Press, 2018.

Kirby, David. *The Baltic World 1772–1993: Europe's Northern Periphery in the Age of Change.* New York: Routledge, 1999.

Kleczewski, Kieran Russell. "Martinique and the British Occupation, 1794–1802." PhD diss., Georgetown University, 1988.

Kleinman, Sylvie. "Initiating Insurgencies Abroad: French Plans to 'Chouannise' Britain and Ireland, 1793–1798." *Small Wars and Insurgencies* 25, no. 4 (2014): 784–799.

Klíma, Arnošt. "Agrarian Class Structure and Economic Development in Pre-Industrial Bohemia." *Past and Present,* no. 85 (1979): 49–67.

Kongl. Maj:ts Krigs-Articlar för des krigsmagt til lands och siös, gifne Stockholms Slott den 31 Martii 1798. Stockholm: Kongl. Tryckeriet, 1798.

Knight, Roger. *Britain Against Napoleon: The Organization of Victory, 1793–1815.* London: Penguin, 2014.

Lacour, M. A. *Histoire de la Guadeloupe.* Basse-Terre: Imprimerie du Gouvernement, 1857.

Lacroix, Pamphile de. *Mémoires pour servir à l'histoire de la révolution de Saint-Domingue.* Paris: Pillet Ainé, 1819.

Landheer, Hugo. "Een maandceelhouder en zijn klanten: De Amsterdamse logementhouder Hendrik Klaver." *Holland: Historisch Tijdschrift* 45, no. 3–4 (2013): 137–145.

Landolphe, Jean-François. *Mémoires du Capitaine Landolphe, contenant l'histoire de ses voyages pendant trente-six ans, aux côtes d'Afrique et aux deux Amériques; rédigés sur son manuscrit, par J. S. Quesné, ornés de trois gravures.* 2 vols. Paris: A. Bertrand and Pillet Aîné, 1823.

Langley, Harold L. "The Negro in the Navy and Merchant Service, 1789–1860." *Journal of Negro History* 52, no. 4 (1967): 273–286.

Laudani, Raffaele. *Disobedience in Western Political Thought: A Genealogy.* New York: Cambridge University Press, 2013.

Laughton, John Knox, ed. *Journal of Rear-Admiral Bartholomew James, 1752–1828.* London: Navy Records Society, 1896.

———. *Letters and Papers of Charles, Lord Barham, Admiral of the Red Squadron, 1758–1813, Volume 1.* London: Navy Records Society, 1907.

Lautard, Laurent. *Esquisses historiques: Marseille depuis 1789 jusqu'en 1815.* Marseille: Marius Olive, 1844.

Lauvergne, Henri. *Choléra-Morbus en Provence.* Toulon: Aurel, 1836.

Lavery, Brian. *Nelson's Navy: The Ships, Men and Organization, 1793–1815.* Annapolis, MD: Naval Institute Press, 1989.

Le Duc, Thomas H. "A Yankee Trader Views the French Revolution in Martinique." *The New England Quarterly* 11, no. 4 (1938): 802–807.

Leech, Samuel. *A Voice from the Main Deck: Being a Record of the Thirty Years Adventures of Samuel Leech.* London: Chatham, 1999.

Le Goff, T. J. A. "Les gens de mer devant le système de classes (1755–1763): Resistance ou passivité?" *Revue du Nord,* special series, no. 1 (1986): 463–479.

———. "Offre et productivité de la main d'œuvre dans les armaments français au 18éme siècle." In *Seamen in Society/Gens de mer en société,* edited by Paul Adam, 95–108. Perthes: Commission internationale d'histoire maritime, 1980.

———. "Les origines sociales des gens de mer français au XVIIIe siècle." In *La France d'Ancien Régime: Études réunies en l'honneur de Pierre Goubert.* Toulouse: Privat, 1984.

———. "Problèmes de recrutement de la Marine française pendant la Guerre de Sept Ans." *Revue Historique* 283, no. 2 (574) (April 1, 1990): 205–233.

Lefebvre, Georges. *The French Revolution: From Its Origins to 1793.* London: Routledge, 2001.

Leiner, Frederick C. *The End of Barbary Terror: America's 1815 War Against the Pirates of North Africa.* Oxford: Oxford University Press, 2004.

Lemisch, Jesse. "Jack Tar in the Streets: Merchant Seamen in the Politics of Revolutionary America." *William and Mary Quarterly,* 3rd series, 25, no. 3 (1968): 371–407.

———. *Jack Tar vs. John Bull: The Role of New York's Seamen in Precipitating the Revolution.* New York: Garland, 1997.

Leunig, Tim, Jelle van Lottum, and Bo Poulsen. "Surprisingly Gentle Confinement: British Treatment of Danish and Norwegian Prisoners of War during the Napoleonic Wars." *Scandinavian Economic History Review* 66, no. 3 (2018): 282–297.

Lévy-Schneider, Léon. *Le conventionnel Jeanbon Saint-André, membre du Comité de salut public, organisateur de la Marine de la Terreur, 1749–1813.* Paris: F. Alcan, 1901.

Lincoln, Margarette, *Representing the Royal Navy: British Sea Power, 1750–1815.* Aldershot: Ashgate, 2002.

Linebaugh, Peter. *The London Hanged: Crime and Civil Society in the Eighteenth Century.* Cambridge: Cambridge University Press, 1992.

———. *Red Round Globe Hot Burning: A Tale at the Crossroads of Commons and Closure, of Love and Terror, of Race and Class, and of Kate and Ned Despard.* Oakland: University of California Press, 2019.

Linebaugh, Peter, and Marcus Rediker. *The Many-Headed Hydra: Sailors, Slaves, Commoners, and the Hidden History of the Revolutionary Atlantic.* Boston: Beacon Press, 2000.

Lloyd, Christopher. *The British Seaman, 1200–1860: A Social Survey.* Rutherford, NJ: Fairleigh Dickinson University Press, 1970.

———. *St. Vincent and Camperdown.* New York: Macmillan, 1963.

Loir, Maurice. *La Marine royale en 1789.* Paris: Armand Colin, 1892.

Lottum, Jelle van. "Some Thoughts about Migration of Maritime Workers in the Eighteenth-Century North Sea Region." *International Journal of Maritime History* 27, no. 4 (2015): 647–661.

Lottum, Jelle van, Jan Lucassen, and Lex Heerma van Voss. "Sailors, National and International Labour Markets and National Identity, 1600–1850." In *Shipping and Economic Growth 1350–1850*, edited by Richard Unger, 309–351. Leiden: Brill, 2011.

Lottum, Jelle van, and Jan Luiten van Zanden. "Labour Productivity and Human Capital in the European Maritime Sector of the Eighteenth Century." *Explorations in Economic History* 53, Supplement C (2014): 83–100.

Lybeck, Otto Emil. *Svenska flottans historia, andra bandet, tredje perioden: Från frihetstidens slut till freden i Kiel.* Malmö: A.-B. Allhems, 1945.

MacCalman, Iain. *Radical Underworld: Prophets, Revolutionaries and Pornographers in London, 1795–1840.* Cambridge: Cambridge University Press, 1988.

Macleod, A. D. "Calenture—Missing at Sea?" *British Journal of Medical Psychology,* no. 56 (1983): 347–350.

Madiou, Thomas. *Histoire d'Haiti.* Port-au-Prince: JH Courtois, 1847.

Magra, Christopher. *Poseidon's Curse: British Naval Impressment and the Atlantic Origins of the American Revolution.* New York: Cambridge University Press, 2016.

Mahan, Alfred Thayer. *The Influence of Sea Power Upon the French Revolution and Empire, 1793–1812.* Vol. 1. 9th ed., 2 vols. London: Sampson Low, Marston, and Co., 1892.

Malcomson, Thomas. *Order and Disorder in the British Navy, 1793–1815: Control, Resistance, Flogging and Hanging.* Woodbridge: Boydell Press, 2016.

Manninen, Juha. "Frans Michael Franzén och franska revolutionen." *Historisk tidskrift för Finland* 74, no. 1 (1989): 31–64.

Manwaring, William, and Bonamy Dobrée. *The Floating Republic: An Account of the Mutinies at Spithead and the Nore in 1797.* Barnsley: Pen and Sword, 2004.

Marcus, G. J. *Heart of Oak: A Survey of British Sea Power in the Georgian Era.* New York: Oxford University Press, 1975.

Markoff, John. *The Abolition of Feudalism: Peasants, Lords, and Legislators in the French Revolution.* University Park: The Pennsylvania State University Press, 1996.

Martin, Jean-Clément. "The Vendée, *Chouannerie,* and the State, 1791–99." In *A Companion to the French Revolution,* edited by Peter McPhee, 246–259. Malden, MA: Wiley-Blackwell, 2013.

Mason, Matthew. "The Battle of the Slaveholding Liberators: Great Britain, the United States, and Slavery in the Early Nineteenth Century." *William and Mary Quarterly,* 3rd series, 59, no. 3 (2002): 665–696.

Masson, Philippe. *Les sépulcres flottants: Prisonniers français en Angleterre sous l'Empire.* Rennes: Éditions Ouest-France, 1987.

Mavidal, Jérôme, Emile Colombey, Louis Claveau, Constant Pionnier, and Louis Lodoïs Lataste, eds. *Archives parlementaires de 1787 à 1860 recueil complet des débats législatifs et politiques des chambres françaises.* 101 vols. Paris: Librairie administrative de P. Dupont, 1862.

McCord, Norman, and David E. Brewster. "Some Labour Troubles of the 1790s in North East England." *International Review of Social History* 13, no. 3 (1968): 366–383.

McKee, Christopher. "Foreign Seamen in the United States Navy: A Census of 1808." *William and Mary Quarterly,* 3rd series, 42, no. 3 (1985): 383–393.

Melville, Herman. *Billy Budd, Sailor, and Other Stories.* Harmondsworth: Penguin, 1970.

Memoirs of Richard Parker, the Mutineer; Together with an Account at Large of His Trial by Court Martial, Defence, Sentence, and Execution and A Narrative of the Mutiny at the Nore and Sheerness, from Its Commencement to Its Final Termination. London, 1797.

Merlin, M. *Répertoire universel et raisonné de jurisprudence.* 3rd ed. Paris: Garnery, 1808.

Meyer, Jean. "Forces navales et puissances économiques." In *Seamen in Society/Gens de mer en société,* edited by Paul Adam, 75–90. Perthes: Commission internationale d'histoire maritime, 1980.

Milo, Taco Hayo. *De geheime onderhandelingen tusschen de Bataafsche en Fransche Republieken van 1795 Tot 1797, in verband met de expeditie van schout bij nacht E. Lucas naar de Kaap de Goede Hoop.* Den Helder: De Boer, 1942.

Morales, Edgardo Pérez. *No Limits to Their Sway: Cartagena's Privateers and the Masterless Caribbean in the Age of Revolutions.* Nashville, TN: Vanderbilt University Press, 2018.

Morison, Samuel Eliot. *The Life and Letters of Harrison Gray Otis, Federalist, 1765–1848.* 2 vols. Boston: Houghton Mifflin Co., 1913.

Morriss, Roger. *The Foundations of British Maritime Ascendancy: Resources, Logistics, and the State, 1755–1815.* Cambridge: Cambridge University Press, 2011.

Morriss, Roger, ed. *The Channel Fleet and the Blockade of Brest, 1793–1801.* Aldershot: Ashgate for the Navy Records Society, 2001.

Mostert, Noel. *The Line Upon the Wind: The Great War at Sea, 1793–1815.* New York: W. W. Norton, 2007.

Mr Livingston's Motion, 20th February 1800. Philadelphia, 1800.

Mutineers of the Hermione. Antigua, 1798.

Naval Documents Related to the Quasi-War between the United States and France. 7 vols. Washington, DC: Government Printing Office, 1935.

Neal, Larry. "The Cost of Impressment during the Seven Years War." *Mariner's Mirror* 64, no. 1 (1978): 45–56.

Neale, Jonathan. *The Cutlass and the Lash: Mutiny and Discipline in Nelson's Navy.* London: Pluto, 1985.

Newman, Simon P. "Reading the Bodies of Early American Seafarers." *William and Mary Quarterly,* 3rd series, 55, no. 1 (1998): 59–82.

Newmeyr, R. Kent. *John Marshall and the Heroic Age of the Supreme Court.* Baton Rouge: Louisiana State University Press, 2001.

Nicolson, Adam. *Men of Honour: Trafalgar and the Making of an English Hero.* London: HarperCollins, 2005.

Notes and Queries: A Medium of Intercommunication for Literary Men, General Readers, Etc., Eighth Series, Volume Tenth, July–December 1896. London: John C. Francis, 1896.

Ojala, Jari, Jaakko Pehkonen, and Jari Eloranta. "Deskilling and Decline in Skill Premium during the Age of Sail: Swedish and Finnish Seamen, 1751–1913." *Explorations in Economic History* 61 (2016): 85–94.

Oliver, William. "A Letter of Dr William Oliver, F.R.S. Concerning a Calenture." *Philosophical Transactions,* no. 24 (May 1704): 1562–1564.

Palmer, R. R. "Much in Little: The Dutch Revolution of 1795." *The Journal of Modern History* 26, no. 1 (1954).

Papon, Jean-Pierre. *Histoire générale de Provence.* Paris: Ph.-D. Pierres, 1784.

Patton, Philip. *The Natural Defense of an Insular Empire, Earnestly Recommended; with A Sketch of a Plan, to Attach Real Seamen to the Service of Their Country.* Southampton: T. Skelton, 1810.

———. *Observations on Naval Mutiny,* 1795.

———. *Observations on the State of Discipline in the Navy, End of the Year 1797. In a Letter to a Friend,* n.d.

———. Anon. [Philip Patton]. *Strictures on Naval Discipline, and the Conduct of a Ship of War. Intended to Produce an Uniformity among Sea-Officers.* Edinburgh: Murray and Cochrane, 1810.

Pelham, Camden. *The Chronicles of Crime; or, The New Newgate Calendar, Vol. 1.* London: Thomas Tegg, 1841.

Penn, Nigel. "The Voyage Out: Peter Kolb and VOC Voyages to the Cape." In *Many Middle Passages: Forced Migration and the Making of the Modern World,* edited by Emma Christopher, Cassandra Pybus, and Marcus Rediker, 72–91. Berkeley: University of California Press, 2007.

Perl-Rosenthal, Nathan. *Citizen Sailors: Becoming American in the Age of Revolution.* Cambridge, MA: Belknap Press of Harvard University Press, 2015.

Pérotin-Dumon, Anne. "Ambiguous Revolution in the Caribbean: The White Jacobin, 1789–1800." *Historical Reflections/Réflexions historiques* 13, nos. 2–3 (1986): 499–515.

Perrin, W. G. *British Flags: Their Early History, and Their Development at Sea; With an Account of the Origin of the Flag as a National Device.* Cambridge: Cambridge University Press, 1922.

Pettit, Philip. "The Tree of Liberty. Republicanism: American, French, and Irish." *Field Day Review,* no. 1 (2005): 29–41.

Pietsch, Roland. "Hearts of Oak and Jolly Tars? Heroism and Insanity in the Georgian Navy." *Journal for Maritime Research* 15, no. 1 (2013): 69–82.

———. "Ships' Boys and Youth Culture in Eighteenth-Century Britain: The Navy Recruits of the London Marine Society Roland Pietsch." *The Northern Mariner/Le marin du nord* 14, no. 4 (2004): 11–24.

Pinckney, Charles. *Three Letters, Written and Originally Published, under the Signature of a South Carolina Planter: The First, on the Case of Jonathan Robbins; Decided under the Twenty-Sixth Article of the Treaty with Great Britain, in the District Court of the United States, for South Carolina. The Second, on the Recent Captures of American Vessels by British Cruisers, Contrary to the Laws of Nations, and the Treaty between the Two Countries. The Third, on the Right of Expatriation.* Philadelphia: Aurora Office, 1799.

Plato. *The Laws.* Edited by Malcolm Schofield. Cambridge: Cambridge University Press, 2016.

———. *The Republic.* Cambridge: Cambridge University Press, 2000.

Pointrineau, Abel. "L'État et l'avenir des colonies françaises de plantation à la fin de l'Ancien Régime, selon P. V. Malouet." *Revue d'Auvergne* 104, nos. 1–2 (1990): 41–54.

Poissonnier-Desperrières, Antoine. *Traité des maladies des gens de mer.* Paris: Lacombe, 1767.

Pope, Dudley. *Life in Nelson's Navy.* London: Unwin Hyman, 1981.

Popkin, Jeremy D. *Facing Racial Revolution: Eyewitness Accounts of the Haitian Insurrection.* Chicago: University of Chicago Press, 2007.

———. "Sailors and Revolution: Naval Mutineers in Saint-Domingue, 1790–93." *French History* 26, no. 4 (2012): 460–481.

———. *You Are All Free: The Haitian Revolution and the Abolition of Slavery.* New York: Cambridge University Press, 2010.

Potofsky, Allan. "Paris-on-the-Atlantic from the Old Regime to the Revolution." *French History* 25, no. 1 (2011): 89–107.

Prétou, Pierre, and Denis Roland. "L'enfermement du large: Les officiers au temps de la marine à voile." In *Fureur et cruauté des capitaines en mer,* edited by Pierre Prétou and Denis Roland, 34–69. Rennes: Presses Universitaires de Rennes, 2012.

———. "Le pouvoir extraordinaire: les fondements culturels de l'autorité à bord." In *Fureur et cruauté des capitaines en mer,* edited by Pierre Prétou and Denis Roland, 14–33. Rennes: Presses Universitaires de Rennes, 2012.

Price, Richard. "Dialogical Encounters in a Space of Death." In *New World Orders: Violence, Sanction, and Authority in the Colonial Americas,* edited by John Smolenski and Thomas J. Humphrey, 47–65. Philadelphia: University of Pennsylvania Press, 2005.

Pürschel, G. Bent. "Træk af flådens retsvæsen." In *Flåden gennem 450 år,* edited by R. Steen Steensen, 308–317. 2nd ed. Copenhagen: Martins Forlag, 1970.

Pyle, Christopher. *Extradition, Politics, and Human Rights.* Philadelphia: Temple University Press, 2001.

Quaritsch, Helmut. "Das Schiff als Gleichnis." In *Recht über See: Festschrift. Rolf Stödter zum 70. Geburtstag am 22. April 1979,* edited by Hans Peter Ipsen and Karl-Hartmann Necker. Heidelberg: R.v. Decker's Verlag, G. Schenk, 1979.

Rancière, Jacques. *On the Shores of Politics.* New York: Verso, 2007.

Rapport sur les peines à infliger dans l'Armée Navale, et dans les ports et arsénaux, fait au nom du Comité de la Marine, dans la séance du 16 Août 1790. Paris, 1790.

Rasmussen, Edit. "Tømrerstrejken i København 1794 og dens omfang." *Historiske meddelser om København* (1984): 69–85.

Ray, William. *Horrors of Slavery, or, The American Tars in Tripoli.* Edited by Hester Blum. New Brunswick, NJ: Rutgers University Press, 2008.

Rea, John. *A Letter to William Bainbridge Esqr., Formerly of the United States Ship George Washington; Relating to Some Transactions Onboard Said Ship, during a Voyage to Algiers, Constantinople, etc.* Philadelphia, 1802.

Recueil des lois relatives à la marine et aux colonies, 18 vols. Paris: L'imprimerie de la république, An V, An VI, An VII, An VIII, An X, and An XII; Paris: L'imprimerie impériale, An XIII, 1806, 1807, 1808, and 1810.

Rediker, Marcus. *Between the Devil and the Deep Blue Sea: Merchant Seamen, Pirates, and the Anglo-American Maritime World, 1700–1750.* Cambridge: Cambridge University Press, 1987.

———. "The Revenge of Crispus Attucks; or, The Atlantic Challenge to American Labor History." *Labor: Studies in the Working-Class History of the Americas* 1, no. 4 (2004): 35–45.

———. *Villains of All Nations: Atlantic Pirates in the Golden Age.* Boston: Beacon Press, 2004.

Reports from Committees of the House of Commons, Vol. X, Miscellaneous Subjects: 1785–1801. London, 1803.

Rheinheimer, Martin. *Arme, Bettler und Vagranten: Überleben in der Not, 1450–1850.* Frankfurt a. M.: Fischer, 2000.

Rions, Albert de. *Mémoire historique et justicatif de M. Le Comte d'Albert de Rions, sur l'Affaire de Toulon.* Paris, 1790.

Roberts, Michael. *The Age of Liberty: Sweden, 1719–1772.* Cambridge: Cambridge University Press, 1986.

Robinson, William. *Jack Nastyface: Memoirs of an English Seaman.* Annapolis, MD: Naval Institute Press, 1973.

Rodger, N. A. M. *The Command of the Ocean: A Naval History of Britain, 1649–1815.* New York: W. W. Norton, 2004.

———. "Mutiny or Subversion? Spithead and the Nore." In *1798: A Bicentenary Perspective,* edited by Thomas Bartlett, David Dickson, Dáire Keogh, and Kevin Whelan, 549–564. Dublin: Four Courts Press, 2003.

———. "Shipboard Life in the Old Navy: The Decline of the Old Order?" In *The North Sea: Twelve Essays on the Social History of Maritime Labour,* edited by Lewis Fischer, Harald Hamre, Poul Holm, and Jaap R. Bruijn, 29–39. Stavanger: Stavanger Maritime Museum / The Association of North Sea Societies, 1992.

———. *The Wooden World: An Anatomy of the Georgian Navy.* New York: W. W. Norton, 1986.

Rogers, Nicholas. *The Press Gang: Naval Impressment and Its Opponents in Georgian Britain.* London: Continuum, 2007.

Roodhuyzen, Thea. *In woelig vaarwater: Marineofficieren in de jaren 1779–1802.* Amsterdam: De Bataafse Leeuw, 1998.

Rose, R. B. "A Liverpool Sailors' Strike in the Eighteenth Century." *Transactions of the Lancashire and Cheshire Antiquarian Society* 68 (1958): 85–92.

Rossum, Matthias van. "'Amok!': Mutinies and Slaves on Dutch East Indiamen in the 1780s." In *Mutiny and Maritime Radicalism in the Age of Revolution: A Global Survey,* edited by Clare Anderson, Niklas Frykman, Lex Heerma van Voss, and Marcus Rediker, 109–130. Cambridge: Cambridge University Press, 2014.

Rouleau, Brian. *With Sails Whitening Every Sea: Mariners and the Making of an American Maritime Empire.* Ithaca, NY: Cornell University Press, 2014.

Rouleau, Brian J. "Dead Men Do Tell Tales: Folklore, Fraternity, and the Forecastle." *Early American Studies* 5, no. 1 (2007): 30–62.

Rousseau, Jean-Jacques. *The Social Contract and Other Later Political Writings.* Edited by Victor Gourevitch. Cambridge: Cambridge University Press, 1997.

Royen, Paul C. van, Jaap R. Bruijn, and Jan Lucassen, eds. *"Those Emblems of Hell?" European Sailors and the Maritime Labour Market 1570–1870 (Research in Maritime History, No. 13).* St. John's, Newfoundland: International Maritime Economic History Association, 1997.

Rydstad, Göran. "1788: Varför krig? Något om bakgrund och 'orsaker' till Gustav III:s ryska krig." In *Gustav III:s ryska krig,* edited by Gunnar Artéus, 9-22. Stockholm: Probus, 1992.

Saint-André, Jean-Bon. *Collection des arrêtes, pris par le républicain Jean-Bon Saint-André, à Brest, concernant la Marine de la République française, depuis le 21 Vendemiaire jusqu'au 21 Floréal, de l'an second de la République française, une et indivisble.* Brest: Gauchlet, An II [1793–94].

Saint-Roman, Julian. "La démocratie turbulente des ouvriers de l'arsenal de Toulon, 1789–1793." In *Peuples en révolution: D'aujourd'hui à 1789*, edited by Cyril Belmonte and Christine Peyrard, 125–138. Aix-en-Provence: Presses universitaires de Provence, 2014.

———. "La précarité des ouvriers de l'arsenal de Toulon à travers leurs mobilités: Fin XVIIIe siècle-début XIXe siècle," *MEFRIM* 123, no. 1 (2011): 103–113.

Schäfer, Eckart. "Das Staatsschiff. Zur Präzision eines Topos." In *Toposforschung: Eine Dokumentation*, edited by Peter Jehn, 259–292. Frankfurt: Athenäum, 1972.

Schama, Simon. *Patriots and Liberators: Revolution in the Netherlands, 1780–1813*. New York: Vintage, 1977.

Schedvin, Johan. "Journal förd om bord på kongliga svenska fregatten Eurydice. Under en sjöresa 1793." SE/SSHM/SME/75, in Sjöhistoriska Museet, Stockholm.

Scott, Jonathan. *When the Waves Ruled Britannia: Geography and Political Identities, 1500–1800*. New York: Cambridge University Press, 2011.

Scott, Julius S. *The Common Wind: Afro-American Currents in the Age of the Haitian Revolution*. London: Verso, 2018.

Selement, George. "Impressment and the American Merchant Marine, 1782–1812." *Mariner's Mirror* 59, no. 4 (1973): 409–418.

Semple Lisle, James George. *The Life of Major J. G. Semple Lisle; Containing a Faithful Narrative of His Alternate Vicissitudes of Splendor and Misfortune*. London, 1799.

Serna, Pierre. "Every Revolution Is a War for Independence." In *The French Revolution in Global Perspective*, edited by Suzanne Desan, Lynn Hunt, and William Max Nelson, 165–182. Ithaca, NY: Cornell University Press, 2013.

Shoemaker, Nancy. *Native American Whalemen and Their World: Indigenous Encounters and the Contingency of Race*. Chapel Hill: University of North Carolina Press, 2015.

Simons, C. H. F. *Marine justitie: Ontwikkelingen in de strafrechtspleging bij de Nederlandse zeemacht, in het bijzonder gedurende de tweede helft van de 18e eeuw en het begin van de 19e eeuw*. Assen: Van Gorcum, 1974.

Smith, James Morton. *Freedom's Fetters: The Alien and Sedition Laws and American Civil Liberties*. Ithaca, NY: Cornell University Press, 1956.

Smyth, Jim. *The Men of No Property: Irish Radicals and Popular Politics in the Late Eighteenth Century*. London: Macmillan, 1998.

Soboul, Albert. *The French Revolution, 1787–1799: From the Storming of the Bastille to Napoleon*. London: Unwin Hyman, 1989.

———. *The Sans Culottes: The Popular Movement and Revolutionary Government, 1793–1794*. New York: Anchor Books, 1972.

Solnit, Rebecca. *A Paradise Built in Hell: The Extraordinary Communities That Arise in Disaster*. New York: Viking, 2009.

Spavens, William. *The Seaman's Narrative*. London, 1796.

Speech of the Hon. John Marshall, Delivered in the House of Representatives, of the United States, on the Resolution of the Hon. Edward Livingston. Relative to

Thomas Nash, Alias Jonathan Robbins. Philadelphia: Printed at the Office of the "True American," 1800.

Spence, Thomas. *One Pennyworth of Pig's Meat; or, Lessons for the Swinish Multitude.* 3 vols. London, 1793–1795.

Spieler, Miranda Frances. *Empire and Underworld: Captivity in French Guiana.* Cambridge, MA: Harvard University Press, 2012.

———. "The Legal Structure of Colonial Rule during the French Revolution." *The William and Mary Quarterly* 66, no. 2 (April 1, 2009): 365–408.

Stedman, J. G. *Narrative of a Five Years' Expedition against the Revolted Negroes of Surinam, in Guiana on the Wild Coast of South America, from the Year 1772 to 1777.* London: J. Johnson and J. Edwards, 1796.

Steele, Robert. *The Marine Officer, or, Sketches of Service.* London: Henry Colburn, 1840.

Suphan, Bernhard, ed. *Herders sämmtliche Werke.* Vol. 18. Berlin: Weidmannsche Buchhandlung, 1883.

Sveriges Rikes Sjö-Articlar. Stockholm: Kongl. Tryckeriet, 1755.

Sydenham, Michael. *Léonard Bourdon: The Career of a Revolutionary, 1754–1807.* Waterloo, ON: Wilfrid Laurier University Press, 1999.

Taillemite, Etienne. *Histoire ignorée de la Marine française.* Paris: Perrin, 2003.

Thompson, E. P. *The Making of the English Working Class.* Harmondsworth: Penguin, 1968.

Thoral, Marie-Cécile. *From Valmy to Waterloo: France at War, 1792–1815.* New York: Palgrave Macmillan, 2011.

Tikoff, Valentina K. "Adolescence in the Atlantic: Charity Boys as Seamen in the Spanish Maritime World." *Journal of Early Modern History* 14, no. 1 (2010): 45–73.

Trotsky, Leon. *History of the Russian Revolution.* Chicago: Haymarket, 2008.

Trotter, Thomas. *Observations on the Scurvy: With a Review of the Theories Lately Advanced on That Disease; and the Opinions of Dr Milman.* Edinburgh, 1786.

Tucker, Jedediah Stephens, ed. *Memoirs of Admiral The Right Honorable the Earl of St. Vincent, G.C.B., etc.* 2 vols. London: Richard Bentley, 1844.

Underwood, Patrick, Steven Pfaff, and Michael Hechter. "Threat, Deterrence, and Penal Severity: An Analysis of Flogging in the Royal Navy, 1740–1820." *Social Science History* 42, no. 3 (2018): 411–439.

Valle, James E. *Rocks and Shoals: Order and Discipline in the Old Navy, 1800–1861.* Annapolis, MD: Naval Institute Press, 1980.

Van Bochove, Christian, and Tom Van Velzen. "Loans to Salaried Employees: The Case of the Dutch East India Company, 1602–1794." *European Review of Economic History* 18, no. 1 (2014): 19–38.

Vergé-Franceschi, Michel. "De l'émeute portuaire à la mutinerie militaire." In *Ruptures de la fin du XVIIIe siècle,* edited by Michel Vergé-Franceschi and Jean-Pierre Poussou, 51–81. Paris: Presse de l'Université de Paris-Sorbonne, 2005.

Vickers, Daniel. *Farmers and Fishermen: Two Centuries of Work in Essex County, Massachusetts, 1630–1850.* Chapel Hill: University of North Carolina Press, 1994.

Vickers, Daniel, with Vince Walsh. *Young Men and the Sea: Yankee Seafarers in the Age of Sail*. New Haven: Yale University Press, 2005.

Voltaire. *Candide, or Optimism*. London: Penguin, 1947.

———. "Man," in *A Philosophical Dictionary*, 2 vols. London: W. Dugdale, 1843.

Wald, Priscilla. *Contagious: Cultures, Carriers, and the Outbreak Narrative*. Durham, NC: Duke University Press, 2008.

Ward, Ned. *The Wooden World Dissected: In the Character of a Ship of War: As Also, The Characters of All the Officers, from the Captain to the Common Sailor*. 7th ed. London, 1756.

Ward, Robin. *The World of the Medieval Shipmaster: Law, Business and the Sea c. 1350–c. 1450*. Woodbridge: Boydell Press, 2009.

Weber, Paul. *On the Road to Rebellion: The United Irishmen and Hamburg, 1796–1803*. Dublin: Four Courts Press, 1997.

Wedgwood, Ruth. "The Revolutionary Martyrdom of Jonathan Robbins." *The Yale Law Journal* 100, no. 2 (1990): 229–368.

Welke, Ulrich. *Der Kapitän: Die Erfindung einer Herrschaftsform*. Münster: Westfälisches Dampfboot, 1997.

Wells, Roger. *Insurrection: The British Experience, 1795–1803*. Gloucester: Allan Sutton, 1986.

Wharton, Francis. *State Trials of the United States during the Administrations of Washington and Adams*. Philadelphia: Carey and Hart, 1849.

White, Jerry. "Pain and Degradation in Georgian London: Life in the Marshalsea Prison." *History Workshop Journal*, no. 68 (2009): 69–98.

Whitman, Walt. *The Early Poems and the Fiction*. Edited by Thomas L. Brasher. New York: New York University Press, 1963.

Wilson, David A. *United Irishmen, United States: Immigrant Radicals in the Early Republic*. Ithaca, NY: Cornell University Press, 1998.

Windham, William. *The Windham Papers, Volume II*. Boston: Small, Maynard and Co., 1913.

The Whole Trial and Defense of Richard Parker, President of the Delegates for Mutiny, etc. On Board the Sandwich, and Others of His Majesty's Ships, the Nore, In May, 1797. Before a Court Martial, Held on Board the Neptune, of 98 Guns, Laying off Greenhithe, near Gravesend, on Thursday, 22d of June, 1797, and Following Days. London, 1797.

Wolfe Tone, Theobald. *An Address to the People of Ireland on the Present Important Crisis*. Belfast, 1796.

Wolfe Tone, William Theobald. *Life of Theobald Wolfe Tone, Founder of the United Irish Society, and Adjutant General and Chef de Brigade in the Service of the French and Batavian Republics, Vol. II*. Washington, DC: Gales and Seaton, 1826.

Young, Alfred F. *The Democratic Republicans of New York: The Origins, 1763–1797*. Chapel Hill: University of North Carolina Press, 1967.

———. *Liberty Tree: Ordinary People and the American Revolution*. New York: New York University Press, 2006.

Zerbe, Britt. *The Birth of the Royal Marines, 1664–1802.* Woodbridge: Boydell Press, 2013.

Zetterberg, Kent. "The Organization of the Army and the Navy in Sweden." In *The Army and the Navy in Spain and Sweden in a Period of Change (1750–1870),* edited by Enrique Martínez Ruiz, Magdalena del Pazzis Pi Corrales, and Juan Torrejón, 15–40. Cadiz and San Fernando: Fundación Berndt Wistedt, Universidad de Cádiz, and Fundación Municipal de Cultura Ayuntamiento de San Fernando, 2001.

Zimmerman, James Fulton. *Impressment of American Seamen.* Port Washington, NY: Kennikat, 1925.

Zysberg, André. "Les gens de mer et l'état: La mobilisation navale en Europe." In *The Sea in History: The Early Modern World,* edited by Christian Buchet and Gérard Le Bouëdec, 825–838. Woodbridge: Boydell Press, 2017.

INDEX

lation (US frigate), 153; *Culloden* (British warship), 114–120, 153; demobilization (1783), 133; demobilization (1802), 207–208; *Defiance* (British warship), 120–124, 153, 179–181, 184–185; *Dordrecht* (Dutch warship), 96; *Dugué-Trouin* (French warship), 68; Dutch fleet in Saldanha Bay, 106–108; *Embuscade* (French frigate), 71–74; *Engagéante* (French frigate), 86; *Félicité* (French frigate), 78–80; *Ferme* (French warship), 62, 72, 74; French fleet in Quiberon Bay, 86; *Havick* (Dutch schooner), 105, 189; *Hermione* (British frigate), 165–172, 190–194; *Illustre* (French warship), 70; *Jackall* (British cutter), 111; *Jason* (Dutch frigate), 97–99; *Jupiter* (French warship), 68; *Lady Shore* (British convict ship), 154; *Léopard* (French warship), 51–55; *Majesteux* (French warship), 58, 64; *Marquis de Carmathen* (British transport), 154; *Monnikkendam* (Dutch frigate), 99–100; *Otter* (Dutch gunboat), 99; *Patriote* (French warship), 63; *Pompée* (British warship), 149–150; *Revolutie* (Dutch warship), 106); *Saturn* (British warship), 159–160, 178; *Savage* (British sloop), 132; *Surveillante* (French frigate), 68; *Temeraire* (French warship), 68; *Terrible* (British warship), 113–114; *Thames* (British warship), 170–171; *Utrecht* (Dutch warship), 189; *Vernieler* (Dutch gunboat), 189; *Winchelsea* (British warship), 111–112, 119; *Windsor Castle* (British warship), 112–113

Nash, Thomas (a.k.a. Jonathan Robbins), 190–192
National Assembly: debate about December 1 insurrection, 45–46; decree of April 4, 1792, 75, 79; decree of March 8, 1790, 48–50; response to Brest fleet mutiny, 59–60
naval arms race, 16–17
naval combat, 1–3, 30, 83–84, 92–93, 168–169

naval discipline, 28–31. *See also* articles of war; *Code Pénal Maritime;* naval reforms; punishments
naval hierarchies, 27–29
naval reforms: in British navy, 110–111, 132–133; in Dutch navy, 95–96; in French navy, 55–58, 87–90
Naval Thanksgiving (1797), 3
Navy Bill (1749), 110
Nore fleet mutiny: collapse of, 150–152; committee system, 143–145; demands, 139–143; influence of 149–150, 153–154, 160–163, 170–171; insurrectionism during, 148–149; justice system, 146–147; position of delegates, 144–145; repression following 154–158; symbolism, 145–146, 147–148
North Sea collier fleet, 122–123, 201

oath-swearing: among mutineers, 119, 134, 143–144, 204–205; loyalty oaths, 64, 91, 98, 101, 205; United Irish conspirators, 179–180
Orangism, 2, 97, 99–100, 107–108
Owen, Edward Campbell Rich, 133, 135

Pakenham, Thomas, 118, 129
Parker, Ann (née McHardy), 155–157
Parker, Richard, 155–157
Patton, Philip, 129–130, 132–133, 137, 164
petitioning: in British navy, 111, 112, 116–117, 169; increasing punishment for, 89–90; *Léopard* mutineers to the king, 62. *See also* round robin
Pigot, Hugh, 165, 167–169, 171, 193–194
Platen, Baltzar von, 21, 37, 40
Plymouth, 148, 160, 172–173, 179–183
political clubs, 65, 123, 174, 180
Posthusfejde, 40
press gangs. *See* impressment
prisoners of war, 33, 103, 108, 148, 154, 189–190
privateers: black seamen onboard, 103–104; French Caribbean privateering, 103–104, 207; mutinies on, 38; plans for Irish

Truxtun, Thomas, 153, 196

United Irishmen, 148, 175–177, 179–186

Vendée, 86, 89, 91
Vengeur du Peuple (French warship), 92–93,
 115–116
violence against officers, 67, 86, 166–167,
 171, 199
Voltaire, 26, 102

Wall, Joseph, 208
William V, Prince of Orange, 2, 95, 96
Wolfe Tone, Theobald, 175–176,
 181–182

xenophobia, 186–187, 189–191

zielverkopers, 19

THE CALIFORNIA WORLD HISTORY LIBRARY

Edited by Edmund Burke III, Kenneth Pomeranz, and Patricia Seed

Founded in 1893,
UNIVERSITY OF CALIFORNIA PRESS
publishes bold, progressive books and journals
on topics in the arts, humanities, social sciences,
and natural sciences—with a focus on social
justice issues—that inspire thought and action
among readers worldwide.

The UC PRESS FOUNDATION
raises funds to uphold the press's vital role
as an independent, nonprofit publisher, and
receives philanthropic support from a wide
range of individuals and institutions—and from
committed readers like you. To learn more, visit
ucpress.edu/supportus.